3/04

D0629158

# FREEDOM ON FIRE

John Shattuck

# FREEDOM ON FIRE

## HUMAN RIGHTS WARS AND AMERICA'S RESPONSE

Harvard
University
Press

Cambridge, Massachusetts, and London, England · 2003

*Library of Congress Cataloging-in-Publication Data*

Shattuck, John H. F.
  Freedom on fire : human rights wars and America's response / John Shattuck.
    p. cm.
  Includes bibliographical references and index.
  ISBN 0-674-01162-7 (alk. paper)
    1. Human rights.  2. Human rights—Government policy—United States.  I. Title.

JC571.S453 2003
303.6'4'09049—dc21      2003049916

In memory of
H. Francis Shattuck, Jr.
(1920–1997)

# CONTENTS

# FREEDOM ON FIRE

# INTRODUCTION

On a gray, sooty day in Prague in August 1988, I huddled over a rickety table at an outdoor café with a woman who spoke in furtive tones. A Stalinist pall still hung over Czechoslovakia. I had come to Prague to find out what was happening to Czech dissidents as freedom began to stir in other parts of Central and Eastern Europe. My interlocutor, Rita Klimova, a close associate of Vaclav Havel, the Czech playwright and leader of the banned dissident organization Charter 77, had made it clear that she would only meet me outdoors. The electronic bugs of the secret police made indoor conversation impossible. I had gotten in touch with Rita through Herman Schwartz, a leading American human rights lawyer well connected to Eastern European dissidents. She briefed me about the Czech dissident movement, especially the harsh repression under which it had to operate and the many Czechs in prison who were paying a high price even as late as 1988 for advocating their political freedom.

Sixteen months later, riding the Metroliner from New York to Washington, I opened my *New York Times* and was astonished to read that the new president of Czechoslovakia, Vaclav Havel, had just appointed Rita Klimova to be the first Czech ambassador to the United States after the Velvet Revolution. (Ten years after our meeting, I too would become ambassador, returning to Prague to represent the United States to the Czech Republic.) Like many other Americans during this magical time, I felt privileged to have a front-

1

row seat in the vast drama of freedom that seemed to be unfolding throughout the world.

Having devoted much of my working life to human rights, in 1989 I had a flash of hope that the right to speak freely, organize politically, vote democratically, and live in safety might finally have a chance of taking hold worldwide. The Cold War was being swept away on the crest of a global democratic revolution. It moved rapidly and reached far. The Berlin Wall fell. Communism collapsed in Central and Eastern Europe and the former Soviet Union. Apartheid was brought down in South Africa, and democratic governments arose in Central and South America and parts of Asia. A new spirit of democracy seemed ready to replace the entrenched forces of totalitarianism. In this climate, euphoria was contagious. During the spring of 1989 even China seemed to be loosening up, as a student-led democracy movement gained momentum. An American commentator famously proclaimed "the end of history." Political evolution, he said, was now complete.[1]

I was less optimistic. I had been a lawyer for the American Civil Liberties Union, vice chair of Amnesty International, and a teacher of human rights law at Harvard. I knew enough about the fragility of political freedom to suspect that what others were characterizing as a global transformation could come to an end at any moment. Still, I remained hopeful that lessons learned from earlier struggles might miraculously sustain this one. In the United States, we knew from our own decades-long civil rights movement that freedom is an elusive goal, not an easy achievement. My experience during the Watergate era had shown me that no battle for freedom is ever permanently won, even when there are strong institutions to protect it. And from my work with Amnesty and other human rights organizations, I understood that the role of the United States and other democratic countries would be crucial in the years ahead if the global freedom revolution was to be defended against inevitable new enemies.

The post–Cold War euphoria was short-lived. In June 1989, just as the popular movement for democracy was gaining ground in Central Europe, the Chinese government moved heavily armed troops and tanks into Tiananmen Square in Beijing, killing, wounding, or imprisoning tens of thousands of students and workers in dozens of Chinese cities who were bravely trying to form their own democracy movement. A chill was felt by rights advocates all over the world. Progress was not going to be easy. A whole new set of threats to human rights would soon arise.

The attacks came fast and furiously, with the mass slaughter of civilians by cynical rulers and modern warlords in nearly every region of the world. Somalia, Yugoslavia, Haiti, Cambodia, Burma, southeastern Turkey, Iraq, Liberia, Angola, Nigeria—these were the post–Cold War killing fields of the early 1990s. In the Rwanda genocide of 1994, as many as 800,000 people were wiped out in less than four months by Hutu extremists determined to destroy their country's moderate Hutu leadership and entire Tutsi minority. At about the same time, ethnic, religious, and political violence began sweeping through Chechnya, Kosovo, Indonesia, East Timor, Sierra Leone, and as had been the case so often before, the Middle East.

A new era of warfare was dawning in which the targets were civilians, not soldiers. Unarmed men, women, and children were being killed and maimed, driven from their homes, rounded up and imprisoned, attacked by marauding gangs, shelled by merciless armies, murdered by cynical leaders. New forms of terrorism were being bred in the failed states and rogue regimes that could be found in the detritus of the Cold War. The clock was being turned back on the long struggle to rid the world of the crimes against humanity that had plagued the twentieth century. These new wars were threatening to destroy the very idea of human rights.

By human rights, I mean the rights of people to be free from torture or arbitrary execution; free from having their thoughts or speech controlled; free from being victimized or discriminated against because of their race, religion, ethnicity, or economic circumstance; and free from being deprived of the basic necessities of life. I also mean the freedom of people to choose their own governments, and the responsibility of governments to protect these rights by developing institutions to promote them within nations and internationally.

The idea of human rights was born in the eighteenth century and came of age during the twentieth—after two world wars, the Holocaust, the Gulag, China's "Great Leap Forward," totalitarian terror, and a seemingly endless scourge of mass killing had destroyed more than 170 million people.[2] In 1948, after the founding of the United Nations, the Universal Declaration of Human Rights was drafted as a charter of freedom based on elements of the world's great religious and ethical traditions. Since its adoption, this far-reaching document has provided the impetus for a growing body of international law, and has been incorporated into the constitutions of many countries.

The Universal Declaration of Human Rights provides a framework for understanding the forces of history that are shaping our world today. Its vision of freedom is juxtaposed with a memory of the "barbarous acts which have outraged the conscience of mankind."[3] Bearing witness to the lessons of history, the declaration proclaims that human rights must be protected "if man is not to be compelled to have recourse, as a last resort, to rebellion against . . . oppression."[4]

Since the end of the Cold War, the competition between freedom and oppression has become more complicated. Over the last decade, freedom has been advanced but also challenged by revolutions in technology, communications, and markets—revolutions that have created new opportunities, tensions, and inequalities across the globe. The forces of globalization have provided many people with new chances to improve their lives and advance their freedom. But these same forces have passed many others by, stimulating powerful reactions as old systems have crumbled, economic inequalities have grown and become more visible, international development assistance has been reduced, nation-states have failed, cultural and religious identities have been eroded, and tyrants have used the fear of change to justify renewed oppression. Despite the expansion of democracy, these forces of disintegration have destabilized the world at the very moment when greater global freedom had seemed within reach. Today, the repressive but relatively stable "order" of the Cold War has disappeared. Crises around the world have exploded with no international framework to contain them.

To prevent the forces of disintegration from prevailing, we need an international system of human rights. Americans have profound economic, political, security, and moral interests in supporting the reinforcement of such a system. Our markets and suppliers span the globe. Our borders are open to foreign capital, and our workforce is full of foreign talent. We are linked by the Internet to a global village in which the world's dreams and disasters are accessible to all. No part of the earth is beyond our reach, and we are fully exposed to all its crises.

Americans no longer can doubt that the United States is directly affected by seemingly distant conflicts. We know that American "homeland security" is vulnerable to terrorism bred in the swamps of foreign repression. We find ourselves paying billions of dollars of emergency assistance to help refugees and the countries overwhelmed by them. From 1996 to 2001, the United States contributed nearly $28 billion to U.N. peacekeeping and humanitarian operations.[5] American soldiers have been pressed into service to help perform difficult and costly peacekeeping work. And the American economy, fueled by trade and investment, has been increasingly affected by global instabilities.

Americans have traditionally preferred to see themselves as spectators of foreign events, but we are today the world's central actors. American economic and military hegemony has thrust upon us the title role on the contemporary world stage; how we play the role will determine whether our security and freedom can be protected from human rights wars and terrorism. Above all, our deepest values are tested each time there is a new outbreak of genocide or crimes against humanity; what we do to translate these values into policy and action will establish whether our commitment to the claim "never again" is genuine, or only passing.

Since September 11, 2001, Americans have drawn a connection between the millions of innocent civilians in Afghanistan who were victimized by the fanatical regime of the Taliban and the thousands of innocent Americans whose lives were destroyed by the Taliban's terrorist partner, al Qaeda. They have grasped the importance of joining with other countries to uproot the terrorists—criminals and human rights abusers who created the Central Asian swamp in which al Qaeda's plan to attack the United States was hatched.

If Americans now understand how what was happening in a failed state like Afghanistan could lead to the events of September 11, what about our understanding of the world's other human rights wars? In the decade before September 11, we received a steady stream of images and information from Bosnia, Rwanda, Haiti, and scores of other places where massive human rights abuses were being committed against millions of innocent civilians. Too often, however, we looked the other way, or acted too late or too little to stop the devastation, believing that there was no direct threat to the peace and security of the United States, that the cost of intervention was too great, and that in any event there was not much we could do from the outside to stop the slaughter.

Since September 11, we have been preoccupied by the war on terrorism, which has overshadowed the struggle for human rights. In prosecuting this war, the Bush administration has pushed rights aside, presenting the United States more as a military power than as a beacon of freedom, and stirring resentment among the world's reformers and freedom fighters, who should be allies, not adversaries, in the battle against terror. As a superpower that now seems intent on ruling alone by force rather than building alliances by persuasion, the United States has become the object of global resentment and the unintentional inspiration for violence. In the Manichaean world of George W. Bush, the risk has grown that human rights wars, terror's breeding grounds, will proliferate.

Since the end of the Cold War there has been much debate inside the U.S. government over whether and how to address local and regional human rights conflicts. The traditional view is that these wars rarely affect U.S. interests in such a direct way that we should intervene to stop them. The traditionalists define national security in military and economic terms, and are reluctant to include the promotion of human rights within that core definition. Their view is that human rights can get in the way of more immediate concerns, such as tracking down terrorists, or promoting foreign trade, and can be pushed aside when necessary to advance other pressing national interests. On the other side of this debate are those who point to evidence that democracies which respect human rights do not go to war against each other, harbor terrorists, or produce refugees. These human rights interventionists advocate policies to head off the failure of both weak and authoritarian countries, and the rise of rogue states, because they are often the breeding grounds of violent ethnic, religious, and political conflict that poses a direct threat to the United States. Before September 11, this threat was perceived in terms of foreign instability, massive destruction of human lives, and irreparable damage to human rights. Now it is also an urgent matter of the security of Americans at home.

I am a human rights hawk. As the pages of this book will recount, I have seen what tools can be used to anticipate and forestall human rights catastrophes. I have also seen how hard it is to muster the political will to address these crises, and how costly they can be when they are allowed to fester. I was at the center of the debate inside the Clinton administration over the role that human rights should play in U.S. foreign policy. I entered the administration in June 1993 as assistant secretary of state for human rights and humanitarian affairs.[6] Unlike most of my political-appointee colleagues, I had no previous State Department experience. My work outside government had sparked my interest in a human rights job in the new administration, and because I knew several of its high officials, including the President himself, I was fortunate to be chosen to serve. By picking me out of the human rights community, Bill Clinton assigned me not merely an office but also a mission. As I took on that mission, I came to understand two basic truths. I learned that evil is a reality, not an abstraction of moral philosophy, and that the killers of innocent people must be held accountable or evil will prevail. I also found how difficult it is to mobilize the U.S. government to promote international human rights, but how essential it is to do so.

My "rights" education began when I was nine and growing up in Hastings-on-Hudson, a small town north of New York City. Not long after I was sporting a kid's "Ike and Dick, Sure to Click" button, I remember my Republican father coming to the defense of a Democratic Party candidate for the local school board, Esther Decker, who had been smeared in the town newspaper for having vague and unspecified "Communist connections." My father, a lawyer and former Marine platoon leader who had received two Purple Hearts for his battle wounds in the Pacific islands during World War II, was deeply disturbed by the articles. In a letter to the newspaper and at a meeting of the school board, he challenged those making the anonymous charges to prove or withdraw them.

When my father did that, some nasty things were also said about him. I remember hearing them from my schoolmates and getting upset. Dad's response was to explain to me his point of view. Late one Sunday afternoon I sat on the arm of his big red-leather chair while he told me that, although he disagreed with Esther Decker about many things and did not know her personally, she had a right to defend herself against the smears coming from people like Senator Joseph McCarthy, who would destroy the freedom Americans had fought for if we didn't stand up for them.

That was when I began to understand that freedom was more than the Memorial Day flag-waving that was an important part of our small-town life. As a Boy Scout with a paper route who played in the Little League, I had a privileged, all-American childhood. But after my father's armchair talk, I sensed that freedom could not be taken for granted; it had to be defended.

The 1960s were bracketed for me by two different kinds of challenges to freedom. In July 1963 I traveled to Moscow with a group of college students in the Yale Russian Chorus during the brief détente between the Cuban Missile Crisis and the assassination of President Kennedy. Our trip was organized under a U.S-Soviet cultural exchange agreement, and we gave impromptu concerts in Red Square and debated into the night with Russians (most of whom no doubt were KGB agents) about freedom in America. We told them about the growing civil rights movement and the struggle to end racial discrimination in our country, and we took on those who loudly insisted that freedom in America was a myth. In a naïve gesture to win the argument by showing that Americans were not controlled by their government, at one point I ostentatiously reached into my wallet, pulled out my driver's license and draft card, and crumpled them up.[7]

Six years later, my faith in the U.S. government was eroded, but not my underlying principles. As a Yale Law School student, I did research for an article published by the *Selective Service Law Reporter,* which argued that prosecuting people who destroyed their draft cards to protest the Vietnam War was an infringement of freedom of speech. I also spent the spring and summer of 1968 working in Senator Eugene McCarthy's antiwar presidential campaign, and a year later helped organize the massive "Vietnam Moratorium" demonstrations in Washington, which together with the increasingly broad-based civil rights demonstrations that grew throughout the decade, tested the American commitment to freedom in new and uncharted ways. I argued with my father about the war, which I felt was a mistake and which he questioned but supported. My mother agreed with me, drawn by her own doubts about the commitment of American soldiers to defend a corrupt regime far from our borders. We remained connected as a family at a difficult time, debating the responsibilities of freedom and the meaning of civil liberties. In 1972, the death of my brother in a drowning accident in Vermont at age nineteen brought my sister, my parents, and me together in tragedy.

In 1969 I met Petra Tölle, a graduate student in political science at Columbia University who had grown up in Germany in the shadow of the Holocaust and World War II. We were married in New Haven in May 1970 in the midst of the demonstrations that erupted after four students were shot and killed by National Guard troops during antiwar protests at Kent State University on May 4. Petra was haunted by the silence of her German family about the horrors of their country's Nazi past, and she had come to America in search of answers. In the years that followed, we became partners not only in marriage, but also in a search to define the meaning of human rights. I went to work for the American Civil Liberties Union (ACLU) and she taught at the John Jay College of Criminal Justice in New York, challenging and inspiring her students, many of whom were New York City police officers.

At the ACLU I became involved as a lawyer in the issues I had come to know as an activist. Freedom of speech and the right of privacy were at the heart of the protest activity of the 1960s and early 1970s, and it was my job to challenge government infringement of these basic liberties. Under J. Edgar Hoover, the Federal Bureau of Investigation (FBI) had sought to disrupt the civil rights and antiwar movements. My clients were among its victims. In one case, I obtained evidence through court proceedings that Muhammad Kenyatta, a civil rights activist in Tougaloo, Mississippi, had received a death threat fabricated by the FBI that had caused him to flee the state with his wife and small children. This evidence opened the way for discovery of an FBI program, "COINTELPRO-Black," aimed at discrediting civil rights leaders.

As the Watergate investigations got under way in Congress, the civil liberties abuses I had been challenging in the courts began to receive national attention. In a widely publicized case, I was part of an ACLU team that represented Morton Halperin, a former aide to Henry Kissinger on the National Security Council staff in 1969 who had sued the Nixon administration for violating his rights by placing a warrantless wiretap on his home telephone for twenty-one months. Halperin later succeeded me as director of the ACLU Washington office and served on the National Security Council staff during the Clinton administration. The evidence of constitutional abuse in his case became a central feature of the articles of impeachment drawn up by the House Judiciary Committee against President Nixon. Two years after Nixon left office, I took his court-ordered deposition in San Clemente, California. During eight hours of testimony, the former President asserted sweeping powers to wiretap whenever he believed it was necessary for reasons of national security. The courts rejected this claim and Halperin eventually won his case. My faith was reinforced in the capacity of the rule of law to hold leaders accountable in a democracy and to enforce the rights of citizens, despite the heavy cost in time and persistence.

I was to learn that the struggle for human rights required advocacy not only in the courts, but also in the political process. In 1977 I took over as director of the ACLU Washington office. My job was to mobilize support for civil liberties and civil rights in the Congress and the executive branch. With all of the interest groups vying for attention on Capitol Hill, I quickly discovered that a civil liberties organization could not command much attention unless it developed a grassroots constituency. I began to travel to ACLU chapters all over the country, outlining the issues we were working on in Washington and leaving behind an agenda for local teams of ACLU members to take up with their congressional representatives.

Out of this was born a new enterprise, the "Bill of Rights Lobby." It had its work cut out for it. In the early 1980s, a major congressional attack organized by Senator Jesse Helms (R-N.C.) was leveled at the federal courts to strip away their jurisdiction over cases involving school desegregation, school prayer, and abortion. The only way to beat back this attack was to mount a grassroots campaign to defend the federal courts. Working with a broad coalition of organizations, including the American Bar Association and the Leadership Conference on Civil Rights, as well as a dedicated band of congressional opponents led by Senator Lowell Weicker (R-Conn.), the Bill of Rights Lobby sprang into action. None of the "court-stripping" legislation was enacted.

I went to Harvard in 1984, as vice president for government, community, and public affairs and lecturer at the law school. At Harvard I expanded my rights work by immersing myself in international human rights law and practice, joining the board of directors of Amnesty International and later becoming vice chair of Amnesty's U.S. section. The anti-apartheid movement was gaining strength on campus, and Harvard was on the defensive because of its investments in companies doing business in South Africa. I worked with Harvard's president, Derek Bok, to change the university's position. Harvard divested its stock portfolio in companies doing business directly with South Africa's apartheid regime and expanded its assistance to racially mixed schools and universities in South Africa. At the same time, I helped Bok organize a group of college presidents to testify in Congress in support of U.S. and international sanctions against the apartheid regime. All of this, of course, was just a small part of the international campaign to bring about fundamental change in South Africa—a campaign whose purpose was to lend support to the movement for racial justice and democracy that was transforming the country from within. Having learned about the importance of grassroots organizing for civil rights and liberties in the United States, I now was witnessing the extraordinary moral power and potential of similar rights movements around the world.

In March 1988 my own world was devastated. Petra died suddenly of a cerebral hemorrhage. We were at the peak of our lives together, and she was showing me what it meant to be wise and beautiful and compassionate. She was my compass on issues of freedom and responsibility. All at once I had lost my love, my partner, and my tutor. I was empty and adrift. I kept dreaming I was waving good-bye to a ship that was setting sail; Petra was on it and so was I. Our three children, Jessica, Becca, and Peter, kept me going as I rallied to drive them to school on rainy days, set up play dates, go to dance classes and Little League games, take them shopping for clothes, and do all the other things any single parent must struggle to accomplish. When the Berlin Wall fell in 1989, it was impossible to believe that Petra would never know the extraordinary changes our world was about to go through.

Three years later my life was restored. I fell in love again, with Ellen Hume, a journalist and teacher who shared my commitment to human rights. Ellen had been recruited as executive director of Harvard's Shorenstein Center for Press and Politics at the Kennedy School of Government, having served as White House correspondent for the *Wall Street Journal*. Her passion for justice and the joy with which she greeted each day were special gifts to me, and our marriage became the place in which life could begin to grow again. After our daughter, Susannah, was born, Ellen encouraged me to think about how I could continue my human rights work. When Bill Clinton was elected and the possibility of a job in the new administration began to take shape, Ellen heroically agreed that we could move to Washington, even though she had been glad to escape five years earlier from the city's political machinations. We left Boston in June 1993, and I entered the complex world of the State Department and American foreign policy.

Soon after taking office, the administration of Bill Clinton was confronted by the post–Cold War forces of disintegration. Within eighteen months, disaster had struck in Somalia, Rwanda, Haiti, Bosnia, and China. Human rights conflicts were erupting or escalating in virtually every part of the world. If the United States was to play a role in stopping or containing these post–Cold War conflicts, it would have to change the nature of its foreign commitments. New resources—diplomatic, economic, and military—would have to be deployed in the promotion of human rights. New alliances—regional and international—would have to be forged to make and keep the peace. Although efforts were made by the new president in that direction, they were often curtailed by resistance from Congress, from within the administration itself, from powerful interest groups, and from public complacency.

The human rights wars of the 1990s took a huge toll. In Bosnia and Rwanda, where war quickly turned into genocide, international action to stop the slaughter came too late, or not at all. In Rwanda, the United States stood in the way of intervention, while in Bosnia the United States eventually led the way toward peace. In Haiti, the United States created a multinational coalition to intervene for the protection of basic human rights and the restoration of a democratically elected government, but it became so preoccupied with fashioning an early "exit strategy" that it allowed the situation to deteriorate again. In China, competing strategic interests and disagreements over the relationships among trade, economic development, and political reform led to a major diplomatic confrontation over human rights, in which the United States backed down.

As the Clinton administration's chief human rights official from 1993 to 1998, I was in the middle of these crises. Although I was never in charge of U.S. policy, I had the power to try to influence it, and I found myself in the thick of many bureaucratic battles. I worked in Rwanda, Haiti, Bosnia, China, and other human rights battle zones where the post–Cold War upheavals were most intense and the level of abuse was highest. In trying to develop ways to contain these conflicts, I confronted obstacles and made mistakes. In each situation, I found that the American government was caught off guard by a series of brutal attacks on civilians that seemed at first to be unrelated to traditional U.S. foreign policy interests. In each case, I learned that the crisis had a profoundly negative effect not only on the region in which it took place, but on all of us. In each crisis, millions of people were killed, wounded, tortured, or oppressed. In Rwanda and Bosnia, many hundreds of thousands were slaughtered. In Haiti and in China after the Tiananmen massacre, thousands were killed and millions more victimized by massive government repression. In other places around the world, horrendous human rights abuses were committed simultaneously on a smaller scale.

What should have been the international response? In an earlier era, the choice in many cases would have been between doing nothing and risking a world war. Since the end of the Cold War, the range of available options has been far wider. This book is written with an insider's view of both the U.S. government and some of the world's human rights crises, and it describes a long and difficult search to define an appropriate role for the United States to play in preventing or stopping these conflicts. This search was conducted not only in Rwanda, Haiti, Bosnia, China, and many other countries, but also in the State Department, the White House, the Pentagon, and other parts of the U.S. government. These are the places where the Clinton administration debated how to fulfill two of the President's 1992 campaign promises: to promote human rights while simultaneously advancing U.S. security and economic interests, and to reduce U.S. military commitments after the end of the Cold War.

Two major themes of the 1992 presidential campaign—"It's the economy, stupid!" and "the Vietnam syndrome"—loomed large over these debates. After the Cold War, many Americans had lost interest in foreign affairs. Since the Soviet empire had fallen, they thought, what more was there to worry about? Now the United States could concentrate on doing business around the world without the distraction of Soviet missiles or Communist threats. In the years after the 1994 congressional elections, when the Republicans took control of the Congress, the entire foreign affairs portion of the federal budget was chopped to less than 1 percent of the total; a successful six-year campaign was conducted by Senator Helms and other powerful anti-internationalists in the Congress to block the United States from paying its dues to the United Nations; and many new members of Congress proudly proclaimed that they did not have passports.

These isolationist signals from Washington increased the sense of suspicion and distrust with which the United States was regarded by its overseas partners. As the remaining superpower and prime mover of "globalization," Washington had become the object of both envy and enmity. New coalitions were formed in the United Nations and other international organizations to hold "U.S. hegemony" in check. At the same time, domestic political forces in the Congress cut American support for international institutions and promoted a more unilateralist foreign policy, raising concerns among traditional U.S. allies in Europe and elsewhere. These concerns extended to the area of human rights. By pursuing human rights objectives unilaterally, the United States opened itself to the charge of using double standards whenever it failed to take as strong a stand on one issue or country as it did on another, or when it failed to be self-critical of its own human rights record.

This book tells the story about how a volatile post–Cold War environment at home and abroad shaped the halting U.S. response to the human rights wars of the 1990s. Although many of the events occurred simultaneously, or within the same time period, there is a logical progression from Rwanda to Haiti to Bosnia to China. Rwanda in the spring and early summer of 1994 exemplified a U.S. policy of catastrophic disengagement heavily influenced by the killing of U.S. troops in Somalia the previous fall. Haiti in the fall and winter of 1994–1995 represented an early step toward a policy of containing human rights wars, although domestic political pressures required the multinational force that intervened in Haiti to exit prematurely, and precluded any sustained follow-through. The U.S. approach toward Bosnia in the fall of 1995 demonstrated a more effective and longer-term commitment to linking diplomacy with the use of military force, after three years of American dithering while ineffective European and U.N. peacekeeping had failed to control the conflict and stop the human rights atrocities. The China chapters come at the end because they review a different kind of human rights war—one where the United States had to respond to the repression of human rights in an authoritarian country with which Americans have a wide range of economic and strategic interests.

Five Washington roadblocks made the task of responding to these human rights conflicts especially challenging. The first was interagency gridlock, a well-known bureaucratic phenomenon whereby no new policy could be adopted unless it was endorsed by all affected government agencies. The only way to break this gridlock was to get a presidential decision. But this path was often blocked by the presidential decisionmaking syndrome, under which a president like Bill Clinton, who had been elected in 1992 by only 43 percent of the popular vote, was unlikely to break an interagency stalemate by deciding to move forward on a controversial foreign policy issue (such as deploying U.S. troops on a peacekeeping mission in Bosnia, or imposing sanctions for human rights abuses on a trading partner like China) that might have major domestic political costs for him. To encourage such a difficult presidential decision, it was necessary to demonstrate strong public support. But this ran into the public opinion syndrome: public opinion about a U.S. response to a foreign policy crisis often cannot be assessed until after the fact. *Not* intervening in Rwanda, for example, proved after the genocide to have had little domestic political fallout for the president; yet conventional political wisdom claimed (without any specific evidence to back it up) that intervention without significant presidential leadership would have been extremely unpopular.

The tendency during the early years of the Clinton administration not to intervene in a human rights war was largely a result of a fourth roadblock, the Somalia syndrome. U.S. participation in international peacekeeping became a political "third rail" issue after eighteen U.S. Army Rangers were killed by a local warlord during a peacekeeping mission in Somalia in October 1993. The domestic political fallout from this military setback was so great that President Clinton felt compelled to issue a directive in May 1994 sharply restricting U.S. participation in any new international peacekeeping operation. Finally, human rights policymaking throughout the 1990s was constantly plagued by a conflict-resolution paradox. This meant that Washington's full policy attention was rarely given to a conflict at an early, controllable stage when there was little pressure to become involved (the breakup of Yugoslavia in 1991). The crisis was only likely to be addressed much later, after it had moved into the international spotlight by spinning out of control and becoming far more difficult to resolve (the war in Bosnia after a quarter of a million people had been killed).

In addition to these Washington roadblocks, the day-to-day bureaucratic impediments of working in the State Department made it hard for mid-level officials to hammer out and implement new ways of responding to human rights crises. Set up as a system of competing micro-enterprises intended to produce "policy" that reflects many points of view, the State Department is constantly in danger of devolving into a dysfunctional organization of warring bureaucratic fiefdoms. Not surprisingly, the strongest fiefdoms are the ones with the most valuable territory. These, of course, are the "geographic bureaus" responsible for U.S. relations with various regions of the world. In rough order of priority based on their importance to U.S. strategic and economic interests, these are Europe, the Middle East, East Asia, Latin America, South Asia, and Africa. Powerless in territorial terms, the "functional bureaus" (administration, diplomatic security, political and military affairs, narcotics and law enforcement, refugee and population issues, environmental affairs, democracy and human rights) are generally ranked in bureaucratic influence according to the size of their budgets. On that scale, the Bureau of Democracy, Human Rights, and Labor ranks near the bottom.

Not surprisingly, in this vast and highly stratified bureaucracy, a central mechanism exists for vetting policy recommendations before they reach the top. That mechanism is called the "clearance process." In order to move a document up the chain of command, an assistant secretary of state must submit it for approval by colleagues in other bureaus to which the subject matter of the recommendation relates. For example, a memo from the Human Rights Bureau recommending specific U.S. actions to respond to atrocities against civilians in Bosnia must be "cleared" by the European Affairs Bureau (as well as the Political and Military Affairs Bureau, if it recommends military action) before it can be submitted to the secretary of state. The "clearing" bureau can block the recommendation or insist on changes. This is the State Department version of interagency gridlock, and it is replicated throughout the government to such an extent that cabinet-level officials or the President are often shielded from a broad range of advice.

As I came to learn the choke points of this sclerotic bureaucratic system during my early months in government, I developed my own guidelines for navigating through or around them. My colleagues were doing the same thing, since bureaucratic warfare is a way of life in Washington. My own tactics for surviving—and sometimes winning—pitched battles inside the bureaucracy were simple and straightforward. I learned to be wary of anyone coming to my office to try to get me to put my initials on another bureau's document. I also learned how to get another bureau's clearance on my document by finding a mole who agreed with my position. I established my own back channels for getting recommendations to the secretary of state or the White House without going through the clearance process. I discovered that the most effective way to make a policy recommendation "up the line" was in person in an informal setting (a private meeting or a phone call), without leaving any paper trail. My favorite bureaucratic tactic for getting high-level attention was to travel to the site of a human rights crisis and phone back to Washington. I learned that I could almost always get my satellite calls returned when I made them from Kigali, or Port-au-Prince, or Sarajevo, or Beijing. In the bureaucracy surrounding U.S. human rights policy, getting through to the top was half the battle.

In short, the political and bureaucratic environment in which the new administration formulated its foreign policy was decidedly hostile to new initiatives or new definitions of national security. In this atmosphere, human rights policies could be overwhelmed by competing economic or traditional security interests. But coalitions inside and outside the government were sometimes able to build resistance to these pressures to get the policies back on track. This book is about how, in the end, after many setbacks and obstacles, human rights advocates elbowed their way into the inner circles of government where they won some battles and lost others, and in the process had a surprising influence on the formulation of foreign policy in the United States.

The rising political profile of human rights issues signaled that they were moving to the center of international relations. As civilians were targeted more and more by political violence, protection of their rights became a significant objective in policymaking. Issues of war and peace not only were decided by political leaders, but now also were influenced by popular movements for freedom and those fighting on their behalf.

As these changes occurred, battles were fought to create new international human rights institutions. The first set of these emerged during the 1990s, and included the new position of U.N. High Commissioner for Human Rights, the International Criminal Tribunals for the Former Yugoslavia and Rwanda, and the International Criminal Court. During the administration of George W. Bush, the U.S. relationship with these new human rights institutions has become increasingly strained and, in the case of the International Criminal Court, downright hostile. An aggressive unilateralism has marked American foreign policy in the Bush years. Multilateral structures and alliances have been cast aside or circumvented by a president skeptical of international entanglements, whose view of the world has been shaped by the events of September 11 and the global preeminence of American power. But the human rights wars of the 1990s present a powerful lesson of the urgency of building international institutions, policies, and relationships to contain the terrorism of our time. Only by working with the rest of the world to address human rights crises that breed terror can we hope to forestall the outbreak of new and more devastating wars against civilians before they become a dominant feature of the twenty-first century.

# CHAPTER 1

# RWANDA

## THE GENOCIDE THAT MIGHT HAVE BEEN PREVENTED

On the morning of April 7, 1994, Joyce Leader, deputy chief of mission of the U.S. embassy in Kigali, heard shouts behind her house and rushed to the back door. There she saw her neighbor, Agathe Uwilingiyimana, the prime minister of Rwanda, scramble to the top of her garden wall with the help of a U.N. peacekeeper. Shots were fired and the prime minister disappeared. Moments later another fusillade rang out, followed by an eerie silence. Then she heard the raucous cheers of gunmen, who had completed their first assignment in the task of starting a genocide.

Many other Rwandans fleeing mobs of soldiers and paramilitaries swarming over the city that day tried to escape into Joyce Leader's garden and the backyards of other foreign diplomats. Several of them made it and then disappeared into hiding from the terror that engulfed the city. One of these was Monique Mujawamariya, a thirty-year-old woman who had spent the last year visiting foreign capitals to try to get the world to pay attention to the growing human rights crisis in her country.

Four months earlier, on December 10, 1993, I had escorted Monique into the White House, where she had been invited to attend President Clinton's official celebration of the forty-fifth anniversary of the Universal Declaration of Human Rights. As we made our way through the West Wing with Eric Schwartz, the National Security Council staff specialist for human rights, we passed my old friend

John Podesta, who was then in charge of the president's scheduling and later became his chief of staff. Podesta flashed a grin and a quick greeting, which reminded me of our conversation several days earlier, when John had given a three-word summary of the administration's foreign policy preoccupation at the end of 1993: "No more Somalias."

Somalia had become a synonym for disaster. Perhaps the lowest point of Bill Clinton's first year in office was the killing, on October 16, 1993, of eighteen U.S. Army Rangers who had been sent in to support a U.N. peacekeeping operation in Somalia. One of the Rangers' bodies had been dragged through the streets of Somalia's capital, Mogadishu, in full view of CNN cameras. The Rangers had been surrounded and attacked by guerrillas connected with a local warlord, Mohamad Farah Aideed, whom they were attempting to capture. Cut off from other U.S. troops in the main U.N. peacekeeping force and lacking adequate intelligence information about their attackers, the doomed Rangers came to symbolize the failure of U.S. policymakers to develop an effective multilateral response to human rights wars. For a long time, the Somalia debacle would cast a shadow over U.N. peacekeeping operations, and for nearly a year it was to paralyze the Clinton administration as it confronted other human rights crises in Rwanda and Bosnia, keeping it from participating in—or even supporting—similar interventions.

I had first met Monique Mujawamariya a few days before our visit to the White House. She had come to my office at the State Department with Holly Burkhalter, the Washington director of Human Rights Watch, which had given Monique an award for her bravery in drawing attention to the Rwandan government's discrimination and promotion of violence against the Tutsi minority in her country. As I listened to Monique describe how extremists from the Hutu majority, abetted by the government, were creating and exploiting the country's ethnic tensions, I thought about our own Ku Klux Klan and the terror it had directed against African-Americans from the last third of the nineteenth century through the 1960s. Monique's message was a familiar one to Americans: unless challenged, the purveyors of hate can become extremely dangerous in any society.

On April 8, 1994, Holly Burkhalter called to tell me that Monique was missing in Kigali. Early reports indicated that violence had broken out following the crash of a plane carrying the Rwandan president, Juvenal Habyarimana, and his guest, the president of neighboring Burundi, Cyprien Ntaryamira. The crash had apparently been caused by a rocket attack launched from the edge of the Kigali airport, and all of the passengers on the president's plane had been killed. These initial reports of the crisis in Kigali did not foretell the staggering dimensions of the cataclysm that was to follow.[1] Because President Clinton had met Monique in December, Holly thought the State Department might be able to track her down. But after Monique had scrambled to safety in Joyce Leader's garden, she had disappeared in the violent chaos that swept over the city. The embassy could not find her.

I called George Moose, assistant secretary for African affairs, to get an update on the situation in Kigali. Moose—one of the highest-ranking African-American officers in the State Department and a consummate foreign service professional—was deeply disturbed by the increasingly ominous reports he was receiving from the U.S. Embassy in Kigali. Within hours of the attack on the president's plane, many Rwandan political leaders, including the prime minister and the president of the constitutional court, had been killed. The government radio station, Radio Television Libres des Milles Collines, was broadcasting venomous messages urging the majority Hutu population to take revenge against the Tutsi minority and against moderate Hutu leaders, who were now being publicly accused of engineering the murder of President Habyarimana. Led by armed militias who seemed to materialize out of nowhere, Hutu groups were attacking Tutsis and moderate Hutus throughout the city and in the countryside. Monique and many of her countrymen were being swallowed up by the expanding disaster, an ocean and a distant continent away from Washington.

What was it like for this young woman, who had been received in the White House four months earlier, to become the victim of the very horrors she had so recently warned us about? Thirty years before, and much closer to home, another young woman named Kitty

Genovese had been stabbed repeatedly outside her New York City apartment building in full view of her neighbors on a warm spring evening. For nearly an hour, her screams were ignored by the residents of her quiet Kew Gardens neighborhood, none of whom called the police. Even for hard-bitten New Yorkers, the story of how thirty-seven people witnessed the murder of a young woman without coming to her rescue came to symbolize how the world breaks down when neighbors ignore desperate appeals for help.[2]

Between April and July 1994 the United States and the rest of the world ignored the warnings of Monique Mujawamariya and others, then stood by and watched as 800,000 Rwandans were murdered.[3] Measured by the number of lives lost, the possibility that many might have been saved, the nature and scope of the crimes committed, and the strategic interest of the United States in preventing the recurrence of genocide, what happened in Rwanda was one of the greatest failures of international human rights protection since World War II.

## The Shadow of Somalia

The story of what happened in Rwanda presents a central theme of this book—that the United States has a strategic and moral interest in preventing or responding wherever possible to the outbreak of genocide. While saving hundreds of thousands of lives may be more difficult than saving one, there are strategies that could have been used to save Rwandans, just as Kitty Genovese could have been saved if her neighbors had responded to her cries for help. As we look back to the events leading up to April 1994, we can identify points along the way where practical and manageable forms of intervention might have made a significant difference.

Before analyzing what could have been done, it is important to understand why it mattered. In addition to the moral cost, the vast loss of life, human suffering, political chaos, social collapse, and regional instability that resulted from the commission of these massive crimes have had a long-term negative influence on international security. When genocide broke out in Rwanda, American policymakers failed to grasp that if left unchecked, the growing wave of killings would ultimately contribute to the destabilization of Central and East Africa, requiring that Americans spend hundreds of millions of taxpayer dollars on peacekeeping operations and humanitarian assistance to sustain the survivors, and destroying all chances of integrating this part of the world into the global economy for a long time. In the eighteen months following the genocide, the United States spent $527 million—more than *twenty* times the amount contributed the year before the genocide—to support U.N. relief and peacekeeping operations aimed at simply keeping alive nearly two million Rwandan (mostly Hutu) refugees.[4] The refugee camps themselves became vast breeding grounds for disease and crime, which spread throughout the region. Nearly a decade later, the Rwanda genocide can be seen as a cataclysm that both precipitated and reflected many aspects of the massive ethnic and political violence that has shaken Rwanda, Burundi, the Democratic Republic of the Congo, and other countries throughout Central Africa for years.

There were two reasons why the United States failed to see the outbreak of genocide in Rwanda as a threat to international security. The first was our experience in Somalia, where we had drawn the wrong lesson from the fatal attack on our troops. A humanitarian mission originally designed to deliver food to a starving population, the U.S.-supported U.N. intervention in Somalia had been slowly transformed during 1993 into a campaign to help the country rid itself of warlords and build the foundations for democracy. This policy shift had occurred without much notice during the transition from the Bush administration to the Clinton administration, and it resulted in part from the new administration's lack of experience, and in part from the zeal of the U.N. secretary-general, Boutros Boutros-Ghali, who as an Egyptian was determined to focus the United Nations on African crises such as the one on Egypt's southern border.

After the Somalia debacle, there was an orgy of finger-pointing in Washington. Since little had been done to build political support for a policy that was at best poorly defined, it should have come as no surprise that both the new administration and the United Nations came under severe attack in the Congress. A leading Republican senator, Mitch McConnell (R.-Ky.), captured this congressional mood when he declared, "Creeping multilateralism died on the streets of Mogadishu."[5] Public support for the administration's foreign policy hit rock bottom. Despite having expressed reservations about the direction of the Somalia policy, Defense Secretary Les Aspin took the fall within the administration for what happened in Mogadishu, and was replaced at the end of 1993 by his deputy, William Perry. But the wounds went deeper than the resignation of a single cabinet official. The most severe casualty was the President's already badly damaged relationship with both the military and the Congress over the deployment of U.S. troops on humanitarian missions. Dogged by the campaign controversy over his draft status and his handling of the issue of gays in the military in the transition after his election, Clinton's relations with the Pentagon brass were strained during the early period of his presidency, making it difficult for him to recover from the Somalia crisis by the time Rwanda erupted.

As a result of these political and bureaucratic upheavals, U.S. policymakers were pushed to draw the wrong conclusion from Somalia. Instead of pulling back from a commitment to peacekeeping, as happened almost immediately, they should have begun to (1) prepare for similar crises in the future, (2) define the criteria for humanitarian intervention (including military intervention as a last resort), (3) broaden the rules of military engagement so that when force is needed, peacekeepers have the mandate and the means to do their jobs, and (4) strengthen U.S. support for U.N. and other multilateral peacekeeping operations. Above all, the lesson of Somalia was that political mobilization back home was essential to the pursuit of humanitarian objectives abroad.

In addition to Somalia, there was another reason why the United States ignored the security threat posed by the Rwanda crisis. Strategic thinking was trapped by an outdated Cold War framework. Former secretary of state James Baker's notorious comment about the crisis in Yugoslavia in 1991, "We have no dog in that fight," could have applied equally to the U.S. strategic view of Rwanda in 1994.[6] When the world was divided into proxy states for the United States and the Soviet Union, Baker's analysis might have made sense. But what happened in Rwanda and Bosnia demonstrated that conflicts after the end of the Cold War in countries with little or no traditional strategic importance can quickly spiral out of control and become sources of regional instability, vast refugee flows, and international terrorism. As the devastating consequences of these two post–Cold War cataclysms became clear, the U.S. strategic interest in preventing or containing genocidal "fights" also came into focus. With significant investment and strategic deployment of resources, the huge long-term moral, political, and security costs that the United States and the rest of the world had to pay for ignoring the outbreak of genocide in Bosnia and Rwanda might have been avoided. To develop a strategy for heading off future genocides, we must begin with a clear understanding of how a modern holocaust can begin.

## Roots of a Genocide

On my many trips to Rwanda from 1994 to 1998, I was always struck by the great beauty of the country. A land of rolling green hills, steep terraced slopes, dark red clay, and rich black soil, Rwanda lies just below the equator but is high enough above sea level to have a mostly temperate climate. Although the country is small (about the size of Arkansas), its hilly terrain has many variations, from dense rain forest to open savanna, undulating heath to volcanic rock. The hills are dotted with villages and farms, and in the distant mountains highland gorillas roam the national parklands. During the rainy season the land is bathed in torrents of water and illuminated by flashes of lightning and the sheen of wet forests.

The people of Rwanda descend from early hunter-gatherers, and from later groups of farmers and herdsmen who are thought to have come to the hills from the east and the north.[7] Over time, and particularly after the arrival of Europeans in the nineteenth century, the two groups acquired the names "Hutu" and "Tutsi," although the accuracy of these ethnic labels is today the subject of much debate. The Hutu were considered by early European colonizers to be a Bantu people who had come from the south and west, composing more than 80 percent of the population, while the Tutsi were thought to be a Nilotic people who had emigrated from Ethiopia and made up about 15 percent.[8] When the Europeans arrived, Rwanda was a relatively stable kingdom that for two centuries had managed to remain isolated from the coastal slave trade because of its mountainous terrain. Over time, Hutus and Tutsis had come to speak the same language (Kinyarwandan), intermarry, and share the same religion and social structure. What differences existed between the two groups were less ethnic than socioeconomic, as many Tutsis gradually emerged as an upper class. In general, while there were tensions, the two groups lived in relative peace with few outbreaks of systemic violence by one group directed at the other.

The recent history of Rwanda is a textbook case of how racism and ethnic hatred can be planted in a society. Formal racial distinctions were brought to the country by the Germans and Belgians, who arrived as colonial masters at the end of the nineteenth century. Although Rwandans had a complex social and political structure in which Hutus and Tutsis were intertwined, the colonizers were influenced by the "race science" of their era, which favored taller, lighter-skinned peoples.[9] The colonial powers ruled in a manner that reinforced their own biases while undermining the structure of Rwandan society. The Germans and later the Belgians used racial stereotyping to select Tutsis for the colony's administrative elite, thereby creating artificial racial distinctions that exacerbated earlier social tensions.[10] This racial system was formalized by the Belgians in 1933, when they took a census of Rwandans in order to issue racial identity cards based on archetypal physical characteristics that prevented Hutus from becoming Tutsis.[11] An American historian of central Africa, Alison Des Forges, describes the social poison that emanated from this system: "Extremist Tutsis, encouraged by European admiration and influenced by the amalgam of myth and pseudo-anthropology, moved from elitism to racism, and a corresponding and equally virulent formulation [developed] on the part of extremist Hutus."[12]

As the wave of independence in Africa reached Rwanda, this climate of racial division grew more political. The suppressed Hutu majority began to throw off their colonial shackles and seek power through political revolution. The theory behind the revolution was simple: in a democracy the majority should rule, and in Rwanda Hutus are the majority. A "Hutu Manifesto" published in 1957 by a group of intellectuals argued that racial indentity cards should be continued after independence to assure the demographic dominance of Hutus.[13] The Hutu political revolution was endorsed by the departing Belgians, who no doubt felt guilty for having previously subjugated the Hutu majority to a colonial Tutsi elite, and no longer subscribed to a philosophy of racial eugenics.[14]

The pent-up social frustrations and racial animosities that flared during the three years when the Belgians were preparing to leave Rwanda produced a spasm of political violence. Nevertheless, the popular uprising of Hutus against Tutsi authorities that began in 1959 and became known in Rwanda as "the wind of destruction" was the first recorded instance of systematic political violence between Hutus and Tutsis in Rwanda's history—it was not, as international commentators would later erroneously claim, a reflection of "age-old animosities" between the two groups.[15]

In 1960, after thousands of Tutsis had been killed and many more driven from Rwanda, one of the leaders of the Hutu revolution, Gregoire Kayibanda, was appointed by the Belgians to be the head of a transitional government. Two years later he was inaugurated as Rwanda's first post-independence president. Kayibanda presided over a weak and corrupt regime that over the next decade allowed the country's colonial infrastructure to deteriorate. Kayibanda's government was overthrown in a 1973 coup led by Juvenal Habyarimana, who as Rwanda's army chief had continued the Hutu political revolution by periodically killing or suppressing Tutsis and driving them into exile.[16]

Once he became president, Habyarimana declared an end to the killing of Tutsis. He consolidated his power by strengthening the racial identity system, blocking the appointment of Tutsis to political or administrative positions, and successfully courting European and American "development donors." By the mid-1980s Rwanda had become economically stronger than other central African countries. But it had created a huge refugee problem: nearly a million Tutsis had been driven out of the country.[17] Habyarimana made clear that he would prevent them from returning. His public rationale was that Rwanda was chronically overpopulated, but his real reason was to protect his power base as leader of the Hutu revolution that had begun in 1959.[18]

The exiled Tutsis increasingly became a problem for Habyarimana after 1987. That year the Rwandan Patriotic Front (RPF) was founded in neighboring Uganda by Tutsi exiles who had played a key role in overthrowing the Ugandan dictator Milton Obote. By 1990 the Tutsi RPF was ready for military action, launching a series of guerrilla attacks against provincial centers in northeastern Rwanda, followed by a full-scale invasion later that year.[19]

The Habyarimana regime responded by rounding up Tutsis in Rwanda and appealing to France and Belgium to send paratroopers to reinforce Rwandan army units fighting the RPF. After helping the army push the RPF into retreat, the French stayed in Rwanda throughout the early 1990s, funneling arms into the country and providing political advice to Habyarimana's regime. During this period Rwanda's one million remaining Tutsis were under constant pressure both from the government, which used the RPF threat as an excuse to crack down on domestic enemies, and from the Hutu extremists, who were emboldened by the climate of anti-Tutsi hysteria.

Several months after the RPF invasion of 1990, the rhetoric of genocide appeared in a venomous tract, "The Hutu Ten Commandments," which was published in Kigali and widely circulated throughout the country.[20] The eighth commandment's dictate, "Hutus should stop having mercy on the Tutsis," was explained in graphic terms by one of the authors of this poisonous creed, Leon Mugesera, a friend of Habyarimana: "We the people are obliged to take responsibility to wipe out this scum."[21]

The RPF reorganized itself after its initial defeat and became an increasingly serious threat to the Habyarimana regime. By early 1993 rebel forces had made substantial gains against the Rwandan army. Meanwhile, European and American diplomats were putting pressure on Habyarimana to negotiate with the RPF by making conditional offers of substantial foreign assistance to his cash-starved government if he would agree to a peace process. After months of resisting, the Rwandan president reluctantly signed an agreement on August 4, 1993, in Arusha, Tanzania, to share power with the RPF, allow Tutsi refugees to return, integrate the Rwandan armed forces, and establish a broad-based transitional government and timetable for elections.[22] Habyarimana's "capitulation" caused a political furor inside Rwanda, with the Hutu extremists condemning the Arusha process as a forced surrender to the Tutsis.

To deal with his domestic problem, Habyarimana obstructed and tried to renegotiate the Arusha accords while the new U.N. Assistance Mission to Rwanda (UNAMIR), which had arrived in October, waited to implement them. At the same time, a secret plan was being developed by Hutu extremists, probably with Habyarimana's approval or at least acquiescence, to derail the Arusha process for good. The plan involved training militias to kill Tutsis and moderate Hutu leaders and inciting the Hutu population by using radio to broadcast the Hutu Ten Commandments and other hate messages against the Tutsis. Apparently, however, the Hutu extremists did not believe Habyarimana was doing enough to advance their objectives. On April 6 the president's plane was shot down as he was returning from Arusha, and the genocide plan was set in motion.[23] Within fourteen weeks, 800,000 people were dead.

## Warnings

The Rwanda genocide did not take the world by surprise. The first condition for preventing a human rights catastrophe was clearly present—there was time to address the mounting crisis before it finally broke out as genocide in April 1994.

For three decades there had been danger signals pointing toward what eventually happened in Rwanda. The country's colonial history illuminated the roots of its ethnic division. The Hutu political revolution against the Tutsi colonial elite—and the subsequent armed Tutsi resistance against the expulsion of Tutsis from Rwanda—previewed the political violence to which this history was leading. The support of Habyarimana's government for Hutu extremists who preached the extermination of Tutsis was a warning posted for the world to see. Although other crises vied for international attention in early 1994, and political constraints limited the world's capacity to respond quickly enough to make a difference, the danger signals in Rwanda should have been visible to France, which had intervened in the early 1990s to shore up the increasingly racist Habyarimana regime; to the United States and the other countries that had sponsored the tenuous negotiating process at Arusha; and to the United Nations, which had assumed responsibility in 1993 for keeping the peace in Rwanda.

Beyond these distant rumblings, there were specific warnings of the impending genocide during the months before it broke. After a wave of political killings in Rwanda in April 1993, a U.N. report prepared by the special rapporteur on extrajudicial, summary, or arbitrary executions, Waly Bacre Ndiaye, concluded that genocide had been committed, and recommended that "[a] mechanism for the protection of civilian populations against massacres should be immediately set up in terms of both prevention and intervention."[24] Ndiaye's report was published by the U.N. Economic and Social Council in August 1993, but there was no mechanism for acting on it until the annual meeting of the U.N. Commission on Human Rights in March 1994. The authority under which this report was produced illustrates a classic U.N. problem: special rapporteurs, who are mandated at a high level but have virtually no support in resources or political clout, are far from the real world of powerful U.N. member states and are rarely given the opportunity to influence international policy.

Another set of warnings was delivered to the United Nations just after the Arusha accords were signed in August 1993. A joint delegation of negotiators representing the Rwandan government and the RPF came to New York to urge the United Nations to send four thousand peacekeepers to Rwanda. The two sides warned that the Arusha agreement was extremely fragile and could fall apart at any time. Weeks later, Secretary-General Boutros Boutros-Ghali recommended a similar but smaller force to the Security Council, which reduced its numbers to 2,500. The new peacekeeping unit was commanded by General Romeo Dallaire of Canada and included a large contingent of Belgian troops. As violence flared and ethnic killings increased toward the end of 1993, Dallaire chafed at the limited mandate of his peacekeepers, which barred them from using force to disarm extremist groups.[25]

In January 1994, three months before the genocide began, Dallaire began to detect signs inside Rwanda of the impending cataclysm. On January 11 he sent a cable to the U.N. Department of Peacekeeping Operations.[26] The cable, entitled "Request for Protection for Informant," told in chilling detail what Dallaire had learned about preparations then being made by Hutu extremists to destroy the Arusha process by unleashing a campaign to kill Tutsis inside Rwanda. Dallaire described his informant as "a top level trainer in the cadre of Interahamwe-armed militia," the Hutu extremist group compiling lists of Tutsis in preparation for the attack. (*Interahamwe* in Kinyarwandan means "those who attack together.") Their plan, according to the informant, was "to provoke the R.P.F. to engage . . . [Hutu] demonstrators and provoke a civil war. Deputies are to be assassinated upon entry or exit from Parliament. Belgian troops are to be provoked and if Belgian soldiers resort to force a number of them are to be killed and thus guarantee Belgian withdrawal from Rwanda." Dallaire also reported that his informant had been "ordered to register all Tutsi in Kigali," and that "he suspects it is for their extermination. Example he gave was that in twenty minutes his personnel could kill up to a thousand Tutsis."[27]

Dallaire's cable predicted the events that were to trigger the genocide three months later. His informant warned that there were no political forces inside Rwanda that could stop the country from hurtling toward the abyss. As the cable put it, the informant "believes the President [Habyarimana] does not have full control over all elements of his old party/faction." In response to the informant's warning, Dallaire made a proposal to the U.N. Peacekeeping Office that was both realistic and straightforward: U.N. troops should be authorized to conduct raids on Interahamwe weapons caches, and the person who had provided information about these caches should be quickly evacuated out of Rwanda.

What could the United Nations realistically have done in response to Dallaire's cable that might have made a difference? It is worth noting that Dallaire's reporting was not always consistent, and that he downplayed the risk of genocide in at least one of his other communications with U.N. headquarters.[28] Nevertheless, Dallaire's January 11 cable was an important warning that could have been acted on by a U.N. Peacekeeping Office that was better organized and better supported by U.N. member states. With a small staff, this office was incapable of responding quickly and effectively to the multiple crises that it had to address simultaneously and the huge volume of cables it was receiving from the field.

Had these constraints not existed, Dallaire's cable might have been processed more effectively in at least three ways. First, an urgent cable from the commander of a U.N. peacekeeping operation requesting action and containing time-sensitive information could have been referred immediately to the secretary-general and the Security Council. Second, the secretary-general could have reviewed the cable and acted immediately to interpret the rules of engagement for the U.N. mission in Rwanda to authorize raids on weapons caches maintained in violation of the Arusha accords and the use of force if necessary to confiscate weapons. This, of course, did not happen, in part because pressure was coming from the United States to limit the mandate and scope of U.N. peacekeeping operations in the wake of Somalia. Third, after the raids were conducted, the United States and other members of the Security Council could have ratified the secretary-general's interpretation and reviewed the mission's rules of engagement to ensure they were adequate to deal with any further contingencies that might arise concerning the mission's enforcement of the Arusha accords. Again, this never happened, because of U.S. concerns about peacekeeping "mission creep."

What actually did happen? In essence, nothing. Dallaire's warning was not given high-level attention by the Secretariat and never reached the Security Council. Paralyzed by the failure of the Somalia mission three months earlier, limited by the tight leash imposed by the United States on post-Somalia peacekeeping activities, and overwhelmed by the seventeen other peacekeeping missions it was then managing, the United Nations' grossly understaffed peacekeeping office, then headed by Kofi Annan, did not give Dallaire the tools he was asking for. Annan's deputy, Iqbal Riza, sent a response denying Dallaire's request to carry out "the operation contemplated" because of the narrow peacekeeping mandate imposed on his troops by the Security Council. When Dallaire challenged this response in a phone call to New York, he was reportedly told that "the United States in particular would not support such an aggressive interpretation of [the peacekeeping] mandate."[29]

Instead of authorizing Dallaire to seize the stockpiled weapons, the U.N. headquarters instructions told him "to immediately contact President Habyarimana" and warn him that the Interahamwe militia activities "represent a clear threat to the peace process" and a "clear violation [of the] Kigali weapons-secure area." The instructions told Dallaire to "assume [Habyarimana] is not aware of these activities, but insist that he must immediately look into the situation."[30] Since the United Nations was giving Dallaire nothing to back up this warning—and Habyarimana had already lost control over the Hutu extremists whose political rise he had sponsored—the headquarters message no doubt rang hollow to Dallaire. As if to make up for the weakness of his rules of engagement, Dallaire was told to pass his warning on to the Belgian, French, and U.S. ambassadors in Kigali, representing the three sponsors of the Arusha process, presumably in hopes that *they* could do something about it.[31]

The United Nations places much of the blame for its downplaying of Dallaire's warning on these three countries. In a 1998 interview,

Iqbal Riza pointed out that he had asked Dallaire to share the explosive information he had received from his informant with the Belgians, French, and Americans. "If those governments, especially the Belgians, had serious fears about what was going to happen, do you think they would have kept quiet? They would have battered down the doors." As for the unwillingness of the United Nations to interpret broadly Dallaire's peacekeeping mandate, Riza explained that it was acting in "the shadow of Somalia," which had influenced Security Council members, particularly the United States.[32]

In December 1999, at the initiative of Secretary-General Kofi Annan, the United Nations took the commendable step of issuing a report about its failure to heed the Rwanda warnings of late 1993 and early 1994. The report faults the U.N. Secretariat for failing to give "the highest priority and attention to the information [in Dallaire's cable] indicating the existence of a plan to exterminate the Tutsi"; U.N. member states for putting "pressure upon the Secretariat" to limit the Rwanda peacekeeping mission; and the U.N. Security Council for its "hesitance in the aftermath of Somalia . . . to support new peacekeeping operations." Above all, the report points out, "the events in Somalia were a watershed . . . for the government of the United States in its policy towards U.N. peacekeeping," which now required "strict conditions for U.S. support" of any new mission.[33]

Looking back on all the unheeded warnings, General Dallaire, in an interview on Canadian television in September 1997, assailed "the apathy and the absolute detachment of the international community—particularly the Western world—from the plight of the Rwandans." He concluded with a blunt question that reflected his amazement that preventing genocide was not defined in 1994 as a global strategic interest: "Fundamentally, to be very candid and soldierly, who the hell cared about Rwanda?"[34]

## What Might Have Been Done

On April 6, 1994, the evening after President Habyarimana's plane was shot down, a "crisis committee" of Rwandan military leaders met until midnight. The meeting was chaired by Colonel Théoneste Bagosora, a Hutu extremist and close friend of the president's wife, Madame Agathe Habyarimana, both of whom had long been suspected of manipulating the president on behalf of their extremist agenda. By the time the meeting broke up, hundreds of soldiers, militia, and presidential guards with lists of high-ranking Tutsis and moderate Hutu leaders had been dispatched throughout Kigali to begin the killing.

Their first target was the prime minister. When the soldiers entered the prime minister's house, a group of ten Belgian peacekeepers tried to rescue her. They were quickly surrounded by a much larger group of Hutu soldiers, who captured, tortured, and murdered the Belgians and then dismembered their bodies. As General Dallaire's informant had predicted in January, this cynical and premeditated attack on the U.N. peacekeepers provided Bagosora and his fellow extermination planners with an insurance policy against any further active U.N. intervention to stop the genocide. Within a week, the Belgians had withdrawn the rest of their soldiers from Rwanda.

It is, of course, impossible to know what might have happened under different circumstances, but there can be no doubt that the U.N. troops would have been better able to defend themselves under rules of engagement authorizing the use of all necessary force if they were threatened with attack. The warning sent to New York had clearly indicated that the Hutu terrorists were already planning in January to head off any further international intervention by killing U.N. peacekeepers once the genocide started. In response to this warning, the United Nations could have beefed up its peacekeeping operation and given it the authority and the means to defend itself. Paradoxically, the most effective way at this point for the U.N. to have avoided being sucked into an endless conflict it could not contain would have been for it to respond forcefully and immediately to the threat against its peacekeepers—both in order to save their lives and to demonstrate to the genocide planners that they would be confronted with force if they continued to pursue their criminal design.

As the peacekeepers withdrew, the genocide spread like wildfire throughout the country. It was ignited according to the plan drawn up by Bagosora's "crisis committee" and fueled by hate radio, mass fear, and efficiently distributed machetes. When the committee gave the order on April 6 to open the caches of small arms shipped earlier to the Rwandan army from France for use against the RPF insurgency, the Interahamwe forces fanned out around Kigali with their lists of Tutsi and moderate Hutu leaders, who became the first victims of the Rwandan holocaust.

The killing escalated as the Hutu extremist radio station, Radio Television Libres des Milles Collines, broadcast that Habyarimana's plane had been attacked by the RPF, that a Tutsi revolution had begun, and that all Tutsis had to be killed in order to stop the revolution and save Hutu lives. A typical radio message broadcast throughout the country on April 7 followed the Hutu Ten Commandments by characterizing Tutsis as "cockroaches" who had to be "exterminated." To ensure that listeners got the point, the broadcaster hammered it home: "You cockroaches must know you are made of flesh. We won't let you kill. We will kill you."[35] Kill or be killed became the slogan of the hate radio campaign. And it worked. Within the first six weeks an estimated 300,000 people were slaughtered, first by the militias and then by terrified and frenzied citizens whose fear of being killed induced them to become instruments of the fastest spreading genocide in recorded history.[36]

The hate-radio broadcasts were another point of potential early intervention to curb the violence. The broadcasts were picked up by the United Nations from the very beginning, and efforts were made both by General Dallaire from the field and by the State Department in Washington to initiate a plan to jam them. But the plan never got off the ground. Prompted by the deputy assistant secretary of state for African affairs, Pru Bushnell, President Clinton's National Security Advisor, Tony Lake, raised the issue with Secretary of Defense William Perry at the end of April. On May 5, Perry's deputy, Frank Wisner, the undersecretary for policy, sent a response to deputy national security advisor Sandy Berger at the White House stating that "we have looked at options to stop the broadcasts within the Pentagon, discussed them interagency and concluded that jamming is an ineffective and expensive mechanism that will not accomplish the objective the NSC Advisor seeks."[37] Meanwhile, the State Department legal adviser's office issued an opinion that jamming would violate international broadcasting agreements.[38] A charitable explanation of these bureaucratic and legal impediments was that this was the first time the national security bureaucracy had been presented with a proposal to use sophisticated technical assets to prevent an incitement to genocide from being broadcast in another country. Unlike peacekeeping, however, radio jamming carried few risks for the United States and in retrospect it is shocking that it was never even attempted.

My own introduction to the Rwanda crisis came on the morning of April 7, 1994, in a conference room on the seventh floor of the State Department, where twenty senior officials were gathered at 9:00 A.M. for our daily staff meeting with deputy secretary Strobe Talbott. When Talbott called on assistant secretaries or their deputies to report on overnight developments, Pru Bushnell announced that the presidents of Rwanda and Burundi had been killed in a plane crash after a possible rocket attack in Kigali, and that "systematic shooting of government ministers" was taking place.

Bushnell had traveled to Kigali in late March to prod Habyarimana's government to comply with the Arusha accords. She had warned the Rwandan president that if he failed to implement the peace agreement, the U.S. Congress was likely to demand the withdrawal of the U.N. peacekeeping force because of political hostility in the United States toward U.N. operations following the Somalia debacle. Based on Bushnell's trip, the State Department was concerned about the growing tensions in Rwanda. When the violence erupted after the president's plane was shot down, this concern deepened. But none of the department's Rwanda experts predicted that the violence would turn quickly into genocide.

On April 8, George Moose (who had returned the night before from Uganda) delivered the Rwanda report at the assistant secretaries' daily meeting. By then the violence was spreading rapidly. "The question," Moose told the group, "is what the U.N. can do." This, of course, depended in large part on what the United States would do. Moose knew that the political firestorm after the Somalia disaster had forced U.S. policy to take a sharp turn away from supporting new peacekeeping ventures. "We're looking into it" was all he could say about what would happen. Meanwhile, the African Affairs Bureau informed Secretary Warren Christopher in a memo the same day that the violence in Kigali was escalating.

The Talbott meeting went on to other major crises in U.S. policy that were breaking that day. On China, political pressure was mounting for President Clinton to grant China the trading status of most favored nation despite its record of massive human rights abuses and its unwillingness to respond to U.S. calls for change. In Bosnia, the Serbs and Croats were encountering no resistance to their ongoing slaughter of Muslims and of each other. Off the coast of Haiti, thousands of boat people fleeing repression were being intercepted and returned by U.S. Coast Guard cutters. As I listened to the report on the new, fast-breaking crisis in Rwanda, I knew that our capacity to respond would be affected by the intense competition for time and resources that we were facing on many fronts.

I also knew that my own political standing within the administration had been undercut by the controversy surrounding our China human rights policy and my role in implementing it. Although I was working to carry out a Clinton executive order linking trade with China to improvements in human rights, I was perceived in some quarters, especially the economic agencies, as operating contrary to a competing policy of promoting U.S. trade and investment in China. Outside of a relatively small circle of people in the State Department and the National Security Council, I had few inside allies in the spring of 1994, and was in a weak position to influence our response to the exploding situation in Rwanda. Furthermore, I did not fully comprehend in those early days what was happening in Rwanda, both because I was preoccupied and overwhelmed by other crises, and because I failed to grasp the full implication of the reports I was hearing.

The reports were both disturbing and confusing. Widespread killings were occurring, but it was not clear to what extent these were being planned and directed, and how they related to the ongoing hostilities between the Rwandan army and the RPF. The key question, as Talbott put it during a staff meeting on April 11, was "What becomes of the U.N. peacekeepers?" After the killing of the Belgian soldiers, pressure was mounting to withdraw the rest. By then, the United States had already evacuated the embassy staff and 250 Americans from Rwanda; other countries were also bringing their citizens home.

Meanwhile, U.N. troops were guarding an ever-growing number of Rwandans trying to escape the killings. But the peacekeepers now numbered fewer than two thousand (of which all but 270 would be withdrawn within a week) and were continuing to operate under sharply restricted rules of engagement. Moose, Bushnell, and I, as well as Phyllis Oakley, the assistant secretary for refugee affairs, and Don Steinberg and Eric Schwartz of the National Security Council staff, took the position that if the United Nations could make a credible case that by staying in Rwanda it could save lives, then the United States should call for it to stay.

In fact, the United States itself, not the United Nations, should have been making that case, but inside the administration the early policy discussions were going in the opposite direction. By mid-April, four thousand foreigners had been evacuated from Rwanda, the Belgians had withdrawn their troops, and the White House, the Pentagon, and the State Department were paralyzed by our own post-Somalia policy on peacekeeping. This policy, which President Clinton would formalize in Presidential Decision Directive (PDD) 25, on May 3 required the United States to work actively against the establishment or continuation of any U.N. peacekeeping mission when hostilities were occurring on the ground.[39] The directive was a peacekeeping straitjacket created to stave off the torrent of congressional criticism of the administration that had followed the Somalia debacle. Its author, Richard Clarke of the National Security Council staff, was given his assignment by Tony Lake, and Clarke argued that his job was to "save peacekeeping" by tightly restricting its use.[40] The drafting of PDD 25 effectively blocked any possibility that the United States would support a continuation of the Rwanda mission.

On April 17 General Dallaire made a last appeal to U.N. head-quarters for five thousand well-armed soldiers backed by a strong mandate.[41] Even at that late date, he asserted, the expanding genocide could have been curtailed. Dallaire's plan was simple: deploy armed peacekeepers on the roads leading out of Kigali to block the genocide instigators from continuing to fan out around the country. Although by then the killing was already under way in many parts of the country, Dallaire's plan might have saved lives.

On April 21, however, the Security Council passed a resolution, with strong U.S. support, virtually disbanding Dallaire's force, by cutting it 90 percent and withdrawing all but 270 soldiers from Rwanda. The rationale for the U.S. position had been set out a week earlier in an "instruction cable" drafted by Clarke and sent by the State Department to Madeleine Albright at the United Nations. "Our opposition to retaining a [U.N. peacekeeping] presence in Rwanda is firm. It is based on our conviction that the Security Council has an obligation to ensure that peacekeeping operations are viable, that they are capable of fulfilling their mandates, and that U.N. peacekeeping personnel are not placed or retained, knowingly, in an untenable situation."[42] Ironically, two weeks earlier a thousand well-armed French, Belgian, and Italian troops had been sent to Kigali for the sole purpose of guarding the evacuation of foreign nationals. Although more than 100,000 Rwandans had already been killed, many more who might have been saved if Dallaire's advice had been heeded were now doomed to die before the genocide finally ran its course three months later.

On April 19, I learned that Monique Mujawamariya had miraculously escaped from Rwanda with one of the diplomatic convoys of evacuating foreign nationals. She had flown to Washington to plead for a stronger U.N. force, arriving the day after the Security Council voted to withdraw all but a skeletal peacekeeping force. Coming to the State Department to see me after meeting with Dick Clarke at the National Security Council, Monique was deeply discouraged by the reception she had received at the White House. The forthcoming presidential decision directive on peacekeeping, of course, would mean nothing to her, nor would the opposition of the Joint Chiefs of Staff and key members of Congress to U.N. peacekeeping activities after Somalia. Monique told me about losing contact with her two children and husband, who were still in the path of the cataclysm in southeastern Rwanda and had no means of escape.

Soon after meeting with Monique, I began to consider traveling to Rwanda. I teamed up with the African Affairs Bureau to get the U.S. and European governments to publicize the staggering rate of killing going on inside the country. We tried to put pressure on the genocide leaders by spotlighting their names and including them on an international watchlist. We proposed an arms embargo on Rwanda to stop the shipment of weapons into the country. Working with a task force chaired by Peter Tarnoff, the State Department's undersecretary for political affairs, we also planned a diplomatic approach to other countries in the region and the Organization of African Unity (OAU) to urge the immediate formation of a regional coalition to press for an end of the killing and to deploy regional peacekeepers once the situation allowed it. I volunteered to travel to Rwanda, Ethiopia, Tanzania, Uganda and Burundi to implement this initiative.

While I was preparing for the trip, I ran into a wall of internal opposition to publicly using the term "genocide" to describe what was happening in Rwanda. I wanted to deliver a statement both in private meetings and in public that stressed the "personal responsibility of the Rwandan military leaders for genocide," but I could not get clearance to use this language from the State Department Legal Advisor's Office or the Bureau of Public Affairs. I was told that an official pronouncement that genocide had been committed might have been understood not simply to be a statement of fact, but to have policy implications. The bureaucracy was obviously nervous. Having received no high-level signal to engage on the Rwanda crisis, it did not want to be drawn into a situation that its political leaders were seeking to avoid. But in my view, there *were* policy implications to be derived from what was happening in Rwanda. The Convention on the Prevention and Punishment of the Crime of Genocide, ratified by the United States in 1988, seemed very clear: under Article 1, parties to the convention "confirm that genocide . . . is a crime under international law which *they will undertake to prevent*."[43]

The semantic debate over "genocide" was an example of what was happening inside the administration on Rwanda. The President was still upset over the peacekeeping disaster in Somalia, which had come at a high political cost for him. The Joint Chiefs of Staff were adamantly opposed to new U.N. peacekeeping deployments. Congress was pressing the administration to avoid similar humanitarian operations in the future and to restrict the ability of the United Nations to mount them. The public was aghast at the media reports about the slaughter in Rwanda, but certainly not clamoring for U.S. intervention to stop it. Both reflecting and creating these political realities, the administration completed its interagency review of the new policy restricting peacekeeping, and the President issued his Decision Directive 25 on May 3.

### Like Logs in a River

On April 29 I went to the White House for a special interagency meeting on Rwanda. I entered the cramped, wood-paneled National Security Council "war room" in the West Wing with Strobe Talbott and George Moose. Just hours before I had lost a battle in that same room with representatives of economic agencies over the administration's changing China policy. Now I was surrounded by a battery of officials from the Defense Department, the Joint Chiefs of Staff, and the intelligence agencies, who had all earlier expressed their opposition to strengthening the tiny U.N. force in Rwanda. Sandy Berger, who was chairing the meeting, recognized that the administration had not given itself any maneuvering room on a crisis that was now playing out in gruesome detail every day in the press. Berger skillfully moved the discussion to a search for actions that could be taken immediately.

With Talbott's help, Berger persuaded the group to endorse a U.N. resolution calling for an arms embargo and an investigation of who was responsible for instigating the killings. (I saw this as an early glimmer that the United States might be willing to support a War Crimes Tribunal for Rwanda.) In addition, the group recommended both endorsing U.N. efforts to keep the violence from spreading to neighboring Burundi by sending additional peacekeepers there if necessary, and working with regional governments and the OAU to raise a local peacekeeping force for possible non-U.N. intervention in Rwanda. This last issue would be one of the three focal points of my trip. The other two would be humanitarian relief for the refugees and justice for the perpetrators of genocide.

We were floundering on many fronts. In his morning meeting of assistant secretaries on May 2, Strobe Talbott expressed frustration with the shackles the administration had put on itself by continuing to follow the military doctrine championed by Colin Powell after the Gulf War—a doctrine that barred the use of force except in very narrowly defined circumstances to counter an immediate threat, like the outbreak of World War III. I knew the problem was not just the political pall cast by Somalia on peacekeeping activities; it was much deeper, and could be traced to the very roots of Cold War military doctrine. Talbott's observation sparked one of the few far-reaching discussions I remember having in the normally clipped daily senior staff meetings. By mid-1994, it had become clear to some of us that the crises in Rwanda, Bosnia, and Haiti had escalated out of control because the United States, the preeminent power in the post–Cold War world, was denying itself the means to address them. Talbott asked the Office of Policy Planning, headed by Jim Steinberg, to produce a paper analyzing the problem. This was not a solution, but at least it was a step toward diagnosing the cause of our chronic inability to deal with humanitarian crises, and it foreshadowed Talbott's aggressive leadership role throughout the summer in building the case for intervention five months later in Haiti.

As I prepared to leave for Africa, I knew there were three big questions about U.S. policy, beyond our failure to act earlier to stop the genocide. Would we now be willing to consider supporting the deployment of a new regional peacekeeping force for Rwanda? Were we

prepared to take steps toward investigating the causes of the genocide and bringing to justice those who had instigated it? And were we
willing to make an immediate commitment of emergency assistance
to the refugees who were streaming across the border into Tanzania?
Although I did not have the answers, I knew these questions would
frame my mission. I was not centrally involved in humanitarian relief,
which was being managed by the U.N. high commissioner for refugees, Sadaka Ogata, and refugee specialists in the State Department,
but I knew that the growing refugee crisis would be a major issue in
my meetings. I felt that the White House interagency meeting on
April 29 had opened the door to a new peacekeeping force, and had
produced a consensus on the need for an investigation and the urgency of providing humanitarian assistance. I confirmed this with
Don Steinberg at the National Security Council, who agreed but was
cautious about how much I could say in East Africa about peacekeeping reinforcements. He reminded me that PDD 25 would be coming
out any day, and that it would impose sharp restrictions on U.S. support for any new U.N. deployment. The biggest question of all was
whether the White House would engage more deeply on the Rwanda
crisis, and whether the President would educate the American public
about how what was happening there should matter to them.

I took off from Washington with a mixture of relief and anxiety. I
was relieved to get away from the backbiting—especially my losing
battle over our human rights policy toward China—but I was filled
with foreboding about Rwanda. Since my trip had interagency approval, it was designated a "presidential mission." This meant an Air
Force plane would take me and my team—David Rawson, our ambassador to Rwanda; Brunson McKinley, principal deputy assistant
secretary for refugee affairs; and Judith Kaufmann, my special assistant—from Rhein-Main Air Base in Frankfurt to Ethiopia, Tanzania,
Burundi, and Uganda. The five-seat plane was not often used for
long distances. The trip would take ten hours, and we would
have to stop for refueling in Naples and Cairo, swinging to the east
over the Mediterranean to avoid flying over airspace controlled
by Libya and Sudan before finally reaching Addis Ababa, our first
destination.

Addis Ababa was teeming with life. Our car snaked its way around crowded market stalls in the blazing midday sun, dodging swarms of pedestrians carrying bundled goods on their heads. Eventually, we arrived at the modest stucco building that served as the headquarters of the OAU, the weak and poorly funded association of African countries. It was May 4, almost a month after the Rwandan genocide had begun.

My first meeting in the region was with OAU Secretary-General Salim Salim. A large, brooding man, Salim had served as Tanzania's foreign minister before taking over the small and relatively powerless OAU secretariat. Having chaired the sputtering Rwanda peace negotiations in Arusha in 1993, Salim was deeply depressed about the latest turn of events in Rwanda. Although he lacked the political authority of a national leader, I knew it was important for me to see him before meeting with any of the regional leaders to whom he reported. As I sat down with Salim, I was intensely aware that I had come ten thousand miles to discuss Rwanda, but had very little to offer. Since the interagency meeting of April 29 had left ambiguous the question of a U.S. role in supporting a regional peacekeeping force, I was constrained in what I could say to Salim or the regional leaders.

Salim opened our discussion by observing that the crisis in Rwanda had been caused by a complex power struggle in which Hutu extremists had gained the upper hand. Over the last month it had spiraled into an unchecked genocide while the international community had pulled out. Salim was well aware of the role of the United States in calling for the withdrawal of U.N. peacekeepers, and I knew that this action would make him disdainful of the U.S. claim to leadership in the United Nations. Now, he told me, the urgent task was to get the peacekeepers back in, but since the crisis had deepened this would be very difficult. I briefed Salim on the new U.N. resolution we were drafting to stop the shipment of arms into Rwanda, authorize a regional peacekeeping mission, and investigate the cause of the killings.

We agreed that precious time had been lost, and that the situation was far worse because nothing had been done to stop it at the outset. Salim doubted that African forces, without U.S. and European logistical support, would be capable of entering Rwanda until a cease-fire had been worked out between the Rwandan army and the RPF. I knew that the U.S. position was weak because we wanted a resolution authorizing a new peacekeeping force only for a "permissive intervention." More generally, I now knew that the African response I was there to engender depended on what the United States was willing to do.

Here was the nub of the problem. I told Salim we were prepared to provide humanitarian assistance and logistical support for the intervention, but the key was getting a cease-fire. I thanked him for his role as mediator in the earlier Arusha peace talks and urged him to use his influence to bring the parties back together. Salim's expression revealed his pessimism about doing this and the depth of his despair about what was unfolding in Rwanda. He said he would try to reconvene the Arusha talks, but that this effort would not be able to get off the ground until I had gotten the support of the leaders of Ethiopia, Tanzania, Uganda, and Burundi. We agreed that the goal of everyone should be to stop the killings. But how to do this without a major forceful intervention seemed impossible.

My exchange with Salim was an example of the diplomatic box the United States had put itself in as a result of our peacekeeping restrictions and Washington's unwillingness to confront what was really happening on the ground. Arranging a cease-fire and reviving the Arusha talks were clearly pipe dreams at that point. What was needed was a plan to stop the genocide.

My only hope for action was to canvass the regional leaders. For the next three days I crisscrossed East Africa on my quixotic mission. Following my talks with Salim and Ethiopian president Meles in Addis Ababa, Tanzanian president Mwinyi in Arusha, Burundian president Ntibantunganya in Bujumbura and Ugandan president Museveni in Kampala, I drafted five separate joint communiqués calling for a cease-fire in Rwanda, an end of the killings, and the creation of a regional peacekeeping force to stabilize the situation. Throughout this whirlwind round of meetings, I was in constant contact with Pru Bushnell in Washington. At each of my stops Pru encouraged me to continue rounding up regional support for what we were trying to do, but also told me that the Pentagon was resisting even this weak formula for peacekeeping in Rwanda. I had the sickening feeling that my mission was doomed because Washington was unwilling to do anything to stop, or even slow, the killing.

By May 7, the last day of our trip, the genocide was proceeding at roughly the rate of five killings a minute, three hundred an hour, 7,200 a day.[44] By that calculation, 21,000 Tutsis had been exterminated while I was in East Africa. On the way from Bujumbura to Kampala our small plane flew low over the Kagera River, which separates Rwanda from the Ngara region of Tanzania. From a thousand feet we could see two terrible manifestations of what was happening on the ground. Where the river turned inward and the border went through open grassland, a great flood of humanity was sweeping into Tanzania. The river itself revealed the deadly truth. Like logs slowly flowing in the current, hundreds of human bodies could be seen heading downstream toward Lake Victoria. David Rawson picked out a bridge below us where he said reports indicated the bodies were being counted at a rate of ten per minute. Rawson pointed toward the lake, fifty miles downstream in Uganda, where boys were reportedly being paid the equivalent of a nickel a body to fish them out at the river's mouth.

Flying out of Africa I was deeply shaken by what I had witnessed. I stopped in Geneva to tell the story. In a press conference on May 8 I decided that even though I had made no progress toward the formation of a new peacekeeping mission, I would do my best to tell the truth about what I had heard was happening in Rwanda and had seen myself. I told the international press that crimes against humanity and acts of genocide were being committed and that those responsible should be investigated and brought to justice. As I expected, this ruffled some feathers in Washington. I called for a special session of the U.N. Human Rights Commission to initiate the investigation, and endorsed the upcoming trip to Rwanda of the new U.N. high commissioner for human rights, Jose Ayala Lasso of Ecuador. Having failed to stop the genocide, I felt at least we could begin to work backward to bring justice to the survivors.

Returning to Washington, I was struck again by the horrors that were unfolding simultaneously in many parts of the world. The immensity of what was happening in Rwanda had put a sharp new focus on the crisis in Bosnia. If Bosnia was a testing ground for post–Cold War morality, I thought, Rwanda was a horror of even greater dimensions, not only because the scale of the violations of basic humanitarian law was so great, but also because the world's response was being tested under the added weight of racism. If our response to Bosnia was grossly inadequate, an even greater evil in Rwanda was now eliciting an even weaker response. Would it be possible to use the consensus I had found during my round of African diplomacy to persuade Washington to do more about Rwanda?

# CHAPTER 2

# RWANDA

## THE STRUGGLE FOR JUSTICE

I came back to Washington with a report that suggested the outlines of a plan of action. I had met with African leaders from the region who seemed ready to participate in a new peacekeeping effort and to assist the United Nations by providing staging areas for refugee and humanitarian relief operations. But I found it difficult to get much attention. Everyone agreed that Rwanda was a disaster, but it was seen as a small country, far away, not connected to any U.S. strategic interest, and engulfed in an orgy of killing that was happening so fast and on such a vast scale that few in Washington could understand or even believe it.

The administration was being pulled in other directions. Warren Christopher was preoccupied with China and the Middle East. Tony Lake and Strobe Talbott were managing the deepening crisis in Haiti. Sandy Berger, who had helped steer the interagency meeting that had provided a reasonably strong mandate for my trip, now reflected the administration's distrust of post-Somalia peacekeeping. In the Pentagon, William Perry and his deputy, Walt Slocombe, were adamantly opposed to new peacekeeping deployments by the United Nations. And Madeleine Albright was in the unenviable position of having to defend the administration's new restrictive policy on peace-keeping in the U.N. Security Council. The system was on overload. It had no time or will to address another crisis, and it was not recep-tive to my human rights field report.

## Paralysis

I summarized the argument in favor of limited intervention in a memorandum to Christopher. I reported that there was a consensus among the African leaders I had met on my trip that practical and immediate steps could be taken to address the Rwanda crisis. Presidents Meles of Ethiopia, Mwinyi of Tanzania, and Museveni of Uganda, as well as Salim of the OAU, all had emphasized the same three points.

First, they were willing to support and contribute troops to a reconstituted U.N. peacekeeping force that would be deployed with U.S. and European logistical help on a "permissive basis" to those areas of Rwanda in which the Rwandan government and RPF forces were not actively fighting each other. The mission of this force would be to create zones of safety for civilians, deter further genocide, and assist displaced persons. I was heartened to learn that Nelson Mandela had raised this same approach with Vice President Al Gore in a meeting in South Africa the week before.

Another point of consensus among the African leaders was the need for an international tribunal to investigate and assess individual responsibility for the genocide. In our meetings in Kampala, Ugandan president Museveni had expressed his view that the deadly cycle of retribution would continue until justice was done. More pointedly, Salim of the OAU had warned that now that the United Nations had established an International Criminal Tribunal to prosecute perpetrators of genocide and crimes against humanity in Bosnia, this effort to bring justice to the people of a European country would have no credibility whatsoever if it was not immediately extended to the survivors of an even greater genocide in Africa.

The third area of agreement among the African leaders was the urgency of providing humanitarian assistance to address the exploding refugee crisis. During my two days in Tanzania, over 250,000 Hutus had fled across the Kagera River bridge connecting Rwanda with Tanzania in order to escape the oncoming RPF forces under the command of General Paul Kagame as they advanced toward Kigali, eventually routing the Hutu Interahamwe and the Rwandan army at the beginning of July. It later became clear that the speed and coordination of this refugee exodus—and the even larger one into Zaire two months later—were attributable to Hutu extremist leaders who were trying to transform themselves and other genocide perpetrators into refugee victims. Once in the camps, they could live off the largesse of international relief agencies. In early May, Tanzania and other countries in the region were appealing for immediate help to deal with this escalating refugee crisis. The U.N. high commissioner for refugees, Sadaka Ogata, and her deputy, Sergio de Mello, were working to mobilize an immediate international response. Although my responsibilities did not extend to refugee relief, the mission I was heading included Brunson McKinley, the State Department's deputy assistant secretary for refugee affairs. McKinley would stay behind to join the U.N. team in surveying the situation in Tanzania and developing a plan of action for Washington and other donor governments.

Throughout this period, the genocide raged on. Following the withdrawal of international troops six weeks earlier, the tiny remaining U.N. peacekeeping force was powerless to stop or slow the killings. In early May the U.N. ambassadors from the Czech Republic, New Zealand, and Spain drafted a Security Council resolution authorizing the limited "permissive" intervention that the regional African leaders were calling for. This presented a major challenge for Madeleine Albright, who worked to find a way to support the resolution within the extremely tight restrictions imposed by the new U.S. policy on peacekeeping. After lengthy negotiations over the mission of an expanded force, the United States finally agreed to sign on as a cosponsor and the resolution was adopted by the Security Council on May 17.[1]

But that was only the beginning of what turned out to be a two-month struggle to deploy the new peacekeeping troops. During this time the Pentagon bureaucracy failed to provide logistical support—specifically, fifty armored personnel carriers (APCs) that the United Nations had requested—to the 5,500 troops from eight African countries who would be recruited for the reconstituted force. The bureaucratic wrangles over the APCs finally ended, but instead of donating them, the Pentagon agreed only to *rent* them to the United Nations for $10 million, including the cost of transporting them from Germany to Uganda.[2] This begrudging gesture was greeted with cynicism by other U.N. members who were well aware that Senator Jesse Helms (R.-N.C.) and other anti-internationalists in the U.S. Congress had succeeded by then in blocking the administration from paying more than a billion dollars of overdue U.N. dues.

Congress was a big part of the problem. The administration's tightly restrictive policy on peacekeeping had been drafted in response to congressional criticism of the United Nations's management of its ill-fated Somalia mission. As the crisis in Rwanda escalated, most congressional leaders—with a few notable exceptions like Senator Paul Simon (D.-Ill.) and Representative Tom Lantos (D.-Calif.), himself a Holocaust survivor—expressed little or no interest in it. The Congress made clear that it was strongly opposed to any U.S. participation in a new U.N. peacekeeping force, particularly after the speed and scope of the killings became fully known in early May. On April 10, Senate Majority Leader Bob Dole (R-Kans.) reflected the prevailing congressional view when he stated that the primary U.S. interest in Rwanda was the protection of Americans. Following their successful evacuation, Dole expressed his satisfaction that "the Americans are out, and as far as I'm concerned, that ought to be the end of it. . . . I don't think we have any national interest there."[3] At the same time, Senator Helms had begun his successful six-year campaign to block the further payment of U.S. dues to the United Nations, setting the United States on a long-term collision course with many of its allies, reducing its leverage in the Security Council, and damaging its credibility in the United Nations.

The mood in the State Department in May 1994 was grim. We were dealing simultaneously with many crises and losing ground on each one. At a staff meeting on May 17, Tim Wirth, undersecretary for global affairs, commented that "we're not responding to criticism, and we're not showing the public what their stake is in foreign policy." Frustrated after my Africa trip by the deafening silence from the White House on Rwanda, I agreed. I published an op-ed on the crisis in the *Boston Globe,* but what I wrote only demonstrated the absence of higher-level voices.[4] Meanwhile, the administration was being battered on Haiti, China, Bosnia, and the Middle East, and it was not effectively identifying and explaining its foreign policy objectives. China policy was in the greatest turmoil. The President was wavering between trade and human rights, and different administration officials were sending competing signals to the Chinese and the American public about what we were trying to accomplish. Backbiting and distrust characterized relations within and among the State Department, the Defense Department, the National Security Council, and other parts of the bureaucracy.

In this turbulent political environment, Rwanda was the new quicksand catastrophe that no one wanted to deal with. As the weeks went by and the scope of the genocide mushroomed, it was difficult to imagine that foreign policy could ever have moral content.

On May 21, I co-signed a "compromise" memo to the secretary of state urging him to settle the semantic debate over "genocide" by authorizing an official statement that "acts of genocide" were being committed in Rwanda.[5] This was another low point for me. I could not get agreement within the State Department to recognize that Rwanda was *engulfed* by genocide. Ironically, the more limited "acts of genocide" was the phrase for which I had been criticized two weeks earlier when I had used it in my Geneva press conference following my trip to central Africa. The compromise memo at least included a paragraph that gave the U.S. delegation to the U.N. Human Rights Commission special session on Rwanda some leeway to use the broader term "genocide." Our memo pointed out, "If we do not . . . use the genocide label to condemn events in Rwanda, our credibility will be undermined with human rights groups and the general public who may question how much evidence we can legitimately require before coming to a policy conclusion."[6]

Looking back, I am again sickened by this debate over terminology, my own participation in it, and the length of time it took to settle the issue. In essence, the strongest country in the world took two months to conclude the obvious, during which time it avoided what was arguably its international legal responsibility "to actually do something" about a genocide in progress.[7]

At the United Nations, there was a leadership vacuum on Rwanda that the French moved to fill by intervening unilaterally. On June 23, a heavily armed French military force of 2,500, Operation Turquoise, entered Rwanda from the west, through Goma across the Zairean border. The rapid deployment of these French troops demonstrated that even at this late date, military intervention to curtail the genocide was still possible, and there is no doubt that the French intervention succeeded in saving some lives. But the French cynically played into the hands of Hutu propagandists by asserting that the killings were the result of a leaderless popular uprising that had erupted after the assassination of President Habyarimana. The French intervention also reinforced the role France had played during the previous decade in propping up Habyarimana and the Hutu nationalists through arms shipments and other forms of military support. By intervening as a surrogate for the United Nations (which voted its approval of Operation Turquoise in a Security Council Resolution on June 22), the French were able to claim the mantle of international rescuer. But most of the Rwandans rescued by French paratroopers were Hutus, many of whom had participated in the genocide and were now fleeing from the oncoming RPF forces.

The acquiescence of the United Nations in the French intervention had three negative long-term consequences for post-genocide Rwanda. First, the Tutsi survivors began to believe that the United Nations favored perpetrators of the genocide over victims. Second, the Hutu extremists and Rwandan army forces who had carried out the genocide were given a boost at a crucial moment as they fled into the sprawling refugee camps in Zaire. And third, the French intervention confirmed the view of the RPF political and military leaders, headed by General Paul Kagame, that the United Nations, which had withdrawn all but a handful of its peacekeepers, was now indirectly helping the enemy. This view would be reinforced in the months ahead as the United Nations helped build up the refugee camps in Goma—camps from which the Hutu extremists were able to launch frequent guerrilla raids into Rwanda to continue their unfinished business of exterminating Tutsis. While Kagame's criticism of the U.N. refugee agency was unfair, since Sergio de Mello, the deputy director, later toured the camps and called for a peacekeeping force to disarm and arrest the extremists, it was symptomatic of the Rwandan leader's increasingly strained relationship with the United Nations after the French intervention.

While the French were helping their Hutu protégés escape, the Tutsi RPF forces were steadily gaining ground. Against great odds and with no international help other than from Uganda, General Kagame and his forces waged a successful campaign to defeat the Rwandan army and take control of the country. On July 2 the RPF took Kigali. Two weeks later, a new government was set up headed by a Hutu moderate, Faustin Twagiramungu, with Kagame as the dominant figure holding the somewhat misleading title of vice president and defense minister. At last the genocide was over. Having failed to do anything to stop it, the United States and other members of the international community now began to assist the vast horde of refugees who had fled the country.

## A Sea of Humanity

As the Hutu refugees poured across the border into Zaire in July 1994, international television images depicted them as the victims of the crisis. Mostly gone from the nightly news were the earlier grisly pictures of the genocide, and in their place were scenes of vast lines of people on the move and setting up makeshift camps on the desolate volcanic terrain in Eastern Zaire. These images created the impression among casual viewers that all the refugees were in fact genocide survivors, and that helping them would assuage the world's guilt for not having intervened earlier. Since it was possible to save living refugees but not dead victims, a consensus emerged in Washington for the United States to provide military logistical support for international refugee agencies as they rushed supplies to the camps that were springing up around Goma.

Brian Atwood, the creative and energetic director of the U.S. Agency for International Development (USAID), probably did more than anyone to stimulate U.S. leadership of this intervention. Atwood visited the refugee camps as they were being set up and met with local representatives of the Office of the U.N. High Commissioner for Refugees and other international relief agencies that were struggling to cope with the greatest single refugee crisis they had ever seen. In a series of television interviews from the refugee camps and then in meetings back in Washington, Atwood made an eloquent appeal for international engagement with Rwanda. Unlike the earlier media accounts that had misled casual observers into believing that Hutu refugees were genocide survivors, not the perpetrators that many of them were, Atwood's interviews were an honest assessment of both the urgency and complexity of the crisis. The security and economic costs of not engaging with post-genocide Rwanda would be enormous, he pointed out, just as the cost of not acting to stop the genocide at the outset had already proved incalculable both in terms of lives lost and regional stability shattered. The refugees needed assistance, but the Hutu extremists among them had to be identified and arrested for their crimes. Most of the refugees were innocent Hutus and not Tutsi genocide survivors, but the presence of extremists made the camps breeding grounds for more anti-Tutsi violence that could be curbed only if U.N. peacekeepers returned and the new Rwandan government was given massive international assistance.

Atwood's arguments were persuasive to President Clinton, who sensed the growing public support for U.S. assistance now that the violence had subsided and the crisis had taken on a broader humanitarian cast. But the Somalia specter still loomed large and the Pentagon continued to insist that U.S. troops be kept out of any new U.N. peacekeeping force. A compromise was struck that called for a U.S. military airlift and logistical support for the refugee assistance operations that would be managed by the United Nations. The United States would not contribute soldiers to the newly reconstituted and expanded U.N. peacekeeping force, but the initial airlift of troops into Kigali would be carried out with the assistance of U.S. planes and military personnel. This represented a significant breakthrough for those who had been arguing for months for some kind of intervention.

In mid-July I was traveling on a long-scheduled human rights mission to Russia, Kazakhstan, and Turkey. I was in the mountains of southeastern Turkey meeting with local Turkish officials and representatives of Kurdish organizations about the human rights crisis in the region when I got a phone call from Nancy Ely-Raphel, my deputy in Washington, who told me that our Rwanda policy was changing. I rushed home to participate in the planning of a U.S. initiative that would be a step in the right direction, but one taken far too late for victims of the genocide.

As Washington made hasty preparations to airlift supplies to the refugee camps, I geared up to return to Rwanda as the first U.S. emissary to the new government. I discussed the rapidly changing situation with Strobe Talbott, Sandy Berger, Peter Tarnoff, and George Moose. General Kagame had won the war on his own while the world stood by and watched the genocide destroy his people, and now he deeply distrusted the international community. It would be my job to demonstrate to him that the United States was concerned about the survivors inside Rwanda, not just the refugees who had fled the country. I would offer our help in setting up a team of international human rights monitors to guard against new outbreaks of genocide, and I would seek Kagame's support for a Security Council resolution to establish an international criminal tribunal for Rwanda to investigate the genocide and bring its leaders to justice. I would also urge Kagame to work with the United States to rebuild the country's shattered justice system. I would offer to initiate contacts between the new Rwandan government and USAID so that a plan of technical assistance and training for Rwandan justice personnel could be developed and a survey could be undertaken to determine the country's law enforcement needs. These points all sounded logical and persuasive, but they would be severely tested in the psychologically devastated environment of post-genocide Rwanda. In that environment, I knew the demand would be greatest for tracking down and punishing the instigators of the Rwandan holocaust.

I assembled a top-notch team for what promised to be a difficult mission. Joining me were Crystal Nix and Josiah Rosenblatt, senior members of the Human Rights Bureau who would also play key roles on later missions to Bosnia, and Rick Barton, head of the new USAID Office of Transition Initiatives, whom Brian Atwood had sent to me after Atwood returned from the refugee camps.

Our first stop was Geneva. There we tried to energize the U.N. Human Rights Center to begin recruiting and training a team of international civilian monitors who would enter Rwanda with the new peacekeeping force. Ibrahima Fall, the Senegalese director of the center, assured me and Dan Spiegel, the U.S. ambassador to the U.N. agencies in Geneva, that he was working on this. We then flew on to Frankfurt and boarded a C-141 Air Force cargo plane at the Rhein-Main military air base. Every square inch of cargo space was loaded with food pallets and water supplies bound for the refugees in Goma, and the plane could not carry a full tank of fuel. The flight therefore required a delicate midair tanker refueling operation over Egypt, which I observed from the cockpit, stunned by the gap between this feat of technology and our failure to try to stop what had happened in Rwanda. We arrived at Entebbe in Uganda at 3:00 A.M. The relief supplies were unloaded next to the burned-out hulk of an El Al passenger jet that had been stormed by Israeli paratroopers fifteen years earlier in a successful hostage rescue.

At the Entebbe airport, while the cargo was being sorted and transferred to a C-5A transport plane for the final flight into Kigali, we were briefed by Johnny Carson, the seasoned U.S. ambassador to Uganda. Carson was an expert on the RPF, which for a decade had launched its military operations from Uganda into Rwanda. He told us that the situation in Kigali was stable and that General Kagame and his forces were firmly in control of the capital. The intelligence reports on Goma, however, were more ominous and indicated that the refugee camps were a powder keg. To make matters worse, neighboring Burundi was increasingly tense. I would travel later to the camps to assess the situation, and to Bujumbura, the capital of Burundi, to urge the government to avoid provocative actions.

Carson knew my task in Kigali would be to persuade Kagame to endorse a War Crimes Tribunal for Rwanda. He was skeptical that this would be possible in light of the Tutsi commander's bitter attitude toward the United Nations and the international community. "Kagame plans to go it alone, since that's how he's gotten where he is," Carson told me. Carson felt that Kagame would try to prevent vigilante justice in Rwanda by being tough on his military and arresting "genocidaires" in the villages. But eventually he would need help. "You may be able to get through to him if you show you understand the pressures he faces from the genocide leaders in the camps and indicate our interest in helping bring them to justice."

## Liberators

We flew in low over the hazy Rwandan countryside and touched down at mid-morning on August 5. As our plane taxied on the same Kigali tarmac from which the genocide had been launched four months earlier when President Habyarimana's plane, also preparing to land, had been shot down by a concealed missile fired from the edge of the runway, I wondered what lay ahead for Rwanda. The airport was eerily quiet. The red-roofed city, sprawling over dusty hills stretching into the distance, was baking in the sun. Apart from one other relief transport plane that had come in ahead of us, the runway was deserted.

A few minutes after our arrival, I saw a badly damaged, ramshackle car lurching along the tarmac toward our plane. As it approached, I realized that we were being met by the new government's minister of justice. The car stopped and Minister Alphonse-Marie Nkubito clambered out of the driver's seat. He shook my hand, and unceremoniously asked me in French to climb in beside him through the missing door on the passenger's side.

Nkubito was a well-respected Tutsi lawyer and human rights advocate who had returned from exile in Belgium to join the new government. He was wary of our mission but interested in getting international help to rebuild the shattered Rwandan justice system. "Since justice does not function," he said flatly, "there is a strong feeling for vengeance. But do not blame the government. Blame the genocide."

The climate of vengeance was being fostered by threats to the new Tutsi-dominated Rwandan government coming from extremists operating inside the refugee camps. As I had been warned, the camps were rapidly coming under the control of the genocide leaders, and now constituted a major security challenge to Rwanda. Nkubito wanted to know what the international community was planning to do about the situation. I told him that the United States was prepared to address the problem by working with regional governments to find the genocide leaders and have them arrested, and by sponsoring the establishment of an International War Crimes Tribunal. The justice minister was dubious that the arrests would be made or that an international tribunal would be created quickly enough to stop the next cycle of violence. He indicated that the new government was rounding up tens of thousands of people who were suspected of having participated in the genocide and planned to begin putting them on trial. The Rwandan prisons were already grossly overcrowded, and the demand for revenge by Tutsi survivors was mounting. I told Nkubito that the United States wanted to help Rwanda rebuild its justice system so that it could conduct its own trials. Putting on local trials before the system was ready for them, however, could destabilize the situation further. This was why the Rwandan government should endorse the creation of an international tribunal. Nkubito said the decision on the tribunal would be made by General Kagame. If I wanted an answer to my question, I should raise it directly with him.

Before leaving his office, I gave Nkubito a draft letter endorsing the tribunal for the Rwandan government to consider sending to the U.N. Security Council. I had prepared the letter with Madeleine Albright's deputy, David Scheffer, and with Crystal Nix, who were both working on the new tribunal's charter. I told the minister that if Rwanda endorsed the tribunal, it would be created. If not, I feared the Security Council might drop the whole effort.

General Kagame had set up his headquarters in an abandoned villa at the top of a hill overlooking the decimated city. Our battered embassy Land Rover wound its way up the dusty road through a series of checkpoints manned by heavily armed soldiers to a veranda where the RPF commander waited for us, surrounded by bodyguards. Rail thin and ascetic in appearance, Kagame looked like a cross between a monk and a monarch as he ushered me to a rickety table and began his effort to educate the United States about the meaning of what had happened in Rwanda. Not far below our hilltop perch, I could see vultures circling over the human carrion that still littered the landscape. As the first American diplomat to meet the Tutsi liberator after his arrival in Kigali, I was acutely aware of my representative status. "You are committing two grave errors," Kagame told me, "leaving us with no option but to correct them ourselves." His voice was soft but firm as he leaned toward me in the oppressive heat. "Your relief workers are sheltering those who committed genocide in the refugee camps at our borders, and you are doing nothing to bring these criminals to justice."

Kagame had cut to the essence. The world had stood by while more than three-quarters of a million people were killed in Rwanda, and now it was prolonging the agony by helping the oppressors at the expense of the survivors. If ever there were a case where justice was a precondition for peace, Rwanda was it. I asked Kagame if he would call for the creation of an international tribunal. He told me he would do so if the world could assure him that the criminals would be arrested and that justice would be speedy. "Otherwise," he said, "we will have to do it ourselves." These few words confirmed what I had anticipated: capturing the genocide planners in the refugee camps was essential to Rwandan stability. Although a tribunal to try them would be created, and some would be captured in neighboring countries, the work of the tribunal would be slow and inefficient, and no arrests would ever be made in the refugee camps.

Instead, the camps would be used by extremists to mount raids on Rwanda until finally the Rwandan government would break them up and sponsor a military effort to eradicate Hutu nationalists in Zaire, all of which would result in massive human rights abuses and long-term destabilization of the entire region.

## The Machete Equivalent of a Neutron Bomb

But in August 1994 it was hard to believe that the world had not learned from its catastrophic mistake in Rwanda. Since my mission was to secure the new government's commitment to an international tribunal, I left my meeting with Kagame encouraged that we would be able to move forward in the Security Council. I told him I would travel the next day to Goma with General John Shalikashvili, chairman of the U.S. Joint Chiefs of Staff (who had come to inspect the U.S. troops providing logistical support to U.N. refugee operations). I wanted to see the refugee crisis firsthand and better understand Kagame's concern about how the camps were harboring perpetrators of the genocide.

On the flight from Kigali I had a chance to speak candidly in the cockpit with General Shalikashvili. Over the roar of the C-5A engines, I asked him how he was able to provide support for humanitarian relief efforts in Goma and still comply with the restrictions of the presidential directive on peacekeeping. He said it was difficult, but told me he supported the restrictions and understood why they had been drafted. "After Somalia, Congress was all over us for allowing mission creep." A peacekeeping mission had turned into a manhunt, with fatal consequences for American soldiers. I asked him if he thought the restrictions had prevented us from stopping the genocide in Rwanda, and he said he doubted that anything could have stopped it. The chairman's view was at odds with General Dallaire's, and I found myself thinking once again about the fatal consequences for 800,000 Rwandans of the withdrawal from Rwanda four months earlier of all but a handful of U.N. peacekeepers. Before we landed, I offered the general my opinion that the peacekeeping restrictions of

PDD 25 would have to be loosened if we were ever to have any chance of preventing future Rwandas. Although he had loyally defended the new peacekeeping policy, I sensed that Shalikashvili's views were not far from my own and was therefore not surprised when several months later, and again the following year, he contributed to the administration's policy changes on peacekeeping in Haiti and Bosnia.

Goma is a small, desolate, and deeply impoverished city on Zaire's eastern border with Rwanda. As we landed, I could see the surrounding rough volcanic terrain on which over a million refugees were sprawled as far as the eye could see. The newly paved airstrip where we touched down looked from above like an asphalt raft bobbing on an endless sea of humanity.

The refugee camps were a scene from Dante's *Inferno*, blasted by incredible heat and the stench of living and dead bodies and raw sewage. I found plenty of evidence on the ground that the camps were still in the grip of the genocide and were being organized by its leaders. Traveling with the local U.N. refugee director through aimlessly wandering crowds, I was told about Hutu politicians pulling up in their Mercedes and paying henchmen to enforce strict discipline and punish anyone trying to leave the camps. At one point I saw a grisly example of this enforcement system at work: a man with brutal machete wounds cowering in a ditch beside the road with a crowd around him and no one coming to his rescue. Meanwhile, the Hutu extremist radio stations that had earlier barked marching orders for tens of thousands of genocide foot soldiers in Rwanda had now set up their broadcast equipment in the camps and were stirring up the refugees to continue the "war against the vermin" inside Rwanda, spreading rumors that the Tutsis were now committing atrocities against Hutus who returned and those who had remained behind.

Beneath the terror and propaganda purveyed by the genocide leaders in their brutal bid to control the camps, a vast sense of collective guilt seemed to be settling over the refugee population. It could be detected in ways both small and large. It was impossible to make eye contact with anyone, and groups of people would shrink away when approached. Vast numbers of people were stretched out on plastic sheeting, most of them too sick to walk, but no one came to help them. In this listless and oppressive atmosphere, everyone seemed guilty.

My trip to Goma showed me graphically that of all the desperate needs of Rwanda, justice was the greatest. A cloud of guilt enshrouded many Hutus, especially those who had been swept up in the frenzy of genocidal killings, and it could only be removed by punishing those who had instigated the killings. Meanwhile, the Tutsi survivors demanded revenge. Kagame's warning that "we will have to do it ourselves" if the international community was unable to move quickly enough to respond to the need for justice rang in my head as I pressed the case for a U.N. tribunal. After returning to Kigali from Goma, I secured a reluctant commitment from Kagame to have the Rwandan government endorse the tribunal, but I had the sinking feeling that the U.N. Security Council, led in this case by the United States, would not live up to its commitment to bring speedy international justice to Rwanda, and that Rwanda would then go its separate way and again hold the United Nations responsible for letting it down.

There was a hard edge to Kagame and the RPF that sometimes kept them from taking responsibility for their actions. Having liberated Rwanda from the grip of the Interahamwe and its genocide leaders, the Tutsi military leaders understandably claimed a moral superiority that they believed absolved them from any share of responsibility for what had happened. But history may not be entirely kind to that claim. While the roots of the genocide certainly lie deep in the extremism of the Hutu power movement, its vicious anti-Tutsi campaigns, and its toxic influence on the Habyarimana regime, these roots can also be indirectly traced to the decision in 1990 of Paul Kagame and his RPF guerrilla fighters to launch a military effort to overthrow Habyarimana and replace him with a Tutsi-led government.

It was the unintended consequences of that decision for which Kagame must bear some measure of responsibility. As an old Tutsi man in a town in western Rwanda told one of the RPF fighters in 1990 who had come to "liberate" him, "You want power? You will get it. But here we will all die. Is it worth it to you?"[8] In essence, the RPF armed liberation movement had put the unarmed Tutsi population inside Rwanda at risk of attack by Hutu extremists.

But in August 1994 the RPF liberators occupied the moral high ground in a devastated country. After finishing my discussions with the new government, I set out with my human rights team to travel overland between Kigali and Bujumbura, the capital of neighboring Burundi. We had heard reports of skittish soldiers at roadblocks and scattered reprisal killings of Hutus who had remained in their villages, but we felt that it was important in this first international trip across Rwanda after the genocide to demonstrate the commitment of the United States to help the new government reopen the country, particularly in the region south of the capital that had been heavily populated by Tutsis. We set off in a battered embassy van, joined by Archbishop (now Cardinal) Theodore McCarrick of Newark, a human rights leader who had traveled to Rwanda to meet with the remnants of the country's shattered and compromised Catholic Church.[9]

We saw and heard powerful evidence of what had happened—vast emptiness and total silence. Traveling through one of the most densely populated countries in the world, we witnessed what Josiah Rosenblatt described as "the effects of the machete equivalent of a neutron bomb." In village after village, not a living soul stirred. The Tutsis had all been killed and the Hutus had all fled. Decomposing bodies were everywhere. And yet the crops in the fields were ripening, standing in homage to the obliterated human hands that had planted them.

When we reached Bujumbura I sent a cable to the White House and the State Department that reflected the emotional exhaustion I felt after this trip. In language both desperate and emphatic, I made a case for addressing Rwanda's justice crisis even after failing to respond to its earlier calls for help. "I cannot begin to come in touch with the consciousness of those few I glimpsed along the roads—or those I saw miserably strewn across the volcanic rocks of Goma.

These powerful and deeply disturbing images have given a new meaning to the already fraught expression, 'Never Again.' While it is too late by far for far too many in Rwanda, an international tribunal and the institutionalization of accountability in the international system can, I am convinced, save lives yet being lived."

On the way back to Washington we stopped in Paris and London to try to stimulate more French and British support for the effort to create the Tribunal that was now coming to a head in the Security Council. Before my meetings with French Foreign Ministry officials at the Quai d'Orsay I had breakfast with Pamela Harriman at the elegant Rothschild Palace residence of the American Ambassador. She was preoccupied with the plummeting opinion poll ratings of President Clinton, who had called her the day before to discuss the growing number of foreign policy problems that were plaguing his presidency. She told me he had said to her that "every time I go abroad my ratings go down," and she wondered aloud to me, "What will pull him out of his slump?" We talked about Rwanda and Bosnia, the challenges these crises posed to the post-Cold War world, and the failure of the efforts the President and the Administration had made so far to address them. I told Pamela that after my week in Rwanda, I was convinced that unless we moved quickly to set up an international tribunal and arrest the leaders of the genocide, a new cycle of vengeance would destabilize all of central Africa. Rwanda was not just a tragedy we had failed to prevent; it was another crisis in the making.

## Justice Delayed

The struggle for justice in Rwanda was a race against time. It was also a battle against bureaucracy. In the fall of 1994 the U.N. Security Council conducted a series of debates over the wisdom and feasibility of creating another ad hoc tribunal to try cases of genocide, crimes against humanity, and war crimes in Rwanda, given that the one it had established the year before for the former Yugoslavia had yet to show any signs of success. Skeptics seemed to be everywhere.

In Washington the week after my return from Rwanda, I attended two meetings that illustrated the difficulties the U.S. government was still having comprehending the full dimensions of the Rwanda crisis. The first was a brainstorming session among refugee experts to consider ways to persuade the refugees in Goma to return to their homes in Rwanda. A volcano above the camps was beginning to smoke, and it was suggested that a seismic warning could be broadcast that would urge people to leave the area. Although it was certainly prudent to prepare for evacuation if the volcano were to erupt (six years later it did), an equally great danger would have come from moving large numbers of Hutu refugees back to Rwanda so soon after the genocide, at a time when ethnic tensions were at their peak. More dangerous than the volcano, too, were the Hutu extremists who dominated the camps. Efforts by U.N. High Commissioner for Refugees Sadaka Ogata to get the international community to take control and arrest the extremists went nowhere. Meanwhile, a position was advanced in an interagency meeting on Rwanda by Justice Department lawyers that U.S. criminal law did not establish a basis for arresting a genocide suspect who had fled to the United States because the crime had not been committed on U.S. territory. Although the arrest was eventually made,[10] here was another example of how the effort to bring justice to Rwanda kept running into bureaucratic roadblocks.

Once the Security Council had finally passed a resolution in November 1994 creating a tribunal, the slow and tortuous process began of actually establishing one. The International Criminal Tribunal for Rwanda and its counterpart for the former Yugoslavia were unprecedented, and it is remarkable that they got off the ground at all. The victors' justice meted out by the Nuremberg Tribunal half a century earlier bore little relation to this novel effort to set up an engine of justice in the middle of two ongoing conflicts that the world had done little to try to stop.

The Rwanda tribunal was in a precarious position. Shortly before the Security Council vote, the Rwandan government withdrew its support for the resolution when it learned that no trials would take place in Rwanda and that the tribunal would not be authorized to sentence genocide leaders to death. These two limitations showed how wide was the gulf between the asserted internal needs of a country recovering from genocide and the evolving international standards for judging the crime. The Rwandan government wanted an immediate and palpable justice they could show their people in the streets of Kigali and the villages of the countryside. This is why it was essential for the United States to assist the struggling Rwanda Justice Ministry in rebuilding the country's devastated domestic justice system. Yet as Richard Goldstone, the first chief prosecutor of both the Yugoslav and Rwanda tribunals, later pointed out, "No fair [international] trials could have been held in the presence of millions of victims calling for blood."[11] As for the death penalty, while many of the countries voting to establish the tribunal had abolished capital punishment, Rwandan prime minister Pasteur Bizimungu protested to Goldstone that "a few months after so many [Rwandans] had been slaughtered was hardly a time to suggest abolition," particularly since "convicted defendants would certainly be sentenced to death when the Rwandan courts were reconstituted."[12]

Rwanda's wariness about international justice posed a challenge for the United Nations. At Goldstone's urging, the tribunal set up its headquarters in neighboring Arusha, Tanzania, and a branch of the prosecutor's office was opened in Kigali. To bridge the gap between Rwanda's dashed expectations and the realities of creating a U.N. agency, Goldstone and his successor, Louise Arbour of Canada, had to concentrate as much on personal diplomacy to secure the cooperation of the Rwandan government as they did on building a new and complex organization to prosecute genocide.

The United Nations itself sometimes created impediments to even the most minimal progress. Goldstone, for example, was blocked for weeks from making his first official trip to Rwanda by Ralph Zacklin, director of the U.N. Office of Legal Affairs, who claimed that the U.N. Secretariat, not the tribunal, should negotiate with the Rwandan government, and that no funds had been appropriated for Goldstone's travel. Another typical hurdle was the U.N. requirement that when a member state offered to contribute its own prosecutors and investigators to the tribunal, it had to pay an additional 13 percent in unspecified "overhead" costs. This created a major problem for the staffing of the tribunal, particularly in the case of the United States (the largest contributor of both personnel and money), because Congress was unwilling to provide additional funds to cover general expenses of a U.N. bureaucracy that it saw as bloated.

If the United Nations was slow in starting the wheels of justice, it was equally slow in addressing the crisis inside Rwanda and in the refugee camps along the border. One of my major recommendations after returning from Rwanda to Washington in August was that a large U.N. human rights monitoring team of several hundred well-trained personnel should be permanently stationed throughout the country to act as an early warning system to guard against the recurrence of ethnic violence. The new U.N. high commissioner for human rights, Jose Ayala Lasso of Equador, who visited Rwanda shortly after I did, made a similar recommendation. Since the United Nations was concerned about the outbreak of reprisal killings, I assumed that a team would be quickly assembled, trained, and deployed. I was wrong. The High Commissioner's office, created in 1993 after the World Conference on Human Rights, was stuck in a U.N. backwater in Geneva. Far from the Secretariat in New York, and without adequate staff or funding, it was largely ineffective.

Three months after the genocide, only two human rights monitors had been sent to Rwanda. The high commissioner was floundering. I tried to mobilize U.S. resources to help, but was only able to come up with $1 million and a promise that the United States would work with European governments to raise additional funds. Six months later there were still only twenty monitors, and the U.N. system had produced such weak field leadership for the team that I began to wonder whether the whole effort should be scrapped. Finally, in July 1995, I managed to persuade my old friend and former secretary-general of Amnesty International, Ian Martin, to transfer to Rwanda after running a highly successful U.N. human rights monitoring mission in Haiti.

Within a few months Martin was able to turn the Rwanda field operation around and galvanize it into the early warning and conflict resolution center that the country so desperately needed. Although U.N. monitors were often in tension with the Rwandan government, which forced them to withdraw from parts of the country where armed clashes were taking place with Hutu guerrillas, they served for several years as an essential part of the international civilian presence in Rwanda. Ian Martin proved that experienced leadership can extricate a new human rights institution from a bureaucratic quagmire, but that new ideas without new resources and the leadership to implement them will sink like a stone.

The challenge of developing adequate funding to support the human rights monitoring mission reflected a larger problem of skewed priorities in the international effort to assist postgenocide Rwanda. From mid-1994 to mid-1995 the United Nations spent an average of one million dollars a day on food and supplies for the refugee camps, and $15 million a month for the 5,500 peacekeepers who had been sent to Rwanda in July 1994 to support humanitarian operations. During this crucial period hundreds of millions of dollars were poured into the Rwanda relief effort, but only a tiny portion of that amount was earmarked for rebuilding Rwandan institutions of justice and civil society.[13]

When General Kagame came to Washington in late September 1994, he decried U.S. support for what he called "the international misery industry" of refugee relief that sheltered genocide killers. If the international community did not take immediate steps to arrest the leaders, Kagame warned Tim Wirth and others in a series of State Department meetings, his government would have to take "appropriate measures" to protect Rwanda from being destabilized. Kagame was annoyed by a report of the Office of the U.N. High Commissioner for Refugees that reprisal killings of Hutus inside Rwanda were a serious threat, pointing instead to the intimidation and violence being directed against refugees and genocide survivors by Hutu extremists inside the refugee camps. Clearly both were threats, and the situation demanded urgent action to confront them.

The immediate need was to arrest the genocide leaders in the camps. Several months after turning over his U.N. command to another Canadian, General Guy Toussignant, General Romeo Dallaire, by now the most experienced international military expert on the Hutu militia, made a proposal to expand the mandate of the U.N. Rwanda mission to authorize it to make arrests. Speaking now on behalf of the Canadian government, Dallaire outlined what he had in mind on a visit to Washington in early October 1994. He told Tim Wirth, George Moose, and me in a meeting at the State Department on October 5 that it was becoming "inevitable that Rwanda will descend into chaos and violence because we are supporting the bad guys in the Zaire camps." Dallaire proposed to reverse this situation by increasing the U.N. force to 8,100 troops and sending them into the camps from Rwanda to disarm and detain the Hutu militia.

Dallaire's plan was no doubt risky and operationally flawed, but it reflected the reality of a situation that the United States and other Security Council members were unwilling to confront. The State Department expressed interest in the plan, but the Pentagon opposed it because it failed to meet the peacekeeping conditions required by PDD 25. Once again, Somalia, the Powell Doctrine, congressional wariness, and above all the lack of high-level leadership within the administration meant that an aggressive approach to a serious peacekeeping problem was never seriously considered.

## Things Fall Apart

I traveled to Rwanda five times more over the next three years, driven partly by guilt and partly by a sense that I could make a difference even after having failed to do so during the time of genocide. I worked with USAID to channel U.S. assistance to the Rwandan justice system, and with the international tribunal to speed up the process of tracking down and arresting high-level genocide suspects. But again and again, both from my discussions in Rwanda and from my efforts to gain high-level attention in Washington, I was left with the impression that from a U.S. perspective, Rwanda was a lost cause.

To be sure, a serious effort was mounted by the United States and other donor countries to strengthen the tribunal and help rebuild Rwanda's capacity to administer justice. Unfortunately, the snail-like pace and limited resources available for these efforts made them largely ineffective as a means of curtailing the violence that continued to increase throughout the region. As Kagame had predicted, the Rwandan government took matters into its own hands and launched its version of rough justice by hunting down Hutu extremists both inside and outside Rwanda. In the fall of 1996 Rwandan troops entered eastern Zaire, broke up the refugee camps, and then in early 1997 joined forces with Congolese rebel leader Laurent Kabila to overthrow the regime of Zairean dictator Mobutu Sese Seko and pursue fleeing Hutu groups.

This chain of events—in which the genocide victims now became perpetrators of new atrocities—was caused in part by the slowness of international efforts to address the justice crisis in Rwanda. On June 13, 1997, I sent the State Department a memorandum from Rwanda at the end of an overland trip through war-ravaged Zaire in which I traced the roots of the ongoing violence that was destabilizing Central Africa. There were no heroes in this seemingly endless chronicle of human failure.

The analysis was simple. The existence of long-term refugee camps just across the border in Zaire, and their domination for years by the very Hutu extremists who had carried out the genocide, caused conditions of increasing instability on the Rwandan and Burundian borders. At the same time, failure by the international community to disarm the camps while assisting the refugees created growing tensions between the United Nations and the Rwandan government. For nearly two years after the genocide, the Mobutu regime supported cross-border attacks into Rwanda and Burundi by Hutu guerrillas, and allowed a vicious Hutu extremist campaign to be conducted against Zairean Tutsis. The Tutsis and elements of the Rwandan army reacted to these threats in late 1996 by breaking up the camps and joining the Kabila insurgency to overthrow Mobutu. As the Kabila forces moved across Zaire, reports grew of widespread killings of Hutu refugees, and hundreds of thousands of refugees mixed with armed Hutu militia dispersed throughout Zaire, Angola, and the Central African Republic. In short, reprisals from the genocide expanded rapidly and proved even more difficult to stop than the genocide itself. The cost of the original cataclysm became even greater.

In March 1998 I traveled with President Clinton to Kigali. This presidential trip was a postscript to the story of Rwanda's agony. Four years after the genocide, the United States and other donor countries had stepped up assistance to the international tribunal and expanded efforts to help the Rwandan government rebuild its justice system. As a result of international pressure on countries like Kenya that had harbored the Rwanda genocide leaders, a large number had been turned over to the tribunal and had been convicted or were awaiting trial in Arusha.[14] At the same time, the Rwandan government had imprisoned in horrendously overcrowded conditions over 100,000 people who were alleged to have participated in the killings.

During his brief visit to Kigali, President Clinton met with a group of genocide survivors. In many ways the president was at his finest, eliciting stories and demonstrating humility and remorse about what had happened. The theme of the discussion was eloquently expressed by a forty-seven-year-old Catholic priest who explained to Clinton that all Rwandans had grown up with the fear of genocide because perpetrators were never punished. "That's why we all feel guilty. After 1994 I feel guilty for even being alive." In his concluding remarks and later in his speech the president stated his priorities clearly: "We must punish the leaders, and then we can have justice for everyone else." He told the group of survivors, "The international community was not organized to deal with this, and it still isn't. We are better organized than four years ago, but we have much more to do." Finally, he apologized for the fact that the United States did not try to stop the genocide and asserted that what had happened in Rwanda should be a lesson to the world.

The president was clearly right that we were not mobilized to respond to the warnings of 1993 and early 1994. After the Cold War was over, the American public was not interested in crises far from home. The Somalia disaster in October 1993 had created a broad consensus in the Congress that the United States should avoid risky U.N. peacekeeping operations on behalf of humanitarian causes. The executive branch was preoccupied with domestic issues and not inclined to take on foreign obligations that might prove to be unpopular. Without presidential leadership in educating the public about how genocide in a small, faraway country could affect American interests, the United States inevitably remained on the sidelines. Indeed, in many ways our own democratic system worked against any serious U.S. engagement with the Rwanda crisis. It was for that reason that I felt my own witnessing of what had happened, and my advocacy for intervention both in Rwanda and in similar situations in the future, was important. But there was no escaping the ugly truth: we had all failed to take action to try to stop a genocide in progress.

Had the result in Rwanda been inevitable, had the countries in the region not been willing to participate in peacekeeping, or had a wider war been likely following international intervention, the decision not to intervene militarily might have been understandable. But the truth is otherwise. The catastrophic consequences of failing to act at an early stage—when minimal intervention might have saved lives—are magnified because the world paid little attention to the warnings coming from Rwanda. By denying General Dallaire and his troops the tools they needed to do their job, and then withdrawing them at the very moment when they might have been able to stop the violence, the international community sealed the fate of 800,000 Rwandans.

# CHAPTER 3

# HAITI

## A TALE OF TWO PRESIDENTS

Repression works. It keeps the lid on freedom and destroys those who try to pry it off. In Haiti it has worked for centuries, ever since a slave revolt at the end of the eighteenth century was put down by the first of an endless succession of brutal, corrupt and dictatorial regimes.

Repression in Haiti has always had a special logic. I got my first insight into Haitian-style rule-by-fear in Port-au-Prince, on December 11, 1993. There I met Evans Paul, an intense young leader of the Haitian democracy movement headed by the exiled president and populist priest Jean-Bertrand Aristide. Paul had been elected mayor of Port-au-Prince in 1990, the same year Aristide was elected president. Eight months later, a military junta headed by Lieutenant General Raoul Cedras overthrew Haiti's first democratically elected government, forced Aristide and other elected officials into exile, and plunged Haiti back into the reign of terror from which its citizens were struggling to escape.

In September 1993, Evans Paul had returned from exile to work against the junta. As a campaigner for democracy, he was a marked man. Having previously been beaten and tortured for his political activities, he knew he would be a target of the thugs who served the military regime and that he would have to be extremely agile to avoid becoming one of the thousands of victims of its omnipresent paramilitary gangs, loosely organized as the Front for Advancement and Progress in Haiti (FRAPH).

When I met him, at the U.S. ambassador's residence, Mayor Paul was eager to educate a visiting American official about Haitian-style repression. To outsmart FRAPH, he told me with a wry smile, he had relied on the timidity of the U.S. military. Two months earlier, the Navy had dispatched a frigate, the USS *Harlan County*, to enforce a diplomatic agreement establishing a timetable for the return of President Aristide, hammered out under U.S. auspices in July 1993 on Governors Island in New York between the United Nations and representatives of General Cedras. But when the American ship reached Port-au-Prince, it had turned around without docking in order to avoid a confrontation with armed FRAPH demonstrators on shore. In the wave of FRAPH-inspired violence that swept over Port-au-Prince after the *Harlan County* sailed away, the wily mayor had arranged to have himself beaten up by his own supporters so that the junta would conclude that he was no longer a political threat to them.[1] Repression in Haiti works in strange ways.

## In Florida's Back Yard

A free and independent Haiti was born in 1804 in the shadow of the French Revolution and a series of slave rebellions against a brutal French colonial elite. Its first constitution was written by Toussaint Louverture, a former slave who cast himself as Haiti's Napoleon. "From the First of the Blacks to the First of the Whites," the founding father had written to Bonaparte announcing the birth of his nation.[2] But the revolution in Haiti was soon brought to a bloody end by the French landowners, and for nearly two hundred years the country fell under the spell of a series of violent and corrupt regimes.

The twentieth-century progeny of this long string of brutal dictatorships were the notorious Duvaliers. "Papa Doc" Duvalier declared himself "President for Life" in 1964, channeling all of the country's resources to himself and his family and ruling by terror through the thuggery of his dreaded Tonton Macoutes. Papa Doc was tolerated by the United States as a "friendly dictator" in a region seen to be constantly under the threat of expanding Soviet influence. His son, Baby Doc, a weaker but equally corrupt and repressive ruler, was toppled by angry mobs in 1986 and spirited off to a well-padded exile in France by his American Cold War protectors.

After four years of a transitional military regime during which a populist movement, Lavalas, gained momentum, U.N.-sponsored democratic elections were held in December 1990. Aristide was elected by 67 percent of the vote and was hailed at home and abroad as the harbinger of a new era for Haiti that would reflect the values of the democratic revolution sweeping the globe at the end of the Cold War. But these accolades were by no means universal. Inside Haiti, Lavalas and Aristide were seen by most members of the country's economic and political elite as a threat to their power base. Inside the U.S. government, Aristide was regarded by some elements of the Pentagon and the CIA as an unstable political leader who risked plunging Haiti into more violence and instability. Since the United States had maintained close Cold War ties to the Duvalier regime, it is not surprising that Aristide was a controversial figure for them. When he was overthrown in September 1991 by General Cedras, they were no doubt relieved. The CIA's view of Cedras was later characterized in an academic journal as highly favorable: "a conscientious military leader who genuinely wished to minimize his role in politics, professionalize the armed services, and develop a separate and competent police force."[3]

The U.S. approach toward Haiti after 1991 demonstrated the competing strains and contradictions of post–Cold War foreign policy. While promoting democracy and human rights—the all-purpose rhetorical mantra after the fall of the Berlin Wall—was the theme of U.S. statements welcoming Aristide's election and condemning the military coup, the Bush administration offered little to back up its words beyond clamping trade sanctions on Haiti after Aristide was deposed.[4] One reason for this limited response was the fact that American Cold War arrangements lingered on in Haiti, shaping U.S. views about both the Aristide and Cedras camps. One of Aristide's chief opponents and the founder of FRAPH, Emmanuel "Toto" Constant, for example, was reportedly an intimate U.S. Defense Intelligence Agency contact on the CIA payroll.[5] CIA reports characterized Aristide as unstable and connected to violent Haitian practices such as "necklacing" political opponents: putting gasoline-soaked tires around their necks and setting them on fire.[6] Because these reports came from Aristide's political enemies, it was difficult for policymakers to separate truth from rumor, and convenient for them to use the reports to discount Aristide's claim to democratic legitimacy over those who had mounted the coup against him, and to avoid spending U.S. resources to help him regain his presidency.

Beyond these Cold War entanglements and preconceptions, U.S. policy toward Haiti was shadowed by Vietnam and the Gulf War. With the vast military mobilization required to confront Saddam Hussein in 1991, the Pentagon was wary of any diplomatic venture in another part of the world that might ultimately require the backing of U.S. armed forces. By this logic, democracy in Haiti was a fine thing, but not if it created instability in America's backyard and might require the intervention of U.S. troops. The chairman of the Joint Chiefs of Staff, General Colin Powell, took as his personal mission shielding the military from political pressures that might push it into engagements of marginal importance to U.S. security.[7] In the case of Haiti, Powell knew that U.S. Marines had been drawn into such a venture in 1915 and had been unable to withdraw for nineteen years. Vietnam was the prism through which Powell looked at all foreign policy decisions. By that standard, Washington's goal for Haiti was to keep it off the screen.

But precisely because Haiti was close to the United States, it kept popping up in domestic politics. As news of the regime's brutal repression began to show up in the American media, the issue that captured the attention of Washington was the growing tide of refugees washing up in small boats on the shores of Florida. Twelve years earlier, Fidel Castro had opened the floodgates in Cuba and 125,000 boat people had made it across the Florida Straits, creating a political crisis for Jimmy Carter as the 1980 presidential election drew near.

Determined to head off a similar crisis, the Bush administration took a hard line against Haitian refugees by intercepting their boats and sending them back to Haiti. Secretary of State James Baker scoffed at claims by immigration lawyers and human rights groups that the Haitian boat people should be allowed to make their case for entering the U.S. as victims of political persecution. The Bush administration's position was that these people were "economic refugees" fleeing from poverty who would become a burden on Florida and U.S. taxpayers if they were allowed to enter, and would set a dangerous precedent for other populations throughout the Caribbean.

## From Candidate to President

Enter presidential candidate Bill Clinton. During the 1992 campaign Clinton branded George Bush a "coddler of dictators," not only in Haiti, but also in China and Yugoslavia.[8] Articulating a new post–Cold War vision to offset his lack of foreign policy experience, Clinton positioned himself as a champion of democracy and human rights who could appeal to an electorate fed up with Cold War politics by telling them that at last the world reflected values that Americans could endorse. "From the Baltics to Beijing," he proclaimed, "from Sarajevo to South Africa, time after time George Bush has sided with the status quo rather than democratic change—with familiar tyrants rather than those who would overthrow them—and with the old geography of repression rather than the new map of freedom."[9] In essence, Clinton as candidate was sketching out for American voters a new era of expanding freedom and global benefits with few costs to the United States.[10]

In campaign speeches Clinton hammered Bush for cruelly rejecting the Haitian boat people and turning a blind eye to the brutality of the Cedras regime. He accused Bush of playing "racial politics" with the refugee issue, asserting, "I wouldn't be shipping those poor people back."[11] It was time, he asserted, for the United States to toughen its position toward dictators like the ones in Haiti, Yugoslavia, and China who were suppressing the forces of democracy that had been unleashed by the end of the Cold War. This appeal to principle struck a chord with voters.

After the election, the candidate's human rights vision had to compete with political realities facing the new administration in a skeptical Washington. On the issue of Haiti, human rights gave way to other voices competing for the President-elect's attention. Among the first to reach him were those of the CIA. According to seasoned Washington observers, December 1992 intelligence reports indicated that Clinton's campaign charge against Bush of coddling dictators had raised the hopes of Haitians that the United States would open its doors to refugees fleeing the Cedras regime.[12] This had accelerated boat building on the island. The reports predicted that hundreds of thousands of Haitian refugees would head for Florida within the next few months unless the United States announced it was continuing its policy of turning them away. This warning no doubt stirred Clinton's memory of the political consequences of the Cuban flotilla thirteen years earlier, not only for Jimmy Carter but also for himself after he had agreed to accept Cuban refugees in Arkansas.[13] A year later, Clinton had lost his bid for reelection as governor. A month before his inauguration as President, Clinton announced that there would be no change in U.S. immigration policy toward Haiti. By the time he was sworn in, the boat building had slowed.

But Haiti was now on the political screen of the United States. The question facing the new administration was what could be done to undermine the Cedras regime without encouraging a new flood of refugees. Complicating this question was the fact that the CIA and the Pentagon had close ties to the regime and were skeptical about Aristide, Lavalas, and the new forces of Haitian democracy. But something had to be done, since Clinton had promised not to "ship back" Haitian refugees and had now reversed himself on this issue. The Congressional Black Caucus and civil rights leaders made it clear that they expected a new policy from Clinton on Haiti. In short, Haiti became a test of whether the incoming administration was serious about campaign-trail commitments to elevate human rights in foreign policy.

As the spring of 1993 arrived, there was little evidence of change. At the end of March, when I was waiting for my Senate confirmation hearing to be scheduled, I got a call from Michael Posner, head of the Lawyers Committee for Human Rights. Mike warned me that Bush administration holdovers in the State Department were working with the White House to prevent the United Nations from expanding its reporting of human rights abuses in Haiti. Posner's suspicion was that Clinton's endorsement of the Bush policy on refugees had led to a decision to downplay the level of repression inside Haiti in order to justify the claim that Haitians were economic, not political, refugees. Since I was in limbo as an unconfirmed nominee, I was not in a position to find out much more. But I did have a conversation with Bernard Aronson, a holdover from the Bush administration and the acting assistant secretary of state for Latin American affairs, who expressed concern about statements by incoming Clinton officials that might stimulate an increase in the number of Haitian refugees. It was clearly going to be difficult to change the Haiti policy.

The tensions in Clinton's own views on Haiti were reflected in divided factions within the new administration. Promoting human rights more aggressively, as Clinton the candidate had promised to do, and I wanted to do, ran the risk of encouraging more refugees. Pressuring Cedras to step down, as the State Department was urging, collided with the concern of Joint Chiefs of Staff Chairman Colin Powell and Secretary of Defense Les Aspin that the United States might be forced to intervene in Haiti to back up its pressure. And bringing about the return of Aristide, which National Security Advisor Tony Lake believed would be the best way to stabilize the situation, threatened U.S. military and intelligence ties to those in Haiti who opposed Aristide.

Throughout 1993, the White House allowed these contradictions to continue. Preoccupied by domestic issues, the President spent little time addressing the Haiti problem. Although Clinton was faulted by commentators for failing to provide foreign policy leadership during this period, international affairs were simply not high on the agenda of a complacent and disinterested American public.

In this political environment, Haiti's emergence as an issue in Washington in 1993 had more to do with the persistence of well-focused pressure groups outside and inside the administration than it did with any broader public perception that U.S. strategic interests were at stake. Indeed, in this respect Haiti won the competition for U.S. attention over Bosnia and Rwanda in 1994 because it had developed a domestic constituency.

There were two unrelated parts to this constituency, pulling at first in opposite directions. The Congressional Black Caucus and civil rights groups campaigned for a U.S. effort to remove Cedras and return Aristide to Haiti, while Florida politicians fearful of a refugee flood pressed for a tougher policy of interdicting Haitian boats on the high seas. Eventually, however, the two groups merged as it became clear that the refugee crisis was being stimulated by the increasingly brutal political repression of the Cedras regime. A strong domestic lobby for policy change began to emerge when the Florida politicians concluded that promoting human rights in Haiti was the best way to protect Florida from being overrun by refugees.

## Telling the Story

One of my responsibilities as the new assistant secretary of state for human rights and humanitarian affairs was to compile and publish an annual report on human rights conditions in countries throughout the world. This put me in a position to assess what was going on inside Haiti, and made my work a focus of the administration's growing policy debate over what to do about the situation. Gathering evidence was difficult, however, since I had to rely mostly on our embassy in Port-au-Prince, where conflicting points of view and differing bureaucratic interests among agency representatives colored the assessment I was receiving.

In the summer of 1993 my human rights reporting was bolstered by a new source of information. An international civilian mission (ICM) had been created earlier in the year in Haiti by the United Nations and the Organization of American States (OAS). Established at the request of Aristide, who as the democratically elected president of his country represented the legitimate government of Haiti in the United Nations and the OAS, the ICM's mission was to "verify compliance with Haiti's international human rights obligations . . . in order to assist in the establishment of a climate of freedom and tolerance propitious to the reestablishment of democracy in Haiti."[14] This was a tall order for a team of civilian human rights workers. Still, the ICM mandate conferred international legitimacy on the effort to restore the fledgling Haitian democracy that Aristide's election had represented. For me, the ICM was also a potential counterweight to the defense and intelligence interests inside the U.S. government that were aligned with the status quo in Haiti. Headed by Colin Granderson, an experienced diplomat from Trinidad with a strong human rights background, and his deputy, Ian Martin, the ICM steadily expanded until by August 1993 it included over two hundred observers deployed throughout the country and had become the best source of information about human rights conditions on the ground.

Our reporting got another boost when Warren Christopher accepted my recommendation on August 1 to send a cable to all U.S. embassies around the world, instructing them to strengthen their country reports on human rights. Sixteen years earlier, when he was deputy secretary of state in the Carter administration, Christopher had supervised production of the first annual State Department human rights report. Earlier in the spring, the Secretary had commissioned an internal review of human rights reporting by the U.S. embassy in El Salvador during the 1980s, where major human rights abuses by the Salvadoran military had been downplayed by the embassy. The human rights record of the military was epitomized by the notorious El Mozote massacre, in which a U.S.-trained Salvadoran army battalion had killed more than five hundred civilians.[15] In order to address the problem of slanted reporting, I recommended to Christopher that he instruct all ambassadors to designate specific human rights officers in each of their embassies. In addition, I suggested that the Human Rights Bureau be explicitly authorized to conduct editorial reviews of embassy human rights reports. I also urged Christopher to inform ambassadors that unless they had substantially new information, they could no longer routinely rewrite the annual reports on their countries to reflect their own editorial perspectives. Christopher endorsed these recommendations and sent them out in the worldwide cable that my bureau drafted for him.

I immediately applied this new authority to the situation in Haiti. I had been surprised that the human rights report published by the State Department in February 1993 had concluded that "the year 1992 did not see the same degree of wide-scale political violence that followed the September 1991 coup d'état," and that "it was difficult to assess the actual number of political and extrajudicial killings."[16] This did not square with reports I was receiving from observers on the ground. I knew we had to supplement our embassy reporting with information from other sources, such as the ICM and nongovernmental organizations, and I set out to establish close ties with Colin Granderson, Ian Martin, and their observer team. Soon I was incorporating some of their findings into the State Department reports.

I saw Haiti as an early test of the Clinton administration's claim that human rights would play a prominent role in its foreign policy. My own views had been shaped by the outpouring of refugees from Haiti that had swelled during the final months of the Bush administration. After Clinton's inauguration, when I was still at Harvard, I had been visited by refugee groups who had described the mounting tension in Haiti and had warned me that the President's reversal of his campaign commitment to open the United States to more Haitian refugees was only making things worse. Now, they told me, the Cedras regime thought it had a free hand and suspected that the new American president had no real intention of taking action to back up his words.

The deteriorating situation in Haiti posed a danger to the United States. Like other parts of the post–Cold War world, Haiti was a failed state teeming with human rights atrocities and on the edge of chaos. But unlike similar crises in the Balkans or Central Africa, this one was not far away. Haiti's geographic proximity, coupled with the threat that increasingly repressive conditions could produce a tidal wave of refugees, would cause Washington to move more aggressively on this crisis in 1994 than on the larger but more distant human rights catastrophes in Rwanda and Bosnia.

The urgency of managing the Haiti crisis was reflected in the administration's early diplomatic maneuvering over the return of Aristide. Working through the United Nations, the State Department's special negotiator on Haiti, Lawrence Pezzullo, had reached an agreement with Cedras and the junta in negotiations on Governors Island in New York City in July 1993. The agreement called for Aristide to return to power by October 30 in exchange for safe passage to exile for Cedras and his regime.[17] The problem with the Governors Island Accord was that it had no enforcement provisions, and therefore no teeth. As the summer drew to a close, it became clear that Cedras saw the accord as just another example of the rhetorical condemnation that both the Bush and Clinton administrations had been leveling at his regime.

As if to make clear that Cedras had no intention of honoring his Governors Island pledge, three dramatic acts of political violence were committed in Port-au-Prince in September and early October. On September 8 armed paramilitary gangs attacked a ceremony at city hall to mark the return of Evans Paul from exile. Several Aristide supporters were killed and scores more wounded. A few days later similar gangs attacked Aristide supporters during a church service, dragging a prominent activist, Antoine Izmery, out of the church and murdering him in front of the parishioners. Finally, on October 14, Aristide's minister of justice, Guy Malary, was assassinated in broad daylight in a public square by masked assailants who escaped into the city under the protection of the junta's police. These three high-profile political killings followed a dramatic increase in the incidence of political violence throughout the country, as reported by the ICM during the summer and early fall of 1993. Cedras and his generals were sending a message: if Aristide returns, this is what he can expect.

## The Ship That Turned Around

Throughout 1993, thousands of small boats brimming with Haitian refugees were interdicted in the Florida Straits by U.S. Coast Guard cutters and sent back to Haiti. In light of this daily show of U.S. force on the high seas, it was a supreme irony that on October 12, a U.S. military ship was effectively stopped and sent back to the United States by a mob of thugs on the wharf in Port-au-Prince, where the ship was supposed to land. But that is exactly what happened, and it marked the low point of Clinton's evolving Haiti policy.

If the assassinations of September and early October were intended to shake the resolve of the Clinton administration to do what was necessary to implement the Governors Island Accord and restore Aristide to power, they certainly hit their mark. In the first week of October, Secretary of Defense Les Aspin told Tony Lake and Warren Christopher that he was against taking any further steps to prepare the way for Aristide's return. Aspin, Powell, and others in the Defense Department were persuaded by a CIA report that Cedras and his generals did not intend to live up to their commitments and were preparing to disrupt U.S. military operations. Specifically, Aspin argued against sending in two hundred lightly armed American soldiers and engineers who, under the terms of the agreement, were to work with the Haitian military and police on confidence-building projects before Aristide's arrival.[18]

This resistance set the stage for one of many skirmishes inside the administration over the question of whether diplomacy to promote human rights and democracy should be backed by force. Lake and Berger disagreed with Aspin's caution—which was reinforced by Powell and the Joint Chiefs of Staff—arguing that the United States had a right under the Governors Island Accord to show some military muscle and that failure to do so would simply play into the hands of the junta.[19] The standoff between the competing positions within the administration led to a disastrous compromise. After much debate, the USS *Harlan County* was dispatched to Port-au-Prince. When it arrived, however, a group of no more than a hundred FRAPH thugs, mobilized by Cedras's security people and controlled by Emmanuel Constant, was able to prevent it from landing.[20] The outcome of this ill-fated mission had the opposite effect of diplomacy backed by force: the ship's about-face reflected a policy of timidity compounded by capitulation.

But the fate of the *Harlan County* had been foreordained by what had happened in Somalia a week earlier. In fact, after eighteen U.S. Army Rangers had been killed in Mogadishu and the Clinton administration had been pilloried in the Congress for allowing the United States to participate in the peacekeeping mission in Somalia, it is remarkable that the *Harlan County* was sent to Haiti at all.

After the ship withdrew, Port-au-Prince descended almost immediately to a new level of repression and chaos, triggered as intended by the assassination of Guy Malary. Since the security of international workers could no longer be protected, the United Nations and the OAS evacuated their two hundred human rights monitors. This prompted Colin Granderson to observe later that the United States had sent "the wrong political and military message to Haiti, and elsewhere, rais[ing] questions about U.S. political capacity to use its military might overseas. This was precisely the message the Haitian military drew from the [*Harlan County*'s] departure."[21] With the monitors gone, it was no longer possible to keep a close watch on the junta and its paramilitary gangs. There was no question, however, as my year-end human rights report later indicated, that "a substantial increase in crimes of violence, including politically motivated killings, [occurred] . . . as tensions rose over the Governors Island Accords and [the junta's] increased efforts to derail their implementation."[22]

As the human rights situation worsened, the administration struggled over its increasingly ineffective Haiti policy. The October 30, 1993, deadline set by the Governors Island Accords for Aristide's return came and went. Having shelved its military option for implementing the agreement, the White House settled for a reimposition of the U.N. sanctions that had been removed during the previous summer as an inducement for Cedras to follow through with his commitments. Meanwhile, under instructions from Lake and Christopher, Lawrence Pezzullo, the Governors Island negotiator, made several unsuccessful attempts to assemble a new Haitian government that would constitute an alternative both to the exiled Aristide and to the junta. By the end of the year the only results of this disjointed policy were increasing levels of Haitian poverty, repression, and the outward flow of refugees.[23]

During much of the fall of 1993 I was preoccupied with other parts of the world. My biggest challenge was gearing up to try to implement President Clinton's ill-fated and short-lived executive order calling for a more aggressive human rights policy toward China. Over the course of three months I held a series of "human rights dialogues" with Chinese officials, traveled widely in China and Tibet, and accompanied President Clinton to his first meeting with Chinese President Jiang Zemin in Seattle in November. In early December I journeyed to the Middle East to meet with Israeli, Palestinian, and Egyptian officials and nongovernmental organizations to discuss human rights problems in the context of President Clinton's new peace initiative, following the historic meeting between Israeli Prime Minister Yitzhak Rabin and Palestinian Liberation Organization leader Yasser Arafat earlier that fall at the White House.

In late November, I made plans to travel to Haiti at the request of U.S. Ambassador Bill Swing so that I could see firsthand what was happening on the ground following the *Harlan County* crisis and the withdrawal of the U.N. human rights monitoring mission. My first annual human rights report was scheduled for publication at the end of January, and the Haiti chapter was certain to attract attention. I wanted to be able to respond to questions about Haiti by offering my own assessment of the human rights situation following my trip.

I flew to Haiti on December 11. The airport in Port-au-Prince was deserted, the escalating violence and U.N. sanctions having all but shut down commercial air travel. I was met by Bill Swing, who had arrived as our new ambassador two months earlier following an equally difficult assignment in Nigeria, where another military regime was committing horrendous human rights abuses while snubbing its nose at the world. Swing was a senior professional diplomat with a strong human rights background, having also served as U.S. ambassador to South Africa when Nelson Mandela was released from Robben Island prison.

With Swing's help, I plunged into my fact-finding mission. The embassy public affairs officer, Stan Schrager, took me to the Sacre Coeur church where weeks before Guy Malary and Antoine Izmery had been assassinated. Standing on the steps of the church, I spoke to the Haitian media, condemning the murders and commending the local pro-Aristide pastor for his courage in continuing to speak out for democracy in the face of personal danger. We then drove and walked through the downtown area, where gangs of FRAPH "attachés" were openly threatening groups of pedestrians and passing vehicles. "These guys are everywhere now," Schrager said, "and Aristide's people are nowhere. They're in hiding or turning up dead." Later, we met with the leaders of one of the few functioning Haitian human rights organizations, Amicale des Juristes. From them I learned that virtually all human rights reporting in Haiti had been shut down by FRAPH violence and threats against anyone trying to collect information about abuses.

Bill Swing was determined to have his embassy fill the vacuum created by the evacuation of the international monitors. On the first evening of my visit he invited a wide array of Port-au-Prince elite to a reception at his residence commemorating the forty-fifth anniversary of the Universal Declaration of Human Rights. The largest gathering hosted by the U.S. embassy in Haiti since the 1991 coup against Aristide, the event was surrealistic. I found myself rubbing shoulders with embassy contacts from the Haitian military and police, as well as businessmen, lawyers, journalists, and a handful of the regime's few remaining open critics, particularly within the Catholic Church. Remarkably, and much to his credit, Swing had arranged to have me join him in presenting a posthumous human rights award to Guy Malary, which was accepted by his seventeen-year-old daughter, as well as an award to Father Arthur Volel, a pro-Aristide priest and longtime advocate of democratic reform. After making brief remarks to the group about the Universal Declaration and reading a letter from President Clinton to the people of Haiti in praise of Malary, Volel, and others who had given or dedicated their lives to the cause of democracy and human rights in Haiti, I stepped back to watch Swing present the awards.

The room grew quiet as Father Volel, framed between the ambassador and an embassy Christmas tree next to the podium, spoke in a soft but firm voice about the repression facing the people of Haiti. I was moved by the bravery of this lonely figure, and shuddered to think about what might happen to him and other priests in the room after they left the safety of the American Ambassador's residence and returned to the streets. Although Swing told me he hoped that the embassy's awards would help protect human rights advocates, nine months later Volel's colleague, Father Jean-Marie Vincent, with whom I had talked at the reception, was gunned down by FRAPH assassins.

### Rebuked but Not Scorned

A major focus of my trip was the refugee crisis. Since the 1991 coup that overthrew Aristide, an estimated 40,000 Haitians had fled the country, many in small boats.[24] Most had been stopped on the high seas by U.S. Coast Guard cutters and forced to return to Haiti, a practice that human rights organizations were challenging in U.S. federal courts as a violation of international refugee law.[25] At the embassy I was told that despite the Haitians' widespread awareness of the strictness of U.S. immigration policy and the likelihood of interdiction, the rate of boat building had gone up dramatically after the *Harlan County* debacle.

It seemed increasingly clear that Haiti's deteriorating political conditions, not the country's abysmal poverty, were responsible for the rapid rise in refugees. Poverty, after all, had been a constant factor in the lives of most Haitians. Nevertheless, U.S. policy called for the repatriation of fleeing Haitians, except for the very few who could obtain political asylum by demonstrating that if returned they would be personally singled out by the regime for especially brutal persecution. The embassy had opened three "in-country processing centers" in Port-au-Prince to discourage boat voyages by making it possible for Haitians to apply for political asylum without fleeing the country. But the underlying policy remained the same, and the number of asylum applications granted continued to be very small. When I visited one of the centers, I noticed that the entrance was swarming with FRAPH thugs whose presence must have made Haitians think twice before applying, and probably made those who did regret it later. Nevertheless, the number of asylum applicants had risen dramatically since October and now was pushing four hundred a week.

Bill Swing told me that the best way to see the refugee crisis up close was to board one of the Coast Guard cutters as it docked with its cargo of returned boat people. With the help of Stan Schrager, I made my way to the waterfront where the second of the week's three dockings was taking place. The deck of the cutter was filled with dispirited Haitians, and an efficient Coast Guard crew was processing the group one by one. I was told by a member of the crew that when the Haitians' flimsy boat had been sighted forty miles off Cap Haitien, he had first judged from its size that it should have no more than twenty-five refugees on board. But when the small boat was lashed to the cutter, he could see that the water came dangerously close to the boat's gunnels because its human cargo was more than four times his estimate.

After the refugees were escorted off the cutter and back onto Haitian soil, the situation grew tense. The bedraggled group began moving slowly and reluctantly toward the end of the dock where a "greeting party" of thirty to forty Haitian police and FRAPH "attachés" were looking them over. To prepare them for their encounter with this ominous-looking group, the Coast Guard crew had suggested to the Haitians that they leave behind any photos of

Aristide or other evidence of their political sympathies they might have taken with them in hopes, now dashed, of persuading U.S. immigration authorities to grant them asylum when they reached Florida. The crew had also interviewed each person to see if any might be a high-profile candidate for asylum (none was identified), and had given to each the addresses of the embassy's three refugee processing centers in Port-au-Prince. After receiving these parting words of advice, the refugees were left on the dock to fend for themselves. I watched for a while and then left when I saw that none was being beaten by the Haitian police. When I reached the embassy, however, I learned that six of the refugees had been carted off by the police after I left, and that the embassy would now have to intervene with the regime to get them released.

I described what I had seen to Bill Swing, who confirmed that this was a typical interdiction, and that the numbers were climbing.[26] I expressed my concern about the safety of those arrested, and then turned to the ramifications of the new wave of boats that was setting off. Clearly, the rate of increase in boat building would soon put a strain on the Coast Guard's capacity to find and interdict refugees at sea. The increase also showed that interdiction was not having a deterrent effect on refugee flows. Indeed, it was only compounding the crisis by reinforcing the claim of the Cedras regime that if the United States was willing to return the refugees, the situation in Haiti could not be so bad. I was troubled by the growing contradiction between our reports about the worsening human rights conditions in Haiti and our policy of effectively preventing Haitians from leaving their country. I told Swing that I intended to call for a review of the refugee policy, and he indicated that he thought this was needed and hoped Washington would be receptive.

As it turned out, I hit a raw nerve in the administration when I told the press before my departure that I was leaving Haiti "with a view that a policy review is necessary," as the *New York Times* reported on December 15.[27] Within weeks, such a review would in fact be under way and I would be pleased to have played a part in prodding the administration to launch it. But in mid-December 1993, the failure of the U.S. effort to return Aristide and embarrassment over the *Harlan County* episode were still fresh, and human rights voices inside the government were resented for keeping Washington focused on Haiti. Reporting on my trip, the *Times* noted in a story headlined "U.S. Aide to Seek New Policy on Fleeing Haitians" that "American officials fear increased repression, especially in the provinces, may force more and more Haitians to take to the seas." I told the *Times* that "the deteriorating situation may cause the United States to seek broader means for assuring that those with legitimate claims for asylum receive attention."[28]

The White House and the State Department reacted quickly and negatively to this story. On my first day back in Washington, I was greeted by a new *Times* headline: "Rebuking Aide, U.S. Says Haiti Policy Stands."[29] An anonymous official was quoted as saying that my call for a policy review "was completely wrong and outrageous and there is enormous anger in the White House and the State Department. . . . There will be no review. It was a completely rogue statement." The article also asserted that I "was given a stern dressing down by Peter Tarnoff, the Under Secretary for Political Affairs." I found this report surprising, since neither Tarnoff nor anyone else in the State Department had called me. In fact, when I saw Tarnoff in the hall on my way to the morning senior staff meeting, he greeted me with a smile and simply said that the existing repatriation policy would have to remain in effect. As we were walking together, he told me the Secretary wanted to hear my views and invited me to a "Haiti Group" meeting later in the morning. Apparently, someone else was the anonymous source of my "rebuke." I had been publicly scolded for doing my job, and could not find out by whom.

As a presidential candidate, Bill Clinton had set the tone for the administration's approach toward human rights. When it came time to make the difficult policy choices and trade-offs necessary to implement the views Clinton had expressed, however, every agency and bureaucratic center had its own interpretation. This meant that those of us who were trying to assess the facts and recommend policy responses were inevitably confronted by resistance from those who considered the administration's commitment to human rights to be primarily rhetorical. When we tried to nudge the policy process forward, as I did on the Haiti refugee crisis, we were accused of being "rogues." If we waited for decisive direction, however, it often came too late or not at all.[30]

When I returned home from Port-au-Prince, exhausted but pleased with my decision to call for a Haiti policy review, Ellen greeted me with a relieved hug at the door. But she was clearly distraught. I didn't have a chance to tell her what I had said in Haiti, which would put me in the news the next day, before she burst out in anguish, "What are we doing about Bosnia?"

As a well-known journalist who had covered Congress and the Reagan administration for the *Wall Street Journal* in the 1980s, Ellen had been dubious from the start about my taking a political appointment. "Just when you think they are going to do what you believe in, they will pull the rug out from under you," she had warned before we left Cambridge. "Then they will make you go out and sell the opposite policy." Ellen had long been concerned about the lack of an effective U.S. response to the ethnic expulsions and slaughter of civilians in Bosnia, as well as our policy of forcing of Haitian refugees to return to the brutal conditions from which they were fleeing. In Washington, when her journalist friends criticized the Clinton administration's foreign policy, she remained silent out of loyalty to me. Privately, she was furious—with the administration's unwillingness to support its own rhetoric, and with her old colleagues, who, she thought, should have been covering the fight I was waging to move the administration forward on human rights.

## The Wind Shifts

Over the next six months the administration's position shifted. Despite the frosty reception I had received when I returned from Haiti in December, many people privately told me they agreed that a refugee policy review was necessary. By April it was under way. There were several reasons for this shift.

First, there was plenty of evidence of the rapidly escalating repression in Haiti. In the first five months of 1994 the ICM reported 340 "extrajudicial killings and suspicious deaths," and many more were informally recorded by human rights nongovernmental organizations.[31] Working closely with Colin Granderson, I filed a series of reports about these killings with the State Department and the White House, which began to use them in the administration's daily press briefings.

At the same time, Haiti had become a Washington political issue. The Congressional Black Caucus, a core leadership constituency for the President as he headed toward what promised to be very difficult midterm elections, was pressing the White House to finish the job of returning Aristide to Haiti, which it had bungled in October in the *Harlan County* debacle. This pressure increased sharply when Randall Robinson, a human rights leader who had played a key role several years earlier in mobilizing support in the United States for the anti-apartheid campaign in South Africa, went on a widely publicized hunger strike in Washington to protest the forced return of Haitian refugees. Clinton knew Robinson and admired what he had done on apartheid. The press began reporting that the White House wanted to stop the erosion of black leadership support by changing its Haiti policy. But the President felt stymied by opposition on Capitol Hill and in the Pentagon to the use of force to help Aristide.

By March 1994, I was deeply frustrated by my job and the seemingly impossible task of getting the U.S. government to address the human rights crises happening all around us. In the three months since being rebuked for suggesting a change in the Haiti policy that was now proving to be an embarrassment for the administration, I had come under attack for my role in trying to carry out the President's human rights policy toward China. Meanwhile, in Bosnia the ethnic atrocities continued unabated, and in Washington a post-Somalia policy review was being completed that would soon put a U.S. straitjacket on all future peacekeeping activities. Then on April 7 genocide broke out in Rwanda.

That same day I called Taylor Branch, an old friend outside of the administration who was close to both Clinton and Aristide, to find out what he thought about the Haiti crisis. Taylor had known Clinton for more than twenty-five years. A Pulitzer Prize–winning historian of the Martin Luther King era, he had drafted Clinton's Inaugural Address, and was greatly respected by the President.[32] I knew Taylor had also met Aristide and after initial misgivings, had been impressed by the Haitian president's deep admiration of Martin Luther King and his aspiration to pattern his own leadership on King's example. I told Taylor how desperate the global human rights situation looked from where I sat, and how urgent I felt it was that at least one of the crises we were facing be addressed with more than words if Clinton's human rights rhetoric was to be regarded as having any meaning.

Taylor told me that he had discussed with Clinton how the administration might work with Aristide to create a democratic alternative in Haiti. Based on conversations with both Clinton and Aristide, he believed that for different reasons both wanted the refugee policy changed and both wanted to spotlight the human rights record of the Cedras regime. What was needed was to keep Aristide and the administration from attacking each other in public. Although this would be very difficult to accomplish when leaks from nameless sources were being used by each side to manipulate the other, I was convinced that if my bureau stepped up our reporting of the atrocities being committed against Aristide supporters by the regime in Haiti, we might be able to curtail the political sniping going on in Washington.

For the next three weeks I was in the middle of a maelstrom of activity around simultaneously breaking crises in Rwanda, China, and Haiti. I huddled with Africa specialists in the State Department and the White House in a desperate but futile effort to jump-start an administration response to the horrific mass killings in Rwanda; I participated in daily interagency meetings in the White House Situation Room about the looming deadline for the President's decision on China's human rights record and its trade status with the United

States; and I coordinated closely with Swing and Granderson to pull together a series of reports on what was happening in Haiti.

During the last week in April, as I was preparing to leave for Rwanda, Burundi, Tanzania, Uganda, and Ethiopia, the Haiti crisis came to a head. By now Tony Lake and Strobe Talbott, both increasingly concerned about the weakness of our approach toward Cedras, were orchestrating a new strategy for dealing with the crisis. In a meeting in mid-April, Talbott outlined the plan. At its heart was the issue of forcibly returning refugees to Haiti. Strobe implicitly agreed with the position I had advocated four months earlier, observing that "the President is now personally anguished about the policy of direct return." Meanwhile, Aristide had begun to make public attacks against Clinton over the refugee issue. Lake and Talbott had called him into the White House to brief him on the policy review and get him to focus his attacks on Cedras, not Clinton.

On April 21, a little-noticed event took place that showed the beginning of a shift. Another severely overcrowded boat packed with 411 Haitians was encountered by a Coast Guard cutter off the coast of Florida. Instead of interdicting the boat, the cutter allowed it to land and the Haitians were processed by U.S. immigration officials.[33] Over the next three months the forced-return policy was slowly changed, and refugee boats began to be escorted to safe havens at the Guantanamo Naval Base in Cuba and other Caribbean destinations, instead of being forced back to Haiti. As my reports indicated, the situation for Aristide supporters who remained in Haiti was becoming desperate. In the last week in April, for example, there were dozens of political killings in Gonaïves, Haiti's second largest city.[34]

There was a surrealistic quality to these events in the spring and summer of 1994. Killing on a vast scale was taking place in Rwanda and Bosnia while the United States and its European allies did little to try to stop it. In Haiti, however, a much smaller human rights crisis was getting far more attention from Washington. Perhaps this was not surprising. Close to U.S. shores, brimming with potential refugees, possessed of a democratically elected president exiled in Washington, and with strong ties to civil rights constituencies in the United States, Haiti was a natural candidate for attention by a U.S. president in the uncertain post–Cold War world—especially one who was influenced by domestic constituencies in setting his foreign policy priorities. In addition, by mid-1994 Bill Clinton badly needed a foreign policy victory. If he concentrated his attention and coordinated an administration that had been rudderless or in gridlock on foreign policy issues for much of the time since taking office, restoring Aristide to Haiti might be within his reach.

Tony Lake and Strobe Talbott spearheaded the campaign to turn Haiti from a foreign policy disaster into a victory for the President. Because of the strong resistance of the Pentagon toward using limited military force to implement or back up diplomatic objectives, the task was Herculean. Not only would the ghost of Somalia have to be exorcised and the straitjacket of Presidential Decision Directive (PDD) 25 removed, but also the perception of Aristide by the CIA and defense intelligence as an unstable leader would have to be changed, and the U.S. Cold War relationships with Cedras and the Haitian military overcome. In addition, for the first time human rights would have to be articulated as a central element in a U.S. foreign policy objective that could be achieved only through a combination of diplomatic and military means. This was a tall order.

But there was growing evidence that the President was ready to take the lead on a human rights issue. In early May, as I prepared for my trip to Rwanda, I could feel the wind shift on Haiti. While the ironic contrast between the administration's approaches to the two situations was not lost on me, I felt that if the political will could be mustered to address the Haiti crisis, this might have a positive effect on how the United States would face other human rights crises.

At a senior staff meeting on May 2, Strobe Talbott announced that in the context of our ongoing review of Haiti policy, the administration would also undertake a review of the Powell-Weinberger "all-or-nothing" doctrine on the use of military force. Strobe had been Bill Clinton's roommate at Oxford and his close friend for twenty-five years, and it was clear he was speaking for the President. "If force can only be used to fight World War III, we clearly need a new doctrine," Talbott offered. In the case of Haiti, he made it clear that "we are dead serious about getting Cedras out and Aristide in," and that to do so, "we need to get it right on the use of force." Two weeks later, Talbott and Harriet Babbitt, the U.S. ambassador to the Organization of American States, led a successful effort to get the OAS, already on record favoring the return of Aristide to Haiti, to support the formation of a U.S.-led multinational force to back up diplomatic efforts to achieve that objective.

Despite these signs of a more robust Haiti policy, there was plenty of resistance both inside and outside the administration. The White House had asked the Pentagon to develop a contingency plan for invading Haiti, both as a way of increasing the pressure on Cedras and the junta, and as a real possibility if the generals continued to shrug off the tightening economic sanctions. Having reached the conclusion that nothing else would dislodge the junta, the State Department was hawkish on military planning. As Warren Christopher later wrote, "Quite simply, as we had feared, the initial premise that the United States could restore democracy to Haiti through sanctions was turning out to be wrong."[35] But Christopher's view was at odds with the position of William Perry and the Pentagon, who continued to see Haiti as another Mogadishu and invasion planning as flatly inconsistent with the post-Somalia peacekeeping policy. On Capitol Hill the skepticism was even greater. With the exception of Florida legislators—led by Senator Bob Graham (D-Fla.), who had been converted to an interventionist as a way of addressing the refugee crisis—and the Congressional Black Caucus, congressional opposition to an invasion was deep and widespread.

## Clinton Agonistes

By the summer of 1994 Haiti had become the administration's top foreign policy headache. Although it was clear that U.S. policy was changing, it was by no means clear where this change would lead. Clinton was now heavily engaged in the effort to force out Cedras and restore Aristide, but it was uncertain whether he would be willing to follow through with the military plan he had ordered, particularly since this would mean overriding the broad opposition to implementing it that was coming from the Pentagon and Capitol Hill.

Nevertheless, for the first time since I had joined the government, I could sense that the President's leadership had opened up more space for me to do my job. I would feel the same way a year later, when Clinton would respond to the mass killings in Srebrenica by authorizing sustained NATO air strikes against Bosnian Serb military targets. Not only were views I had expressed about Haiti now being championed by Warren Christopher and Strobe Talbott, but also at the National Security Council Tony Lake was eager to use my human rights reporting to strengthen the case for removing Cedras, and at the United Nations Madeleine Albright and her team were in regular contact with me about redeploying Colin Granderson's human rights monitoring team. Another ally arrived in late spring, when Clinton appointed Bill Gray, president of the United Negro College Fund and former House Democratic whip, to be the president's special envoy to Haiti. All this political muscle at the top of the administration helped produce a string of human rights victories in the internal battle over Haiti policy. These included a whole new approach toward refugees and the shelving of PDD 25 so that military planning could go forward. The best evidence of what the President's involvement meant to our overall effort was the heavy White House lobbying that led to the defeat on June 30 of a Senate resolution that would have barred the United States from sending troops to Haiti.

Not surprisingly, Clinton's new policy began to draw strong criticism from many quarters. A favorite target was the administration's handling of the refugee crisis. After the Coast Guard stopped forcing refugee boats to return to Haiti, and instead began escorting them to temporary safe haven camps elsewhere in the Caribbean, the numbers of refugees leaving the island skyrocketed. On July 3 and 4, more than six thousand boat people took to sea.[36] Many in Congress blamed Clinton for creating this new wave through a combination of liberalized refugee policy and tightening of economic sanctions. It fell to me once again to demonstrate that the brutal repression of the Cedras regime was driving Haitians away. In a report to Christopher and Lake on July 7 that was later made public, I pointed to the dramatic increase in human rights abuses over the preceding year. This included many new atrocities, such as rapes against family members of political activists, abduction of children, disfigurement of victims' faces, and dismemberment of their bodies. My report also cited numerous cases of repatriated Haitians who had suffered severe reprisals. Its conclusion was indirectly bolstered by Sadaka Ogata, the U.N. high commissioner for refugees, who told me and other State Department officials that in the spring of 1994 her agency was completely overwhelmed by the surge in refugees fleeing from political strife in many parts of the world, particularly Rwanda, Bosnia, and Haiti.

As the summer wore on, the President's focus on Haiti intensified. To achieve his objective of forcing out Cedras and returning Aristide, Clinton had to overcome two major obstacles—Aristide himself, and the Pentagon.

The forty-year-old Haitian president was an impressive, charming, and mercurial figure whose connection to the people was both charismatic and ideological. As a practitioner of "liberation theology," Aristide professed his commitment to freeing impoverished Haitians from centuries of bondage to an oppressive elite. Although he knew he needed the assistance of his host country, he was determined to return to Haiti from his Washington exile strictly on his own terms. He was dependent on but deeply ambivalent about U.S. power, and throughout the summer he resisted endorsing a U.N.-mandated multinational force for fear that it would make him a puppet of the Americans who would lead it.

More problematic for Clinton were Aristide's public attacks on U.S. refugee policies, and his human rights record during the brief period he had served as president. Although Aristide ended these public criticisms when the Coast Guard finally stopped making forced returns of refugees to Haiti—and his human rights record was certainly better than that of the Duvaliers[37]—Clinton was irritated by what he regarded as the Haitian president's unreliability and by the ammunition his unpredictable behavior gave to Senator Jesse Helms (R-N.C.) and other congressional critics of the administration's new approach to the Haiti crisis.

The military aspect of the President's policy was questioned in many quarters. The Pentagon, the Congress, and the U.N. Security Council all stood in the way of Clinton's plan to remove Cedras and restore Aristide by backing a diplomatic ultimatum with military force. William Perry and his deputies, John Deutch and Walt Slocombe, were concerned about the prospect that a military force could get caught between contending Haitian groups and trapped in an open-ended occupation. Fortunately, General John Shalikashvili, who had succeeded Colin Powell as chairman of the Joint Chiefs of Staff in October 1993, proved to be more flexible, and his position made it easier for Perry eventually to fall in line behind the White House.

Congressional opposition to the President's military strategy was fueled by the Pentagon's skepticism and by Republican leaders working overtime to put Clinton on the defensive as the midterm elections approached. A whispering campaign, "Another Somalia," was used to attack the new Clinton Haiti policy. The Pentagon's concern about the possibility that an invasion force could get stuck in Haiti without an exit strategy was echoed on the Hill in a barrage of criticism of Clinton's "nation-building" aspirations. Senator Sam Nunn (D-Ga.), a respected Democratic expert on national security and military issues, told the *New York Times* that he had "warned the White House to consider any invasion plans 'very carefully,' and said Haiti is not a 'vital' American interest."[38]

The "exit strategy" problem posed a dilemma for the administration. Clinton had to choose between a policy of providing long-term support for Haitian democracy, which might be scuttled by the Congress, or short-term military assistance for the return of Aristide, which had a chance of getting congressional approval. In order to assure victory on the Hill, Wendy Sherman, the politically astute assistant secretary of state for congressional relations, recommended the short-term military plan. The White House had the same view, and that is the approach the administration took. While this may have been the right choice for tactical reasons, the long-term cost was high: Congress was promised an exit strategy that would limit the U.S. commitment to Haiti once Aristide was safely back in the country. This meant that essential elements of democracy-building, such as police training, judicial reform, and elections supervision, would get a burst of U.S. attention, but not the development assistance needed for democracy in Haiti to have a chance of taking hold.

As intervention planning proceeded in Washington, Madeleine Albright had her hands full at the United Nations. The pall of Somalia hung heavily over the Security Council. In addition, Russia and China, for opposite reasons, resisted the U.S. plan to authorize a multinational force to use "all necessary means" to dislodge Cedras and restore Aristide. Russia was opposed because it wanted U.S. support for resolutions authorizing it to intervene in Georgia and other former Soviet republics, which the United States was not about to give. China was wary of a resolution authorizing armed intervention into a sovereign state. Furthermore, apart from the resolution itself, there was the sticky problem of who would command a multinational force. The U.S. position that there must be a U.S. commander was non-negotiable, and this made Albright's consultations extremely difficult. Fortunately, Talbott's earlier work with the OAS in May meant that the United States now had a solid bloc of Latin American countries behind its position. By July 31, Albright had skillfully used this advantage to obtain the Security Council resolution that we wanted. This was a moment to savor: for the first time the United Nations had gone on record authorizing the use of "all necessary means" to defend democracy.[39]

Meanwhile, the Congress refused to budge. Wendy Sherman summarized the prevailing attitude toward Clinton on the Hill after the U.N. vote as "you've now got your U.N. authorization; how about ours?" Jesse Helms and other hardline enemies of the President made it clear they would bide their time and wait to sabotage the President's policy at the earliest available opportunity.

Clinton was not happy. Although everything was in place for military action by the end of the summer, the President began to balk. Preoccupied by the coming elections, he told George Stephanopoulos and other White House political advisors that he felt trapped by a situation that carried political risks in every direction, and wondered why the Haiti crisis required him to act during the congressional campaign.[40] But if his political instincts made him cautious, his strategic sense kept him focused. Clinton recognized that the military planning had significantly increased his leverage over Cedras and that it was time to issue an ultimatum now that the plan was in place.

The strategy had many opponents inside the Beltway, but the President knew it was time to reach over their heads and take it to the public. Christopher had persuaded him to address the nation on September 15 to explain his objectives in Haiti and how he planned to achieve them.[41] A week before the speech, Eric Schwartz and Tara Sonnenschein of the National Security Council staff asked me to prepare a briefing paper on the human rights crisis that the White House could use to support the President's message. The next day Schwartz called again to say that Tony Lake wanted me to brief the President and to bring photographs of human rights atrocities that would illustrate life under the Cedras regime. Eric, who had done a terrific job managing the NSC response to the refugee flood, suggested that I focus my briefing on the regime as the root cause of the mass exodus of boats from Haiti. I called Bill Swing in Port-au-Prince to see if the embassy could assemble the photos. In the end, however, it was Jim O'Dea, the Washington director of Amnesty International, who produced the best set culled from various sources. Since a military operation to protect human rights was new territory for Amnesty, O'Dea wanted to know whether U.S. troops would be instructed to follow human rights standards in carrying out the operation. I assured him that was part of their training, thanked him for the photos, and told him they would be put to good use.

Early in the afternoon of September 14, I spread my photos of the disfigured faces and bodies of Haitians who had recently been attacked by the FRAPH on a coffee table in the Oval Office. Examining them closely one at a time, the President swore quietly, "Those bastards," and vowed that Haiti's reign of terror would be brought to an end. The statistics I summarized for the President spoke for themselves—more than three thousand killed since the 1991 coup against Aristide, including nearly a thousand in the first eight months of 1994; mass graves found by human rights monitors; an estimated 300,000, or 5 percent of the population, driven into flight or hiding; and thousands of cases of mutilation, rape, and beating of Aristide supporters by the regime's network of gangs. As I talked, the President stared at the hacked and mutilated bodies of men, women, and children trapped on an island ruled by thugs.

Later that afternoon I worked with Taylor Branch and the White House speechwriting team to hone Clinton's television message. The speech should appeal equally to American values and American self-interest, pointing out that in a country near the coast of Florida human rights and refugee crises were also threats to U.S. security. Clinton's response should be measured, firm, and deliberate. "The nations of the world have tried every possible way to restore Haiti's democratic government peacefully," the President would say. "The dictators have rejected every possible solution. The terror, the desperation, and the instability will not end until they leave." Then would come the ultimatum: "The message of the United States to the Haitian dictators is clear. Your time is up. Leave now or we will force you from power." On September 15, 1994, the President delivered this message in a televised address to the nation.

## Uncertain Victory

The administration was managing a delicate balancing act. The U.S.-led multinational force would have to make every effort to enter Haiti without violence. The Cedras regime would have to leave "voluntarily." And Aristide would have to agree to return to Haiti only after American troops had cleared the way for him. It was not going to be easy. And, as was often the case with Clinton foreign policy changes, the scenario would be heavily improvised.

In mid-September 1994, the improvisation centered around the role of Jimmy Carter, who had earlier been contacted by Cedras for help in brokering a settlement with Washington. Carter volunteered to lead a negotiating team to Port-au-Prince to arrange for the junta to leave peacefully. Eager to avoid casualties, Clinton decided to give the negotiating track one last try. Carter proposed to take his fellow Georgian, Sam Nunn, as well as General Colin Powell. Although Clinton was concerned that the Carter team might give Cedras the impression that there were two American presidents, two secretaries of state, and two commanding generals who could be played off against each other, he dispatched the mission to deliver the ultimatum with a deadline of noon on September 18.[42] After that, the military operation would be launched.

On September 18, the deadline arrived and Carter called to ask for an extension. Clinton agreed to extend the time on an hour by hour basis. Late that afternoon, Powell phoned to say that an agreement had been reached. When the text was faxed to the White House, however, it was unacceptable. The agreement negotiated by the Carter team would have allowed the junta members to remain in Haiti until the Haitian parliament approved an amnesty for them.[43] This would have left Cedras effectively in control and free to negotiate the terms of his amnesty with the parliament. At Christopher's suggestion, Clinton set October 15 as the unconditional date for the generals to leave, without amnesty, and for Aristide to return.[44] Perry—now committed to a strategy of using military force to back up diplomacy—summarized the administration's position succinctly: "We're not going in on the basis of trust, but on the basis of overwhelming arms."[45] As the deadline arrived for the invasion to begin, the President ordered the negotiating team to leave within thirty minutes. Before departing, Carter called once more, this time to report that the junta had finally agreed to Clinton's terms.[46] At 2:00 A.M. on September 19, the U.S. Army 82nd Airborne Division and other troops from the multinational coalition entered Haiti without opposition.

There was a clarity to Clinton's victory—he had, after all, forced the junta out and restored a democratically elected president with a strong show of force and not a single casualty. In addition, the victory was the result of an impressive exercise of presidential leadership on an issue of democracy and human rights that had little popular support at home. Not surprisingly, however, an air of uncertainty hung over the situation. As soon as the multinational force was on the ground, Congress began sniping at its mandate. Having previously forced the President to set a date for its withdrawal within six months, congressional appropriators now sharply limited the "nation-building" capacity of the U.S. part of the multinational force. Several leading Democrats, including House Foreign Affairs Committee Chairman Lee Hamilton (D-Ind.) and Senators Chris Dodd (D-Conn.), Edward Kennedy (D-Mass.), and Bob Graham (D-Fla.), mobilized to protect Clinton's fragile foreign policy victory against the full-scale assault being mounted against it. But on the eve of the disastrous 1994 midterm elections, the administration found little congressional support for the kind of long-term U.S. engagement that would have given Haiti a better chance of becoming a stable democracy.

If Clinton was shackled by congressional resistance to his Haiti policy, Aristide was liberated by the success of the military operation. Five days before the exiled Haitian president's scheduled return to Port-au-Prince, Taylor Branch and I met with him in his modest apartment on the edge of Washington's Chinatown. I had seen Aristide at earlier stages of the crisis in official meetings in the State Department and the White House, but this was the first time we had met in a private setting where conversation could proceed naturally. Aristide greeted me warmly and said he had wanted for some time to thank me for drawing attention to Haiti's worsening human rights situation the previous December, and for calling for a review of U.S. policy. He said my trip to Haiti after the *Harlan County* crisis had been a "turning point," and that he had been confident after then that his return was just a matter of time. He spoke about the need to change political behavior in Haiti by "changing the hierarchy."

As it turned out, my visit to Aristide's apartment took place at the very moment when Cedras and the junta generals were leaving Port-au-Prince. Aristide and I sat together on the sofa and watched Cedras on CNN make a few self-serving remarks at the president's palace that were largely drowned out by jeering crowds. Aristide remarked to Taylor and me that by leaving in disgrace and without amnesty for his crimes, Cedras symbolized the fall of the discredited military hierarchy that was at the root of Haiti's political problems. The first order of business in building democracy, Aristide offered, would be to dismantle the Haitian military and rebuild the country's police and court systems on the basis of "their loyalty to democracy, not their thuggery against the people."

This was exactly what the United States would try to do during the very limited window of opportunity offered by the presence of the multinational force (MNF) before its scheduled withdrawal the following March. An immediate task was to establish rules of engagement for the force that would allow it to counter acts of violent resistance by groups tied to the old regime. In interagency meetings in late September, I worked with Bob Gelbard, assistant secretary of state for international narcotics and law enforcement, to make sure these rules authorized the use of force to respond to human rights atrocities committed in the presence of MNF troops. At the highest level, the administration now seemed ready, at least in the case of Haiti, to scrap the restrictions imposed on peacekeepers in Somalia, Rwanda, and Bosnia. On October 2, two weeks after their deployment, the new rules of engagement were tested when American soldiers mounted an armed assault on the headquarters of FRAPH. Reporting on the successful raid, the *New York Times* observed that "by striking decisively at the headquarters of the most belligerent and feared [of Haiti's paramilitary groups], the American forces that began landing here two weeks ago scored a significant political victory and raised their stock among the populace."[47]

Creating a new civilian police force proved to be a much greater challenge. Soon after the MNF troops arrived, they identified a ranch on the outskirts of Port-au-Prince that American and Canadian law enforcement experts could use as a police training academy. The ranch had been built by Baby Doc Duvalier, and its new use seemed a symbol for a new era, as a team of international instructors headed by Ray Kelly, a former New York City police commissioner, moved in.[48]

But it was easier to recruit outstanding instructors than to find adequate trainees. The problem was simple: most of the potential pool had been poisoned by working in or with the Cedras regime's security forces. During the fall, a process for screening out human rights violators was established by the international law enforcement team in coordination with Colin Granderson's international human rights mission, but progress on developing even a barely adequate Haitian police force was slow. Even slower was the process of reforming the deeply corrupt Haitian judicial system, a project undertaken by USAID Assistant Administrator Mark Schneider. Unlike police training, this project never seemed to get much support from Aristide.

As the months went by, the enormity of the task of building democracy in Haiti became ever clearer. On a trip throughout the country in early December 1994, I was struck by the contrast between the great progress we had made in ending the reign of terror and the glacial pace of change in Haiti's political infrastructure. Human rights conditions were vastly improved in large part because of the presence of the multinational force. Driving through the streets of Gonaïves in an Army humvee with my son, Peter, escorted by heavily armed Major Tom O'Neill of the U.S. Army's Tenth Mountain Division, we were greeted by throngs of waving pedestrians in a city that only months before had been a center of political assassination, torture, and violence. When I asked O'Neill how six Army Rangers could have brought stability to a city of fifty thousand, our Rambo escort answered succinctly: "We go everywhere and we show the flag and the gun." Later, at the Port-au-Prince city hall, Evans Paul told me he could not have reclaimed his mayoral office without the support of the MNF, and Aristide made the same point in his meeting with me at the presidential palace. I found myself elated and sobered by these comments, since they indicated how relatively easy it had been for us to change the human rights dynamic in Haiti, but how hard it would be for the Haitians to build a democracy that could protect human rights once all the international assistance they were getting had dried up.

Haiti was an imperfect victory for human rights, but it was a building block for a new American foreign policy. By building an international consensus and assembling a multinational force to intervene in a human rights crisis that was breeding terror, causing massive civilian suffering, and creating substantial regional instability, the Clinton administration finally broke free from its post-Somalia straitjacket and laid the foundation for a new doctrine of humanitarian intervention. This doctrine would later be implemented again in Bosnia, Kosovo, and East Timor. In the case of Haiti, heavy pressure from a skeptical and politically hostile Congress forced the administration to withdraw most American troops within six months of their arrival, and to scale back its democracy-building assistance to the government. Although the human rights conditions in Haiti are generally better today than they were in early 1994, the country has slid back toward its long tradition of political corruption and government repression, exacerbated by extreme poverty. This tradition has gripped Haiti for more than two hundred years. Tragically, some observers say Aristide looks increasingly like its contemporary representative.[49] But the short attention span of the international community in assisting the Haitians in the hard task of nation building has also contributed to the fate of their struggle for democracy.[50] The lesson of the Haiti intervention is that while diplomacy backed by force can make a difference for human rights, democracy in a shattered country cannot be built overnight without sustained and well-coordinated outside help.

# CHAPTER 4

# BOSNIA

## THE PARIAH PROBLEM

The air in the cinderblock schoolhouse was hot and putrid. A strong odor of dried sweat arose from the floor where scores of bedraggled figures lay in a state of exhaustion. In the corner a mother slept beside her two heavily bandaged children. Only the dull thudding of artillery shells in the mountains broke the torpid atmosphere. It was July 30, 1995. These were the survivors. They held the key to a terrible past and a better future.

I had come to Tuzla, in central Bosnia, to a schoolhouse that was now serving as a makeshift refugee center, to find out what had happened in Srebrenica, a Muslim town thirty kilometers to the east that had been taken by the Serbs two weeks earlier. Sitting on a rickety wooden chair in the back of the room, I listened to the story of Hurem Suljic, a fifty-five-year-old farmer with a lined and leathery face, deep-set dark eyes, and a slightly crippled right leg. The grizzled Bosnian Muslim looked and sounded like a biblical witness to an apocalypse, punctuating his sentences with cringing gestures of fear and ghastly memory. Two weeks earlier in their village outside Srebrenica, Suljic and his family had been ordered by Bosnian Serb soldiers to go to the nearby U.N. "safe area" compound. When they arrived, they had found the area teeming with soldiers who were busy separating Muslim women and children from men and herding the women and children onto buses. Suljic was told to join a group of men who were taken to the unfinished frame of a new house and made to sit on the concrete floor.

A Serb soldier asked, "Who knows Commander Mladic? If you don't, you'll meet him soon and get to know him well." Within minutes a short stocky man in a uniform with epaulettes came and stood on a wooden box in the middle of the house frame. "Hello, neighbors," he said, "180 of my people are in prison in Tuzla, and I want to exchange them for you, probably by tomorrow. You won't be harmed. The exchange will be done in a peaceful way, and you'll soon be back with your families." Suljic knew that Mladic was a powerful man, and he remembered feeling relieved by what he had heard him say.

An hour later Suljic and his group were hustled onto buses and driven to an empty warehouse in Bratunac, a Serb-held town north of Srebrenica, where they were joined by hundreds of other Muslim men and forced to sit virtually on top of each other on the dirt floor. Then came the first indication that Mladic's promise would not be kept. During the night soldiers pulled Suljic and other men outside in groups and beat them with iron bars and axe handles until some were unconscious and then threw them back onto the crowded dirt floor.

In the morning Suljic looked around and saw that most of the younger men were no longer there. Mladic appeared again. The older men who remained asked, "Why are you torturing us?" Mladic replied that the Bosnian army in Tuzla had been unwilling to organize a prisoner exchange. "But now we've persuaded them, and the buses are on the way to pick you up." After the prisoners had spent another day in the warehouse, new buses arrived at night. But again, they went north, further into the Serb-held areas, not west toward Tuzla where the supposed exchange was to take place. Suljic and his companions were unloaded at a high school gym, blindfolded, and pushed to the floor. Telling them the blindfolds were to prevent them from seeing a military installation, the guards ordered them out of the building one by one.

When his turn came, Suljic edged up his blindfold enough to see that he was being herded into a pickup truck with about twenty other men. As the truck drove through the fields, he could see bodies in the ditches beside the road. He remembered hearing a Serb soldier shouting, "Don't turn around," as he was hustled off the pickup truck. "My mind went blank as the shots came," Suljic rasped to me in an exhausted voice. "I thought I was dead when I fell into the ditch with all the other bodies on top of me. But they had missed me, and I lay there for hours. I saw Mladic ordering his soldiers to finish off the wounded. I saw my best friend lying dead near me. I saw the end of the world." Still afraid to be heard, he described to me in a halting whisper how he had waited until the soldiers left, then pulled himself out of the pile of bodies and crept with two other survivors through miles of dangerous forest to reach the Bosnian side of the confrontation line.

Outsiders knew little about what had happened after the fall of Srebrenica. My interviews with Hurem Suljic and other survivors in the Tuzla refugee camp were among the first concrete accounts of the Serbs' systematic slaughter of Muslim men. Staggered by the stories I had heard, I reported them at a press conference on July 31 in Zagreb. Most of the international reporters who were there were preoccupied by the long-anticipated Croatian offensive against Serb forces in northwestern Bosnia and the Krajina, and after four years of covering this war were only marginally interested in "another ethnic cleansing story."[1] But David Rohde, an enterprising reporter for the *Christian Science Monitor,* picked up immediately on the significance of the vast and unprecedented scope of the mass executions in Srebrenica that I was describing. Two weeks later, he located the first mass grave site in Nova Kasaba.[2]

Back in Washington on August 1, I gave the findings of my Srebrenica mission to Secretary of State Warren Christopher. I hoped this fresh evidence of the worst genocide in Europe since World War II would finally lead to a change in U.S. policy toward Bosnia, but I feared that the years of genocidal warfare in what was once Yugoslavia would continue to drag on.

My week had begun with Christopher granting my request to lead an urgent mission to Tuzla to investigate the fate of thousands of men reported missing from the Srebrenica area. In approving my mission, Christopher had overruled objections by midlevel officials in the State Department's European Affairs Bureau (but not the bureau's chief, Assistant Secretary of State Richard Holbrooke, who supported what I was trying to do), as well as protests by diplomatic security experts who did not want to authorize any State Department official travel to the Bosnia combat zone.

I knew the stakes were high. I had asked Josiah Rosenblatt, a foreign service officer who directed the multilateral affairs office in the human rights bureau, to accompany me. Josiah had traveled with me a year earlier on a trip across Rwanda in the aftermath of the genocide. We were joined in Zagreb by Dubravka Maric, a Croatian-American officer posted at the U.S. Embassy, and Anthony Holbrooke (Richard Holbrooke's son) of the International Rescue Committee, one of the leading international relief organizations operating in Bosnia. Our group of four had been able to interview scores of Srebrenica refugees. We had pieced together horrific details and common themes from many stories like the one told to me by Hurem Suljic. As we flew back to Washington, there was no doubt in our minds about what had happened in Srebrenica.

My written report to Christopher was graphic:

I have heard credible eyewitness accounts of mass executions of men and boys by Bosnian Serb soldiers with many of the victims buried in mass graves dug on the spot by bulldozers. I have also heard first-hand accounts of horrible brutalities committed against people who were trying to flee, including slitting of throats, cutting off of ears, noses, jaws and limbs of persons still alive, and tying people to landmines. I have heard many credible accounts of the shelling of large columns of civilians attempting to flee, and four separate accounts of the possible use of chemical weapons that severely disoriented fleeing people, causing several to commit suicide. Information was presented to me by both victims and witnesses of rapes and sexual abuse of Muslim women by soldiers. I also heard several accounts of Bosnian Serb soldiers luring Muslim residents to follow them by wearing U.N. helmets and then attacking them. Finally, I heard detailed information about the existence of Bosnian Serb detention centers and concentration camps for an undetermined number of men and boys from Srebrenica and Zepa at Potocari, Bratunac, Batkovic, and Rogatica. Based on this information I am very concerned about the safety and fate of a very large number of people who are missing. It is impossible at this point to estimate accurately how many have been killed, but clearly that number is very substantial. . . . We need to draw immediate lessons from the fall of the so-called "safe areas": preventive measures can save lives. The magnitude and horror of the human rights abuses of Srebrenica must not be repeated.

The overwhelming evidence of vast new crimes against humanity in Srebrenica contributed to a long-overdue shift in U.S. policy. On August 2, the day after my press conference in Zagreb, Balkan specialists at the Central Intelligence Agency began an urgent search for spy satellite photographs that would confirm the existence of mass grave sites in the area north of Srebrenica, which the survivors had described to us as the killing fields. One analyst later told me that after reading my report he had stayed up all night closely studying photos of the Nova Kasaba area, finding several that showed large numbers of men gathered on July 13 on a soccer field which two days later was empty, while nearby mounds of freshly moved earth were clearly visible. When these photos were circulated to policymakers in Washington, U.S. Ambassador to the United Nations Madeleine Albright sought and obtained a White House decision to release them at a U.N. Security Council meeting on August 10. Hurem Suljic's story was now confirmed before the world.

Eighteen days later, a crowded Sarajevo market was blown apart by a mortar shell that killed thirty-eight Bosnian Muslim vendors and shoppers and severely mangled eighty-five others.[3] On August 30, with Washington taking the lead, the North Atlantic Council in Brussels ordered NATO planes into the air to begin bombing Bosnian Serb military targets. At the same time, an aggressive new American initiative, characterized by Christopher as "diplomacy backed by force," was launched by President Clinton with Richard Holbrooke as its point man. Holbrooke's objective: to try at last to end a war that had seemed endless and had killed or devastated the lives of hundreds of thousands of Bosnian civilians. Many factors contributed to this policy shift, including the deaths on August 19 of three American peace negotiators in an accident on a treacherous mountain road high above the besieged city of Sarajevo. But no single factor was more important than the unfolding truth about what had happened at Srebrenica, where more than seven thousand Bosnian Muslims had been murdered in the largest single act of genocide on European soil since the Holocaust.

In August 1995, Srebrenica riveted the attention of the world, demanding and finally receiving the kind of international response that had been lacking during four years of systematic attacks on entire sectors of the Yugoslav civilian population, who had been singled out solely because of their religion and ethnicity. But if the response to Srebrenica was a triumph for the most basic principle of human rights—that genocide must never be committed with impunity—it was a triumph preceded by seemingly endless failure.

## The Making of a Human Rights Disaster

From the very beginning the crisis in the Balkans was treated as a pariah problem by the U.S. foreign policy establishment. The breakup of Yugoslavia coincided with the fall of the Berlin Wall. But these two revolutionary events marking the end of the Cold War were vastly different. In the late 1980s, popular demands for democracy had powered peaceful Central European movements for change in Germany, Poland, Hungary, and Czechoslovakia, but in Yugoslavia, appeals to ethnic and religious nationalism by cynical communist leaders seeking to perpetuate and enhance their own power had sparked violence. When the smallest Yugoslav republic, Slovenia, broke away from the central government in Belgrade in November 1989, and the predominantly Albanian-speaking province of Kosovo asserted its longstanding status of autonomy within Serbia, Slobodan Milosevic seized the opportunity to fan the flames of nationalism, force out reform-oriented Belgrade leaders, and begin his climb to power by manipulating the Serb national identity that had been suppressed during four decades of Tito's communism. Other former communist politicians, including Franjo Tudjman in Croatia and Alija Izetbegovic in Bosnia, applied their own nationalist tactics to consolidate their power.

The four Balkan wars that ensued—in which a quarter of a million people were killed and nearly two million more were driven from their homes—were depicted by many commentators in Europe and the United States as the inevitable product of "ancient hatreds" among a population long divided by both religion (Orthodox, Catholic, and Muslim) and national identity (Serb, Croat, and Bosniac). In fact, the Balkan wars were the consequence of a series of complex power struggles by communist leaders who stimulated religious and nationalist conflict as they scrapped over the spoils of a disintegrating Yugoslavia. Milosevic launched these conflicts by using the state-controlled media in Belgrade to stir up nationalist resentments and historical grudges, and then by employing police, military, and paramilitary forces to unleash human rights crimes against non-Serbs in Bosnia, parts of Croatia, and Kosovo. Tudjman and others followed suit in an endlessly vicious spiral of reprisals.

The Bush administration, underestimating the instigating role of Milosevic in the early stages of the Yugoslav crisis, chose to see the conflict as one of "ancient hatreds" that could not be contained. In 1991, Secretary of State James Baker summed up his view of what was at stake for the United States in Bosnia with his notorious comment, "We don't have a dog in that fight."[4] Baker's comment reflected the view of many policymakers at the time, who failed to grasp that the U.S. interest was not in picking the right dog, but in entering the fray to stop the fight before it engulfed all of Yugoslavia. This outdated Cold War perspective proved disastrously wrong. By failing to develop an aggressive diplomatic strategy with European countries to stop the breakup of Yugoslavia, the Bush administration allowed Milosevic to start the first of four wars that would eventually destabilize all of southeastern Europe and put at risk the transatlantic alliance that had been the foundation of European and American security for more than four decades.

The power struggle that incinerated Yugoslavia after 1989 had actually begun a decade earlier after the death in May 1980 of Josip Broz Tito, the country's founder and maverick communist dictator. If the Tito regime had survived until the fall of the Berlin Wall in 1989, events in Yugoslavia arguably might have taken a different course. Milosevic, Tudjman, and other communist politicians might not have had time to consolidate their power in the face of external pressures for reform coming from the anticommunist revolutions in Central and Eastern Europe. Instead, because Tito died nearly a decade before the collapse of communism, his heirs had time to transform themselves into extreme nationalists and crush moderate opponents who were in favor of preserving a multiethnic Yugoslavia.

Traditional instruments of communist control—the state media, the police, and the military—were used to advance the dangerous ambitions of these new nationalist leaders. In the early 1990s, vast projects of "ethnic cleansing" were launched in Bosnia and Croatia by Milosevic and Tudjman and their Bosnian Serb and Bosnian Croat surrogates. By the end of 1992 hundreds of thousands of people had been forced from their homes, tens of thousands slaughtered, many thousands rounded up in concentration camps, women raped, and entire population groups terrorized solely because of their religion or ethnicity. Although 12,500 lightly armed U.N. troops were deployed in March 1992 to supervise a tense cease-fire in Croatia and later to watch over humanitarian shipments and the establishment of U.N. "safe areas" in Bosnia, the rules of engagement drawn up for the white-helmeted peacekeepers by their thirty home countries sharply limited what they could do.

When the Clinton administration came into office in January 1993, the horrors of ethnic cleansing were continuing unabated under the eyes of a paralyzed international community. In March I began commuting from Cambridge to the State Department as President Clinton's nominee to be assistant secretary of state for human rights and humanitarian affairs. In Washington I found that Bosnia was regarded as a sinkhole that would drag down anyone who got involved with it. Clinton as a candidate had criticized the Bush administration for "turning its back on basic violations of human rights in Bosnia," and had urged air strikes against the Serbs for blocking humanitarian convoys to Sarajevo.[5] But Clinton as President seemed uncertain about how to address the crisis.

In one of the early staff meetings I attended at the State Department I raised the question of when and how we were going to fulfill the President's pledge to be more proactive on Bosnia than the Bush administration. I was surprised to hear from Tim Wirth, the former Colorado senator who had been nominated to be undersecretary for global affairs (my immediate superior), that the prevailing view within the administration was that our capacity to deliver humanitarian assistance in Bosnia would be undermined if we became more engaged politically or militarily in the Balkan crisis. Warren Zimmermann, the last U.S. Ambassador to Belgrade, was at the same meeting. Zimmermann indicated to Wirth that he disagreed with this low-profile and relatively neutral position. Later, over lunch in the eighth-floor State Department dining room, I asked Zimmermann where he thought Bosnia policy was headed and what we could do to strengthen it. It's a morass, he said, and no one wants to deal with it.

Earlier U.S. and European efforts to address the crisis had been fruitless. In February 1993 a new peace initiative had been put forward by former secretary of state Cyrus Vance and former British foreign secretary David Owen to create ten separate ethnic cantons in Bosnia divided among Serbs, Croats, and Muslims. The plan was widely accepted in Europe but attacked by parts of the Congress and the American press as a Munich-style sellout.[6]

Clinton administration officials expressed ambivalence about the Vance-Owen plan and sought an alternative. In May, Clinton sent Christopher to London, Paris, and Bonn to sound out European leaders on a two-part American proposal: to lift the arms embargo so that the Bosnian Muslims could strengthen their military defenses, and to launch NATO air strikes against the Bosnian Serbs to break the Serbs' siege of Sarajevo. The purpose of this "lift and strike" proposal, in Christopher's words, was to "level the military playing field between Muslims and Croats; once the Muslims had better means to defend themselves, the logic went, there would be less need for outside intervention."[7] But a key ingredient was missing. Neither the President nor any of the new administration's top decisionmakers, as Christopher later wrote, "had enthusiasm for commitment of U.S. ground troops to force a settlement. Many, including myself, were concerned that American public opinion would not support a prolonged and risky operation for such a purpose."[8]

Christopher's mission to Europe was doomed from the start. Not wanting to overcommit the United States when the President was unwilling to contribute ground forces, the Secretary of State had traveled to Europe to consult, not to lead. U.S. reluctance to share responsibility for solving the Bosnia crisis was clearly demonstrated, the Europeans felt, by the American "lift and strike" proposal, which carried serious risks for the safety of European peacekeeping troops, without any comparable risk for Americans.[9] Christopher returned empty-handed. The failure of his mission reinforced the position of those in the administration who believed that the crisis in Bosnia was insoluble and should be left to the Europeans to manage. The plug was pulled on an activist American approach to Bosnia before I had even been confirmed by the Senate as assistant secretary for human rights.

## Early Lessons in Diplomacy

I learned something important from this early setback: there are no magic "policy wands" in Washington. The battle to set foreign policy can be as protracted as the struggle to implement it on the ground. Within the U.S. government, hundreds—even thousands—of people from different agencies and bureaus are likely to be involved, each defending a piece of turf that will be needed for a major policy shift to occur. Outside the government, a wide range of constituencies can make or break a policy, augmenting their voices by speaking through members of Congress, high officials in the administration, or the media.

In the case of Bosnia, the path toward implementing the President's campaign commitment to do more for human rights was blocked in four ways. The White House was wary of being drawn into a messy Balkan conflict, particularly in light of Clinton's 43 percent popular vote. The Joint Chiefs of Staff, led by General Colin Powell, were strongly opposed to military involvement in situations where the United States was not able to "win" through overwhelming force superiority. The State Department had no independent means of enforcing diplomatic efforts on behalf of human rights. And Congress after the end of the Cold War was shying away from new American military commitments to intractable international situations like the Bosnia war.

Beyond these roadblocks stood an additional bureaucratic hurdle—an "interagency process" managed by the White House through which the new administration planned to vet all major policy initiatives. In one of my earliest White House meetings, my notes reflect that I was warned by Dick Clarke, the National Security Council senior director for global affairs, that "our human rights policies will have to be consensus-driven. All agencies will have a right to comment on proposals in this very sensitive area." This sounded like a prescription for mush, gridlock, or both.

How could I move forward in this environment? I was largely an outsider in the State Department. In the spring of 1993, when I was still mastering the elaborate color-coded wall system of Foggy Bottom, I received some advice from one of my oldest friends in the human rights field, Aryeh Neier, who was then in transition from directing Human Rights Watch to becoming president of George Soros's Open Society Foundation. Aryeh, my first boss when he hired me right out of law school in 1971 to be an ACLU staff lawyer, was blunt: "Don't allow yourself to become the public spokesman for positions that you fundamentally disagree with. That's what they'll want you to do, and if you do that you'll lose your credibility."

He urged me to draw this line and stick to it, and then focus on the daily grind of trying to make progress. He counseled me to form alliances, be prepared for criticism both from inside and outside the government, and to take risks and seize opportunities without reaching beyond the limits of what I could do at any given moment. Bosnia, he said, would be very difficult, and I would have to start pushing right away.

I saw my first opportunity in the emerging debate over how to handle the issue of war crimes. In early 1993, the United States had begun to champion the creation by the U.N. Security Council of an International War Crimes Tribunal for the Former Yugoslavia. The leader of this effort was Madeleine Albright, then the U.S. ambassador to the United Nations, whose strong views on the Balkan crisis had been shaped in part by her own family's experience of having twice been forced to flee her native Czechoslovakia, first under the Nazis and later under the communists.

A tribunal had been proposed as early as 1992 by Human Rights Watch and the Lawyers Committee for Human Rights as a way of signaling that crimes against humanity could not be committed with impunity.[10] Drawing from the example of the Nuremberg Trials after World War II, proponents of a tribunal argued that international justice was needed to lift the burden of collective guilt that settles on a nation whose leaders have committed genocide. Another argument drawn more directly from the Balkan crisis was that in the absence of justice, a vicious cycle of ongoing reprisals would perpetuate itself. On the other side of the debate were those who saw an international tribunal as an impediment to peace that would block the possibility of giving amnesty to the warring parties as an incentive for their participation in negotiations.

My civil liberties background, and especially my experience with issues of public accountability during the Watergate crisis, drew me instinctively to the search for Balkan justice. As an early advocate of a War Crimes Tribunal, I seized on Albright's project even before I was confirmed as assistant secretary. I started working with Albright's assistant, David Scheffer; State Department Legal Adviser Conrad

Harper; and Harper's deputies, Mike Matheson and Jim O'Brien, to draft the tribunal's mandate, raise funds from the Congress and other governments to support it, and mount a search for its prosecutor and judges. Driven by our conviction that the war crimes being committed daily in Bosnia required an international response, our group formalized itself as the first human rights coalition inside the Clinton administration.

In these early days of the new administration, the policymaking process was both chaotic and opaque. Daily meetings of assistant secretaries were discontinued in 1993 during the brief tenure of deputy secretary Clifton Wharton. It was not until the administration had been in office for a full year that assistant secretaries began to meet regularly as a group under Wharton's successor, Strobe Talbott, to discuss policy issues. In addition to the confusion over policy coordination, I soon encountered another problem that was specific to my position. During much of the Reagan and Bush administrations, the human rights bureau had been marginalized and largely cut out of the policy process; this legacy made it difficult to get access to key Bosnia meetings during the first two years of the Clinton administration.

One lesson that took me several months to learn was that I had to force my way into the policy process, not simply wait to be asked to join it. In addition to using my newfound strategy of traveling to a crisis area and then sending my recommendations back to Washington, I found that I was more likely to get into high-level meetings if I had just returned from or was planning a trip than if I was trying to maneuver through the Washington bureaucracy. In the case of Bosnia, however, my travel before 1995 was generally blocked for reasons I will explain that illustrated the profound problems in U.S. policy.

## In the Spotlight: A World Conference on Human Rights

Bosnia was the toughest foreign policy issue that the new administration faced in mid-1993. Failure by the Christopher mission to persuade the Europeans to support the "lift and strike" proposal had effectively forced the Clinton administration back to the position taken earlier by the Bush administration: that the crisis was a morass from which Europe would have to extract itself without American help.

This was the view I encountered on the seventh floor of the State Department when I set out to persuade Christopher to deliver the administration's first comprehensive speech on human rights at the U.N. World Conference on Human Rights in Vienna in mid-June. The conference, a massive gathering of 160 governments and two thousand nongovernmental organizations with a mandate to examine international human rights norms in the post–Cold War world, was certain to become a forum on Bosnia. As assistant secretary, I would be responsible for managing the U.S. delegation, negotiating the text of the conference document, and delivering our positions in the drafting and plenary sessions. Although Tim Wirth planned to attend the opening days of the conference as head of the U.S. delegation, and former President Jimmy Carter would be there in his private capacity, I wanted the Secretary of State to deliver the main U.S. speech to show that our delegation had administration backing at the highest level.

I ran into a brick wall. Tom Donilon, Christopher's chief of staff, told me he saw nothing but trouble in the conference and another chance for the Secretary to be embarrassed on human rights and Bosnia. He relented only slightly when Wirth intervened, and made clear that Christopher could focus on global democracy-building themes but had to stay away from "the Carter trap" of scolding other countries on human rights. Above all, Donilon warned, Bosnia was off limits. "If this is screwed up, you're fired," he said in a parting shot as I headed to Vienna.

When the conference opened on June 6, it quickly turned into a cauldron of controversy. Countries like China, Malaysia, Indonesia, Syria, Iraq, Iran, and Cuba were using it as a forum to attack the principle of universality—the idea that human rights standards apply equally in all countries. A caucus of authoritarian regimes had been formed to promote "cultural relativism" as a shield against charges of censorship, torture, and other blatant human rights abuses.

While this assault was being mounted by the world's authoritarian governments, activists from all over the world were crammed together in the basement of the Vienna conference center, trying to get access to the meetings so they could lobby delegates and shine their spotlight on repressive governments. Amnesty International, Human Rights Watch, the Lawyers Committee for Human Rights, the International Human Rights Law Group, and other U.S. organizations with which I had close ties were at the forefront of these efforts. I decided that the best way to fight the authoritarian caucus was to champion the activists' demands for access to the official meetings. The U.S. delegation assembled a loose coalition of democratic countries to get nongovernmental representatives into the meetings. We also began holding daily public briefings on what had happened in the delegate corridors and behind closed doors, working with friends and former colleagues in human rights organizations outside of government to gain support and leverage to fight the inside battles.

We needed all the help we could get. As predicted, Bosnia emerged as a major issue at the Vienna conference. The rules precluded "country-specific resolutions." Many European countries and the United States wanted to avoid an acrimonious debate on Bosnia that would put them on the defensive, and other countries wanted to keep their own human rights records out of the spotlight. Any effort to break the ban on "country-specific resolutions," therefore, risked having the whole conference collapse. But the Bosnia crisis was too big to be kept off the agenda. The Bosnian delegation used its position in the Organization of Islamic Countries to press for an exception to the conference rules in the case of "crimes against humanity right here in Europe," as they described the situation, calling for a vote on a resolution condemning the international community for failing to stop the war. Emotional appeals swung many delegations toward Bosnia's position, and the conference began to teeter on the edge of collapse as Iran threatened to introduce a resolution on Israel, and India and Pakistan traded charges over Kashmir.

Most democratic governments and many human rights activists did not want the conference to fail. This would have handed a victory to the authoritarian caucus by preventing resolutions from being adopted on fundamental principles like the universality of human rights, which they were refusing to accept. Failure would also have meant a lost opportunity to create the new position of U.N. high commissioner for human rights, a major objective of both democratic governments and human rights leaders.

I began to look for a way of saving the conference while using the energy in Vienna to press for a more activist American policy on Bosnia. In several transatlantic telephone conferences with Madeleine Albright and Tony Lake, I recommended that we hammer out a plan to have the conference appeal to the U.N. Security Council for stronger measures to address the crisis in Bosnia, including strengthening the War Crimes Tribunal and, if possible, adopting the U.S. "lift and strike" policy. Albright liked this approach, and Lake did not object to it. Although we failed to get agreement on "lift and strike," I was able to announce to the press on June 21 that the United States advocated "a conference dialogue with the Security Council over the human rights catastrophe in Bosnia." By forging a consensus on Bosnia, we were able to clear the way for conference approval of resolutions reinforcing the Universal Declaration of Human Rights and calling for the establishment of a U.N. high commissioner for human rights. By learning how to maneuver at the conference, I gained credibility in Washington while strengthening, ever so slightly, the administration's weak Bosnia policy.

Another challenge was preparing for Christopher's speech. A battle over the text was waged in a series of tense conference calls between Christopher's staff, led by Tom Donilon, who wanted the Secretary of State to steer clear of Bosnia and other human rights controversies, and others like Eric Schwartz, the human rights specialist on the National Security Council staff, and myself who felt strongly that at a world conference on human rights the United States should claim the mantle of a human rights leader by squarely addressing the Bosnia crisis. Bennett Freeman, Christopher's speechwriter, was caught in the middle of this debate and helped to bridge the gap. Christopher was visiting Istanbul the night before he was to arrive in Vienna. Discussing his speech with Freeman, Christopher reflected on his days in the Carter administration when as deputy secretary of state he had helped create the human rights bureau. Looking out over the balcony of his hotel at the twinkling lights of the ancient city below him, Christopher told Freeman that he wanted his speech to address *both* human rights *and* democracy, because each was an essential element of freedom. "You're right," said Freeman, seizing on the chance to remind the Secretary that there are democracies with horrendous human rights records. Pointing off to the distance, Freeman observed, "Turkey's a democracy, but I'm sure someone out there is being tortured tonight."

My side won the debate over the speech. The next day in Vienna, Christopher spoke publicly about Bosnia for the first time since his ill-fated European mission. In light of the policy morass in Washington, what he had to say was surprisingly strong:

> Fresh horrors abound around the world. We have only to think of the enormous costs of regional conflict, ethnic hatred and despotic rule. We have only to think of Bosnia—just a few hundred miles away from this meeting hall, but worlds away from the peaceful and tolerant international community envisioned in the Universal Declaration of Human Rights.
>
> A lasting peace in the Balkans depends on ensuring that all are prepared to respect fundamental human rights, especially those of minorities. Those who desecrate those rights must know that they will be ostracized. They will face sanctions. They will be brought before tribunals of international justice. They will not gain access to investment or assistance. And they will not gain acceptance by the community of civilized nations.

These were tough words. But it would take more than two years for the Clinton administration to back them up with action. The situation on the ground would not wait. By mid-July 1993, Sarajevo was being cut off from the world by Serb mortars and snipers, and the designation of the city as a U.N. "safe area" had become a cruel joke.

After returning from Vienna I decided to make another move on Bosnia inside the State Department. Using reports compiled by my bureau, I sent a memo to Christopher on July 15, citing the growing evidence of genocide in central Bosnia and the urgency of strengthening the War Crimes Tribunal so that it could investigate, arrest, and prosecute those responsible. The European Affairs Bureau (EUR) and its assistant secretary, Steven Oxman, at first tried to block my memo, saying I was wrong to focus on the tribunal at a time when efforts were being made to get the Balkan leaders to participate in peace negotiations. But because I had framed what I had written as an "information memo," one not calling for specific "action," EUR could not prevent it from reaching the Secretary. After much internal debate in which EUR (by then rocked by resignations in protest of U.S. policy)[11] was pitted against the Human Rights Bureau, Christopher tentatively agreed to put the United States on record in favor of an "unfettered tribunal" and against offering amnesty to participants in the sporadic peace negotiations in Geneva. Nevertheless, the public statement I had drafted about the tribunal and its independence from the peace negotiations was repeatedly postponed at the request of U.S. negotiators, who claimed it would get in the way of what they were trying to do.

By the fall of 1993, the efforts of our State Department war crimes working group were slowly beginning to show results. The United States was now providing financial and staffing assistance to the tribunal, which had been formally established by the U.N. Security Council on May 25, 1993.[12] But we were still getting nowhere on the underlying policy question: would the United States lead an effort to stop the war and arrest war criminals in Bosnia? Since President Clinton seemed unwilling to authorize further U.S. involvement in Bosnia beyond our limited diplomatic engagement, and his Joint Chiefs of Staff chairman, Colin Powell, was flatly against committing U.S. troops to another peacekeeping effort when he was already managing a crisis in Somalia (one that would end in disaster), our struggle to move the War Crimes Tribunal to center stage seemed doomed. The mood in Washington on Bosnia became increasingly grim after the Somalia debacle. When Tim Wirth announced at a staff meeting on October 28 that "the President is not pleased with his foreign policy," I knew he was connecting Bosnia with Somalia.

## Disaster on the Ground

One of the many difficulties I encountered in late 1993 was getting approval for a human rights mission to the Balkans. By then, my frustration with our policy was well known and my colleagues in EUR, who had primary responsibility for implementing it, did not want me to use a trip to the region to spotlight the evidence of genocide that I had been forwarding to Christopher's office on the seventh floor. During the first year of the Clinton administration my bureau had produced five separate human rights reports on atrocities in the former Yugoslavia. These were pieced together from materials prepared by our embassies in Zagreb and Belgrade; by foreign service officers who conducted interviews in the refugee camps in Bosnia, Serbia, and Croatia; and by human rights organizations active in the region. We sent each report to Christopher's office, and simultaneously to the U.N. War Crimes Commission for the Former Yugoslavia, a precursor to the War Crimes Tribunal.

Although most people in the State Department agreed that war crimes were being committed in the Balkans, genocide was a term few were willing to use to describe what was actually happening. Those who did so either resigned in protest against the weakness of U.S. policy, or, like me, stayed on to fight for change. The genocide debate, which had begun in the Bush administration and would be repeated in the spring of 1994 in the case of Rwanda, reflected the reluctance of U.S. policymakers to confront the responsibility of countries that had ratified the Genocide Convention "to prevent and punish" crimes determined to constitute genocide.[13] For this reason I could not get State Department clearance to use the term "genocide" to describe what was happening in Bosnia or Rwanda.

As a human rights fact-finder, I saw the danger that truth would become a victim of this debate. I wanted to assess the situation for myself. Throughout the fall, however, I was blocked by EUR, which refused to clear my request to travel to the Balkans because it felt a human rights mission would complicate the peace negotiations. The roadblock to my trip was finally removed when Madeleine Albright invited me to join her in early January 1994 to review the U.N. mission in Croatia, and witness firsthand the devastation in Vukovar and other parts of eastern Slavonia where Serb forces had slaughtered or evicted virtually all of the ethnic Croats. Incredibly, this was to be the first U.S. cabinet-level trip to the Balkan war zone since the breakup of Yugoslavia.

The brief flight from Frankfurt over the Alps to Zagreb showed how close the Balkan crisis was to the heart of Europe. Except for the fleet of white U.N. planes and helicopters parked on the airport tarmac and the humanitarian relief vehicles plying the city's streets, Zagreb looked like any other provincial European city slowed by the dull, gray cold of winter. It was a grim time for Croatia, much of whose territory had been seized two years earlier by Belgrade-directed Serb paramilitary groups, an act that fueled the authoritarian nationalism of Franjo Tudjman, the Croatian president. Tudjman was playing the same lethal game as Milosevic, pursuing his territorial ambitions in Bosnia, where he was supporting the Bosnian Croats in their campaign of ethnic cleansing against the Bosnian Muslims. The U.N. peacekeeping force had neither the mandate nor the means to stop the brutality. The European comfort and elegance of downtown Zagreb, where the U.N. mission was headquartered, mocked the total ineffectiveness of the peacekeeping effort.

Peter Galbraith, the U.S. ambassador to Croatia, conveyed a mood of frustration in briefing our team. Peter was a tightly wound advocate of greater U.S. involvement in the Balkans who had done effective human rights work on behalf of Kurdish victims of Saddam Hussein in Iraq when he had served on the staff of the Senate Foreign Relations Committee in the 1980s and early 1990s. He told Albright that the situation in eastern Slavonia was tense, and that Tudjman was using it to build up Croatian military strength and public support for his ethnic cleansing campaign in Bosnia.

The area around the devastated city of Vukovar, which we would visit two days later, was a powder keg. Family members of missing Croats were angrily campaigning for government action. In central Bosnia, Bosnian Croat troops were blocking or hijacking humanitarian convoys right under the noses of U.N. peacekeepers. Galbraith encouraged Albright and me in our meetings and press comments to focus on the issue of Serb war crimes against Croats. By demonstrating U.S. concern for the Croatian victims of Serb atrocities in Vukovar, we might be able to persuade Tudjman to cooperate with the new war crimes tribunal, which was simultaneously beginning to investigate Croat atrocities in Bosnia. Albright agreed with Galbraith's strategy, but also pointed to another problem that demanded attention: What was happening to humanitarian relief shipments, and what was the United Nations doing to protect them from hijacking?

Early the next morning, in the makeshift Zagreb office and warehouse of the U.N. High Commissioner for Refugees (UNHCR), Albright and I got a firsthand account of how international humanitarian workers were being used as pawns by both Milosevic and Tudjman. The UNHCR staff told us that the two leaders were accusing the United Nations of "assisting the enemy" through food shipments, and that delivery convoys were constantly coming under attack from both the Serbs and the Croats. The shortage of food and medicine in remote villages was becoming a political and military problem as well as a humanitarian issue. Since the U.N. Protection Force was operating under extremely limited rules of engagement imposed by its political masters in the Security Council, there was simply no way to protect the relief convoys against hijacking.

Later that morning Albright raised these issues with Yasushi Akashi, the U.N. secretary-general's senior representative in Zagreb. The atmosphere was tense. Under the mandate of the U.N. Protection Force, Akashi had the power to authorize or veto any military response to an act of aggression or human rights abuse committed in Bosnia. Under U.N. procedure, this meant that he could block recommendations by the United States or any other Security Council member to conduct air strikes against Serb or Croat military forces that were committing human rights atrocities or attacking humanitarian convoys. Albright told Akashi bluntly that the situation on the ground was deteriorating rapidly and that if the United Nations was to remain in control, air strikes might have to be conducted on short notice to respond to the rampant abuses. She lit into a recent public statement by Akashi's boss, Secretary-General Boutros Boutros-Ghali, who had boasted that he was authorized "to control or veto the U.S. in Bosnia."[14] Akashi responded that the peacekeeping review then under way in Washington in the wake of the Somalia crisis had made the United States "an unpredictable participant" in U.N. peacekeeping operations. "I see the pendulum swinging the wrong way," Akashi told Albright. Reflecting her frustration both with the United Nations and with her own government, Albright replied that it was time for greater military flexibility and a more rapid response to the growing human rights and humanitarian disaster on the ground. "We are reviewing peacekeeping operations," she asserted, "so they can be become *more,* not less, effective."

In a later meeting with Albright and me, the U.N. commander in Zagreb, French general Philippe Cot, personified the weakness of the entire U.N. operation. "We often don't know why we are here," he told us, "but at least we are witnesses who hope to have a deterrent effect on further atrocities."

## Vukovar and Ovcara

The next morning Albright and I flew by helicopter over the roofless and burned-out farmhouses around Erdut, seventy-five miles northeast of Zagreb. It was clear that U.N. "witnessing" was having no effect on the ongoing devastation. The local U.N. commander described the situation in eastern Slavonia as "incipient anarchy and chaos." Most of the majority Croat population had been forced out of their homes by Belgrade-controlled troops and paramilitary forces, Serb gangs were running towns and villages, terrorism was being conducted against pockets of remaining Croats, and ragtag groups of Serb soldiers under no command were roaming the countryside looking for targets and plunder. In short, the U.N. mission was not keeping the peace.

As if to illustrate the point, our visit to Vukovar, ten miles away, and a suspected mass gravesite outside the city was being blocked by the local "Serb regional council." They had told the United Nations that the safety of our convoy could not be guaranteed unless we negotiated directly with them. The U.N. commander had balked at allowing our trip to go forward with this threat hanging over it. Neither the United States nor the United Nations officially recognized any of these local Belgrade-directed Serb warlords, who were carrying out Milosevic's order that Croats be removed from eastern Slavonia. When the self-styled Serb regional council demanded a meeting with Albright and me, we responded that this was out of the question. To keep our mission on track, however, we agreed to have Peter Galbraith, as ambassador to Croatia, conduct a discussion with the Serbs as Croatian citizens, not Serb nationalists. Albright and I would be silent, and Galbraith would emphasize the U.S. condemnation of Serb aggression against Croatia and the people of eastern Slavonia.

The meeting took place in a deserted and heavily damaged schoolhouse on the outskirts of Vukovar. A disheveled group of armed Serbs took their seats opposite us in the bleak and bitter cold in what was once a classroom, and their leader launched immediately into a diatribe. "The Croats are capitalist crooks who stole our land. Before that, they were fascists who killed our grandparents." Galbraith pointed out that hundreds of thousands of Croats had been forced by Serbs from the homes they had lived in for generations. "Every ethnic group in a nation is entitled to its human rights," he said gamely. The Serb warlord snarled back, "We Serbs have finally got our human rights, and the Croats have got what they deserve."

The city of Vukovar, once a bustling small metropolis of 75,000 Croats, Serbs, Hungarians, Czechs, and other Central European minorities, had been turned into a jumble of bombed-out apartment buildings and burned cars and trucks abandoned on deserted streets.

Its assault by Serb forces in 1991 had been shorter and more immediately disastrous than the ongoing siege of Sarajevo. As we approached the devastation, I wondered whether Vukovar represented the future of the Balkans.

Our convoy snaked through the devastated city on its way to Ovcara, a village fifteen kilometers to the north. We were to be the first international officials to reach the desolate site of a mass grave near the village. There, Russian U.N. troops were guarding an abandoned garbage dump that was believed to contain the bodies of 250 Croatian soldiers who had been taken from the Vukovar hospital by Serb militia two years earlier, after the city had fallen. The badly wounded men had been seized in their hospital beds and loaded into trucks on the pretext that they were being "transferred." One man who was less severely wounded had escaped from one of the trucks just before it reached the Ovcara field where the others were shot and buried in a shallow bulldozed mass grave, and his story, told later at a refugee camp, provided the lead for an international investigation. The investigation established that the Serb militia had killed the wounded Croats under orders from Zeljko Raznatovic, the notorious Belgrade paramilitary leader and close associate of Milosevic known as "Arkan," who was indicted by the War Crimes Tribunal for crimes against humanity in 1997, and killed in January 2000 in Belgrade by unknown assailants thought to be connected to Milosevic. My State Department bureau had referred to the Ovcara mass gravesite in our 1993 human rights report on Croatia, but when Albright and I arrived in January 1994 the site had not yet been investigated because the Serbs were blocking efforts by a U.N. war crimes forensic team to excavate the field.[15]

We reached Ovcara at nightfall. Grinding in over a mud track in a white U.N. armored personnel carrier under the wary stares of gaunt Serb men with Kalashnikov rifles, we emerged at the edge of a field surrounded by barbed wire coils and guarded by three nervous Russian soldiers. Flooded by the lights of the CNN television crew accompanying us, the refuse-strewn field looked eerie and yielded only a few of its secrets—rotting shoes, bits of clothing, and the bones of a human foot. A cold rain was falling as Madeleine Albright offered a bleak summary of the situation: "The fact that people suffer and then end up in something that is basically a garbage dump is symbolic of the tragedies of this country."[16]

On the helicopter trip back to Zagreb I reflected on what we had seen. The Ovcara field is five kilometers from a large collective farm and fifteen kilometers from the hospital in Vukovar where the wounded Croatian men had been herded into trucks and carted into the night. This isolated field was a typical site on the roadmap of human rights at the end of the Cold War: it had been turned into a mass grave containing the victims of ethnic cleansing. The most chilling aspect of this trip was our realization that this grave had existed undisturbed for nearly three years in an area where the people responsible for the crime were living undetected day by day, enshrouded by the guilt of their shamed community.

Back in Zagreb the situation seemed in many ways as bleak as the Ovcara countryside. The Mothers of Vukovar, a human rights organization founded to support families searching for tens of thousands of missing persons in the shattered city we had just visited, warned in an emotional meeting organized for me by Peter Galbraith that Americans were being manipulated by the same propaganda that the Europeans were swallowing. "We are not being killed by ancient hatreds," one of the mothers exclaimed. "We are being slaughtered by our own leaders."

The evidence we had seen certainly pointed to the massive culpability of the Balkan leaders. President Tudjman provided his own corroboration when we met him on the last day of our trip. While complaining that Croatia was under attack by the Serbs, he undermined his own position by boasting that he would liberate Bosnia from the "barbaric Muslims." When we raised the issue of war crimes committed by Croats in central Bosnia, Tudjman snapped that this was anti-Croatian propaganda. Other examples of cynical maneuvering by the Balkan leaders, especially Milosevic, were laid out for us later that day by the U.S. commander in Europe, Admiral Jeremy "Mike" Boorda.[17] The admiral told us that Milosevic and his Bosnian

Serb surrogates, having achieved significant territorial gains, were now renting out tank units, artillery, and other lethal material to both the Bosnian Croats and the Bosnian Muslims, in an effort to get them to kill each other off.

## Battle in Washington

Back in Washington, the "Balkan ancient hatreds" mantra was more in vogue than ever. At a staff meeting at the end of January Tim Wirth recommended I read Robert Kaplan's *Balkan Ghosts*,[18] the book that had popularized this view among American policymakers, including President Clinton.[19]

I read *Balkan Ghosts* and was disturbed by it. Kaplan had written an absorbing book about centuries of Balkan war that emphasized the deep roots of religious and ethnic conflict, but said little about the responsibility of Milosevic, Tudjman, and other Balkan political bosses and their henchmen for designing and carrying out vast programs of "ethnic cleansing." These leaders were conducting a war against the entire civilian population of Yugoslavia which I did not believe could be explained solely, or even principally, as the product of "ancient hatreds."

Influenced by Kaplan's explanation of what was happening in Bosnia, many people at high levels in the administration conveniently believed in 1993 and 1994 that we should stay out of the fray and limit our role to providing humanitarian relief. In their view, my effort to spotlight human rights atrocities and build support for the prosecution of war crimes ran counter to this objective. Not surprisingly, therefore, in the month following my return from Croatia with Madeleine Albright, I was unable to get State Department clearance for another mission to Bosnia and Serbia.

I felt that the Clinton administration had painted itself into a corner. Lacking credibility with the United Nations and the Europeans because we were unwilling to commit troops to the peacekeeping effort, we now were undercutting our own diplomatic leverage with the regional leaders by downplaying their responsibility for what was happening.

The weakness of U.S. policy toward Bosnia was on display during a trip by Secretary Christopher to Paris at the end of January. In meetings that I attended, Christopher reviewed the Bosnia situation with French foreign minister Herve de Charette, and conducted separate bilateral talks with Chinese foreign minister Qian Qichen, who was visiting France at the same time. At a dinner with de Charette and other French officials hosted by Ambassador Pamela Harriman, Christopher made points similar to the ones Albright had raised with Akashi in Zagreb about the need for more aggressive U.N. peacekeeping. He also restated U.S. support for lifting the arms embargo and conducting air strikes when necessary to respond to acts of aggression. The French were dismissive, however, reminding Christopher that they had previously rejected these same points. Unlike the Americans, de Charette pointed out, France was participating in the peacekeeping mission by committing ground forces to the United Nations, and was therefore in a far better position than the United States to assess the situation in Bosnia. Furthermore, as de Charette remarked acerbically in response to Christopher's renewed appeal for support of the American "lift and strike" strategy, French troops would be vulnerable to attack or hostage-taking in the event of U.S.-led NATO air strikes in Bosnia.

Later, in his meeting with the Chinese foreign minister, Christopher made a telling comment that spoke volumes about the U.S. view that the Bosnia conflict was a pariah problem. It's hard to bring about an end to the war, the Secretary mused to his Chinese counterpart, so long as the parties want to continue fighting.

My own view, which I had voiced within the State Department following my trip to Croatia, was that ending the killing would be impossible until the Balkan leaders were made to pay a price for their war crimes. This meant strengthening the War Crimes Tribunal by giving it more political and financial support and protecting its independence from the peace negotiations. It also meant providing international military support to the tribunal's operations on the ground in Bosnia, including arrest of indicted war criminals.

It was not clear to me what more could be done to raise the price of committing war crimes without a major change in our policy on military intervention. Our approach toward Bosnia was having little effect on the rate of the ongoing mass killings. Comprehensive economic sanctions had already been imposed on Serbia in an attempt to punish Milosevic for instigating and feeding the Bosnian Serb war-crimes machine. The United States was also trying with mixed success to negotiate an end to the fighting between Bosnian Croats and Muslims and to create a federation of the two groups to resist further attacks by the Serbs.

But the United States would never be able to play more than a limited role in Bosnia so long as the deployment of U.S. ground forces continued to be ruled out. With no troops on the ground, the maneuvering room for U.S. diplomacy was very limited. The only thing that seemed possible was to continue spotlighting the atrocities to make sure that truth itself did not become a victim of this genocidal conflict. Flying back to Washington from Paris on January 25, I was nagged by the enormity of our failure in Bosnia. The day before, eight children playing in the snow in Sarajevo had been gunned down by Serb artillery, while the French, the United States, and the United Nations continued to dicker over how the U.N. peacekeeping force—of which we were not a part—could protect the U.N. convoys that were delivering relief to "more secure" parts of Bosnia.

Bosnia was on fire in the spring and summer of 1994, but so were many other parts of the world, including Rwanda, Haiti, and China. In the thick of this seemingly endless series of crises, I frequently asked myself whether the United States would ever be prepared to use its diplomatic and military power to protect basic human rights from the new threats of the post–Cold War world. A particularly low point came when the *Washington Post* refused to publish my reply to a devastating opinion piece by E. J. Dionne announcing the death of Clinton's human rights policy after the President's decision on May 25 to renew China's most favored nation status.[20] I was told by the editor that the *Post* would be willing to accept my article if it explicitly criticized Clinton, but I rejected this because I had decided not to resign but to stay and fight from within.

I began to push my point of view harder within the State Department. I increased my efforts to use my relationships with political appointees in the administration to develop informal channels into the policy process, and to become more aggressive in seeking allies on the outside, particularly in Congress, where there was growing support for strong human rights policies.

In late March, after two months of near-total preoccupation with China, I learned that the War Crimes Tribunal was in danger of being scuttled. Heavy pressure to offer amnesty to the Balkan leaders to induce them to enter "serious" peace negotiations was coming from the five-power (United States, Great Britain, France, Germany, and Russia) Bosnia Contact Group that had been set up in 1993 to coordinate diplomatic peacemaking efforts. In a staff meeting on March 29 and a telephone conversation the same day with Sandy Berger, the President's deputy national security advisor, I pointed out that offering amnesty to war criminals to get them to the peace table was contrary to the position approved earlier by Warren Christopher that the tribunal should be independent of the peace process. In addition, amnesty would only play into the hands of Milosevic and Tudjman by further demonstrating the weakness of the international will to hold them to account for what was happening on the ground.

In a series of tense meetings inside the State Department at the end of March, I argued that because the United States had earlier called for establishing the tribunal as an instrument of peace as well as justice, we should not allow it to be undercut before it had even begun its work. Jim Steinberg, director of the Policy Planning Office and Christopher's key advisor on this issue, agreed with me, as did Madeleine Albright. Berger and Strobe Talbott told me they agreed with my point of view, but were not sure amnesty could realistically be avoided in the long run if that was all that stood in the way of peace. Since the tribunal now had broad support on Capitol Hill, I alerted several key members of Congress, including Representative Tom Lantos (D-Calif.) and Senator Joe Biden (D-Del.), that they might soon have to come to the tribunal's defense. For the time being this seemed to create enough Washington buzz to prevent any short-term change of policy.

Meanwhile, the situation on the ground was getting increasingly grim. Hardline Serbs were uniting under the military leadership of General Ratko Mladic, and they began to form a pincer movement around the Muslims and Croats. Sarajevo, Gorazde, and other designated U.N. "safe areas" were being strangled, and appalling human rights atrocities by Serb troops and paramilitaries were being reported almost daily in the international press. Administration policy vacillated between lifting the U.N. arms embargo and strengthening the Bosnian Muslims, on the one hand, and maintaining the embargo and trying to get Russia to restrain the Serbs from continuing their territorial aggression, on the other.

In the midst of this flailing about, a policy debate slowly took shape over whether the administration should alter standard Cold War military doctrine about the use of force. At a State Department senior staff meeting on May 2, Strobe Talbott observed that none of the human rights crises we were facing in the spring of 1994 fit the Cold War mold. But we had tied our hands in each of them by precluding the use of force to back up our diplomatic objectives. Commissioning an analysis of the problem, Talbott signaled that the State Department would push for a new approach.

## The Vicious Cycle of War Crimes

But a decision to use military force to stop the genocide in Bosnia was still a year away, and in the case of Rwanda no such decision was ever made. My first trip to Rwanda in early May 1994 gave me a searing firsthand look at what that was at stake in these two post–Cold War genocidal conflicts. Rwanda showed how urgent it was not only to prepare for the use of force to stop a genocide, but also to bring to justice those who were responsible for it. Although I never managed to change the administration's hands-off approach to Rwanda during the genocide, what I saw and learned had a profound influence on my thinking about Bosnia. In a memo prepared after my return from Africa, I argued that there was an urgent need for international justice to hold accountable those who commit genocide or crimes against humanity:

> There are three fundamental reasons why individual leaders must be held responsible for the ethnic crimes and genocide in Bosnia and Rwanda. *First,* the spiral of retribution must be stopped. If responsibility is covered up or ignored, it will never be possible to have peace, reconciliation or democracy. Those who have seen their parents, brothers or sisters targeted for ethnic killing are never going to reconcile with killers who are not identified and brought to justice. *Second,* the oppressive atmosphere of collective guilt must be lifted. The air must be cleared so that those who are innocent can breathe freely and not be seen to be guilty by ethnic association with the criminal leaders who are personally responsible. Collective guilt not only destroys individuals, it makes whole peoples the target for retribution. Those who were the planners and instigators of genocide must be held responsible for their actions; those who were misled by them should not be punished by collective guilt. *Third,* international human rights law must be enforced. If these crimes against humanity can be committed with impunity, there can be no rule of law and no deterrent against any conceivable form of international terrorism.

During the summer of 1994, a major step was taken to advance the justice agenda. After a long and politically charged search, a prosecutor for the War Crimes Tribunal was finally appointed. Richard Goldstone, a distinguished jurist and anti-apartheid activist from South Africa, took up his position in September and began the enormous task of gathering evidence for the tribunal's first indictments, which were issued at the end of the year.

Getting support for Goldstone's appointment required a major diplomatic campaign. Orchestrated by David Scheffer and me, this effort was led by Madeleine Albright. In a Moscow meeting on

July 6 with Sergei Lavrov, the Russian deputy foreign minister, I nailed down Russia's crucial vote later that month in the U.N. Security Council by drawing Lavrov's attention to Goldstone's central role in the long battle against apartheid in South Africa and pointing out that because he was neither an American nor a European he would be immune from direct influence by Contact Group countries.

Despite the progress on justice issues, 1994 ended much the way it had begun for the Bosnia crisis. The U.N. peacekeeping force was seen as increasingly ineffective and unpopular. The United States and Europe were divided over the arms embargo and the use of air strikes. And the Contact Group had little to show for its efforts to develop a process for negotiating peace.

Jimmy Carter waded into this morass in December, announcing that he would go to Pale, the Bosnian Serb capital, to attempt to negotiate a cease-fire with Radovan Karadzic. The State Department's reaction was cool. I was concerned that without a military threat to back it up, Carter's message could unintentionally encourage more Serb aggression. President Carter proposed that as an inducement for Karadzic to agree to a cease-fire, U.N. peacekeepers should replace the Bosnian troops on Mount Igman over Sarajevo. Reacting from Belgrade, Milosevic warmed to this proposal and said that with a few more concessions he might be able to persuade Karadzic and the Bosnian Serb Assembly to support the plan. Carter returned from Pale after four days of discussions with Karadzic with a four-month cease-fire, which was broken by the Serbs less than two months later. With their limited mandate, the U.N. peacekeepers were powerless to enforce the cease-fire. Although lives were saved during this short respite, the longer-term effect of negotiating with Karadzic was dangerous. The Bosnian Serbs saw more clearly than ever how little there was to back up the rhetoric of the international community.

The arrival of 1995 brought a new political atmosphere in Washington. The revolution in Congress produced by the 1994 election results had weakened the President, strengthened his Republican opposition (which now controlled both the House and the Senate), increased the partisan polarization of foreign affairs, and created a formula for gridlock on virtually all policy issues in Washington. In this highly charged domestic political environment, distant crises like the one in Bosnia seemed more intractable than ever and less likely to receive high-level political attention.

On January 9, sensing the mood of uncertainty and frustration among my overworked and undervalued colleagues in the Bureau of Democracy, Human Rights, and Labor, I decided to turn a routine staff meeting into a pep talk. The next day I was scheduled to leave for China on another difficult mission that was bound to stir up controversy for the bureau. I told the staff that these were tough times for what we were trying to do, but we needed to keep at it. I reminded them that later in the month our bureau would publish a 1,200-page report on human rights conditions in 193 countries around the world. Doing this would be a triumph, I told them, because two months earlier several regional bureaus had tried to persuade the State Department leadership to scale down the report by eliminating its coverage of "democratic countries." Warren Christopher had rejected these proposals. I pointed out that Christopher's decision reaffirmed that human rights should be an integral part of U.S. foreign policy, and it was up to us to keep fighting to make that a reality.

During the winter and spring of 1995, I plunged into this fight by traveling to some of the most challenging human rights crisis areas. I went to Beijing to press for the release of political prisoners and register the objection of the United States to ongoing religious repression in Tibet; to Indonesia to protest recent political killings in East Timor and express support for the country's press and nongovernmental organizations, which were struggling to survive under the Suharto regime; to Geneva to spearhead an effort to pass a U.N. Human Rights Commission resolution condemning China's human rights record; to Northern Ireland to participate in a program bringing together both sides in the conflict to discuss disarmament and police reform issues; to Colombia to investigate human rights abuses by military units receiving U.S. assistance; and to Rwanda with the

U.N. prosecutor, Richard Goldstone, to deliver U.S. funding for the start-up of the new U.N. International Criminal Tribunal for Rwanda and the rebuilding of a domestic justice system that had been destroyed by the genocide. Throughout this period, I kept an eye on the situation in Washington, looking for indications of a break in the deadlock over Bosnia policy.

### The Hostage Crisis and Pressure for Withdrawal

The break came in May 1995, but it was not a welcome one. While I was in Rwanda, I got word from our embassy in Kigali that hundreds of U.N. troops in Bosnia had been taken hostage by the Bosnian Serbs. The Serbs were clearly testing to see how far they could go in their attacks on U.N. "safe areas." They claimed that their hostage-taking was a retaliation for NATO air strikes against the Serb artillery units that were active above Sarajevo. The air strikes had been requested by the British U.N. commander in Sarajevo, General Rupert Smith, and authorized by NATO's governing body, the North Atlantic Council. In reality, the bombing had amounted to little more than pin pricks because Akashi and the top U.N. commander, French general Bernard Janvier, had insisted on sharply restricting NATO's action in order to avoid endangering the U.N. troops.

The weakness of NATO's response had emboldened the Bosnian Serbs. By seizing 350 soldiers as hostages, they obviously wanted to prove that they were in charge and to warn the United Nations and NATO what would happen if peacekeeping got more aggressive on the ground or in the air. In the Kigali living room of Ambassador David Rawson, I watched scratchy television images of CNN's coverage of the crisis and saw U.N. soldiers chained to trees and telephone poles or waving white flags of surrender. Reflecting on these appalling images on my way back to Washington, I sensed that the dynamic of the entire Bosnian conflict was changing for the worse.

After a week of humiliation in the glare of the international media, the U.N. hostages were released on June 4 following a secret meeting between Janvier and General Mladic, the Bosnian Serb commander. Janvier made no public statement about these negotiations, but anonymous comments to the press suggested that he had given assurances to Mladic that the United Nations would not use air strikes again.[21] Akashi seemed to verify that this was the U.N. position when he told his staff that "the events of May had shown the ineffectiveness [of air strikes]."[22] The final blow to the air strike policy was delivered by U.N. Secretary-General Boutros-Ghali, who announced after the hostage crisis that he was taking away from ground commanders like General Smith in Sarajevo the power to call for air strikes, and that in the future all such military decisions would be made at U.N. headquarters in New York.

Back in Washington our policy was in turmoil. At the daily staff meeting chaired by Strobe Talbott on June 5, I joined Richard Holbrooke, Jim Steinberg, and others in pointing out that the taking of U.N. hostages by the Bosnian Serbs should remove all doubt about whether what was happening in Bosnia was a "civil war," as the opponents of intervention had been calling it. Two days later, however, the Talbott meeting received a report from the European Affairs Bureau about a "discordant and rudderless" discussion of Bosnia at the North Atlantic Council in Brussels, where the United States was in no position to lead because we had no troops on the ground. This report came on the same day as the dramatic rescue in Bosnia by U.S. special forces of an American F-16 pilot, Scott O'Grady, who had been shot down on June 2 by Bosnian Serb artillery. The saving of Lieutenant O'Grady reminded our European allies what the United States could do on the ground when it was motivated to act to save an American soldier—in sharp contrast to its inaction for more than three years while European troops were deployed on the ground and hundreds of thousands of Bosnians were slaughtered.[23]

In the aftermath of the hostage crisis there was a rush toward withdrawal by U.N. troop contributors. Two years earlier, following the ill-fated Christopher trip to persuade European leaders to back our "lift and strike" policy, President Clinton had made a commitment to send U.S. ground troops to assist in the eventual withdrawal of U.N. peacekeepers. Although vague at the time, now it looked as if this commitment would have to be honored. But how? Congress seemed more firmly set than ever against any commitment of U.S. ground forces, and Senator Bob Dole and other supporters of the alternative strategy of arming the Bosnians so they could defend themselves seemed to be very close to having enough votes to make it happen. At a State Department senior staff meeting in mid-June, it became clear to me that the White House wanted to press the Europeans to stay in Bosnia, in part so that the President would not be faced with sending American soldiers to implement a humiliating U.N. withdrawal. At the meeting, I expressed the need to push equally hard for eliminating the U.N. restrictions on responding to human rights atrocities. That week French president Jacques Chirac arrived in Washington for a state visit, and a round of high-level discussions began concerning the future of the United Nations in Bosnia and Chirac's proposed U.N. Rapid Reaction Force as an alternative to outright U.N. withdrawal. I was not on the list of U.S. participants.

My own thoughts during this period turned increasingly toward resigning. To be in charge of human rights in the U.S. government while being excluded from discussions about the government's response to human rights crises was intolerable. My frustrations over our Bosnia policy were well known, and I now felt I had less access than ever to the small group in the White House, the State Department, and the Pentagon where policy was being made. I was proud of my role in helping establish the War Crimes Tribunal, but I knew that the tribunal itself was a hostage to the events unfolding on the ground.

Instead of resigning after the hostage crisis, I decided instead to make a last-ditch effort to strengthen the tribunal so that it might be able to influence the international response to the war crimes it had been established to prosecute. I knew that the prosecutor's office, headed by Richard Goldstone, was assembling evidence of crimes committed or orchestrated by the Bosnian Serb leadership during their sustained assault on civilians in Sarajevo, Vukovar, Gorazde, and other population centers. For this reason I saw the importance of having the United States and other countries step up their information sharing with the tribunal and adopt a policy of isolating and refusing to negotiate with anyone under indictment. I discussed this approach with Lee Sigal, a friend who had served in the Pentagon in the Carter administration. Sigal agreed that a policy of isolating criminal leaders was worth pursuing, but warned that it would be difficult to get such a policy adopted because of the political pressure to negotiate a settlement of the war at almost any price—for example, by trading the War Crimes Tribunal and sanctions for a permanent cease-fire.

I could feel this pressure whenever I raised the tribunal issue in the State Department. At the end of June I had a meeting in my office with Bob Frasure, a skilled senior Foreign Service officer who was tragically killed a month and a half later in an accident on a treacherous mountain road in Bosnia—the only road leading into besieged Sarajevo. Bob was the U.S. point person in negotiations with Milosevic and the Bosnian Serbs. I wanted to discuss with him how to protect the tribunal in the negotiations. He was very candid. "There's no gas in our negotiating tank," he said. Following the hostage debacle and the rush to withdraw U.N. troops, he was pessimistic about stopping the Serbs from gaining a free hand in Bosnia. I told him that the tribunal was close to issuing indictments of the Bosnian Serb leadership, which would greatly weaken their negotiating position. I recommended that Milosevic be required to cooperate with tribunal investigations as a condition for lifting U.N. sanctions against Serbia. Bob said this condition was not in the negotiation package, and that if we tried to add it now we would create a firestorm with the British, French, and Russians. He warned against adding "new conditionalities." Milosevic already knows he's negotiating with a weak and divided alliance, Frasure said, and this would only make us look weaker.

In a conference call later that day with Madeleine Albright and Peter Tarnoff, I learned what I already suspected. Albright reported that there was growing opposition to the tribunal. She suggested that instead of trying to include active cooperation with tribunal investigations as a condition for Serbian sanctions relief—a position for which we had no internal support—we should now push for a policy whereby active efforts to disrupt the tribunal (by attacking its investigators, for example) could lead to the reimposition of sanctions. This showed how much pressure we were under to abandon the tribunal, although I was confident Albright would never allow that to happen.

On July 5 I took off for The Hague to meet with Goldstone. I had an idea that if Karadzic, Mladic, and other Bosnian Serb leaders were indicted for war crimes, the political dynamic in Washington might change. I wanted to find out from Goldstone whether and when these indictments might be coming. I also wanted to brief him about my unsuccessful efforts to get the United States to support a stronger sanctions mechanism for getting the Serbs to cooperate with his investigations.

Our meeting was sobering for both of us. Although Goldstone told me that the indictments were only "a few weeks away," he reported that the U.N. representative in the ongoing negotiations with Milosevic, Thorvald Stoltenberg of Sweden, was saying that the tribunal's investigations should be negotiable. Stoltenberg had apparently raised the tribunal issue with Milosevic, suggesting that he could "expect understanding from the tribunal" if he cooperated with the peace negotiations. This seemed to go even beyond the ominous warnings I had been hearing in Washington. I discussed with Goldstone the tribunal's financial and administrative support requirements, as well as his need for better information from the United States and other governments. I also visited the bulletproof courtroom to observe the trial of Dusan Tadic—the first accused war criminal brought to justice—and imagined what might unfold in that courtroom in the years ahead if the world would only allow this new U.N. institution to do its job.

From The Hague I traveled on a personal journey to Westphalia, in the center of Germany, to the farm near the village of Herringsen where my late first wife, Petra, had grown up in the shadow of Hitler and the Holocaust. Reflecting on the spiraling disaster in Bosnia and the advance of Bosnian Serb forces as they moved to attack the last remaining U.N. "safe areas," I sensed the impending disaster. I wrote:

> I have thought a great deal about this in recent weeks, but here in Germany my thinking is clearer and more intense. Here, after all, is where the Holocaust began, where people were taught to separate blue eyes from brown, to keep lists, to blame those who were on the lists for the problems of everyone else. . . . It's time to change the way we think about Bosnia. The U.N. force, guided by European countries that have committed the bulk of the troops, has in essence become an excuse for inaction in order to protect the troops, and an invitation for new aggression and human rights abuse, because its response to what has already happened has been so weak. The U.S. has postured endlessly about airstrikes and lifting the arms embargo, but with no commitment of ground forces our warnings sound increasingly hollow. The signal to aggressors by both Europe and the U.S. is clear: we want you to stop the killing, but we won't do anything to make you. The price for the release of U.N. hostages three weeks ago seems to have been a permanent cessation of NATO airstrikes. Now the Contact Group negotiates with Milosevic with no real political, military or moral authority to back it up. I am trying to get a policy decision to protect the war crimes Tribunal through sanctions linkage, but so far only Madeleine Albright is an ally. Now that I have learned from Richard Goldstone that he will indict the Bosnian Serb leaders within the next few weeks, I can step up my campaign for the tribunal by showing that there will soon be a clear moral price for negotiating with war criminals.

As I wrote these words in my diary on July 10, 1995, General Mladic and his troops were beginning to round up the men and boys of Srebrenica. Hurem Suljic and more than seven thousand other Muslims were starting what for almost all of them would be a journey of death. Two weeks later, in the cinderblock schoolhouse in Tuzla, Suljic would tell me his staggering story. Within a month this story and many others like it would influence the highest levels of government. At last, the United States would change its policy on Bosnia.

# CHAPTER 5

# BOSNIA

## FACING REALITY

Throughout the spring of 1995, the takeover of U.N. "safe areas" by Bosnian Serb forces had been a catastrophe waiting to happen. The weakness of U.N. peacekeeping operations had become clearer than ever during the June hostage crisis. In order to free the U.N. peacekeepers from their Bosnian Serb captors, the U.N. commander, French general Bernard Janvier, had secretly promised that no further air strikes would be conducted against Serb targets around Sarajevo.[1] This had signaled to the Bosnian Serbs that they would not be challenged if they moved against the Muslim enclaves of Srebrenica, Zepa, and Gorazde. During June and early July, Bosnian Serb president Radovan Karadzic and his commander, General Ratko Mladic, continued their military buildup in preparation for taking over all of eastern Bosnia.

The takeover began on July 10, when Mladic and his forces entered Srebrenica, easily overrunning a Dutch U.N. peacekeeping brigade of 350 soldiers. Having repeatedly called for a NATO air attack to repel the Bosnian Serbs as they amassed their troops around Srebrenica, the Dutch commander, Colonel Tom Karremans, finally got his wish on July 11, when eighteen U.S. F-16s flew over the town. The planes dropped several bombs without hitting any significant targets. At that point, the Bosnian Serbs threatened to kill the Dutch soldiers if further air strikes occurred. This produced a U.N. surrender.[2]

Within days, rumors began to circulate in the international press about the fate of thousands of Muslim men and boys trapped in Srebrenica. The speculation was that they were either being held prisoner by the Bosnian Serbs or had been killed in battle. Reacting to these rumors, French president Jacques Chirac telephoned President Clinton on July 13, proposing that American helicopters carry French troops into Srebrenica to relieve the town and free the survivors. Although Chirac's proposal did not have the support of the French military and was rejected by the British and the Pentagon, it showed how desperate the situation was and how chaotic was the allied response.[3]

False information about what was happening in Srebrenica was circulated by the Bosnian Serbs. On July 17, Mladic's troops drafted a "Declaration" that was signed by the deputy commander of the Dutch battalion, Major Franken, certifying that "the evacuation [of the Srebrenica civilian population] was carried out by the Serb side correctly . . . and the Serb side has adhered to all the regulations of the Geneva Conventions and the international law of war."[4] This document was used as part of a Bosnian Serb campaign to stir up international confusion about the fate of the missing men.

Taking advantage of the disarray, Bosnian Serb forces on July 19 expanded their attacks to other parts of Bosnia, moving against Zepa, another U.N. "safe area," and Bihac, a Muslim enclave in the northwest. The British announced that day that they were preparing to pull their troops out of Gorazde, and the French indicated they would follow suit if their Srebrenica relief plan was not accepted by the allies.[5] All hell was breaking loose, and nothing was being done to stop it.

On July 19 British prime minister John Major announced that Britain would host an emergency conference on the crisis. The London conference was called as an alternative to the French proposal to send international reinforcements to the besieged "safe areas," but it had the effect of providing a forum for those who wanted the allies to respond to the new Serb aggression by the use of force. Starting in mid-July, Washington had begun to signal a shift in U.S. policy. After

Srebrenica, the view that there was no more room to negotiate with the Serbs began to prevail in the State Department.

When I returned from The Hague and Germany on July 12, I sensed this shift as stories about the Srebrenica atrocities broke in the Washington press. I sent a memorandum to Christopher reporting what I had learned in The Hague about the imminent indictment by the War Crimes Tribunal of the Bosnian Serb leaders Karadzic and Mladic, and pointing to new evidence that they had orchestrated the crimes in Srebrenica. I was concerned that European peace negotiators would be tempted to capitulate to the Serbs in a desperate effort to end the crisis at any cost. I argued that the United States should oppose all further negotiations and restate the policy announced in 1993 by Christopher and Albright of refusing to negotiate with war criminals. I concluded my memorandum by pointing out that the new atrocities in Srebrenica required military intervention to protect Gorazde and other remaining "safe areas."

In the growing international outrage over Srebrenica, I began to see the issue of war crimes as a vehicle for changing the whole U.S. approach toward Bosnia. I convened a meeting of the interagency war crimes working group in my office on July 13. With David Scheffer, Jim O'Brien, Mike Matheson, and others, the group hammered out a strategy to strengthen the War Crimes Tribunal. Our plan would involve publicly highlighting the tribunal's indictments of Karadzic and Mladic; having the United States issue a new "no-negotiation-with-indicted-war-criminals" statement; urging European governments to arrest any indicted war criminals entering their jurisdictions; holding congressional briefings on the tribunal; and arranging for the tribunal's chief prosecutor, Richard Goldstone, to visit Washington and New York at the end of July. These ideas would all be implemented over the next few weeks. The most important part of the strategy—no negotiation with indicted war criminals—would be put into play by Richard Holbrooke in a stormy meeting in Belgrade on August 30 with Slobodan Milosevic.[6]

But the War Crimes Tribunal did not have an army, and the burning question in mid-July 1995 was how to confront the new Bosnian

Serb aggression. When I mentioned the impending indictments of Karadzic and Mladic at a senior staff meeting on July 14, Strobe Talbott observed that the tribunal's lack of power to bring war criminals to justice underscored the weakness of the international position in Bosnia. Talbott's point was graphically illustrated by the refugee crisis created by the fall of Srebrenica and the threatened Serb attack on Zepa, another U.N. "safe area." Sadaka Ogata, the widely respected U.N. high commissioner for refugees (UNHCR), announced from Tuzla on July 17 that while her organization could handle the emergency situation in Tuzla, it could not shed light on the fate of the thousands of men and boys missing from Srebrenica. That same day, the Geneva-based International Committee for the Red Cross (ICRC), whose mandate includes searching and accounting for prisoners of war, reported that Bosnian Serb forces were blocking the ICRC from getting to areas around Srebrenica where they were attempting to search for the missing.[7]

Against this backdrop of expanding catastrophe and international confusion, the London conference got under way on July 21. Two questions loomed large. How was the Bosnian Serb assault to be stopped? And what actually happened at Srebrenica? The U.S. delegation headed by Warren Christopher came to London with a proposed answer to the first question. The U.S. position was essentially a robust reframing of the Clinton administration's longstanding advocacy of using air power to respond to Serb aggression: NATO should launch massive air strikes if the Bosnian Serbs attacked Gorazde, the last remaining "safe area," and NATO alone—with or without U.N. approval—should make the decision when to initiate the strikes. After a contentious day of debate, the conference adopted a communiqué reflecting the U.S. position.

What happened at Srebrenica was another matter.

### Search for the Missing

Beginning on July 13, reports of missing men were discussed at Strobe Talbott's daily senior staff meetings. I began an intensive effort with the ICRC and the UNHCR, both of which had officials on the ground in central and eastern Bosnia, to track down leads. Using what little intelligence information was available from U.S. government and international sources, we tried to locate the men.[8] Through frequent communications with ICRC president Cornelio Sommaruga and his deputies in Washington and Geneva, I began to piece together reports. Some of the reports claimed prisoners were being held in warehouses, school gymnasiums, or open fields, but all were sketchy and none stated explicitly that the men had been killed. Since the ICRC officials on the ground were unable to locate any organized prison camps similar to those seen earlier in the war, or any large groups of prisoners, the situation was increasingly ominous.

On July 19, I sent another memorandum to Christopher, reporting what I had found out from my ICRC sources. While the truth turned out to be far worse, the information was still devastating: "The human rights abuses we are seeing hearken back to the very worst, early days of 'ethnic cleansing.' In Bratunac [a town near Srebrenica], 4,000–5,200 men and boys are incarcerated and the Bosnia Serbs continue to deny access to them. Another 3,000 soldiers died as they fled Srebrenica, some taking their own lives rather than risk falling into Serb hands. There are credible reports of summary executions and the kidnapping and rape of Bosnian women." My memo was entitled, "Defense of the Safe Areas in Bosnia," and I argued that if the United States let Gorazde and other Muslim areas fall to the Serbs, countless additional lives would be lost, the Europeans would begin to withdraw their troops, and the United States would have to follow through on its earlier promise to assist with their evacuation. Failure to act now would mean an even more serious crisis for the United States later: "U.S. troops will be on the ground helping the U.N. force pull out," I warned, "while Bosnian Serbs fire upon them, and fearful Muslims block their exit." I hoped that this increasingly plausible nightmare scenario would finally be enough to change U.S. policy.

Appalled by what I was learning, I decided to go to Bosnia myself. I knew it would not be easy to get clearance for the trip, since I had been discouraged from traveling to the Balkans for more than a year. I discussed my plan with Dan Spiegel, our ambassador to the U.N. agencies in Geneva, who had accompanied Sadaka Ogata on her refugee mission to Tuzla. Spiegel backed me up by sending a cable to Washington arguing that a U.S. human rights mission to central Bosnia would put pressure on the Bosnian Serbs to cooperate in the search for the missing. On July 17 I raised the idea of my mission with Strobe Talbott and Sandy Berger, who cautioned that it might overload the circuits if I was in Bosnia at the same time the United States was trying to gain allied support for defending Gorazde at the London conference, then four days away. Reluctantly, I postponed my departure.

For the next week I continued to work in Washington to energize the stalled search for the missing men by meeting with and telephoning U.N. and Red Cross refugee workers and human rights organizations. But I was increasingly frustrated by a feeling that I, too, was being held hostage and could not do what was necessary at this moment of maximum danger. If I could not pursue the truth, how could I do my job? On July 25, when the London conference was winding up, I heard from Phyllis Oakley, the assistant secretary for refugee affairs and principal U.S. contact with the U.N. high commissioner for refugees, that a few men were at last beginning to arrive at the jerry-built refugee camp in Tuzla. I knew that I had to go there immediately to find out what had happened to the thousands of others who were still missing.

Dan Spiegel urged me to get on a plane right away, as did Peter Galbraith calling from Zagreb. I spent a final day rounding up Washington support to maximize the influence of my trip on the shifting U.S. policy. I talked to Richard Holbrooke, who was leading the effort in the State Department to toughen our diplomatic stance, and persuaded him that it was time to launch a high-profile human rights mission to central Bosnia. Holbrooke and I had differed a month earlier when I had tried unsuccessfully to get our negotiators to include cooperation with the War Crimes Tribunal as an explicit condition for lifting the sanctions against Serbia. Now we saw eye to eye on what was to become a key part of the strategy for ending the war—shining a U.S. spotlight on human rights atrocities and confronting those who had committed them. With Holbrooke leading the way and our policy becoming more interventionist, I was at last able to overcome the resistance I had been getting from lower levels in the European Affairs Bureau.

The situation was grim. Just before a senior staff meeting on July 27, an ominous report came in from the Red Cross office in Tuzla that more than two thousand Muslim men had been trapped by the Serbs in a forest north of Srebrenica. At the meeting I briefed the senior State Department staff on my mission. Holbrooke expressed his support for my "enormously important trip." Strobe Talbott agreed that I should go. What we were hearing, he said, recalled reports about the massacre of thousands of Polish officers by the Soviets in Katyn Forest in 1940, when truth itself was buried in a mass grave until it was finally exhumed by Gorbachev in 1989.

To make sure all the signals were straight I telephoned Bob Frasure in London so that he could inform the Contact Group about my plans. Bob wished me well. It was the last time we would speak before his death a month later in a road accident high above Sarajevo. I also spoke again to Sandy Berger, and called Joe Nye, a former colleague from Harvard and now the assistant secretary of defense for international security affairs, to be sure that the Pentagon would support my mission. Then, just when I was ready to leave Washington, I heard that the diplomatic security bureau was trying to get Christopher to cancel my trip for security reasons. I called Holbrooke to find out what was going on. I was relieved when he told me the Secretary had overruled the bureau.[9] I finally left Washington for the Balkans on the evening of July 27, 1995, more than two weeks after the Serbs had seized Srebrenica.

Josiah Rosenblatt and I arrived in Zagreb on July 28. We were met by Peter Galbraith, who plunged immediately into the crisis by telling us he was convinced that genocide had been committed in Srebrenica. When we reached the embassy, we were joined by Tone Bringa, a Norwegian anthropologist working for the United Nations who had just returned from Tuzla, where thousands of refugees were still streaming in from Srebrenica. Peter asked Tone to brief me about what she had seen and heard, and to give me the names of the Bosnian Muslim men she had spoken to the previous day. I sensed from her briefing that the truth was terrible and close at hand.

The forty-five minute helicopter trip east to Tuzla showed graphic evidence of the war below and above. In the hills and valleys of western Bosnia, burned and ravaged farmhouses stood side by side with untouched structures, testimony to the deadly precision of ethnic cleansing. Far off in the distance, to the north, there was smoke where the destruction continued around Bihac. As we approached Tuzla, an American pilot's voice crackled over the helicopter radio. Our Norwegian crew told us over the intercom that an F-16 flying above us had spotted a Croatian military plane violating the "no-fly zone" over Bosnian air space and was ordering it to return to Croatia or risk being shot down.

When we reached the Tuzla airport tarmac I was hit by the full force of the war. In the blazing noonday sun thousands of gaunt and disheveled figures, mostly women and children, were lining up for food. I could see a steady stream of new arrivals stumbling out of the woods from the east, making their way slowly across the fields beyond the airport, then collapsing into the Red Cross tents once they reached the camp. Serb gunners on the hill to the north had sporadically shelled the airport in recent weeks, and the risk of new atrocities was growing by the hour as the tents swelled with refugees. U.N. and Red Cross workers were feverishly trying to move this sea of humanity into makeshift shelters like the cinderblock schoolhouse where later that day I interviewed Hurem Suljic and the other Muslim men whose first-hand accounts of the mass killings at Srebrenica would shock the world—and finally lead four months later to an end of the war in Bosnia. But getting to that distant point would be a long story whose outcome was never certain.

When I returned to Washington on August 3, Strobe Talbott asked me to brief the senior State Department staff on what I had seen and heard in Bosnia. As I described the horror of Srebrenica, the deputy secretary's elegant seventh-floor conference room became deathly silent. This time, no one challenged my use of the term "genocide" to describe what had happened.

## Diplomacy Backed by Force

Just as the immensity of the crime in Srebrenica was becoming widely known, the Croatian army launched an offensive during the first week of August against Croatian Serbs in the Krajina region. Meanwhile, the Bosnian Serbs intensified their assault against the Muslim population in Bihac. This was the war that was raging below my helicopter as we flew out of Tuzla, the war that by then had killed more than 200,000 people and driven more than a million others from their homes, the war that international diplomacy had been powerless to stop because negotiators had never been backed by credible threats of force to stop criminal leaders from committing atrocities against the people of the former Yugoslavia.

A year and a half earlier, after witnessing the devastation of Vukovar and seeing the mass graves at Ovcara, it had begun to dawn on me that this terrible war would probably drag on until most of the basic elements of civilization in what was once Yugoslavia were destroyed, or until force was brought to bear from the outside to challenge the aggressors. It had taken the world a long time to learn this truth. Had it acted earlier, hundreds of thousands of lives might have been saved, and the physical, economic, and political devastation of this part of southern Europe might have been averted. Europe and the United States had stood by for nearly four years while Yugoslavia burned and was carved up—its cities, towns, villages, neighborhoods, and families devastated and torn apart by leaders bent on enhancing their own power through the manipulation of differences and suspicions generated over centuries of Balkan conflict.

The United States had always had a strong interest in ending the war in Bosnia, but it was not until August 1995, after the genocide in Srebrenica, that it finally began to act in accordance with that interest. Although the integration and consolidation of democracy in

Europe after the fall of communism depended on the maintenance of European peace and stability, the crisis in Yugoslavia had never gotten the attention it deserved.

In 1990 and 1991 the Bush administration had walked away from the crisis. It failed to respond to entreaties for support from the moderate administration of Yugoslavian prime minister Ante Markovic; it told Slobodan Milosevic in June 1991 that the United States would not act to prevent the breakup of the country; it refused to respond to Serb attacks on Dubrovnik and Vukovar in the summer of 1991; it ignored the request by Bosnian president Alija Izetbegovic for U.N. peacekeepers in the fall of 1991; and it did nothing to stop Germany from recognizing Croatia and Slovenia in October 1991, the diplomatic event that left Bosnia no choice but to declare its own independence and gave Milosevic and Tudjman the excuse they needed to begin their campaigns of ethnic cleansing to carve up multiethnic Bosnia.[10]

Two years later, just after coming into office in 1993, the Clinton administration had attempted to persuade European countries to authorize NATO air strikes against Bosnian Serbs engaged in ethnic cleansing. But Clinton's effort to develop a more robust policy had been abandoned in the face of European resistance stemming from the new administration's own unwillingness to contribute troops to the U.N. peacekeeping force in Bosnia. In short, from late 1991 until August 1995, the United States had done nothing to prevent the war from starting, and little else to try to stop it.

Following the London conference and the shock of the international community in discovering the truth about Srebrenica, two events in August propelled a change of U.S. policy toward Bosnia. The first was the tragic death of three U.S. diplomats on August 19, 1995, in a road accident. High above Sarajevo, the armored personnel carrier in which they were traveling overturned and exploded as they were setting out on a new American negotiating effort after Srebrenica to stop the hostilities. Bob Frasure, Joe Kruzel, and Nelson Drew were part of a team headed by Richard Holbrooke whose mission was to try to persuade the parties to accept the division of

Bosnia into two entities, with 49 percent of the land going to the Bosnian Serbs and 51 percent to the Muslim-Croat Federation. The funerals of the diplomats in Washington on August 24 poignantly captured the impotence of a policy that for more than three years had precluded U.S. military involvement in the Balkans, stiffening the resolve of those within the administration who knew that any new U.S. diplomacy in Bosnia had to be backed by force if it was to have a chance of succeeding.

Four days after the three American diplomats were buried, thirty-eight Muslim civilians were killed and eighty-five wounded in a mortar attack on an open market in Sarajevo. By August 30, the United States had persuaded its NATO allies to join in authorizing sustained air strikes against Bosnian Serb military positions. The intensive NATO air campaign continued for more than two weeks. At last there was a military price to be paid for waging war against civilians.

The NATO intervention changed the dynamic of the Bosnia conflict. By punishing the Serbs for their attacks on the civilian populations of Srebrenica, Zepa, Sarajevo, Gorazde, and Bihac, NATO opened opportunities for the Croat-Muslim Federation forces to push back against the Bosnian Serb army in central Bosnia. But even more important was the effect of NATO's action on the diplomatic situation. For the first time, international diplomacy in Bosnia was being linked to military force, creating pressure on the parties to agree to a cease-fire. If the pressure was successful, it could be followed by a diplomatic campaign to forge a peace agreement. For nearly four years these objectives had eluded a long line of European and American diplomats. Now, at last, they seemed to be within reach.

Three people were crucial to the rapid series of decisions that led to NATO's intervention at the end of August and the launching of a new U.S. diplomatic strategy to end the war. The overall leadership came from President Clinton, who was shocked by the news from Srebrenica, concerned about the waning credibility of NATO as the war dragged on, and moved by the deaths of the American diplomats on Mount Igman and the Muslim civilians in the Sarajevo market. In addition, the President had been emboldened by a related foreign policy initiative he had taken the year before in another part of the post–Cold War world. In October 1994 he had bucked domestic public opinion by authorizing the deployment of twenty thousand American troops in a multinational force to stop a military junta from terrorizing the civilian population of Haiti and facilitate the return of the country's democratically elected president. The Haiti intervention had been carried out without American casualties for more than nine months, and this successful military operation had increased Clinton's confidence that an eventual deployment of U.S. soldiers in Bosnia need not be plagued by the Somalia syndrome, nor haunted by the larger and more ominous specter of Vietnam.

The President's shift toward a more interventionist stance on Bosnia opened the way for proponents of diplomacy backed by force to devise a strategy for ending the war. Warren Christopher, who had loyally reflected the reluctance of the White House over the first two and a half years of the administration to commit U.S. military and diplomatic resources to Bosnia, now took the signal from Clinton that the United States should adopt a more aggressive approach toward the crisis. Christopher took the lid off the State Department and empowered his team to act.

Christopher's contribution to this effort was to join with Clinton in designating Richard Holbrooke as team leader for implementing Bosnia policy, giving him broad responsibility for managing all aspects of a new American-led diplomatic offensive that was initiated after the collapse of the Contact Group negotiations and the chaos on the ground following the Bosnian Serbs' capture of Srebrenica and other U.N. "safe areas." Holbrooke's energy, wit, ambition, and bulldog assertiveness made him an ideal choice for this job, which would involve shaking up Washington and confronting the Balkan leaders in ways that no one had done since the war began. Christopher recognized the potential of Holbrooke's contribution, and he delegated full authority to Holbrooke's negotiating team throughout their many months of forceful, tumultuous, and controversial shuttle diplomacy.

## Confronting the Balkan Leaders

The intervention by NATO provided the cornerstone on which to build a new strategy of confrontation and negotiation with the Balkan leaders. That strategy took many twists and turns, but led eventually to the Dayton Peace Agreement of November 21, 1995.

Holbrooke understood that Bosnia was a human rights war, and he supported my participation in the new American-led drive for peace when others sought to exclude me. I had to spend much of the first half of September working on Haiti, including making a trip to Port-au-Prince to help prepare for the presidential elections scheduled for December. During this time, however, I was able to have several long discussions with Holbrooke and his staff about how to increase the pressure on Milosevic, Tudjman, and their Bosnian Serb and Croat surrogates by spotlighting the ongoing human rights atrocities in Bosnia and Croatia. Out of these discussions came a plan for Holbrooke to confront the leaders with fresh evidence of their criminality, warning them that they along with their subordinates and field commanders were now likely to come under investigation by the War Crimes Tribunal, and pressing them to begin negotiations to end the war. To help implement this plan, I would travel to the areas of conflict in both Bosnia and Croatia on a series of high-profile human rights missions, staying in close touch with Holbrooke and providing him with information about what I saw and heard so that he could use it to increase the pressure on the leaders to stop the atrocities or face further military or economic punishment.

Having witnessed the results of the ethnic expulsion campaigns conducted by the Serbs in Vukovar and Srebrenica, I thought I knew the depths of horror into which the people of the Balkans could be plunged by their leaders. But over the next six months I learned even more about the forces of evil that were driving this conflict and their destructive effect on every aspect of human behavior. At the core of the crisis was a simple but lethal idea: people should live only with other members of their own ethnic groups. Serbs should live with

Serbs, Croats with Croats, and Muslims with Muslims. This idea was the seductive heart of the authoritarian Balkan nationalism practiced by the two post-communist power brokers of Yugoslavia—Milosevic and Tudjman. It was also the means by which they manufactured the weapon that enforced their rule: fear. A pervasive social fear, growing ever larger over the four years of brutal ethnic engineering that began with the siege of Vukovar in 1991, could be seen and smelled in thousands of Bosnian and Croatian villages, where the smoke or charred ruins of burned houses and disturbed earth of mass graves was everywhere. Fear drove the "ethnic cleansing," whereby local paramilitary groups stole or destroyed the homes of neighbors; raped their wives, sisters, or mothers; shot or tortured their fathers, brothers, or sons; and drove everyone like them out of town. The fear that motivated these horrendous attacks was the fear of the first strike—if we don't take their land and destroy their families, they will attack ours. It was a fear I had first come to know in Rwanda, and now in Bosnia I could see that it had no national or ethnic boundaries.

In the Balkans, Milosevic was the prime mover of this diabolical world. When Yugoslavia began to break up in 1990, he was the first to recognize that he could stay in power by appealing to Serbs throughout the crumbling nation to protect their communities by making preemptive attacks against other ethnic groups. In pursuing his territorial ambitions under the banner of Serb nationalism, Milosevic had an asset that no other regional leader was able to claim: Belgrade, the capital city of Yugoslavia, with all its bureaucratic and military power. Because he was able to turn the Yugoslav army and the paramilitary forces that it spawned into instruments of ethnic warfare, Milosevic gained an early advantage over other nationalist leaders, particularly Tudjman. By 1991 he had begun to demonstrate the devastating results of manipulating the ethnic fear of the greater Serb population. And he did so with a vengeance. In Bosnia, from 1991 to mid-1995, Serbs violently expelled Croats and Muslims from 3,700 previously mixed towns and villages. By contrast, Serbs themselves were only forced out of fifty mixed Bosnian communities by Croats, and none by Muslims, while Croats and Muslims forced each other out of another three hundred communities. Over 90 percent of the ethnic expulsions in Bosnia before the summer of 1995 were carried out by Serbs who were stimulated, controlled, and often supplied by Belgrade.

But Croatia's Tudjman was no choirboy. The brutality of his commanders in Bosnia and in the Krajina—where they drove out over 150,000 Serbs, many from their ancestral homes—was later the basis for a series of indictments by the War Crimes Tribunal.[11] At home, Tudjman used Milosevic-style nationalist-authoritarian tactics, particularly censorship and economic pressure on the press, to shore up his rule. In one respect, Tudjman outdid Milosevic, asserting that Croatian sovereignty extended into the Croat-inhabited areas of Bosnia where residents who could prove their Croat ethnicity were allowed under the Tudjman-era constitution to vote in Croatian elections. While Milosevic maintained the fiction that the Bosnian Serbs were operating independently from Belgrade (despite the fact that their military commanders were often active-duty members of the Yugoslav army), Tudjman explicitly included the Bosnian Croats at the center of his vision of a Greater Croatia, and by doing so ensured that they would provide his strongest base of political support.

The third member of the triangle of leaders vying for control of Bosnia in 1995 was Alija Izetbegovic. A Muslim dissident who had spent eight years in prison in Tito's Yugoslavia, Izetbegovic was a hardline defensive nationalist. But unlike Milosevic and Tudjman, he did not start out by aggressively promoting policies of ethnic expulsion. After the war, his government fell prey to the ethnic cleansing disease when it blocked the return of Serb and Croat refugees to Sarajevo and other predominately Muslim population centers. From the point of view of Milosevic's Bosnian Serb surrogates and Tudjman's Bosnian Croat subordinates, Izetbegovic stood in the way of their respective efforts to affiliate with Serbia and Croatia. Back in 1991, Izetbegovic had inflamed the Serb leaders by making clear in a speech to the Bosnian parliament that he "would sacrifice peace for a sovereign Bosnia-Herzegovina, but for that peace . . . I would not sacrifice sovereignty."[12] During the war Izetbegovic stubbornly and courageously represented the interests of the Muslim victims of a Bosnia butchered and carved up by Milosevic and Tudjman.

Holbrooke's shuttle mission was to prod the three antagonists toward a cease-fire and then move them toward permanent peace negotiations. Following the brutal Bosnian Serb campaign in eastern and northwestern Bosnia over the first six months of 1995, culminating in the genocide at Srebrenica, three military events in August and September put the Serbs on the defensive. First was the NATO bombing. Second was the Croatian army's August 1 attack on the Serb regime that had been holding the Krajina region south of Zagreb since its capture from Croatia in 1991. And third was the counteroffensive of Muslim and Croat forces against the Bosnian Serbs in central and western Bosnia. When the new U.S. diplomatic campaign backed by NATO force was launched in August, war was raging everywhere. But the balance of power and territory was finally beginning to shift away from Bosnian Serb dominance.

My own mission was to support our peace campaign from the field. In doing so I would operate independently from Holbrooke and his negotiating team, but would coordinate all my trips and meetings with them. Holbrooke and I had a long discussion in his office on September 22, 1995, in which we mapped out my role of helping to implement key aspects of the overall strategy: spotlighting ongoing atrocities against civilians wherever they occurred; securing immediate commitments from leaders to end the atrocities or face the prospect of more NATO bombing and further economic sanctions; moving the War Crimes Tribunal to center stage as a way of raising the personal costs of criminal leadership; and assuring that there would be no negotiations with indicted war criminals.

## Croatia and Western Bosnia

I began to implement this strategy immediately by traveling to Croatia and western Bosnia at the end of September 1995. To demonstrate the evenhandedness of the peace process, I would call Tudjman to account for forcibly expelling more than a hundred thousand Serb civilians from the Krajina region of Croatia. At the same time, I would draw attention to the crimes committed by Bosnian Serbs against Bosnian Croats and Muslims in western Bosnia. I would be the first international official to travel to the Krajina after the Croatian offensive, and the first to go into Muslim and Croat areas recently liberated from the Bosnian Serbs in western Bosnia, where the fighting continued.

On the eve of my trip, Holbrooke and I met in New York. After two days of negotiations, on September 26, he and Christopher had just concluded a "framework agreement" with the three Balkan foreign ministers. The agreement contained language about the importance of observing international human rights standards in ongoing military operations. Holbrooke urged me to test the agreement by going as close to the areas of continued fighting in Western Bosnia as I could. I would take special mobile communications equipment so that I could reach him before his meetings with Milosevic and Tudjman. Since my State Department bureau was starved for travel funds, this and all my future Bosnia trips would be funded directly by the office of the Secretary of State. Human rights were no longer on the sidelines.

As I packed to leave home on September 25, Ellen questioned why I was making another trip to Bosnia. For a long time she had resented Washington's unwillingness to do more to stop the slaughter of civilians that was being endlessly chronicled by the international press. I told her I believed the situation was changing and that at last I would have the chance to do what we both felt should have been done long ago—confront the Balkan leaders with the horrors of the ethnic conflict they were causing and threaten them with *real* consequences (not just more talk) if they did not end it. Although this would be my third trip to the Balkans (I would take five more before 1995 was over, and many more in 1996), I was well aware that it would be the first time I would be fully supported by all parts of my own government.

Ellen asked me about the security problems of a high-profile diplomatic mission in a war zone. She also reminded me that I had already been overseas many days during that year. When we checked my calendar together I realized that by September I had already been out of the country for eighty days in 1995 on fifteen separate trips (it would be 128 days by the end of the year), in virtually every part of the world—Beijing, Tokyo, Indonesia, East Timor, Kenya, Rwanda, Haiti, Panama, Colombia, Geneva, The Hague, Germany, Northern Ireland, Bosnia, and Croatia. All that time, Ellen held our family together and listened to the endless Washington criticism and backbiting about Clinton administration policies and actions. Our partnership was as strong as her support for what I was doing, but in many ways she had a harder job than I did.

I arrived in Zagreb on September 28. This time I was accompanied by Steve Coffey, an experienced Foreign Service officer whose passion for human rights was unrivaled among the many career professionals with whom I worked. Steve was my principal deputy in Washington, and later would serve as my deputy chief of mission in Prague. Steve and I were met at the airport by Peter Galbraith, and we took off immediately by car through the cold and rainy Croatian countryside toward the devastated Krajina region.

As we drove south, Galbraith briefed us on the two human rights crises that Tudjman had provoked in the wake of the Croatian army's successful military campaign in August to retake the Krajina region from the Serbs. The first involved the killing of large numbers of unarmed Krajina Serbs, including sick and elderly people, women, and children, by Croatian soldiers and armed gangs marauding throughout the province. The second was a refugee crisis. In retaking the Krajina from the Serb military regime that had seized it in 1991 at the instigation of and with military support from Milosevic, the Croats were determined to exact from the Krajina Serbs a devastating retribution in human suffering. Over 150,000 Serbs, most of whose families had lived in the Krajina for centuries, had been forced to abandon their homes and make the long trek across war-torn Bosnia to Serbia in search of refuge. The Tudjman government had confiscated their property and was beginning to turn the Serb houses over to Croat refugees from Bosnia. Meanwhile, Tudjman was moving in other ways to create an ethnically pure Croatia by closing down Bosnian refugee camps and forcing their inhabitants to move back across the border to western Bosnia, where the fighting was more intense than ever.

Galbraith was outraged by these developments and pleased that Washington had sent me to investigate them. Somehow, he said, Tudjman always managed to hide behind the dark shadow of Milosevic. By allowing Zagreb to be used as a staging area for international assistance to Bosnia and the entry point for U.N. troops, Croatia had escaped the sanctions that were directed at Belgrade. But Tudjman's human rights record was only slightly less egregious than Milosevic's, and if the peace process was to move forward, the Croatian government would have to be held accountable for the brutal treatment of the Krajina Serbs.

As we drove through heavily shelled and burned-out towns, past deserted Serb houses, we talked about how to put pressure on Tudjman to respect human rights. Galbraith pointed to Tudjman's four areas of vulnerability: his interest in getting international recognition of Croatia's claim of sovereignty over Vukovar and eastern Slavonia; his need for World Bank, European, and U.S. assistance to rebuild the Croatian economy; his frustrated dream of reintegrating Croatia with Europe; and his fear of indictment by the War Crimes Tribunal.

Two days earlier, on September 26, I had tested some of these pressure points in a meeting in New York with Croatian foreign minister Mate Granic. I had warned Granic that the United States was concerned about Croatia's treatment of Serb and Muslim refugees and expected a pledge from his government that no more would be forcibly repatriated. Now, as we pulled into the nearly deserted town of Glina, where large numbers of Krajina Serbs had been killed and many others driven away, I got an answer to my refugee question from the newly installed Croatian mayor: no Serbs had been massacred or expelled in the Croatian army's August offensive—they had simply "decided to leave." When Galbraith asked what had happened to a Serb World War II monument that he had seen in the town square on a previous visit, he was told by the straight-faced Croatian mayor that it had been removed "because it was out of keeping with the local architecture." Back in the car Galbraith said, "Welcome to ethnically pure Croatia." Further south we encountered more evidence of Tudjman's handiwork: a squalid refugee camp of twenty thousand Bosnians under increasing pressure from the government to move back across the border into the middle of the conflict from which they had fled.

In Zagreb I met with Tudjman's hardline deputy prime minister, Ivica Kostovic. I asked Kostovic about reports concerning the Croatian army's mass killings and expulsion of Serbs from Krajina. His response exemplified the Tudjman-style Croatian nationalism that was stoking the fires of ethnic conflict throughout the region. Kostovic denied that Serb civilians had been killed by the army, but said it was difficult for the government to stop roving gang attacks in the Krajina "because of the strong feeling people have against the Serbs." As for the Serb refugees, Kostovic said their property had been confiscated by the Croatian government when they fled the country. At the same time, he told me, the government had revoked the refugee status of Bosnian Muslims living in Croatia because they were a burden on the government and were being "asked" to relocate to recently liberated areas of western Bosnia.

I told Kostovic that his response was totally unacceptable. Under international law the Croatian government had an obligation to stop the killings in the Krajina, allow Serbs who had lived in Croatia for generations to return to their homes, and protect the refugee status of Muslims who would be at risk if they were made to go back to areas of ongoing conflict in Bosnia. The United States wants to help Croatia rebuild its country after the war, I said, but you will get no help from us if you build on a foundation of ethnic purity and expulsion. Kostovic tried to deflect my points by claiming that his government had to protect the security of Croatia. I told him that if this was the way Croatia continued to act, his government should forget about receiving any international assistance.

Sobered by the Krajina crisis, I turned my attention to western

Bosnia. In many ways this was no-man's-land. The fighting between Bosnian Serb and Muslim-Croat Federation forces was continuing. The U.S. embassy in Bosnia was trapped by the siege of Sarajevo and could not get to western Bosnia, and our Zagreb embassy was limited to covering events in Croatia. From Zagreb I called John Menzies, the U.S. ambassador in Sarajevo, and outlined the plan Holbrooke and I had discussed for me to enter Bosnia by road across the Croatian border and try to get as far as possible into the "confrontation area" so that I could assess the human rights and refugee conditions in recently liberated towns. Menzies welcomed my mission, but said I faced the Hobson's choice of risking the security of our group by getting too close to the conflict, or staying away and not getting enough information to make the trip worthwhile. I told him I would try to be careful, but also useful.

The road through Bihac in northwestern Bosnia was lined with slow-moving columns of exhausted and bedraggled civilians fleeing from recent fighting and ethnic expulsions in both Bosnia and Croatia. Burned-out farmhouses and the wrecks of cars and military vehicles were everywhere, and here and there dead horses lay where they had dropped from exhaustion or gunfire. Bihac had been liberated ten days earlier when the Bosnian Serb army was forced back by Federation forces, but shooting continued to the east around Sanski Most and Prijedor, where four years earlier the Bosnian Serbs had conducted brutal ethnic cleansing campaigns against Muslims that had ignited all of Bosnia.

I stopped to meet the Danish U.N. commander at his headquarters south of Bihac. He told me that all three sides in the area were playing politics with refugees, trying to resettle them in dangerous frontline towns in order to stake out territorial claims, ready to assert human rights violations against the enemy if civilians were harmed in the fighting. He was glad to hear that I had come to check out the situation in frontline towns like Bosanski Petrovac, where Muslim refugees were reportedly being forcibly resettled. I also wanted to see if there were mass graves in the area, given reports I had heard about Muslim civilians being executed by Bosnian Serb soldiers before they had fled. The commander provided us with a U.N. military observer, an Italian soldier, to guide us toward the front, but warned that we should not try to go much farther than Bosanski Petrovac, which was at the edge of the fighting.

As we made our way east, the scenes of devastation increased. Muslim villages had been razed, their mosques bombed, and wrecked cars abandoned. The only signs of recent human life were occasional pieces of clothing and refuse along the road, marking the route the Serbs had used to flee. Signs of life returned as we entered Bosanski Petrovac, where over two thousand terrified Muslim refugees had been dropped off two weeks earlier by the Bosnian Muslim army. I spoke to several of them and learned that most had been expelled from the city of Banja Luka during a storm of ethnic cleansing in September carried out by paramilitary groups sweeping through Bosnian Serb areas to ensure that they were now "ethnically pure." The refugees' situation in this frontline town was extremely perilous. The U.N. military observer who was traveling with us told me that land mines had been found in the town's buildings and surrounding fields. Serb snipers in the hills were a constant threat, and the fighting was only ten kilometers away. I concluded that these refugees were being used as pawns by the Bosnian government in a high-stakes territorial game; weeks before, they had been pawns of the Serbs when they were forced from their homes in Banja Luka. This is what Bosnia is all about, I said to Steve Coffey as we walked through the town—everyone is an ethnic pawn.

On a desolate dirt road a few kilometers beyond Bosanski Petrovac near the frontline town of Klujc, I encountered another grim Bosnian reality. Two days earlier soldiers from the Bosnian Muslim army had discovered a mass grave, and now I joined our U.N. military observer in making the first international visit to verify the site. We clambered a hundred yards down a muddy hillside in a driving rain to a ditch dug out along the edge of a field. There we saw tattered bits of clothing, a ribcage, a skull, and several hands and feet protruding from the mud. A Bosnian Muslim soldier told us that more bodies had been found in a cave nearby. I asked the U.N. observer to make sure that War Crimes Tribunal investigators were notified so that they could excavate the site as soon as local military conditions allowed it. Further on, we stopped at a clearing in the forest near the Croatian border, where the U.N. observer told us he had found fifteen bodies the day before, including several women and children. Three had been decapitated. All had been killed within the last two weeks, probably by Serbs before they fled from the oncoming Croat-Muslim Federation forces. The smell of death was omnipresent and overpowering.

During four days in Croatia and western Bosnia, I now had witnessed or seen evidence of fresh human rights crimes by all three sides in this seemingly endless conflict. Croatian against Serb in the Krajina. Serb against Muslim in Bihac and Klujc. And in Bosanska Petrovac, the Bosnian Muslim government was resettling Muslim refugees dangerously close to the front lines of fighting in order to extend its territorial claims. On the route back to Zagreb, in a scene that matched the Bosnian army's use of Muslim civilian refugees as territorial pawns, I came across an example of aggressive ethnic cleansing within the supposedly allied Croat-Muslim Federation. A Muslim town, Kulen Vakuf, had been liberated from the Serbs by Croat-Muslim Federation forces the week before, but since then, Croatian soldiers had seized the town and now refused to allow any of its Muslim residents to return. All of these incidents provided depressing evidence that despite the NATO bombing and more aggressive international diplomacy, the engines of war were driving on inexorably in Croatia and western Bosnia.

Back in Zagreb I hammered home two points to the Croatian government: we won't help you rebuild your country until you stop violating the human rights of Serbs and Muslims, and we won't help the Serbs until they stop violating the rights of Croats and Muslims. At a well-attended press conference before heading to the airport, I described in detail what I had seen. Then I delivered my punch line: the Tudjman and Milosevic governments are responsible for the human rights crisis in the Krajina and western Bosnia, and they must solve the crisis now or face the consequences.

At the airport I met with the Holbrooke team for an hour on their plane before they flew on to Belgrade and I returned to Washington. I told Holbrooke I had plenty of evidence of fresh human rights atrocities that he could use to put pressure on Milosevic and Tudjman. He was particularly struck by my description of what was going on in the Krajina. We agreed that my account would be a useful way to demonstrate to Tudjman that he risked the same kind of isolation as Milosevic unless he reined in his forces. As for Milosevic, Holbrooke would put him on the defensive by informing him that I had seen evidence of new ethnic cleansing by the Serbs in Banja Luka as well as mass killings of Muslims in western Bosnia. He would emphasize that our human rights investigations were evenhanded, and that we were simultaneously pressing Tudjman to stop the Croatian atrocities against Serbs in the Krajina and to allow Serb refugees to return to their homes. When Holbrooke returned to Zagreb the following day, he found that the statements I had made in my press conference had infuriated Tudjman.[13] Our strategy seemed to be working.

## More War Crimes

For years the fighting in the Balkans had been affected by seasonal changes. Each fall, as the leaves began to turn and mists descended on the rugged mountains and valleys of Bosnia, the war would intensify as armies clawed for advantage, and then go into remission during the harsh Balkan winter. The most dangerous time of the year was October, when criminal commanders and politicians would use tactical brutality to steal a march on the changing season.

In October 1995 the pressure of the coming winter was greater than usual because the situation on the ground was more complicated than ever. The Bosnian Serbs were on the defensive militarily, reeling both from NATO's September bombing campaign and from the counteroffensive of the combined Federation forces of Bosnian Muslims and Bosnian Croats. At the end of September and the first few days of October the Holbrooke team was pressing all parties for a cease-fire. On October 5, after a whirlwind round of negotiations in Belgrade, Sarajevo, and Zagreb, Holbrooke managed to broker a cease-fire agreement in return for promised exchanges of prisoners, restoration of gas and electricity for Sarajevo, and a peace conference in the United States in November. This was a huge breakthrough. But it was followed by a month of uncertainty and danger as winter approached and the parties jockeyed for position, testing the will of the United States to break the deadly grip of violence and recrimination that had controlled the former Yugoslavia for years.

Since the United States had stood on the sidelines for so long, this testing was serious. We had to meet it decisively or the peace process would never get off the ground. Over the next month, we would have to get the political leaders to stop their ethnic cleansing and start cooperating with us, and eventually with each other. This would not be easy. Tudjman was still busy expelling and confiscating the property of hundreds of thousands of Krajina Serbs, Milosevic and his surrogates were scrambling to complete the expulsion of Croats and Muslims from Banja Luka so that it would remain a Serb stronghold, and Izetbegovic and his revived military forces were resisting the cease-fire.

During the first several days of October I cancelled a long-planned trip to the Middle East and went to Warsaw to begin an effort to mobilize the Organization for Security and Cooperation in Europe (OSCE) to play a role in the fledgling peace process. As the only regional human rights organization of governments from North America and western and eastern Europe (including Russia), the OSCE would be essential to the effort to stabilize and rebuild Bosnia. Since we knew that the credibility of a new peacekeeping operation would depend on Russian involvement, or at least acquiescence, the OSCE was a key forum for ending the war.

I laid out for delegates to the OSCE's annual human rights conference the results of my trip the previous week to western Bosnia and Croatia. I described the evidence I had seen of fresh atrocities committed by Serbs and Croats, explaining the relationship between Holbrooke's negotiations and my fact-finding activities, and asking for the support of member states for an eventual OSCE role in human rights and elections monitoring once a peace agreement was signed. Although several delegates expressed support in their remarks to the conference after I had spoken, in private discussions many of them raised questions about the ability of the OSCE to organize and deploy a large-scale monitoring effort in the near future. Key countries like Britain, Canada, and the Netherlands were clearly skeptical about the capacity of OSCE to play the role we were creating for it. I returned to Washington with the message that we had a long way to go to assemble the human rights parts of a peace implementation plan.

But events on the ground were intensifying the pressure to move quickly. On Thursday, October 12, John Menzies called from Sarajevo to tell me he was beginning to hear reports of a new round of Serb ethnic cleansing in Banja Luka, including mass killings of men and rapes of women and girls, that sounded ominously reminiscent of Srebrenica. John urged me to travel as quickly as possible to Zenica in central Bosnia, where refugees—mostly women and children—were beginning to arrive. Since the road from Sarajevo to Zenica was still blocked, we agreed that I should enter Bosnia through Croatia, as I had done on my previous trips. After talking to Menzies I called Peter Galbraith in Zagreb to tell him my plan and urge him to send ahead Dubravka Maric, the Foreign Service officer from his embassy who had been with me when I had interviewed the Srebrenica refugees in July. Dubravka would meet with refugees as they arrived from Banja Luka.

I knew my trip would have to be coordinated closely with Holbrooke's next round of negotiations with Milosevic if we were to have any chance of stopping the Banja Luka atrocities. I talked with Holbrooke from my office in Washington on Friday, October 13. We agreed the situation was grim, and decided I should travel immediately to Bosnia to gather as much information as possible from the refugees. On Tuesday evening, October 17, I would call Holbrooke from Zenica to tell him what I had learned, just before his meeting with Milosevic that night in Belgrade.

Since Milosevic was certain to press Holbrooke to begin to lift the international sanctions against Serbia in return for playing a constructive role in the upcoming peace conference, I knew we had leverage over him. But I also knew that Holbrooke and I had disagreed in the past about linking sanctions relief with war crimes cooperation. This time our views were in lock-step. We both knew that not only was the peace process in jeopardy; the specter of Srebrenica was close as thousands of lives were again at stake. If I could get the ammunition for Holbrooke to use against Milosevic, he could pull the trigger. Holbrooke would tell Milosevic that sanctions and war crimes were linked, and that Serbia would get no relief from sanctions until it stopped committing or abetting war crimes in Bosnia. We also agreed that my human rights missions should continue to focus on all of the leaders, not just the Serbs. In Bosnia I would be on the lookout for evidence that the Bosnian government was allowing the Mujahedeen and other Islamic extremists to foment violence. After calling Holbrooke from Zenica, I would travel again to Croatia to investigate fresh atrocities in the Krajina and then confront the Tudjman government about its continuing abuse of the Krajina Serbs.

To contribute to our pressure on the leaders, my movements on the ground would have to keep pace with Holbrooke's frantic shuttling between Washington and the Balkan capitals. By mid-October, Wright-Patterson Air Force Base in Dayton, Ohio, had been selected as the site of the peace talks, which were to begin on November 1. But peace was nowhere in sight. Despite the cease-fire, paramilitary forces linked to Milosevic and Tudjman were committing war crimes throughout Bosnia and Croatia. The political climate was turning increasingly ugly as all of the parties jockeyed for position. If this vicious cycle of violence could not be broken, the war might start up again and continue for years.

Before taking off for Zagreb on October 15, I asked my staff to assemble all the recent unconfirmed reports of Serb and Croat atrocities around Banja Luka and the Krajina. They produced a half-inch-thick folder of grim information: the rounding up by masked men in early October of between three and six thousand Muslim men and boys, mass rapes of Serb women married to Muslim men, the forcible resettling of Croat and Muslim refugees by their own governments in recently seized towns near the front, the reopening of prison camps by the Bosnian Serbs, the killing of elderly Serbs in the Krajina and the seizure of tens of thousands of Serb-owned houses by the Croatian government so that Croat refugees from Banja Luka could be permanently resettled in them. These reports told the story of the continuing recrimination going on beneath the cease-fire, and belied the claim that peace was at hand.

On October 16, a Norwegian-piloted U.N. helicopter took me from Split, on the Dalmatian coast, over the rugged terrain of western Bosnia. The leaves were turning gold and snow had fallen in the mountains. Remote villages appeared below the blue haze enshrouding the valleys. With the roofs of many houses burned off, these outposts of civilization now looked like sentinels of terror. As we landed in Zenica, I hoped we still had a chance to save lives before the engines of ethnic cleansing once again put them at risk. But we would have to act quickly.

Dubravka Maric met me at the helicopter landing pad and took me immediately to meet the commander of a battalion of Turkish troops who were serving as the U.N. peacekeepers in central Bosnia. I was not sure how I would be received. I had traveled to Turkey twice the previous year on high-profile human rights missions and had publicly criticized the Turkish military for its human rights abuses against the Kurdish population in southeastern Turkey. The commander opened our meeting by saying that he disagreed with my human rights work in Turkey, but respected what Holbrooke and I were trying to do in Bosnia. "There will be no peace until the killing of Muslims is stopped," he said, "and right now terrible things are happening in Banja Luka." He told us that between October 6 and 12 over six thousand terrorized Muslim women and children from Banja Luka had arrived in Zenica. No men were with them. Shades of Srebrenica. "You must force Milosevic to pull back Arkan [Zeljko Raznatovic, the notorious Belgrade paramilitary leader and Milosevic henchman] and his paramilitaries before it is too late," he said. The commander also warned me that foreign Mujahedeen terrorists were beginning to operate in Zenica. If Arkan continued his rampage, the Mujahedeen might begin to foment violence against the United Nations and international humanitarian workers in central Bosnia. These dark observations were echoed by U.N. and Red Cross refugee workers, who told me that several thousand Muslim men were being held by the Bosnian Serbs in or near Banja Luka and that, as in Srebrenica, their whereabouts were unknown.

The only way to get the full story was to interview the refugees. But first I needed permission from the mayor (with whom I had met during my previous trip in July when I had interviewed the Srebrenica survivors), because the Bosnian government was sensitive about giving access to its "war information." Having fought back on the ground after the disasters of the summer, the Bosnians now wanted to protect their victim status in the upcoming peace talks. This meant asserting control over the recently arrived Muslim refugees.

The mayor met me in his office in the run-down communist-era Zenica city hall, surrounded by deputies and photos of assorted leaders, including Bosnia president Alija Izetbegovic and Yugoslavia's former president Josip Broz Tito. I knew I was in the politburo. In contrast to our July meeting, the mayor seemed genuinely pleased to see me. With a big smile he said he now understood why I had asked all the questions earlier about Srebrenica. "Thank you for bombing the Serbs," he said bluntly. "We welcome your visit because we have been waiting a long time for the United States to help us." I told him that the United States was now trying to save lives in Banja Luka and I needed to interview refugees to find out what was happening there. He gave me detailed statistics about how many refugees had arrived in Zenica each day in October, and how many of their male family members were still missing. He avoided my question about interviews, but after I reminded him how the stories of Srebrenica survivors had changed the course of the war, he finally agreed to let me visit several new refugee "collection centers" in Zenica and the nearby village of Kakanj.

As a foreign stranger I had no right to expect these victims of fresh terror to pour out the personal details of their shattered lives. But they did. Huddled in corners of crowded makeshift shelters, a dozen terrified women and a few elderly men told Dubravka Maric and me what they had been through. Many of them broke down repeatedly as they struggled through their stories, telling of husbands, brothers, and sons forced to stay behind when they had been violently expelled from their homes in Banja Luka.

The refugees painted a grim picture of what had happened. Two weeks earlier, just as the cease-fire was taking effect, masked paramilitary men had stormed through the remaining Muslim neighborhoods in Banja Luka and nearby cities and towns. The paramilitaries were organized and had lists of Muslims to be rounded up. They forced them from their homes, taking the men to unknown locations. They raped women and beat the elderly before pushing them onto buses, where they were robbed and their clothing and underwear searched for valuables. The buses drove them to the front line, where skirmishes continued between Bosnian Serb and Federation forces. They were then forced to walk for miles through swamps and rivers, sometimes beaten and shot along the way by Serb soldiers. Finally, they reached Federation territory and made their way to Zenica. Throughout our grueling day of interviews we heard examples of horrific cruelty (soldiers drowning elderly people by pushing them into a river) and extraordinary bravery (Serb neighbors sheltering Muslims in their basements). The most chilling theme of all was the intense cynicism of the Bosnian Serb leaders and their patron, Milosevic, who while agreeing to a cease-fire in order to avoid further losses of territory had simultaneously unleashed the "Arkan Tigers" to force out the last vestiges of ethnic diversity from northern Bosnia in the run-up to Dayton.

As I prepared to make my call to Holbrooke on October 17 to arm him for his meeting that night with Milosevic, I encountered another form of terror. Coming out of the refugee center, I was approached menacingly by two tall bearded figures dressed in camouflage outfits. One of them pointed his finger at me and shouted in heavily Arabic-accented English, "You fucking Americans are destroying Bosnia. Who's in charge here? You'll all soon be dead unless you get the fuck out of this country." Before I could open my mouth, my security guards had pushed me into our waiting car and gunned the motor. They told me later they had heard a report that day about an armed mujahedeen terrorist training camp across the street from the refugee center, but until that moment had not seen any evidence of it. That night the mayor of Zenica apologized for the threat against us, which he said had come from "foreign elements who are violating our law." Later, the Turkish U.N. commander told me that Izetbegovic's Bosnian government was doing little to prevent Afghan mujahedeen—linked, as we later learned, to al Qaeda—from operating in Bosnia and infiltrating the Bosnian Muslim army. Arkan's terror to the north was feeding an environment of recrimination in the south in which mujahedeen operatives were finding increasing support. It was clear that the human rights war in Bosnia was becoming a breeding ground for international terrorism.

I had plenty to tell Holbrooke. Using the satellite equipment I had brought with me from Washington, I made my call from the barracks of the Turkish battalion. I waited to be connected by the State Department Operations Center to Holbrooke's plane as it approached Belgrade from Moscow. I had the feeling the peace process hung in the balance. The information I had gathered about Serb paramilitary operations in Banja Luka was good material for Holbrooke to use that night against Milosevic, who was testing us to see if we would try to stop him. I thought about how often Milosevic had called the bluff of the international community, and how often we had failed to use our leverage to block or counter his latest moves. I hoped tonight would be different.

The satellite connection was bad and we spoke only briefly, but it was enough to prepare Holbrooke for the meeting. Based on what I told him, he confronted Milosevic directly: the United States would not discuss sanctions relief for Serbia until Arkan's forces were called off and the Muslim prisoners released. When Milosevic claimed my information was wrong and his government had no connection with Bosnian Serb paramilitaries, Holbrooke confronted him again two days later with an unclassified CIA report confirming the latest round of Banja Luka ethnic cleansing. Since our intelligence reports showed that Belgrade was continuing to supply the Bosnian Serb forces, we knew we had caught him red-handed. Holbrooke held the line on sanctions relief.

Two weeks later we got a signal that our human rights strategy was beginning to produce results. On October 29, just before the Dayton talks got under way, the Bosnian Serbs released 324 Muslim men who had been rounded up in Banja Luka a month earlier.[14] Although it would be weeks more before the Serbs would release other prisoners, I felt a step at last had been taken toward ending the vicious cycle of war crimes and ethnic cleansing.

# CHAPTER 6

# BOSNIA AND KOSOVO

## BREAKING THE CYCLE

Early in my tenure as assistant secretary, Ellen gave me a scrap of paper to carry in my wallet. On it she had written the Talmudic commentary, "He who saves one life saves the world." When I first encountered this phrase, many years earlier, it had seemed remote, but as I reread it on October 18, 1995, during a grueling overland trip on the rugged mountain road between central Bosnia and southern Croatia, its meaning came into focus.

In the fall of 1995, the United States had adopted a strategy of spotlighting the brutality of the Bosnia war and confronting the leaders with their personal responsibility for the crimes being committed against an entire civilian population. The goals of this strategy were saving lives, breaking the cycle of violence, and creating incentives to end the war. If we could get the leaders to recognize that each of them had a stake in pulling back, we might actually have a chance of breaking the cycle.

By the end of October, our strategy had come to a head. We had succeeded in showing all three sides that each had a self-interest in stopping the war crimes that were being committed. The Bosnian Muslims wanted the Serbs to release the Muslim men seized earlier that month in Banja Luka and to know the fate of the men taken from Srebrenica in July. The Serbs wanted the release of the Serb prisoners taken when Sanski Most fell to Federation forces in September and they wanted the Krajina Serbs who had been expelled by the Croats in August to be able to return to their homes. The Croats wanted the Muslim refugees in Croatia to go back to Bosnia and they wanted to find homes for the Croats expelled during the summer and fall from Banja Luka and other Bosnian Serb areas.

These objectives were not mutually exclusive. In fact, they were mutually reinforcing. The rewards for pursuing them would be postwar assistance and the lifting of sanctions. The punishment for ignoring them would be indictment by the War Crimes Tribunal and resumption of NATO bombing.

## Milosevic and Tudjman

Milosevic and Tudjman were our targets. To get to them we would not only use all of our carrots and sticks; we would also go out of our way to demonstrate that we were evenhanded in helping all victims of the war—Serb, Croat, and Muslim alike.

In his meeting with Milosevic on October 17, 1995, Holbrooke had stressed that my human rights missions were focused not only on the atrocities committed against Muslims by Serb paramilitaries in Banja Luka, but also on the continuing abuses being committed by Croats against the Krajina Serbs. When I reached the Krajina region on October 18, after an exhausting ten-hour drive over the mountainous smuggling routes between Bosnia and Croatia, I found a shattered and desolate landscape. Tens of thousands of Serb ancestral homes had been destroyed during the Croatian offensive that had swept through the Krajina in August. Of the three thousand Serbs who had stayed behind, most were elderly. Several hundred had been killed by roving gangs.[1]

Local U.N. officials told me there was no law in the Krajina. By condoning lawlessness, the Croatian government was sending a signal to the Serbs not to return—a signal made even clearer by the government's confiscation of all Serb property that was not reclaimed within ninety days of its abandonment by Serbs forcibly expelled from the Krajina. In Zagreb, I again confronted Croatian deputy prime minister Ivica Kostovic, warning him for the second time that the War Crimes Tribunal was preparing to investigate the Krajina killings and that the United States would block all assistance to Croatia if it tried to build an ethnically pure state. Before returning to Washington on October 21, I held a press conference in which I again blasted both Tudjman and Milosevic for the criminal behavior of their regimes.

As they jockeyed for position before the Dayton Peace Conference, the Balkan leaders clearly did not like the kind of human rights spotlight we were aiming at them. But our strategy was bringing results. The day after I returned to Washington, I was back on a plane headed to Belgrade and Zagreb. Exhausted, I was nevertheless exhilarated because Milosevic and Tudjman had both told Holbrooke that they were now willing to discuss our human rights demands. Rudy Perina, the U.S. chargé d'affaires in Belgrade, confirmed in a phone call to my special assistant, Peter Eicher, that Milosevic had agreed to a meeting in Belgrade on October 24. I asked Peter to come with me and prepare the political and logistical briefing materials for the trip. Perina told Eicher that Milosevic knew he was losing the public relations battle over the October ethnic expulsions from Banja Luka and was now prepared to discuss my demand to open the area to the international press and international humanitarian organizations. The invitation from Zagreb was less clear: Tudjman had informed Holbrooke that his government wanted to brief me about the steps they were taking to "stabilize the situation" in the Krajina. In response, I would go to Zagreb to tell the Croatian government once again that international human rights standards required them to protect those Serbs who remained and others who wished to return.

Milosevic had clearly decided to go on a charm offensive to rehabilitate himself before Dayton. Having lost the upper hand in Bosnia, where his Bosnian Serb clients were in retreat, and having been forced out of Croatia, where his Krajina puppet regime had been routed by the Croatian army, he was now focusing on how to negotiate the most favorable deal for his government at the peace talks. He wanted to carve out a Serb state from Bosnia, to have the sanctions against Serbia lifted, and to entice international donors to begin providing assistance to his government. But Milosevic had a huge problem: he was now seen to be the architect of the war in Bosnia and the patron of the Bosnian Serb leaders who were responsible for the genocide in Srebrenica and the latest round of ethnic expulsions in Banja Luka. In agreeing to meet with him, I knew I was running a risk of becoming a tool in Milosevic's rehabilitation campaign. But I also knew that I had a chance to use his new vulnerability to advance our own campaign to save lives, release prisoners, promote freedom of movement, and strengthen important human rights institutions like the War Crimes Tribunal.

Before heading to Belgrade, I stopped in Brussels to enlist the European Union (EU) to put more pressure on Milosevic over human rights. I told the EU representatives that my mission to Belgrade was to convey a message to Milosevic that we were holding him responsible for the dangerous situation in Banja Luka. He had to solve it by calling off the paramilitary groups, opening the area to international organizations, and providing access to the missing Muslim men. My plan was received politely by the EU "troika" (officials representing France, Spain, and Italy as the current, immediate past, and next EU presidencies), but I did not exactly sense that an army of European diplomats would be marching beside me as I entered the lion's den.

Peter Eicher and my secretary, Lynda Walker-Johnson, had managed miraculously, on less than twenty-four-hours' notice, to procure a small U.S. Air Force plane for our trip from Brussels to Belgrade, which was inaccessible to commercial airlines. Peter and I huddled in the tiny cabin during the two-hour flight and mapped out the points I would make to Milosevic. Most important was what I would *not* do: no negotiations, no concessions, no joint press conferences, no positive public statements without concrete actions. I would confront Milosevic with the issue of Serb war crimes in Banja Luka and Srebrenica. To demonstrate evenhandedness I would also tell him about my plan to confront Tudjman the following day on the issue of Croatian war crimes committed against the Krajina Serbs.

Rudy Perina predicted that Milosevic would be jocular and disarming. He was right. But there were other more distinctive elements in Milosevic's demeanor that evening as he welcomed us to a darkened receiving room in the presidential palace and gestured vaguely for us to be seated in the typical communist-era overstuffed armchairs. Settling into his own chair, Slobodan Milosevic assumed the air of the Yugoslavian banker in New York that he had been for three years in the 1970s during the Tito era. He spoke in tones that implied bottomless ineptitude on the part of everyone but himself, projecting a vast and conniving self-confidence blending into arrogance. Here was a leader surrounded by enemies but assured by knowledge based on experience that he knew how to manipulate them. Predictably, he began our discussion by exploding with a diatribe against Croatia's "worst genocide against the Serbs since the Second World War, and the largest genocide in Europe in fifty years." He seemed quite familiar with his own world of ethnic cleansing, I thought, although he conveniently managed to leave out Srebrenica.

To get beyond the diatribe, I told him I would travel to Zagreb in the morning to press the Tudjman government about war crimes against the Krajina Serbs. But now, I said, I was in Belgrade to discuss the war crimes crisis in Banja Luka. I was not here to negotiate but to insist on immediate access to the Bosnian Serb areas where these crimes were being committed. Lives were at stake and urgent action was needed to save them. The missing Muslim men must be found immediately and allowed to reunite with their families.

While I was speaking, I watched Milosevic for signs of his reaction to my blunt demands. His wiliness and instinct for self-preservation pointed him toward agreeing with me. Protecting his flank, he said he was not "in the chain of command" in the "Republika Srpska" (the Bosnian Serb political authority), but would "do my best" to secure the arrest of those guilty of any crimes. He claimed he had been told by the Bosnian Serbs that individual soldiers had been "guilty of excesses," but he did not necessarily accept this point of view and would "search for the truth." He would insist on immediate access for international humanitarian organizations and the press, and he instructed his foreign minister, Milan Milutinovic, who was at the meeting, to see that the missing men, whose names were now on International Red Cross lists, were found.

Struck by the agility with which Milosevic seemed able to maneuver on territory that lesser tyrants would have found threatening, I pushed on with my argument. The only way to get to the bottom of these crimes was to allow the War Crimes Tribunal to investigate them. Sidling up to my position, as his instinct no doubt told him his interest required for the moment, Milosevic responded that he would not obstruct war crimes investigations. "All criminals will be arrested," he asserted. But then he made a big qualification that would become his principal defense against the tribunal in the months and years ahead: "The constitution of Serbia prohibits the extradition of its citizens." To get around this roadblock I suggested that he agree to discuss with the tribunal prosecutor how to assure Serbia's cooperation with tribunal investigations consistent with its constitution and its international obligations. When he responded that this sounded like a reasonable proposal, I pressed on and urged him to allow international investigators to get access to the mass graves that had been reported near Srebrenica. I sensed I was on sensitive ground, but Milosevic replied airily that he saw "no reason why access should not be granted" and said he would raise the issue with "Republika Srpska leaders" the next day.

Milosevic's cunning acquiescence to my demands was remarkable. Clearly he had calculated that he could dump the Bosnian Serbs overboard—and protect himself against association with their crimes by cooperating for the moment, at least, with our human rights agenda—then sail smoothly into Dayton as a champion of peace. I tested the limits of his tactical congeniality by asking him about political repression inside Serbia. He snapped back, demanding that I be "objective" and asserting that there is "more freedom of the press in Yugoslavia than in the countries that surround us."

I could sense the meeting was coming to an end, so I decided to shift back to the plight of the Krajina Serbs. I told Milosevic I would seek a commitment the next day from Tudjman to protect Serbs who were still in Croatia and allow those who wanted to return to their homes to do so. He seemed pleased, and moved to another level in his calculus of cynical cooperation by saying he would make a public statement after our meeting restating his commitments to me. I told him that a statement was fine, but would be meaningless without immediate action on granting international access to Banja Luka. Access was imperative because lives were at stake. Furthermore, I said, investigators must be allowed to visit Srebrenica so that the truth about what had happened there could be uncovered. "No problem," he replied, waving his hand confidently, but also as if to dismiss the subject. "You will have access by tomorrow."

Although I did not know it at the time, aerial photos taken on October 20, four days before my meeting with Milosevic (later introduced into evidence in the trial of General Radislav Krstic, the Bosnian Serb commander at Srebrenica), showed that while Milosevic was making his promise of access, a massive coverup of the Srebrenica killings was being attempted by the Bosnian Serbs.[2] Bodies buried in mass graves at the massacre sites were being dug up and reburied in remote areas along the Drina River on the Serb border. The fuel required by the backhoes and bulldozers that were used to carry out this work was supplied by Mladic, who in turn generally obtained his military support from the Yugoslav army in Belgrade. When I met with Milosevic on October 24, the photos taken on October 20 showed that the reburial work was under way. This may help explain the reason for the Serb dictator's blithe promise to me that international investigators could be given access to Srebrenica: he may have been told by the Bosnian Serbs that the evidence of what had happened on July 11 and 12 would soon be removed from the area.

Milosevic was—and for five more years continued to be—at the center of the Balkan crisis. Although he was finally ousted by a popular democratic revolt in Serbia in October 2000, I often agonized during the long years when Milosevic continued in power over whether we were right to deal with him as we did in the fall of 1995, coercing him to cooperate on human rights in Bosnia in order to negotiate the terms of peace with him at Dayton.

By 1995 Milosevic had started three wars that had led to the destruction of Yugoslavia, and he was widely regarded as the unseen force behind the Bosnian Serbs and their criminal conduct in Srebrenica and elsewhere. Should we have simply refused to deal with him, and worked only to support his opponents? Should NATO's military campaign against the Bosnian Serbs have been taken directly to Belgrade in 1995 in order to punish and isolate Milosevic instead of enhancing his status by negotiating with him, as we did at Dayton? If we had taken this approach, what would have happened on the ground? Would thousands more have been killed? Would the Banja Luka crisis have exploded? Would the war have widened? Or would we have stood a better chance of stopping Milosevic before he started his fourth war, this time in Kosovo, three years later? These are questions I have never been able to answer, least of all for myself. The bottom line is that we made a choice in 1995 to save lives and secure peace in Bosnia, but Milosevic survived and the larger crisis continued.

After the Milosevic meeting, I began the frenzied planning of next moves that characterized all my Balkan missions. First, I had to reach Washington so that I could work out a coordinated press strategy with Holbrooke and Nick Burns, the State Department spokesman. I wanted to make sure Holbrooke did not exaggerate Milosevic's commitment to me. At this point Holbrooke and I were again disagreeing over our policy on U.N. sanctions against Serbia, and the following morning there was to be a White House meeting to decide whether to lift the sanctions before Dayton. I was against any form of sanctions relief for Belgrade until Milosevic had taken major human rights steps, such as arranging for the release of prisoners, accounting for the missing, cooperating with War Crimes Tribunal investigations, and reining in the Bosnian Serbs in Banja Luka. Holbrooke, on the other hand, wanted to suspend (but not lift) the sanctions before Dayton as an inducement for Serb flexibility on territorial issues at the negotiating table.

From Belgrade I reached Holbrooke, and later Sandy Berger, and argued that we would undermine our entire human rights strategy if we suspended sanctions now. Holbrooke agreed not to hype Milosevic's promises to me, but he made clear that he felt we now had Milosevic on the hook and wanted the sanctions suspended to keep him there. At the White House meeting the next day the sanctions were kept in place on the strong urging of Madeleine Albright and Leon Fuerth, Vice President Gore's national security advisor, whose views were similar to mine.[3] I felt relieved.

I was fogged in at the airport as I waited to leave Belgrade for Zagreb after my meeting with Milosevic. The fog seemed to symbolize the political distance between the two capitals, as well as the difficulty of getting to Banja Luka where the war was still playing out. I used the morning to plan a trip to Banja Luka two days later to test Milosevic's commitment. I called Milutinovic, the Serbian foreign minister, and told him I was not prepared to say anything positive about Milosevic's public statement unless concrete steps were taken to implement it. This meant allowing freedom of travel immediately for me, for the Red Cross, and for the international press throughout all areas held by the Bosnian Serbs. Milutinovic told me he would "work out the technologies" with Nikola Koljevic (a Milosevic protégé in the Bosnian Serb leadership group in Banja Luka) and get back to me as soon as possible through our embassy in Belgrade.

When the fog lifted I flew to Croatia to repeat my message to Tudjman's deputy prime minister, Ivica Kostovic (Tudjman himself was on vacation)—protect the Serbs in Croatia and allow them to return to their homes. As an incentive I told Kostovic I had gotten commitments from Milosevic to find and release the missing Croat men in Banja Luka and to allow Croatia to increase the size of its "liaison office" in Belgrade so that it could process applications of Krajina Serb refugees to return. With the Dayton talks fast approaching, Kostovic was more accommodating than he had been in our last discussion. He agreed to allow some Serbs to return (as it turned out later, very few) on "humanitarian grounds," to extend the ninety-day limit for Serbs to reclaim their property, and to provide more police to "protect the safety" of the several thousand Serbs who still remained in the Krajina.

After my discussion with Kostovic, I whirled through a series of meetings—first with the Red Cross, to review lists of missing persons and suspected locations of detention camps; then with the U.N. high commissioner for refugees, to brief the Zagreb representative on my interviews with the Muslims who had been forced out of Banja Luka; and finally with Bosnian Federation vice president Ejup Ganic, to urge the Bosnian government to accept the voluntary return of Bosnian refugees from Croatia. After all these discussions I had only twenty minutes before a scheduled press conference to talk to Holbrooke again to make sure we were saying the same thing about Milosevic's commitment to me to open up Banja Luka and other Bosnian Serb areas.

I told Holbrooke I wanted to play down what Milosevic had said in Belgrade because it was still just a promise. We decided that I would use the press conference to hit the Croatians hard for causing the human rights crisis in Krajina, keeping the public pressure on Tudjman just as we were keeping it on Milosevic. Since I knew the U.N. sanctions against Serbia were not going to be lifted until a peace agreement was signed, I felt I had Washington's support for maintaining a tough position on human rights.

## Banja Luka

During the early fall of 1995, Banja Luka was at the heart of the Bosnia crisis. The largest Serb-held city, it had come to symbolize the endgame of the war. Revitalized Croat-Muslim Federation forces were pushing hard to capture it and reverse years of Serb territorial conquests. Banja Luka was also the place where the spiral of ethnic brutality had begun four years earlier.

The antiseptic term "ethnic cleansing" had first been used in 1991 to describe the brutal Serb paramilitary campaigns of rounding up, expelling, torturing, and murdering Muslims and Croats in Banja

Luka and the nearby towns of Prijedor, Sanski Most, and Omarska. What happened in Srebrenica in 1995 was the logical outcome of what had happened earlier in Banja Luka. Since no one had tried to stop it then, the ethnic war against civilians continued until it finally encountered resistance. When NATO at last responded to Bosnian Serb aggression by sustained bombing of military targets during the first half of September 1995, in addition to the genocide at Srebrenica it was the atrocities four years earlier in Banja Luka that everyone remembered.

Two fateful decisions were made in the second half of September that shaped the path to Dayton. The first was made by the Croat-Muslim Federation forces *not* to extend their ground offensive against the Bosnian Serbs to Banja Luka. The halting of Federation troops west of the Bosnian Serb stronghold was influenced by Richard Holbrooke and his negotiating team, who had told Tudjman on September 17 that the seizure of Banja Luka would further destabilize the region by creating two hundred thousand more Bosnian Serb refugees. This would make the peace process even more difficult since, as Holbrooke later wrote, "the city was unquestionably within the Serb portion of Bosnia."[4] The second decision was made by the Bosnian Serbs, probably abetted by Milosevic, to unleash a final round of ethnic expulsions of the Muslim and Croat minorities in Banja Luka to shore up Serb control of the city.

As a result of these two decisions, Milosevic came to Dayton with Banja Luka still in his pocket. Furthermore, he was now in a position to earn points from the West for being cooperative on human rights by ultimately reining in the Bosnian Serb ethnic cleansing in Banja Luka, in which he himself was complicit. This was vintage Milosevic—using every opportunity to create crises and then gain tactical advantage by solving them.

Looking back, I can see more clearly than I did at the time that October 1995 was an especially dangerous period of testing for both local and international actors in the Bosnia conflict. We were testing the Balkan leaders and they were testing us. Having finally demonstrated the political will to use military force to stop the atrocities, the United States was now showing its diplomatic will to exact a price from the Balkan leaders for our sponsorship of the peace process.

But once again, in retrospect, there are legitimate questions about this strategy. Did we insist on enough? Milosevic and Tudjman were both eager to get the best possible territorial deal for themselves and their surrogates at Dayton, and they proved willing to make concessions where necessary. But by pressing them to make gestures on human rights as the price of admission to Dayton, were we also giving them a legitimacy that would prolong their stranglehold on Balkan politics? Did we have a choice? Short of further military action, what could we have done to reduce the power of Milosevic and Tudjman on the eve of the peace talks while at the same time inducing them to end nearly four years of war? The intense debates in Washington in the fall of 1995 over sanctions policy and the feasibility of holding the Balkan leaders accountable for their war crimes reflected all of these fateful questions.

On October 25, in Zagreb, I began planning my Banja Luka trip. I set up a conference call with the State Department's Balkan Task Force in Washington and the U.S. embassy in Belgrade to get agreement on my message to the Bosnian Serbs. Since their leaders were under indictment for war crimes and we were refusing to negotiate with them, I would focus my mission exclusively on saving civilians and locating the missing.

No U.S. diplomat had made the trip to Banja Luka since the beginning of the war in 1992. Since sporadic fighting was still going on across the "confrontation line" separating Federation-held territory from the Bosnian Serb areas, security was a huge concern. Many questions had to be answered quickly. What weapons should our security officers carry? How should we travel—by U.N. helicopter, with the risk of being shot at or fogged in; or by ground transport from Zagreb, Belgrade, or Sarajevo, avoiding the fog but running an even greater risk of being fired on or hitting a land mine when we crossed the confrontation line? Another issue was whether I should take the press with me. Could I get Washington to approve? Could I get the United Nations to waive its rule limiting travel on U.N. helicopters in combat areas to government officials? Finally, the Red Cross was skittish about cooperating with my mission for fear of compromising its independence. Could I persuade them to come in order to implement Milosevic's commitment to me to open the Bosnian Serb area to international inspection? These questions had to be answered right away, and a trip more complex than diplomatic missions planned far in advance had to be organized overnight.

Thanks to an all-out effort by the staff of the Zagreb embassy, the logistical arrangements quickly fell into place. But as I sat down to an interview at Galbraith's house with Roger Cohen and Ray Bonner of the *New York Times,* I still had no clearance from Washington to make the hazardous trip to Banja Luka. To complicate things further, during the interview I received a call from Matt Hodis, head of Bosnia operations for the War Crimes Tribunal, who had heard about the trip and wanted to brief me immediately on how my meetings in Banja Luka could lay the groundwork for arresting Karadzic and Mladic. I knew that until there was a peace agreement with troops to enforce it, arrests would be impossible. But I wanted to coordinate with the tribunal. I told Hodis to come over.

The scene in Galbraith's dining room was surreal. While I huddled in the corner with Hodis—Cohen and Bonner straining to hear our conversation—Galbraith took a call from Washington giving me the green light for my mission. The State Department Press Office wanted me to take Cohen with me, but no other reporters. Cohen declined but passed his invitation on to Bonner, who immediately accepted. I decided to ignore Washington's effort to micromanage my passenger list, and told Bonner to be at the airport the next morning at 6:00 A.M. I also called Christine Spolar of the *Washington Post,* who was in Zagreb, and asked her to join us. By midnight my mission was set to go. I felt like a human rights explorer setting out for the frontier.

Long after midnight I got a call from Nancy Ely-Raphel, my former deputy in the human rights bureau, who was now on Holbrooke's staff in Washington. Nancy told me that Warren Christopher wanted me to postpone my mission, because of new security reports that increased shooting along the confrontation line over the past two days now made conditions too dangerous for travel outside Banja Luka. This meant I would not be able to reach the prison camps, nor establish the freedom of movement throughout Bosnian Serb territory that I had fought for with Milosevic. Feeling defeated by this last-minute setback, I slept fitfully for a few hours. As I prepared to leave for the airport before dawn, I debated whether to go ahead with a scaled-back mission, but soon another stubborn Balkan fog had settled in and blocked all movement.

I had to wait for another day. But the following morning was no better for different reasons. The U.N. relief helicopter we were to fly on was shot at as it took off from Banja Luka, and the refugee van that was to drive us around the Bosnian Serb areas was hijacked. Grounded in Zagreb, I spent the time with Ray Bonner and Christine Spolar, giving them material for stories in the *New York Times* and *Washington Post* about our efforts to keep the pressure on Milosevic and Tudjman before Dayton.

Late in the morning I reached Nikola Koljevic, the Bosnian Serb official who had been designated as my contact, by phone in Banja Luka. He had been waiting for me to arrive and seemed relieved when I told him I had had to postpone my trip. Ironically, the fact that Koljevic did not have to host me in person in Banja Luka may have made it easier for him to deal with my requests. In exchange for my promise to get U.N. military observers into northern Bosnia towns where he said the Serbs were being harassed by the Croat-Muslim Federation forces, Koljevic agreed to open Bosnian Serb checkpoints to international reporters and allow the Red Cross access to six suspected Bosnian Serb detention centers. By the end of the day my intervention with Koljevic had opened the door for Jane Perlez of the *New York Times* to become the first reporter to get past the Serb checkpoints.[5]

I returned to Washington on October 28 without having gotten to Banja Luka, but I felt that at last I had begun to crack open the Bosnian Serb border. Holbrooke called as I was leaving Zagreb.

"The Secretary wants you to establish freedom of movement as soon as possible. Let's assess the situation again next week. Maybe you can go in then."

## Dayton

Washington, as always, was a cold bath even compared to the challenges and frustrations of the Balkans. My four days in the city before leaving for Dayton on November 2 were filled with reminders about how little political support we still had for what we were trying to do.

Particularly chilling was a round of visits and phone calls to members of Congress. At the request of Wendy Sherman, the State Department's assistant secretary for legislative affairs, I concentrated on members of both parties who had shown interest in human rights, sounding them out on the deployment of U.S. troops as part of a NATO peacekeeping force. A typical response reflecting the mood of the House majority was Representative John Porter's assertion that "people see Bosnia as Clinton's Vietnam." Since I had worked closely on other human rights issues with Porter, a moderate Republican from Illinois and co-chair (with Republican senator Alphonse D'Amato of New York) of the congressional Helsinki Commission, his opinion was especially discouraging. Porter and other members were skeptical about the peace process, claiming there was little domestic interest in Bosnia and casting blame on the President for failing to articulate to the American people what was at stake in the Balkans. While it was true that Clinton had not addressed Bosnia as a bully-pulpit priority and had ruled out sending U.S. ground troops two years earlier, the sniping on the Hill was typical of the preemptive Washington blame game that was taking place on the eve of a momentous foreign policy decision.

Off the Hill the climate was somewhat less harsh but still turbulent. I had several meetings with my old colleagues from human rights organizations who were heavily involved in Bosnia. Jim O'Dea, the Washington director of Amnesty International, on whose board I had once served, complimented me on my tough public messages about the ethnic cleansing in Banja Luka and the Krajina, but he, like other human rights leaders, was reluctant to address the military aspects of the peace process. A decade earlier, Amnesty had sharply criticized human rights atrocities arising from the U.S. military role in Nicaragua and other parts of Central America, and now it was reluctant to embrace a different kind of U.S. military intervention to protect human rights in Bosnia. Amnesty had no policy on military intervention, O'Dea said. That was also true of the other major organizations like Human Rights Watch and the Lawyers Committee for Human Rights that were following the Balkans. Mike Posner, executive director of the Lawyers Committee, had long been active in pushing for a strong War Crimes Tribunal, but the Committee had not yet endorsed the role of an international military force to arrest war criminals.

Despite the cool reception our policy was receiving in Washington, I felt increasingly optimistic that we were on the right track. On October 29, the Bosnian Serbs released the first of the Banja Luka prisoners we had been pressing Milosevic about. The next day Alex Braunwalder, head of the regional Red Cross office, met in Banja Luka with Nikola Koljevic, my Bosnian Serb contact. Koljevic told Braunwalder that on the basis of my earlier appeal, the Red Cross would now be given access to all suspected detention sites in the Banja Luka area, and that any Muslims remaining in the area "would be allowed to stay or leave without condition or interference." These concessions would have to be tested, but Braunwalder gave me credit for them in his message to the Red Cross headquarters in Geneva. Meanwhile, the opening of Bosnian Serb areas to the international press now also seemed to be occurring. Stories were being filed from Bosnian Serb territory by Jane Perlez of the *New York Times,* Christine Spolar of the *Washington Post,* Jane Wilkinson of the *Los Angeles Times,* Martha Raddatz of National Public Radio, as well as reporters for ABC News and the Associated Press, all of whom had crossed for the first time through Bosnian Serb checkpoints.

Back in Washington, Bosnia interventionists had passed through an important bureaucratic roadblock. After a battle lasting many months, proponents of a more aggressive Bosnia policy had finally won interagency approval of language for the U.S. position going into Dayton that reflected the realities of what had happened on the ground. Instead of standing above the fray, casting blame on all sides, and professing to be "neutral," as the United States and the Europeans had done for the past four years, our position as articulated on October 31 by Nick Burns, the State Department spokesman, was blunt and specific: "We are not neutral—we are evenhanded. We believe the Serbs are the aggressors."[6]

On Thursday, November 2, I flew to Dayton in an Air Force plane from Andrews Air Force Base. The rest of the U.S. delegation had gone earlier for the formal opening of the talks on November 1, but I had stayed behind to finish my round of consultations on the Hill and meetings with human rights groups. Looking out the window at the Appalachian Mountains ablaze in fall colors, I savored the journey from my days of isolation earlier in the year to this moment when human rights finally seemed to be at the center of our newly aggressive Bosnia policy.

When I landed at Dayton's Wright-Patterson Air Force Base, I was met by the State Department's Bosnia desk officer, Phil Goldberg, who had been a key supporter of my human rights work throughout the fall. As we drove together to the conference headquarters, Goldberg briefed me on the negotiating dynamic that was beginning to develop at the conference.

The Bosnians were making international action on human rights a condition of their participation in the talks. Izetbegovic had told Christopher the day before that the Bosnian government was counting on my missions to open up Banja Luka and Srebrenica to international investigations. The Bosnians' willingness to negotiate in Dayton on territorial issues would depend on continued U.S. efforts to bring to light all that had happened in these two symbolic centers of the war and hold accountable those who had committed the war crimes and genocide of the past four years. To help get the talks on track, Holbrooke wanted me to meet immediately with representatives of the Contact Group countries (Britain, France, Italy, Germany, and Russia) to brief them on my travels, and then to press Milosevic and Koljevic for more progress on the Banja Luka missing. After that, I was to return to Bosnia to keep the spotlight on human rights while the talks were proceeding.

As I went through this first round of Dayton meetings I felt like a skunk whose unpleasant message nearly everyone wanted to avoid. As our Bosnia strategy had demonstrated throughout the fall, human rights were by definition at the center of every issue that the peace conference would face. Still, it was obvious that not only the Balkan leaders (except Izetbegovic), but also the Europeans and some Americans were not pleased to find themselves discussing war crimes and missing persons on an American military base with an American human rights official.

During my twenty-four hours in Dayton before leaving again for Bosnia, I attended three bizarre meetings that captured the mood of the negotiations and the character of the Balkan players in the Dayton drama.

The first was a meeting of the Bosnia Federation leaders, Izetbegovic and Tudjman, and their delegations, chaired by Richard Holbrooke. Both leaders complained endlessly about what the Serbs had done to the Muslims and Croats, and as usual they found nothing good to say about each other and offered no ground for cooperation. Holbrooke pressed them to make progress on allowing the return of Muslim and Croat refugees to two Federation towns—Jajce, held by the Croats, and Bugojno, held by the Muslims. "If we can't make progress on this, we can't make progress on anything," Holbrooke told the group. As Izetbegovic and Tudjman argued back and forth, Holbrooke scribbled a note to me. "The guy across from you [Croatian defense minister Gojko Susak] is a dangerous war criminal who ought to be indicted." After an hour of this, Holbrooke stood up and threatened to end the talks if the two sides were not willing to allow at least a hundred Croat and Muslim refugees to return to the two towns. "You'll never get anywhere with Milosevic if you go on like this," he said. Finally, after another round of recriminations against the mayors of Jajce (by the Bosnian delegation) and Bugojno (by the Croats), an agreement was struck for the return of a hundred refugees each. I was asked to implement it by going to Bugojno and Jajce on my way to Banja Luka. I was not optimistic about the outcome.

The second meeting was even more bizarre. After talking to him over the phone several times during the previous ten days about our search for the missing in Banja Luka, I arranged a meeting with Nikola Koljevic, who had been given a seat on the Serb delegation. He insisted on meeting in his room. When I got there I could see why. Completely drunk and barely able to talk, Koljevic, a devotee of Shakespeare who had once taught in a Cleveland high school, opened our meeting by complaining about having no phone in his room (on Milosevic's orders, I was later told). After telling him this was a problem for him, not for me, I explained to Koljevic that I planned to travel to Banja Luka the next week and wanted him to help arrange meetings for me. This opened the floodgates. Koljevic babbled on about how my trip could help *him,* how I could "intervene" on his behalf with Karadzic and the Bosnian Serb military, and how they "might even be willing to release" the American reporter, David Rohde, who had been arrested in Bosnian Serb territory on October 29. Realizing that Koljevic was a dead end (but certainly not a dry hole), I told him that Karadzic was an indicted war criminal whose only meeting with an international official would be when he was arrested, and that Milosevic knew that David Rohde must be released immediately or the Serb side would not be allowed to participate further in the peace talks.

After my strange encounter with Koljevic, I sought out the Serb strongman himself. Ensconced in the barracks suite set aside for the head of the Serb delegation, Milosevic seemed to be savoring the irony of his overnight transformation from warlord to peacemaker and the strong position he had managed to carve out for himself with minimal concessions as the conference got under way. He had been invited to the United States; his rival, Karadzic, was now firmly under his control; and his enemies, the Croats and Muslims, were bickering with each other. Although my presence was an unpleasant reminder of the many scores that remained to be settled with him at Dayton and beyond, Milosevic was in an expansive mood as he responded to my questions about cooperating with international investigations, guaranteeing me access to Banja Luka and Srebrenica, and releasing David Rohde. He told me he would meet with Izetbegovic "*tonight*—to arrange the release of *all* prisoners." As for Banja Luka and Srebrenica, "your security is assured, although I'm not responsible for all that has gone on there." The deftness Milosevic demonstrated in deflecting the crimes and problems of his own making to his Bosnian Serb subordinates was breathtaking. As for David Rohde, "He will be released once I get Karadzic to cooperate." Sure enough, on November 8, when I was on my way to Banja Luka, the Bosnian Serbs turned Rohde over to an officer from our Sarajevo embassy. There was no question about who was in charge.

## Keeping the Pressure On

My trip back to Bosnia after the first week of Dayton was intended to keep the pressure on Milosevic to open up the Bosnian Serb territory to international scrutiny and pave the way for NATO forces to enter. The situation was extremely tense along the confrontation line, where a month earlier Federation troops had halted their advance toward Banja Luka. The road north of the bombed-out city of Mrkonic Grad went through a mountainous ten-kilometer no-man's-land that no international official had crossed in four years.

I set out from Sarajevo to travel this route. By crossing through the confrontation zone I would be able to demonstrate the stability of the cease-fire and show the Serbs in Banja Luka (who had begun to break away from Karadzic and his hardline nationalists) that there were benefits to be gained from cooperating with the Dayton process. On the way I would stop in the Federation towns of Bogojno and Jajce to prod their mayors to allow Croat and Muslim families to return to their homes.

The roads were already icy in the early Balkan winter as we moved out of Sarajevo on November 7 in two armored humvees, the squat military vehicles used for hazardous interior travel in Bosnia. Joining me were Crystal Nix, head of the war crimes office in the human rights bureau, who had traveled with me to Rwanda and had been instrumental in setting up the International Criminal Tribunal for Rwanda, Rob Malley, a National Security Council aide who later became special assistant to National Security Advisor Sandy Berger and the NSC specialist on the Middle East; and two foreign service officers from the embassy in Sarajevo, Karen Decker and Phil Laidlaw. Our humvees were driven by three intrepid Sarajevo-based diplomatic security agents. While not exactly Mission Impossible, our trip would prove to be difficult, and our team would perform well.

The devastation of central Bosnia was overwhelming, even to hardened Balkan observers. Everywhere we saw destroyed houses, scattered and broken furniture, burned-out cars, cratered roads, animal carcasses—the landscape of four years of massive killing. Here and there, figures bundled in rags against the bitter cold could be seen picking over the ruins of their homes, while crows and vultures circled overhead. The poisoned atmosphere of ethnic distrust was captured in a comment to me by the Bosnian Croat mayor of Jajce when I urged him to allow Muslim families to return to his town: "As soon as Croats are allowed to return to Bogojno, Muslims will be allowed to return to Jajce. But Bogojno must go first because we don't trust the Muslims."

North of Jajce we entered the zone of confrontation. Soldiers with the British battalion of U.N. peacekeepers helped us negotiate our way through a series of tense Croat checkpoints and barricades as far as Mrkonic Grad. From there, we were on our own. Earlier that morning, Phil Goldberg, the Bosnia desk officer, had called me from Dayton over my secure satellite phone to pass on an unconfirmed report that fighting had broken out to the west of our location in the confrontation zone. Phil told me to assess the situation and decide whether to continue or turn back. After getting in touch with the British commander, who told me his intelligence indicated that the road north to Banja Luka was quiet, I called a brief meeting of our team. Everyone agreed to go ahead with our mission.

The two humvees wound slowly along a deserted icy road that snaked above the ravine of the Vrbass River. The only sign of life was a small group of disheveled, heavily armed Serb soldiers who appeared to be drunk as they stopped us in front of a makeshift wooden barrier. After checking our documents, they pulled landmines out of the road in front of us and lined them up one by one, glinting in the sun at the base of a rocky cliff—our first concrete evidence that Milosevic had passed the word to give us safe passage. At this point Crystal and I began rehearsing how to deal with Karadzic if, as Holbrooke predicted, he showed up in Banja Luka with television cameras to try to take credit for allowing my trip. No handshake. "I don't recognize you or your government," I would say. "I'm here to save lives." Suddenly, we were jolted in our seats as our diplomatic security agent, driving the lead humvee, sped up the caravan. He was clearly agitated. For the next few minutes we were deathly silent. Our agent finally broke the silence by telling us that he had spotted a Croat sniper on the hillside above the road who had looked as if he might take a shot at the landmines. Had he done so, this would have given the Croats a golden opportunity to blame the Serbs for blowing up an American diplomatic convoy trying to cross the border.

As we pulled into Banja Luka we were greeted not by Karadzic but by Milosevic's deputy interior minister, Drago Dragicevic, and twenty heavily armed Serb red beret troops from Belgrade. Dragicevic shook my hand with a bone-crushing grip, proclaiming more loudly than seemed necessary, "Your security is one hundred percent guaranteed." Relieved after our harrowing race across the confrontation line, I nevertheless wondered whether our newfound security was a sign of progress at Dayton or simply another effort by Milosevic to outmaneuver his opponents. Probably both, I thought.

My Belgrade escorts took me through a round of meetings with assorted Banja Luka municipal officials. I secured a "pledge" from the mayor—a typical communist city boss surrounded by deputies straight out of central casting—that he would work with the Red Cross to locate missing people on their list of victims of the September ethnic expulsion campaign. I also raised the issue of war criminals with the mayor and the police chief, warning them that life would not return to normal in Banja Luka until Karadzic, Mladic, and others responsible for all the problems they had been through were arrested and sent to The Hague. My one unescorted meeting was with the local Catholic bishop, Tomas Komarica, a Bosnian Croat who had spent the fall under house arrest and was released after my departure.

On the way back to Sarajevo our humvee slid off the icy road twice, barely avoiding hitting a tree and hurtling down a cliff as we raced to reach the city before it was barricaded at curfew by U.N. troops. After one of our near disasters, my security agent turned to me with a wry grin and offered up a motto for our mission: "You know, if you're not living on the edge, you're taking up too much space."

## The Cost of Peace

I flew back to the United States on November 12. The Dayton negotiations were entering a prolonged period of deadlock and the spotlight had swung back to Washington, where Richard Goldstone, the chief prosecutor of the War Crimes Tribunal, was beginning a four-day visit. Goldstone had come at David Scheffer's and my suggestion to build public support for the Tribunal during the peace negotiations. Since I had just returned from Bosnia, where my message on war crimes had been widely reported, the press was speculating that I was trying to put pressure on the negotiations to enhance the tribunal's role after a settlement. After my meeting with Goldstone, Holbrooke asked me to come back to Dayton and stay until the end of the negotiations. I was reluctant to go because I was afraid I would be sidelined. When I agreed, I made it clear that I wanted to ensure that language would be inserted into the peace treaty that would require all parties to Dayton to cooperate with the orders of the tribunal.

The arrest and prosecution of war criminals was one of the most important and far-reaching issues of the Bosnia peace process. I held the view, which I frequently expressed, that peace would not come to the Balkans until those who had instigated and committed genocide and crimes against humanity were held accountable for what they had done. This was the lesson of the Nuremberg Trials, and it was the message of the hundreds of thousands of victims of ethnic killings and their survivors in Bosnia, Croatia, and other parts of the former Yugoslavia. Until the instigators of genocide were held responsible for their crimes, the cycle of revenge would continue and the mantle of collective guilt would remain tightly wrapped around each ethnic group, blocking the path toward peace. At the local level, extreme nationalists like Radovan Karadzic would be able to prevent the rise of moderates and continue to fan the flames of ethnic and religious hatred. Refugees would not want or be able to return to their homes. Criminal violence and instability would hamper international policing and peacekeeping. This is why we had created the War Crimes Tribunal in the first place, and now it was time for it to do its work.

But another point of view on war crimes surfaced at Dayton. In many ways it symbolized the underlying weakness and fragmentation of the coalition behind the entire peace process. On a philosophical level, opponents of the tribunal argued that peace can only be built on compromise, and that the way to get people to stop killing each other is to focus their attention on the future, not the past. On a practical level, they argued that the threat of prosecution would drive the parties away from the negotiating table. It would prevent the lifting of sanctions and the resumption of normal economic relations. It would require international soldiers to act as police.

These objections revealed a deep split in the coalition over how to finish the job of making peace. The conservative governments of three key European countries had soft spots for the aggressors—the British and French for the Serbs, and the Germans for the Croats—and all were suspicious of the Bosnian Muslims, whom they regarded as promoters of dangerous Islamic politics in Europe. In some ways the U.S. position was not much stronger. Defense Secretary William Perry and his deputy, Walt Slocombe (who had worked with me twenty years earlier on Mort Halperin's wiretap case against Richard Nixon and Henry Kissinger), made it clear that the Pentagon would oppose any mandate for peacekeeping in Bosnia that might require U.S. soldiers to act as policemen and arrest war criminals. President Clinton was preoccupied by the congressional opposition to sending U.S. troops to the Balkans. And Warren Christopher and Richard Holbrooke, although supportive of my position, were worried that pushing the tribunal issue too far might make Milosevic and Tudjman less cooperative at the negotiating table.

But the war crimes issue would not go away, and I did my best to keep it alive in Dayton. On November 16, Richard Goldstone announced in The Hague that the tribunal was issuing a new indictment of Radovan Karadzic and Ratko Mladic for genocide and crimes against humanity for their central roles in planning and executing the premeditated mass murder of seven thousand Muslim men from Srebrenica. Goldstone's meetings in Washington with Warren Christopher, Tony Lake, and CIA Director John Deutch were covered extensively by the press, which editorialized about the danger that the Dayton negotiations could undermine the tribunal just as it was getting serious.[7] Goldstone called me in Dayton to tell me that his meetings in Washington had been productive. He was particularly pleased that Lake had promised to have a secure phone line installed connecting Goldstone's office in The Hague directly to the offices of Lake, Christopher, and Deutch so that the prosecutor could request information and evidence about war crimes without going first through endless bureaucratic channels.

Meanwhile, Milosevic and Tudjman played their roles to the hilt as the heavies in the war crimes drama. Milosevic told Holbrooke that the best way to get rid of war criminals was to allow them to run for office—a not-very-veiled appeal on behalf of his erstwhile protégé, Karadzic, to compete for the presidency of the Bosnian Serb entity that was widely expected to be created at Dayton. This infuriated Holbrooke, who had earlier sidetracked Karadzic and refused to deal with him because of his status as an indicted war criminal. Holbrooke told me after this exchange that he would do everything possible to protect the tribunal in the negotiations. Meanwhile, Tudjman thumbed his nose at the tribunal by announcing at Dayton that he was promoting his favorite general, Tihomir Blaskic, who had been indicted for war crimes a month earlier. Since it was widely speculated that Milosevic and Tudjman were themselves under investigation in The Hague, their actions at Dayton gave the tribunal an unexpected boost.

Our battle to protect the War Crimes Tribunal during the negotiations was fought on two fronts. Even though it was an independent institution created by the U.N. Security Council, the tribunal's ability to function in the Balkans would have been severely compromised by an agreement that either explicitly provided amnesty to war criminals or was silent on the tribunal's authority to prosecute them. Since four of the five permanent Security Council members (Britain, France, Russia, and the United States) were involved in the negotiations, failure to reaffirm the tribunal's authority at Dayton would have been seen as a major setback of the effort to bring war criminals to justice.

The second front in the war crimes battle was the debate over the future of the U.N. sanctions against Milosevic's government. Along with the NATO bombing, the sanctions had been the main source of pressure to bring Milosevic to the negotiating table. Before coming to Dayton, Milosevic had made clear that he expected the sanctions to be lifted. In response, Holbrooke had indicated that sanctions relief would be his reward for full cooperation with the peace process and the signing of an agreement. But what did "cooperation" mean? Did it include cooperating with the War Crimes Tribunal? If so, what would be the consequences down the road of failing to cooperate with the tribunal? These were the issues I had discussed five months earlier with Bob Frasure.

The pressures in Dayton to capitulate on both fronts were enormous. The focal point of the negotiations was the territorial struggle over the future map of Bosnia. The Serbs, Croats, and Muslims each had territorial claims over the entities that would make up the post-Dayton state of Bosnia and Herzegovina, and the political energies of the international negotiators headed by Holbrooke were almost entirely consumed by trying to resolve these conflicting claims. Most other contentious issues were set aside or ignored, to be decided by technicians or left unresolved. Problems such as how to administer and police the peace agreement, how to define the mandate of a new peacekeeping force, how to draft a legal framework and constitution for the new state of Bosnia and its constituent entities, and how to deal with war criminals were kept off the negotiating table for most of the three-week peace conference and left largely to a team of U.S. experts to address in drafting a "Framework Agreement" and set of annexes.

The war crimes issue was particularly vulnerable to indecision because no one at Dayton wanted to deal with it except the Bosnian Muslims and the Americans, and the Americans were internally divided on the issue. The Pentagon wanted to make sure NATO troops would not be required to hunt down and arrest war criminals. Christopher and Holbrooke hoped to protect the tribunal by explicitly requiring the warring parties to cooperate with it, yet they felt that because of congressional resistance to committing U.S. troops to peacekeeping in Bosnia, they were powerless to take on the Pentagon on the arrest issue.

But there were strong counterpressures to reinforce the tribunal at Dayton. Goldstone's visit to Washington and the new indictment of Karadzic and Mladic for their role in the Srebrenica genocide galvanized the human rights community and the tribunal's congressional supporters and captured the attention of the U.S. press and editorial writers. After I called her from Dayton, Madeleine Albright connected with Christopher from the United Nations, underscoring that the United States had led the way in creating the tribunal in 1993 during the dark early days of the Bosnian war and should now work to strengthen it as an instrument of peace.

Albright's intervention made a difference. Jim O'Brien, her staff representative on Holbrooke's negotiating team, a young lawyer on loan from the State Department Legal Adviser's Office, drafted language for the Framework Agreement and the Bosnia Constitution requiring "all competent authorities in Bosnia and Herzegovina [to] cooperate with and provide unrestricted access to . . . the International Criminal Tribunal for the Former Yugoslavia."[8] Working with David Scheffer and me O'Brien also devised a formula for enforcing this "cooperation" requirement by maintaining a credible threat of renewed sanctions for noncooperation. We knew that the sanctions on Belgrade were likely to be lifted by the U.N. Security Council once a peace agreement was signed, so we began to promote a position that called for periodic Security Council review of compliance with the agreement, including cooperation with the tribunal, and an affirmative vote by the council to continue the sanctions relief. That way the United States would be able to get the council to reimpose sanctions for noncompliance simply by vetoing a resolution for continued relief. Christopher, Holbrooke, and the White House accepted this approach.

In the eye of the storm, when the negotiations were temporarily stalemated over territorial issues, Christopher invited me to go for a walk with him in the bitter cold around the drab Air Force barracks that had become our prisonlike home. I was awed by the formidable stamina of the seventy-year-old Secretary of State, who was locked in around-the-clock negotiations with the Balkan scorpions in the Dayton bottle. As we walked he gave me his trenchant assessment of the three leaders: Milosevic, evil and completely untrustworthy; Tudjman, the scavenger, hunting for prey in the shadow of Milosevic; Izetbegovic, the prisoner of a desperate and victimized past. The Secretary commended me for spotlighting the horrors of Bosnia and propelling human rights to the center of our policy. He then commented on a memo I had sent him earlier in the week questioning whether Bosnia would be ready for elections within nine months, as required by the draft Framework Agreement, unless leading war criminals like Karadzic were arrested well before then. Christopher urged me to be realistic, to recognize that the elections had to take place within the next year because Congress would not support the commitment of U.S. troops for longer than that, and to understand the limits of what we could expect to accomplish at Dayton on the issue of war crimes. I was pleased by the Secretary's praise, but sobered by his cautionary message about war crimes. I realized he was warning me that we might not be able to accomplish everything I was pushing for.

A day later the stalemate broke as Milosevic abandoned a key territorial demand in order to strengthen his position on other issues. The future of the city of Brcko, which he had insisted must be part of the Bosnian Serb entity, would now be determined by a separate international arbitration to be managed by a senior member of Holbrooke's team, Roberts Owen, a former State Department legal adviser. In a scramble of eleventh-hour negotiating, the war crimes issue was resolved by requiring the parties "to cooperate" with the tribunal. But an important clause, "and with its orders," was deleted from the Framework Agreement (it remained in the Bosnia Constitution) at the insistence of Milosevic. This deletion had the effect of appearing to exempt Serbia and Croatia from the tribunal's orders.[9]

The military annex to the agreement was silent on whether the new International Force (IFOR) could arrest indicted war criminals in Bosnia, but there was plenty of language to support an enterprising commander who chose to do so.[10] Disastrously, IFOR's first commander, Admiral Leighton "Snuffy" Smith, made clear from the moment he arrived that he had no intention of arresting anyone. In his first weeks on the ground Admiral Smith came to view the issue of war crimes investigations, as well as the War Crimes Tribunal that was pursuing them, as threats to his mission. The signal that he sent by defining his authority as narrowly as possible could not have been lost on Karadzic, Mladic, and other criminal architects of the Bosnian war.[11] Nor can it be assumed that Smith was acting on his own; his cautious approach to his mandate was a reflection of views that had been prevalent in the Pentagon and the White House ever since the Somalia disaster two years earlier.[12]

The benefits of Dayton outweighed the costs, thanks to the persistence of Richard Holbrooke and his negotiating team. Above all, it created a legal framework for breaking the cycle of violence that had gripped Bosnia for more than four years. By authorizing the entry into Bosnia of a large NATO-led peacekeeping force with more robust rules of engagement than its U.N. predecessor, the Dayton agreement at last provided the effective means for making peace. The disarmament requirements of the agreement defined IFOR's major task—moving the Serb, Croat, and Muslim military forces back into their barracks, locking up their weapons, and promoting the process of demobilization.[13] Within six months of IFOR's arrival in December 1995, this task was well on its way toward completion.

But the costs of Dayton were high. Because the negotiations had focused almost exclusively on the issue of territory, the agreement was vague on a wide range of other important issues. On balance, however, Dayton was a victory for human rights because it finally ended the genocide that had been raging in the heart of Europe for nearly four years and had by then claimed nearly a quarter of a million lives. Instead of settling such different matters as the authority of the international organization that would administer the treaty, the return of refugees, and the creation of new government institutions, the parties at Dayton left them to be worked out on the ground in Bosnia.

## Pursuing War Criminals

The most significant unfinished business of Dayton was the issue of war criminals. Although the mandate of the War Crimes Tribunal had been reaffirmed by the peace agreement, its work was made difficult in two key ways. The Dayton requirement of "cooperation" with the tribunal was vague and hard to enforce. More important, the mandate of the International Force in the agreement's military annex left indicted war criminals free to roam through Bosnia without fear of being hunted down by international troops. In fact, as I discovered myself when I went to make the first international investigation of the sites of the Srebrenica mass executions, the U.S. commanders of IFOR were going out of their way to keep their troops from coming into contact with war criminals or appearing to assist the tribunal in its investigative work.

I went to Srebrenica in January 1996 with the support of Richard Holbrooke and General Wesley Clark. They agreed with me that opening up eastern Bosnia and making progress on establishing accountability for what had happened at Srebrenica were essential for the Dayton agreement to begin to take hold. General Clark, a key member of the Dayton negotiating team who represented the Joint Chiefs of Staff in the peace process before, during, and after Dayton (and later was the supreme allied commander of NATO forces during the Kosovo conflict), was a strong proponent of war crimes prosecutions and my principal ally in the Pentagon. Unfortunately, Clark's views on war crimes differed from those of most other U.S. military leaders.

While planning my Srebrenica mission, I was surprised to learn that the IFOR commander, Admiral Smith, would not provide me with an IFOR escort. His ostensible reason was that IFOR had just arrived in Bosnia and was not yet familiar with the territory. I suspected that the real reason was the presence of two tribunal investigators on my team and the possibility that we might encounter war criminals during our mission. I had made a commitment to myself in July to go to Srebrenica to open it to war crimes investigators as soon as possible. Since IFOR would not escort me, I worked with Holbrooke to get Milosevic to allow me to go there from Belgrade. I knew there were risks involved in going to the site of the worst genocide in Europe since World War II under the protection of the man who had instigated it. But there were also benefits. Milosevic's commitment to Dayton would be tested, and I would be able to confront him with what I had witnessed.

After a long and grueling trek over ice and mud in eastern Bosnia, during which I retraced the death march of the seven thousand Muslim men, I met with Milosevic in Belgrade and recounted in excruciating detail what I had witnessed. I had seen the schoolhouse in Karakaj where Hurem Suljic was blindfolded on July 11 and led to the killing fields. I had also seen the burned-out warehouse in Bratunac where hundreds were herded in the night and assaulted with hand grenades and rocket launchers so that spattered blood was visible on the walls and the thirty-foot ceiling. When Milosevic tried to persuade me that the Muslims had been killed in battle, I told him that no battles had been fought by unarmed men in these places. For once, the Serb dictator fell silent and seemed trapped by what I was telling him.

When I returned to Sarajevo, Admiral Smith invited me to meet with him at his headquarters. My trip to Srebrenica had been widely praised in the media and in Washington for cracking open the site of the genocide.[14] Perhaps feeling under pressure, Smith somewhat softened his previously uncooperative position and agreed to allow the tribunal to begin war crimes investigations in eastern Bosnia. But on the issue of arrests, the admiral and other IFOR commanders adamantly refused to help, asserting that tracking down war criminals was not in their mandate. They were wrong, and their position was undermining the peace process.

The time to rid Bosnia of the leaders who had instigated and committed the massive crimes against humanity that had fueled the war was in the months immediately after Dayton. This was the time when war criminals like Karadzic were most discredited among their own supporters, and when IFOR's strength and credibility were greatest. Those months offered the best opportunity to stabilize the peace process by removing disruptive elements before they could regroup. But the failure of the Pentagon, the White House, the Congress, and the governments of other IFOR troop contributors to move quickly to arrest the war criminals sent a dangerous signal that they and their political patrons were safe in Bosnia, and beyond the reach of IFOR in Serbia and Croatia.

It is true that the war crimes issue was complex and there were no easy ways to resolve it. Logistically, the tracking of war criminals presented a major intelligence challenge. Operationally, arresting them required a combination of careful planning, surprise, and targeted use of force more suited to police work than peacekeeping. Politically, arrests of high-level figures like Karadzic would have to be authorized at the highest levels of the governments of participating IFOR troops because of the possibility of casualties and the effects on the peace process. In this risk-fraught environment caution ruled the day, and those who opposed the arrest of war criminals as a potential source of disruption were able to block all significant action in this area for more than a year after Dayton.

During this time I worked with other allies of the War Crimes Tribunal in the United States and Europe to try to reverse the situation. In February 1996, Holbrooke, Clark, and I succeeded in persuading the IFOR commander in Sarajevo to transport Bosnian Serb general Djordje Djukic and another lower-ranking Bosnian Serb officer, Aleksa Krsmanovic, to The Hague at the request of the tribunal. The two had been arrested by the new Bosnian government for their role in shelling civilians in Sarajevo. Flying the two Serb military officers to the tribunal was clearly preferable to leaving them in the hands of the Bosnians. Since they had not been arrested by IFOR, this kind of assistance did not imply a change in IFOR's basic policy of not tracking down war criminals. During the year after Dayton, IFOR troops did arrest four low-level people indicted by the tribunal who were "encountered" during routine peacekeeping activities, but Karadzic, Mladic, Croat general Dario Kordic, and other well-protected leaders under indictment remained at large.

Because of IFOR's intransigence, we turned to other strategies to try to remove war criminals from Bosnia. One idea pushed by Goldstone was to develop a special international police unit attached to the tribunal that would be able to conduct arrests with the help of an elite commando team. Goldstone broached this idea with me in The Hague in June 1996 and raised it simultaneously with Dutch defense minister Hans van Mierlo, who called me to his office to discuss it. Van Mierlo told me the Dutch would contribute personnel and train the commando team if it also had American and British members. I told him I would explore his proposal in Washington, and urged him to send an emissary to take it up directly with Lake, Christopher, Perry, and Deutch. In a memo to Christopher on June 19 arguing for the arrest of Karadzic before the Bosnian elections scheduled for September, I wrote that "the picture of an international community clutching desperately for diplomatic and economic tools [to oust

Karadzic] while the strongest military force in the world stands idly by is not an appealing one. The risk of inaction implicates our entire Bosnia policy and the credibility of NATO."

The Dutch proposal ran into the usual White House–Pentagon opposition to war crimes risk-taking. Instead of authorizing the arrest of Karadzic, the White House dispatched Holbrooke to Belgrade in July 1996 to work out an arrangement with Milosevic to have Karadzic removed from office as Bosnian Serb president before the elections. Karadzic stayed in Bosnia, however, and was later reported to have voted in the elections, which were won by hardline opponents of Dayton in many areas, particularly in the Bosnian Serb "Republic."

By mid-July 2002, the number of indicted war criminals in custody in The Hague had increased to 120.[15] Still, there was little change in the basic arrest policy of the NATO Stabilization Force (SFOR) that had succeeded IFOR after its one-year mandate ran out at the end of 1996. In most cases, arrests resulted from SFOR "encounters" with war criminals, or economic pressure on governments. Until the fall of the Milosevic regime in October 2000, this pressure had little effect on Serbia, where a number of key Bosnian Serbs such as General Mladic and Arkan (until his mysterious murder in January 2000) traveled freely. Serbia was a haven for war criminals, including Milosevic himself, following his indictment in June 1999 for war crimes in Kosovo. Economic pressure was more effective in Croatia. Tudjman's government was persuaded by the threat of losing international aid and World Bank loans to turn over to the tribunal generals Blaskic and Kordic, as well as several other high-level Croat officers and paramilitary leaders who had engineered the ethnic cleansing of central Bosnia.

As the tribunal's prison population swelled, so did U.S. contributions of money and personnel to help the tribunal conduct investigations and trials. By 2002, twenty-seven defendants from the former Yugoslavia had been convicted, and forty-three additional accused war criminals were in custody awaiting trial.[16] Clearly, the institution that we had started against great odds in 1993 had become a success.

But the cost of early inaction on war criminal arrests after Dayton was high. Although peace has slowly come to Bosnia, it would have come sooner if the international community, led by the United States, had moved early and decisively against war criminals. Many political hardliners were able to stay in power at all levels of government, and moderates were forced back for years on all sides. Corruption and organized crime flourished among the same groups that had led the campaigns of ethnic expulsion that sparked the war. Refugees were more hesitant to return to their homes in the years following Dayton when they knew that the war criminals who had expelled them were still at large. The credibility of international peacekeepers was lower than it should have been in the early years of peace because they allowed war criminals to roam freely: crossing through military checkpoints, defying arrest, and maintaining their own private security forces. Paradoxically, international troops have had to stay longer and in larger numbers in Bosnia because they did not arrest war criminals at the beginning of a mission that has now extended for nearly eight years.

Finally, and above all, Milosevic and Tudjman, the grand architects of war in the Balkans with whom we had to deal at Dayton in order to break the cycle of violence in Bosnia, were given new leases on their political lives in the years immediately following the peace agreement. Their renewed political vitality stemmed from the failure of the international community to root out the criminal networks they had established to carry out their earlier territorial ambitions. The signal that was sent when these networks were allowed to remain in place after Dayton was that the price of committing war crimes and crimes against humanity was still relatively low. Although an opening for democratic change in Croatia was created by Tudjman's death in 1999, Milosevic had calculated the year before—erroneously, as it turned out—that he could afford to start another war of ethnic expulsion, this time in Kosovo.

In September 1998 Madeleine Albright, now the Secretary of State, asked me to go to Kosovo to investigate reports of new ethnic cleansing and human rights atrocities. I traveled with Senator Bob Dole, the 1996 Republican candidate for President. By then, I had been working with Dole for more than a year in his capacity as chair of the International Commission on Missing Persons, tracking down records of the hundreds of thousands of Muslims, Croats, and Serbs who were still unaccounted for three years after Dayton. Our mission was to travel through the devastated villages and hamlets of Kosovo to find out who was responsible for forcing more than 250,000 Kosovar Albanians from their homes. We heard many accounts by victims and eyewitnesses of the systematic shelling of villages by Serb paramilitary forces, and the rounding up of military-age men—dramatic new evidence of an organized campaign to terrorize and drive out the non-Serb population of Kosovo. At the end of our fact-finding mission, we traveled to Belgrade to confront Milosevic with what we had learned about the role of Serb forces in Kosovo, and to warn him that the expulsion campaign must be stopped. His explanation was that his government was fighting terrorists. When we presented him with detailed evidence of attacks by Serbian security forces on the civilian population of Kosovo, including extensive house-burnings and the shelling of unarmed fleeing women and children, Milosevic angrily asserted that this was the propaganda of anti-Serb terrorists. He abruptly ended our meeting and signaled to an aide to cancel the formal luncheon he had planned for us. Before Senator Dole and I were unceremoniously escorted out of the presidential palace, I told Milosevic that his war crimes were catching up with him.

In Washington, our report was one of many factors that led to a strengthening of the U.S. response to the human rights crisis in Kosovo. Thanks to Senator Dole's stature and credibility, our testimony before the congressional Helsinki Commission helped build bipartisan support in the Congress for a final confrontation with Milosevic. During the fall of 1998 and winter of 1999, the Clinton administration made a series of decisions that led to a sustained NATO air campaign and eventually forced Milosevic to withdraw his forces from Kosovo, permitting the deployment of U.N. peacekeepers, and paving the way for the return of nearly a million Kosovar refugees.

Milosevic had now lost his fourth war. This time there was no Houdini escape for him. In September 2000, the people of Serbia overwhelmingly voted him out of office despite his own best efforts to rig the election. A year later he was arrested on the orders of a brave Serbian judge, flown to The Hague, and put on trial for genocide and crimes against humanity. A decade of Balkan war crimes had at last come to an end. From Prague, where I was serving as U.S. ambassador to the Czech Republic, I looked back on eight years of witnessing genocide in the remnants of what was once Yugoslavia, and hoped that the long nightmare of the people of the Balkans would finally be over.

# CHAPTER 7

# THE CHINA SYNDROME

Suppression of human rights is the defining characteristic of most authoritarian regimes. Throughout the twentieth century, many governments have resisted pressures for democratization and human rights over a long period, and then become internally unstable or threatening to their neighbors.

China is the largest and most important authoritarian country in the world today. Descended from an ancient and advanced civilization, modern China struggled for two centuries under a barrage of Western exploitation before consolidating itself as a nation under communist rule in 1949, following a revolution led by Mao Tsetung. After the revolution, the United States refused to recognize the legitimacy of "Red China" until 1972, when Richard Nixon and Henry Kissinger began establishing diplomatic relations with the communist regime. Over the next two decades, a succession of U.S. Presidents strengthened these ties and broadened them to include a variety of economic, military, and even some private-sector exchanges. But U.S.-China relations were managed from the top down by a small number of officials and experts on both sides who focused exclusively on establishing closely controlled geopolitical cooperation during the Cold War.

## Tiananmen

The issue of human rights remained in the background of this tightly scripted U.S.-China relationship until the spring of 1989. On June 4, beginning in Beijing's Tiananmen Square and continuing in cities around the country, the Chinese army killed thousands of unarmed Chinese citizens who were peacefully demonstrating for democracy. In cities throughout China, tens of thousands of workers, students, and intellectuals who were guilty of nothing more than engaging in basic forms of political expression were rounded up and sent off to prison, or in some cases, summarily executed.[1] That these events unfolded in June 1989—just as nonviolent democracy movements were beginning to sweep away communist regimes in Eastern Europe and Gorbachev's efforts at "perestroika" were opening up the Soviet Union—only served to enhance worldwide outrage at the actions of the Chinese government.

Tiananmen marked the triumph of repression over reform at the top of the Chinese government. During the 1980s, the steady process of economic development and market liberalization championed by Mao's successor, Deng Xiaoping, had been accompanied by some loosening of the totalitarian restrictions on speech and expression. Foreign trade began to open China's economy to the outside world. Tens of thousands of students were allowed to study overseas, many in the United States, and increasingly open political discussion began to take place at universities. Many international observers, particularly in the United States, became convinced that the economic and social changes fostered by Deng's policies would lead to expanding political freedom and respect for human rights.

Throughout this period American policymakers believed that the most effective way to promote a more open China was to support Deng's efforts to expand foreign trade and investment as a way of developing the Chinese economy. Rising living standards and the growth of a middle class, it was thought, would inevitably lead to improvements in human rights and the eventual development of democracy in China.[2] Tiananmen disproved this assumption. While it is true that economic growth helped create a demand for greater social and political freedom, the Chinese government's response to the Tiananmen democracy movement clearly showed that there was nothing inevitable about foreign trade and investment leading to the expansion of human rights under an authoritarian regime.

In the mid-1980s, popular demand for democratic reform grew among a broad range of Chinese citizens, starting with students and intellectuals. Soon the ranks of those characterized as dissidents swelled as their views became more mainstream. Even Deng's hand-picked successors, Premier Zhao Ziyang and Communist Party Secretary Hu Yaobang, were receptive to this trend toward greater political openness and intellectual freedom.[3] But the regime eventually disapproved. Hu was forced out in 1987 after a wave of student demonstrations in Shanghai, and Zhao was overruled, ousted, and later imprisoned for favoring negotiations with the Tiananmen demonstrators.[4]

The Bush administration misjudged the nature of the Tiananmen crisis and the effects it would have on U.S.-China relations. In the early days of U.S. diplomatic relations with Mao's China, George Bush had served as head of the U.S. liaison office in Beijing. Now, he was motivated by an instinct to preserve the long-term investment that he felt the United States had made in its fifteen-year policy of coaxing China to open itself to the world. The theory behind Bush's caution was that China's size, history, culture, strategic importance, and economic potential made it unique among nations, requiring a U.S. policy that left plenty of room for accommodating the authoritarian government's suppression of basic freedoms.

President Bush dispatched his national security advisor, Brent Scowcroft, on two secret missions to Beijing, in July and December 1989, to convey to the Chinese that the Tiananmen crisis would not affect the basic structure or tone of U.S.-China relations. Scowcroft's message was that the United States would not allow differences over human rights to get in the way of its longstanding positive relationship with the aging Deng Xiaoping and the Chinese government.[5]

The Scowcroft secret meetings in Beijing came to symbolize the

Bush administration's response to Tiananmen. Winston Lord, who had served as ambassador to China during the last years of the Reagan administration and the early months of Bush, wrote a scathing op-ed in the *Washington Post* condemning Bush's deemphasis of the human rights crisis. Lord characterized Scowcroft as "a fawning emissary" who encouraged repression by "pay[ing] tribute" to a brutal government.[6] Lord's point of view was worth heeding. Three years later Bill Clinton would tap him to be his assistant secretary of state for East Asian and Pacific Affairs and an architect of the new administration's China policy. Equally important was the reaction of Senate Majority Leader George Mitchell to the Tiananmen crisis. Mitchell fashioned a tough congressional response to China's crackdown on dissent that influenced and was eventually folded into the Clinton policy. Mitchell denounced Bush's approach, and especially the Scowcroft missions, as "an embarrassing kowtowing to a repressive Communist government."[7]

The Tiananmen massacre opened up a deep fissure in American policy toward China. Before 1989, a broad bipartisan consensus had backed the tightly controlled strategy of engaging with the Chinese leadership in order to secure their Cold War cooperation without confronting them over the suppression of human rights. Tiananmen shattered that consensus by planting seeds of doubt that the Chinese government would ever allow reform to occur from within, or would ever match its aggressive pursuit of global economic markets with a new commitment to the rule of law. The television images of unarmed students racing through the streets of Beijing pursued by Chinese tanks and soldiers captured the attention of millions of Americans and turned China into a major domestic political controversy in the United States. Supporting freedom of expression in China and signaling to those trying to exercise it that Americans were on their side became the key objectives of those advocating a change in U.S. policy toward China.

George Mitchell epitomized the outrage felt by ordinary Americans about what had happened in Tiananmen Square. A respected congressional leader with no previous involvement in the formulation of U.S.-China policy, Mitchell represented a fresh perspective that was unwilling to accept the brutality of a regime that crushed all reformers. The day after the tanks opened fire on the democracy demonstrators near their cardboard replica of the Statue of Liberty, Mitchell told reporters on Capitol Hill that the U.S. practice of winking at China's human rights record while condemning similar repression in the Soviet Union and other countries must end. Calling for broad economic sanctions and other tough measures to respond to the mass killing of Chinese civilians by their own government, Mitchell insisted that "we . . . make it very clear that the United States government stands with and in support of those who seek freedom and democracy in China and throughout the world."[8] Earlier he had told his staff that what was happening in Beijing was "outrageous. It's murder."[9]

Tiananmen was a clear threat to American interests. During the previous decade the United States had forged economic, political, and military ties to China based on an assumption that the country would move slowly away from its totalitarian past. An evolving and increasingly pluralistic China, with its vast human resources and economic potential, could become a source of regional stability and a participant in global market development. But a reactionary and authoritarian China that violently suppressed internal movements for reform could become a breeding ground for unrest, terrorism, and external aggression.

The issue of human rights was squarely in the middle of this great divide. More than any international event in the early post–Cold War years, China's destruction of its internal democracy movement following Tiananmen brought home to Americans the urgency of the struggle for human rights in authoritarian countries and the importance of finding appropriate ways from the outside to encourage reform while condemning repression. The advocates of a new approach called for the United States to work with other countries in the U.N. Human Rights Commission to censure China's human rights record, while linking trade and economic relations—including China's access to international lending through the World Bank—to the improvement of its record.

During the Bush years, a significant China human rights caucus emerged in the Congress. Reflecting the views of academic experts, human rights organizations, and the public at large, this caucus was led by Mitchell and California Democrat Nancy Pelosi, as well as several Republicans, and it steadily pressed the Bush administration to put greater emphasis on human rights in its diplomatic relations with China.[10] The caucus considered itself to be connected directly to China's suppressed democracy movement through tens of thousands of Chinese students studying in the United States, some of whom were veterans of Tiananmen Square.

By the time Bill Clinton came into office, a changing political and economic situation inside China had intensified the debate over what kind of policy the United States should adopt toward the regime that had carried out the Tiananmen massacre. The Chinese government had begun to emerge from its defensive crouch. A power struggle to succeed Deng Xiaoping, whose health was rapidly failing, was under way. Out of this struggle would emerge Jiang Zemin, who had been selected by Deng in 1989 to replace the reformer Zhao Ziyang as Communist Party General Secretary, after Zhao had been forced out for opposing military action against the democracy movement. Most observers expected Jiang to be a weak caretaker who would be unable to control internal party jockeying over how to manage the legacy of Tiananmen inside China and internationally, particularly since the Chinese economy had taken a sharp nosedive immediately after 1989.[11]

But as Jiang emerged as China's new leader, he had an ace in the hole. In a 1992 "last hurrah" tour of the southern provinces, Deng had rallied China's industrial heartland and called for an influx of foreign investment to revitalize Chinese industry and open the country's vast markets to the world. The result was dramatic and almost instantaneous. As one observer, Patrick Tyler of the *New York Times,* wrote: "The explosion of manufacturing along China's southeastern coast—textiles, plastics, toys, shoes, and electronics—was difficult to capture in any familiar metaphor. . . . Armies of bulldozers assaulted vast vistas of rice paddies and mountains as Patton had assaulted the plain of Europe. Mechanized brigades engorged red-clay landscapes to make bricks; mammoth rock-crushing machines shredded promontories into aggregate gravel to be poured into the concrete foundations of factory skeletons."[12] Thanks to Deng's farewell push and hordes of new foreign investors, China relaunched itself in 1992 with an economic boom that continued through the 1990s.

## Proclaiming a "New Covenant"

In 1992, American domestic politics focused on two issues involving China—human rights and trade. At the Democratic National Convention in New York in July, Bill Clinton proclaimed a "New Covenant for America." Among its major points was a commitment to an "America that will not coddle dictators, from Baghdad to Beijing." Saddam Hussein and Tiananmen Square became the rallying cries for Clinton's attacks on George Bush's foreign policy. The Democratic candidate scored significant gains by accusing Bush of failing to finish the job in Iraq and of cozying up to "the butchers of Beijing."[13]

But Clinton won the election not because of his positions on foreign policy; instead, the weakness of the American economy was what drove his voters to the polls. The famous sign outside James Carville's office—"It's the economy, stupid!"—not the candidate's statements about coddling dictators, was the bumper sticker for the Clinton campaign. Strengthening the American economy would become the centerpiece of the new administration. In the case of China policy, the emphasis on economic issues would eventually require tradeoffs on human rights. As a candidate, however, Clinton expressed confidence that he could have it both ways. He invited Chinese student leaders from the Tiananmen democracy movement to address the Democratic National Convention, and strongly endorsed the position taken by George Mitchell, Nancy Pelosi, Richard Gephardt (D-Mo.), and other congressional Democrats that China's most-favored-nation trade benefits should be linked to human rights improvements.[14] At the same time, Clinton made clear that he wanted to do everything possible to support U.S. companies doing business or investing in China. And the foreign investment pouring into China in 1992 was predominantly American.

Clinton's position on China was not particularly new, but rather reflected mainstream Democratic Party thinking. What *was* novel about the way China policy was evolving in the early 1990s was that for the first time Congress was playing a role in shaping U.S.-China relations. In the two decades since Nixon had opened the door to China in 1972, Congress had generally supported the White House and stayed out of the way of presidential initiatives. That all changed after Tiananmen. With the prodding of congressional Democrats and a few Republicans, an alternative China policy was hammered out in the Congress that required the United States to take a firm stand on human rights and arms sales and signaled the end of the broad consensus over how U.S.-China relations should be conducted.[15]

The vehicle for this new congressional policy was China's status as a most-favored-nation (MFN) trading partner of the United States. Since 1979, one of the mainstays of U.S.-China relations had been the annual renewal of MFN. In 1991, legislation was passed by both houses of Congress to make the extension of China's MFN benefits conditional on progress on human rights and a reduction of arms exports. Although Bush vetoed the bill, the Senate came within six votes in March 1992 of overriding his veto.[16] Clearly, the President was no longer the only one driving U.S. China policy.

By endorsing the congressional MFN strategy in 1992, Bill Clinton's presidential campaign was partly bowing to political necessity. Many key congressional Democrats were pressing the candidates to be tough on China. After receiving the Democratic Party nomination, Clinton skillfully used the MFN issue to put George Bush on the defensive. Beyond the immediate political advantage of adopting the views of congressional Democratic leaders, Clinton was instinctively drawn to a position that minimized the likelihood that as President he would get trapped, as Bush had, in a confrontation with Congress over China.

After his election, the new President made clear that unlike Bush he was aggressively going to promote *both* human rights *and* trade with China. A roundtable discussion led by Clinton in Little Rock in December 1992 with American business representatives a month before his inauguration showed how confident he was that he could have it both ways. One of the participants, Jill Barad, the president of Mattel, a U.S. toy company, expressed her concern about the MFN policy Clinton had endorsed.[17] If Clinton were to withdraw MFN because China failed to make progress on human rights, Barad said, Mattel would have to pay more than five times the tariff it now doled out on Chinese-made toys and would risk losing its share of the toy market to foreign competitors.

Clinton answered the Mattel executive by making two points. First, he said that he would not revoke China's MFN status "if we can achieve continued progress" on human rights, adding, "I think we've got to stick up for ourselves and the things we believe in."[18] Second, he asserted that since China's exports to the United States were $15 billion greater than American exports to China, Beijing had a greater stake in good trade relations than the United States did.[19] In hindsight, both points were unrealistic: the first, because China had shown no willingness to ease up on dissent after Tiananmen; and the second, because regardless of the favorable U.S. trade balance with China, the American business community was certain to put pressure on Clinton to renew MFN even if China did not meet his human rights conditions. The incoming President may not have considered what it would take for him to achieve both his human rights and his trade priorities. He would have to stand up to a recalcitrant Chinese government and resist the pressure of the American business community—a two-pronged strategy that would require him to be willing to spend a great deal of his own political and diplomatic capital to achieve.

Soon after taking office, Clinton set out to forge a consensus around this all-encompassing China policy. Appealing to congressional sponsors of the MFN legislation, the administration drafted an executive order whose purpose was similar. When the order was being drafted, I had not yet been confirmed by the Senate and therefore was not able to participate in any of the discussions in the State Department or on Capitol Hill about the evolving China policy. I certainly favored an approach toward China that demonstrated U.S. support for human rights reform, but I was uncertain about the proposed new MFN policy. I had heard warnings about it from several reliable sources. Pat Hotze, a Foreign Service officer and China specialist who had represented the Human Rights Bureau at the State Department meetings on MFN, told me he did not see how the order could be enforced, since it would be virtually impossible to cut off MFN without a major disruption of U.S.-China relations. Joshua Rubenstein, the Northeast regional director of Amnesty International, put it more bluntly: "It's a nuclear weapon you'll never be able to use."

Clinton's effort to create a strategic alliance on China policy between the new administration and the Congress had an internal logic. The White House wanted to make good on the President's pledge to elevate human rights issues in U.S.-China relations while bringing an end to the annual stand-off between the President and the Congress over MFN. In addition, Tony Lake, who was shaping the new policy as the President's national security advisor, and Winston Lord, who was now the State Department point person on China, wanted to preserve the administration's flexibility by embedding the policy in an executive order rather than in the permanent legislation that Mitchell and Pelosi were pushing. Since Mitchell and Pelosi had enough votes to pass their bill, the White House clearly had to deal with them.

A deal was struck. The legislation would be dropped and China's MFN status extended for another year, until May 1994. In exchange, Clinton would commit himself to renew MFN the following year only if he could certify that China had met the human rights conditions specified in his executive order. Two of the conditions were "mandatory" (promoting freedom of emigration and curbing the use of prison labor), while five others required "overall, significant progress" (adhering to the Universal Declaration of Human Rights; releasing and accounting for political prisoners; providing access to prisons by humanitarian and human rights organizations; protecting the religious and cultural heritage of Tibet; and permitting international broadcasting into China). These terms were favorable to the White House because Mitchell and Pelosi agreed not to include in the executive order any of the additional conditions on trade and arms sales that had been in their original legislation, leaving progress on human rights as the sole basis for the President's MFN certification. From a human rights standpoint, the executive order certainly looked like a nuclear weapon.[20]

The White House signing ceremony on May 28, 1993, was the high point of Clinton's China MFN policy and the only time when the policy received universal accolades from its diverse constituencies. Congressional leaders, Chinese students, human rights groups, and representatives of the business community all joined in welcoming the new executive order. Of course, everyone had a different reason for applauding what Clinton had done, and that was the way he liked it. Pleased that the Congress no longer faced a presidential veto of his human rights legislation, Mitchell proclaimed, "For the first time since the events of Tiananmen Square, nearly four years ago, we have a president who is willing to act in order to bring about positive change" in China.[21] At the same time, business leaders expressed their gratitude that the President had renewed MFN for another year, while dropping some of the conditions of the Mitchell-Pelosi legislation. Robert Kapp, the incoming president of the U.S.-China Business Council, asserted that "the President has done a great service."[22] A Boeing spokesman said simply, "We are encouraged."[23] Even Henry Kissinger, not known as a human rights advocate, lauded the new executive order as "statesmanlike."[24] Basking in the apparent unity he had created, Clinton was in an expansive mood. "It is time that a unified American policy recognize both the values of China and the values of America," he said. In a comment that soon came to haunt him, the President declared that "starting today, the United States will speak with one voice on China policy."[25]

Drafting the executive order had not been easy. The order had to be specific enough to be credible and measurable, but general enough to be flexible and realistic. It had to satisfy Congress, appeal to human rights groups without alienating the business community, and avoid being rejected out of hand by the Chinese government. The balancing act that Winston Lord and other administration negotiators had to perform to produce the order proved impossible to sustain once it was completed.

The façade of unity that existed when the President signed the order in the Rose Garden masked three fundamental problems. First, the business community had not been extensively consulted during the drafting process and felt no real stake in the outcome other than a sense of temporary relief that the new President was continuing MFN for another year.[26] To the extent that a compromise had been struck, it was between the administration and human rights advocates in the Congress. Others who opposed altogether the linkage between human rights and trade had no reason to support the new policy. And Europe, which was rapidly expanding its trade with China, was on a competing course.

Second, underlying the executive order was the assumption that the Chinese would comply with its conditions. As Winston Lord observed at a State Department senior staff meeting in early June, the United States had never conditioned MFN before. "The idea is to use it, not lose it."

Third, the executive order had no real teeth. The only penalty available to the President if the Chinese defied him was total revocation of MFN, a result the Congress had never had to face because legislation to revoke MFN had always been vetoed. In drafting the order, the administration might have proposed less extreme penalties that would have been more credible and therefore more effective in keeping up the pressure for human rights improvements in China. Although it is not clear whether such penalties could have been worked out with congressional negotiators, they might have included a gradual increase in tariffs for noncompliance, or even a partial revocation aimed at specific sectors of the Chinese export economy.

## Skirmishes

Shortly after being sworn into office in June 1993, I had a warm-up encounter with Chinese diplomacy at the U.N. World Conference on Human Rights in Vienna.

The Vienna conference was the first global human rights gathering in twenty-five years. The Chinese government saw the conference as an opportunity to try to push back the international human rights movement that it regarded as an instigator of the Tiananmen crisis and a threat to its ability to keep the lid on internal pressures for reform. The Chinese delegation worked overtime with other authoritarian regimes to mount an attack on the principle that human rights are universal, lobbying to get the conference to adopt resolutions recognizing cultural and economic differences around the world as the basis for differences in the way governments treat the issue of political and civil rights at home.

As head of the U.S. delegation, I worked to organize resistance to this attack. At one point I suggested to the Chinese delegation (as President Clinton was to warn Chinese President Jiang Zemin four years later) that resisting the Universal Declaration of Human Rights would put them "on the wrong side of history."[27] Although the Chinese did not succeed in watering down the Universal Declaration, the delegation's behavior in Vienna showed that the regime was not about to apologize for having crushed a peaceful internal movement for democracy and human rights in China.

During the summer of 1993 the Clinton administration found itself skirmishing with China on several fronts. The CIA uncovered what it thought was evidence that a Chinese freighter was carrying weapons-grade chemicals to Iran. When the ship was inspected in Saudia Arabia, however, no chemicals were found, and the Chinese accused the United States of "bullying."[28] In another confrontation over weapons issues, Undersecretary of State Lynn Davis announced at the end of August that the United States would impose sanctions on China for selling missile parts to Pakistan. The sanctions barred the export of American-built satellite components, creating tensions not only with China, but also with American companies who made satellite parts and wanted to complete the sale.[29]

This marked the first time the Clinton administration had clashed with the American business community over China policy. In a harbinger of things to come, the administration's senior economic team, led by Robert Rubin, chairman of Clinton's National Economic Council, persuaded the President to back down and begin granting waivers from the missile sanctions on a case-by-case basis. Despite this softening of the missile sanctions, U.S.-China friction increased even more when the House of Representatives passed a resolution condemning China as unfit to host the 2000 Olympic Games because of its human rights record.[30]

As these tensions mounted, the White House began searching for a new strategy of "engagement" with China that might soften the confrontation and create a framework for achieving multiple objectives. Plans for implementing the president's executive order on MFN were put on hold while the China policy was reviewed. As the person who would be most directly involved in implementing the executive order, I welcomed the new approach of high-level engagement that Tony Lake conveyed to Chinese Ambassador Li Daoyu on September 25 at the White House. But I also saw that engagement could be a recipe for confusion. If the administration was to "engage" with the Chinese government on a wide range of issues, how would the message be delivered to Beijing that progress on human rights was of paramount importance if MFN was to be renewed?

The day before Tony Lake met with Ambassador Li, Lake asked me to join him and Winston Lord in his office for a discussion of the new policy. Since I was scheduled the following day to have my first meeting with Chinese assistant foreign minister Qin Huasun at China's U.N. mission in New York, I was eager to hear how Lake thought I should present the requirements of the President's MFN executive order to the Chinese. What I heard was both encouraging and disappointing. I was pleased that my upcoming human rights dialogue was getting attention from the White House and that the executive order would now be a priority for U.S. diplomacy with China. Lake urged me to have an open and honest discussion with the Chinese about our own struggle for civil rights in the United States as well as China's human rights record since Tiananmen, and this gave me more latitude than I had expected.

But I was also sobered to hear that the human rights dialogue would be only one of many diplomatic avenues that the administration would be pursuing in the coming months. Lake told me that a number of cabinet-level visits to China would take place. In addition, the ban on military contacts would be lifted and Clinton would meet President Jiang Zemin in Seattle in November. In theory, this meant that human rights would have many messengers. In practice, it turned out to be an invitation for different parts of the administration to deliver mixed messages. For example, the upcoming discussions by Treasury Secretary Lloyd Bentsen about strengthening economic and trade relations between the United States and China were likely to encourage the Chinese to believe that they could finesse Clinton's MFN policy, even if Bentsen raised the issue of human rights, as he did, in his meetings. To get the Chinese to move on human rights, they would have to be told that complying with the executive order was more important at that moment than anything else in their relations with the United States. Unfortunately, that is not what they would hear.

I met with Assistant Minister Qin Huasun in New York on September 26, four days before Warren Christopher was scheduled to have his first meeting with Chinese Foreign Minister Qian Qichen. Stiff and formulaic, Qin read a long script that boiled down to a single point: "We can talk about human rights, but I won't agree with anything you say; don't tell us what to do and don't expect our relations to improve so long as your president threatens to cut off MFN if we don't do what he wants on human rights." The Chinese were testing our resolve. My message on MFN was reinforced by Christopher, who opened his presentation by telling the foreign minister that we needed to see progress on human rights if U.S.-China relations were to improve. Breaking the ice, the foreign minister invited me to China the following month to continue our "dialogue."

## Delivering the Message

A week later, I landed in Beijing and was immediately whisked off for a ritual duck banquet hosted by a transformed Qin Huasun. Cordial and informal, the assistant minister clearly had been told to change his tone and make his American guest feel welcome. When I expressed my surprise to Stapleton Roy, our ambassador and the leading U.S. government expert on China (who had also been with me at the New York meeting), he explained that the Ministry of Foreign Affairs had decided to switch tactics on me. In an effort to steer our dialogue into shallower water, Qin was now to play Mr. Nice Guy. Roy's advice was to stay on message, and show Qin how we could work together to put the MFN controversy behind us by having China take several specific steps on human rights.

After the banquet I huddled with the ambassador; Don Keyser, the State Department's China director; and Eric Schwartz, Tony Lake's human rights specialist on the National Security Council staff who had come with me from Washington. We mapped out a message for our meetings the next day that would emphasize Clinton's achievement in getting the Congress to work with him on China policy, his promise to improve U.S.-China relations, and the importance of human rights progress in China for him to be able to keep his promise.

I would be very specific about the contents of Clinton's executive order. The order appealed to China to allow close relatives of exiled dissidents to leave the country and agree to stop exporting prison labor products to the United States. In addition, it urged China to demonstrate "overall significant progress" on accounting for and releasing Tiananmen political prisoners, allowing an arrangement for an international humanitarian organization such as the Red Cross to be given access to Chinese prisons, discussing with the Dalai Lama or his personal representative the protection of Tibetan religion and culture, and ending the jamming of Voice of America radio broadcasts into China. I would emphasize that President Clinton's executive order should be seen as part of the process of "engagement" that Tony Lake had outlined in his meeting with Ambassador Li in September. Finally, and above all, I would make it clear that our delegation represented the position of the President himself, and that the message we were delivering was coming directly from him.

For nearly four hours the next day I went over all these points with Qin Huasun. Qin repeated China's objection to the linkage we were drawing between human rights and MFN and went on at great length about the differing perspectives of China and the United States on the meaning of human rights. Still, the length of the meeting and the fact that Qin listened intently to my "message from our President" represented something of a breakthrough. Two developments during the morning seemed to point in opposite directions. On the positive side, Qin accepted the prisoner list that we had prepared for him, and confirmed that our delegation would be invited to visit Tibet later in the week. In a more negative development, he warned that if we were serious about having a human rights dialogue, we should abandon our effort to censure China at the annual meeting of the U.N. Human Rights Commission in Geneva. My response was clear, but not what he wanted: the United States would be willing to drop its support of a China resolution in Geneva if China took steps to improve its human rights record.

That evening I got a taste of Chinese official charm at a banquet in honor of our delegation at the Daioyutai Guest House, an elaborate government compound in the former royal gardens of the imperial emperor on the outskirts of Beijing. Hosted by Vice Foreign Minister Liu Huaqiu, the veteran American "handler" of high-level U.S. visits, whose daughter was a student at Stanford, the banquet gave me a chance to show my commitment to a two-way dialogue by broaching the subject of human rights issues in the United States as well as China. I told Liu that Americans had great admiration for what China had achieved in raising the standard of living for an enormous and impoverished population, and that the ongoing development struggle in China was similar to our own efforts in the United States to improve the conditions of equal justice for all Americans. Liu agreed, but spoke of "the gap between the views of developed and developing countries on human rights," asserting that "in your country there are no economic rights."

I disagreed, and the debate sharpened. Pointing to the programs implemented by the U.S. Social Security, Medicare, and public education systems, I suggested that while the United States could learn from China's commitment to economic development, China could also learn from our commitment to political freedom. Liu countered that homeless Americans have the freedom to sleep under bridges, while rich Americans have the freedom to ignore the homeless. I responded that freedom to disagree with the government was an essential safety valve in the United States, and that China would eventually pay a price if it continued to deny this freedom. The evening ended with an exchange of toasts in which we professed the importance of dialogue between those who disagreed about fundamental issues.

The next six days were a whirlwind of meetings, events, and travel. In Beijing I met with intellectuals at the Chinese Academy of Social Sciences, who encouraged me to make broad contacts in China. One participant told me that "open discussion is the best way to seek progress on human rights." Curious advice, I thought. What does it mean?

I had heard that China was loosening its restrictions on religion, and wanted to see for myself. On Sunday, I cycled two miles with Ambassador Roy through crowded Beijing streets to an officially sanctioned Christian church. A week later, in Guangzhou, the center of southern China's economic boom, I visited an "underground" church at the invitation of its well-known dissident pastor, the Reverend Samuel Lam, and addressed the Chinese congregation from a makeshift pulpit. I commended them for being brave in the pursuit of their beliefs, wondering whether this was the kind of "open discussion" the Beijing intellectuals had in mind.

At the Chinese Bureau of Religious and Nationalities Affairs I was told by an aging bureaucrat who read from a prepared text that the church I had attended in Beijing was one of eight thousand authorized Christian places of worship in China. As if reciting a catechism, my interlocutor assured me that China recognized freedom of religion. But there were two limitations that he said any reasonable person would understand—no religious activity was permitted that affected the public order or interfered with education, and no religion was allowed that was "subject to foreign domination." The embassy had prepared me for the rigidity of this meeting by telling me that these dour bureaucrats were the gatekeepers to Tibet to whom I had to pay my respects in order to be able to accept the invitation of the Ministry of Foreign Affairs to travel to Lhasa. After they had spent more than an hour telling me that China was liberating Tibet from the slavery and serfdom imposed by the Dalai Lama, I came away with no doubt that the government was intent on destroying traditional Tibetan religion and culture.

My round of meetings in Beijing also included stops at the Ministries of Justice and Public Security and the Peoples' Procuratorate, where I was briefed on the Chinese justice system. In contrast to the Religion and Nationalities Bureau, the Justice Ministry seemed interested in having a real discussion. In a session that lasted nearly two hours, I covered a wide range of topics with the young deputy minister, Jia Jingping. I asked about the prisoners on my list who had been convicted of "counterrevolutionary crimes," the difficulties the International Red Cross was having in arranging access to Chinese prisons, whether China was willing to stop exporting prison-made products to the United States, and what efforts were being made by the ministry to reform Chinese criminal law. At the Peoples' Procuratorate, a sort of chief prosecutor's office, I was told that I would be able to visit the Drapchi Prison in Lhasa during my trip to Tibet, and that visits to other prisons by the International Red Cross were now being discussed "at higher levels." This sounded positive, but it was difficult to tell whether any real commitments were being made that would satisfy the human rights conditions for renewal of MFN.

"Dialogue" with the Chinese government was as complicated as communication with our own far-flung bureaucracy. But these meetings had the effect, if not the intention, of softening the U.S.-China confrontation over human rights. At one point, a bizarre note of informality was struck when our hosts at the Foreign Ministry realized that we did not have time for the official lunch they had prepared, and suggested that we go instead to a popular McDonald's restaurant across the street for a quick snack between meetings. This lowbrow gastronomic improvisation illustrated the relatively relaxed and informal way we were being received. As a seasoned observer of Beijing atmospherics, Stapleton Roy was pleased that I was able to explain in detail the requirements of Clinton's executive order without getting an overwhelmingly negative reaction. I had succeeded in delivering the message. Now it remained to be seen how it would be interpreted.

The rest of my trip gave me a steady stream of fascinating glimpses of the dynamic changes occurring throughout China and the pressure tactics being exerted by Beijing to try to control them. In Chengdu, the southwestern city from which we would take off for Tibet, the economy was sagging and many younger people were struggling to get approval to leave and seek work in the coastal areas to the east.

On the roof of the world in Lhasa, where I was the highest-ranking U.S. executive branch official ever to visit, economic development was being force fed by Beijing. Tens of thousands of fortune-seeking workers were pouring into the city from China, dramatizing the slow strangling of traditional Tibetan culture. After being officially guided through the seventh-century Jokhang Temple and the Dalai Lama's Potala Palace, I learned later from confidential sources that the Bureau of Religious and Nationality Affairs in Beijing had secretly restricted Tibetan monks to giving tours, and barred them from studying or teaching Tibetan Buddhism. Later, a note was thrust into the hands of our embassy escort, Don Camp, the U.S. consul general in Chengdu. The crumpled paper read in hastily scrawled Chinese, "more than thirty monks from this monastery are in prison."

The next day, and a world apart, I visited Guangzhou, the industrial city on China's southern coast near Hong Kong, where I could feel the energy being unleashed by the country's economic boom. The city was a forest of construction cranes, and its residents were clearly proud of what they were accomplishing. I heard remarkably similar comments from local officials, like the head of the municipal "Systems Reform Office," and local dissidents, such as the Reverend Samuel Lam, who said in essence: "Beijing is far away and we want to do things our own way here."

## Centrifugal Forces

While I was in Beijing explaining the President's MFN policy, the Chinese were getting a very different message from other American visitors. How dare we go around telling the rest of the world that it must accept our position on human rights, former Secretary of State Alexander Haig fulminated to the press in Beijing, where he was introducing the new president of United Technologies Corporation to the Chinese leadership. Commenting on the Clinton administration's position, reflected in my public comments the week before, that the United States would have to find signs of human rights progress in China in order to be able to renew MFN, Haig made it clear that the U.S. business community did not like Clinton's MFN policy. "I think the time has come to take a different tack here," the former Secretary of State insisted. "And Tiananmen is a long way behind us."[31]

American investment was pouring into China. In 1993, U.S. companies signed a record 6,700 new contracts totaling $10 billion, including nearly $800 million in new commercial aircraft sales that boosted the ailing U.S. aircraft industry.[32] The Commerce Department estimated that by the end of 1992 over 150,000 American jobs depended entirely on the Chinese export market. That number continued to grow throughout 1993. The message about China from American business was that everyone would benefit from increasing U.S.-China trade and investment. Footwear import lobbyists, for example, were telling members of Congress that by buying inexpensive shoes made in China, American consumers would save over $16 billion in 1993.[33] The attraction of the Chinese market was enhanced by stiff competition from other countries. On October 20, the day I left China to return to Washington, Hong Kong's *South China Morning Post* carried separate front-page articles about my meetings in Beijing and about British investment in China with side-by-side headlines that said it all: "Beijing Not Doing Enough for MFN— U.S. Envoy" and "Britain's Exports to China Soar 90 Percent."[34]

In this highly charged economic environment, the paper-thin consensus around Clinton's MFN policy began to disappear. Not only was the business community impatient with the uncertainty about China's trade status, but Congress and the administration itself also began to show cracks in what I had gamely been asserting to the Chinese was a united front in Washington. When the administration began to back away from the missile sanctions it had announced in August so that Hughes Aircraft and other manufacturers of satellite parts could stave off European competition for Chinese contracts, it was clear that the economic agencies inside the administration were gaining the upper hand in the growing battle over Clinton's China policy. Hughes got California senator Dianne Feinstein (D-Calif.), one of the administration's most important congressional supporters from a key state with a struggling economy, to push for the relaxation of sanctions and announce that she and others in the Senate felt that using a stick with China would be counterproductive.[35] This growing anti-sanctions sentiment in Washington emboldened the Chinese to toughen their position on the human rights conditions in Clinton's executive order.

Winston Lord was holding weekly meetings of the interagency China Steering Group. I attended regularly. As the fall went by, it became obvious that there were many China policies, and that each agency was essentially pursuing its own China agenda. In the aftermath of the missile sanctions battle, an unidentified "White House official" was quoted in the *New York Times* as saying that American business interests in China were so important that "we're not going to let something like MFN stand in our way."[36] Lord angrily repudiated this comment, and warned that "China has got to understand that movement is required [on human rights] or we're all going to be in trouble next spring."[37] But the damage was done: the White House leak showed that Clinton's policy was not only being defied by the Chinese; it was also being undermined from within. Although the China Steering Group had been set up to impose discipline on the administration, the effect of the new "engagement strategy" was becoming clear—differing approaches to U.S.-China relations were proliferating. Human rights were nominally on the menu of every meeting, but only as a sort of required hors d'oeuvre.

At a steering group meeting on October 28, I could see evidence of the centrifugal forces that were making it increasingly difficult for Lord to manage the process. Lord opened the meeting with a review of where things stood on MFN, warning that the Chinese were growing complacent. Unless the administration spoke with one voice, he predicted, the Chinese were not likely to do what was necessary for Clinton to certify the human rights progress required by his executive order. This should be the main item on the agenda of all upcoming meetings, Lord stressed, because "we won't be able to do much else if MFN can't be renewed."

What followed was a surrealistic review by each agency of its China objectives. The Defense Department representative, for example, reported that Charles Freeman, Jr., the assistant secretary for international security affairs, was then engaged in a series of meetings with the Chinese about reestablishing direct military-to-military contacts. As an afterthought, he claimed that human rights had been "mentioned" at the beginning of the first meeting. Similar reports were made by the Departments of Agriculture, Commerce, and Treasury. The staff person from the U.S. Trade Representative's Office pointed out that the business community was upset with the President's linkage of MFN and human rights. Then, in a remark that captured the uncertainty of the situation, she asserted, somewhat incongruously, "The Chinese are prepared to lose MFN."

# CHAPTER 8

# CHINA

## COLLISION COURSE

Two major China conflicts were shaping up at the end of 1993. The first was a diplomatic collision between China and the United States over human rights. The second was a clash within the U.S. government between the economic agencies and the State Department over the President's policy of linking human rights and trade.

Warren Christopher could feel the tension mounting. He had supported the approach Tony Lake and Winston Lord had taken when they drafted the MFN executive order, and after the President had signed it, Christopher considered the order his legal mandate. For the first nine months of the year when the policy was in effect, Christopher worked hard to protect the integrity of the President's position. His loyalty to Clinton and to the rule of law, which he felt the executive order represented, was steadfast, making him both a standard bearer for the policy and a scapegoat for its eventual failure when others undercut its implementation.

The Secretary's forthrightness was on full display when he met with a large group of business leaders in the State Department auditorium on October 20. He urged them to join with the administration in pressing the Chinese to make progress on human rights. Warning his high-powered audience of the disaster that lay ahead if they gave the Chinese a different message from the one in the executive order, Christopher said, "I don't believe we can sustain the position [of MFN] beyond next June unless we see continued improvements in the human rights field by the Chinese."[1] These brave words fell on deaf ears. Christopher's audience saw China not as a human rights problem, but as a vast market opportunity.

## Seattle

Despite the growing conflict over China policy, I hoped a full-scale collision could still be avoided. Trade promotion and human rights diplomacy, after all, were not inherently inconsistent; properly balanced, they could be mutually reinforcing. The key was to tell the Chinese government that it could not keep locking up dissidents and reformers and expect to receive continued preferential trade benefits from the United States.

I was guardedly optimistic about Clinton's upcoming meeting in Seattle with Jiang Zemin. Here was a chance to boost the diplomatic process on human rights that Christopher and I had started in New York and Beijing. Throughout the summer and fall the President had been preoccupied with domestic issues, and had remained above the controversies swirling around his China policy. Now, in mid-November, buoyed by a surprise victory in Congress on the North American Free Trade Agreement in a vote many had expected him to lose, Clinton headed off to the Seattle meeting of Asia-Pacific leaders with a badly needed foreign policy win under his belt. The first Clinton-Jiang summit would be an opportunity for the President to make clear to the Chinese that for the United States to extend China's most favored nation trade status, China would have to demonstrate "overall significant progress" on human rights.

What did this mean? Critics of Clinton's MFN policy have sometimes asserted that the Chinese were never told what they had to do to satisfy the terms of the executive order.[2] But my six meetings with Qin Huasun between September 1993 and March 1994 in New York, Seattle, and Beijing; Christopher's three meetings with Foreign Minister Qian Qichen; and Clinton's Seattle summit with President Jiang Zemin left no room for the Chinese to claim confusion about

Clinton's policy.[3] In Beijing on October 11 and again in Seattle on November 18, the day before the Clinton-Jiang meeting, I went over in great detail with Qin the human rights position we had hammered out in Washington through the China Steering Group and in my discussions with Winston Lord, State Department China office director Don Keyser, Eric Schwartz and Richard Schifter of the National Security Council staff, and Pat Hotze, the China officer in the human rights bureau.[4]

During the weeks leading up to the meetings in Seattle I received plenty of unsolicited advice, much of it conflicting. The CIA told me that the power struggle going on inside the Chinese leadership over Deng's succession meant that I would never get a clear response to my points, since the leadership was divided over whether MFN was important and whether China had to make significant human rights concessions in order to keep it. President Carter called to advise me not to berate the Chinese, but to make my points indirectly and show respect for their economic achievements. Several academics, particularly Andrew Nathan of Columbia University, urged me to be very precise about our bottom-line negotiating position, while others suggested that I should avoid being too specific because doing so would only stir up the Chinese hardliners. Orville Schell, an expert on Tibet, told me to be both friendly and tough. Pierre Pont of the International Red Cross said his organization welcomed my intervention with China on their behalf, but other Red Cross representatives told me they worried that U.S. pressure could retard their ability to open a dialogue with China over access to its vast prison system. Some members of Congress called to make special appeals on issues outside the executive order like forced abortion, eugenics, and the persecution of Christians; others advised me to stick to Clinton's conditions. I felt that I had an enormous weapon strapped to my back, with everyone claiming expertise but no one really knowing how to use it.

On Tuesday, November 16, I was in Chicago to deliver a speech to the World Affairs Council. When I reached the Oak Park house of my friends John and Ann Gearen, there was a message waiting for me to call the State Department Operations Center. Within moments I was connected to Sandy Berger, the President's deputy national security advisor. Berger told me he was flying with the President to Seattle and wanted to be sure I would be there to brief Clinton before his meeting with Jiang on Friday. I said I would be fresh from my third round of talks with the Chinese on Thursday and ready to give the President anything he needed to get ready for Jiang.

When I arrived in Seattle the next day I met with Winston Lord to go over the President's briefing papers. I was pleased to find that the State Department draft prepared by the China office emphasized the importance of "early and steady progress on human rights . . . in order to realize the great potential" of U.S.-China relations. But the President's key briefing point seemed ambiguous: "You are serious about human rights, *and not looking for an excuse to get out of your commitment.*" To insure that the message was clear, I redrafted it to read: "You are serious about human rights progress, *and want to leave Jiang with no doubt about your commitment. Emphasize that this is the position of both you and the Congress, and it will not change.*"

On Thursday, November 18, I met with Assistant Foreign Minister Qin Huasun to lay the groundwork for the Clinton-Jiang summit on Friday. I told Qin that we had not yet seen the "overall significant progress" called for in the executive order and therefore could not yet recommend the renewal of MFN. I also told him I felt we could still get there, saying that in the next few months we could achieve the kind of progress that would allow us to remove the annual debate on MFN from the center of U.S.-China relations. I pledged that "the U.S. will not move the goalposts," and would stay within the framework of President Clinton's executive order.

I made seven points. First, I welcomed the statement a week earlier by Chinese Foreign Minister Qian Qichen that China was now ready to give "positive consideration" to allowing Red Cross visits to three thousand "counterrevolutionary prisoners," and I signaled to Qin that it would be an extremely positive development if definite confirmation of these visits could be announced.[5] Second, I urged the government to provide an accounting of the crimes and status of these prisoners. Third, I requested the release under "medical parole" of the political prisoners on the list I had handed over in Beijing in October, many of whom were known to be ailing.[6] My fourth point was about Tibet. While reaffirming Chinese sovereignty, I suggested that the Dalai Lama or his personal representative be invited by the Chinese government to engage in discussions about how to safeguard "the religious and cultural integrity of Tibet."[7] Next, I presented Qin with a list of nine cases of family members of dissidents who had been denied permission to leave the country, and suggested that their right to emigrate under international law be respected by China.[8] Sixth, I requested that China sign an agreement with the U.S. Customs Bureau authorizing inspection of Chinese factories suspected of using prisoners to manufacture goods to be shipped to the United States.[9] Finally, I asked for a meeting between technical experts from the United States and China to determine a means of solving the problem of "frequency crowding"—the diplomatic term for "jamming"—that was preventing Voice of America broadcasts from being heard in large parts of China.[10]

Qin's response was predictable. He again rejected the linkage between MFN and human rights, and observed with obvious pleasure that "China knows many U.S. companies who are sending letters to President Clinton supporting MFN for China." During three hours of diplomatic fencing, it became clear that Qin was probing to see how little the Chinese could do on human rights and still achieve their objective of extending MFN. He told me, for example, that "China has normal business contacts" with the Red Cross, but said nothing about scheduling prison visits. He said that he had passed on my request for a prisoner accounting to the Ministries of Justice and Public Security, with whom I had already met on the subject. On Tibet, he said nothing about the Dalai Lama, but spoke about how much money China was spending to restore the Potala Palace. He gave similarly deflecting responses to my other points, while complaining about "the U.S. attacks on China" at the U.N. Human Rights Commission and in the State Department annual Human Rights Report.

After my three-hour meeting with Qin, I went straight to the President's hotel suite to join the presummit briefing. The meeting room was filled with economic and defense officials who I knew were eager to expand their contacts with China and were impatient with the impediment posed by the human rights conditions of MFN. Entering, I encountered Bob Rubin, U.S. Trade Representative Mickey Kantor, and Secretary of Commerce Ron Brown—the team that had fashioned Clinton's NAFTA victory—and Charles Freeman, the Pentagon's point person on China. Clinton was poring over his papers with Sandy Berger at his side, while Freeman briefed the President about military-to-military contacts.

When Freeman had finished, Berger nodded to me to begin. I summarized for the President my meeting with Qin. I told him I was confident the Chinese now knew exactly what was required by the executive order, but that he would have to demonstrate forcefully to Jiang that he was serious about implementing it. I emphasized that Jiang needed to be told that a collision would occur in which China stood to lose its trade advantage if it ignored our policy on human rights and the commitments the President had made to the Congress and the American people that MFN would not be extended unless China made progress on human rights. If we held firm in our position, I told the President, I was sure progress could occur. Clinton thanked me for the briefing and for my work on China, and said that in his meeting with Jiang he would take the approach I was suggesting.

The next morning I was invited to go jogging with the President's entourage. As we circled a park on the outskirts of Seattle, wedged at the front of a large pack of staff, Clinton friends, and Secret Service agents, the President asked me what I thought of the op-ed by Wei Jingsheng that had appeared in the *New York Times* the day before.[11] Puffing for breath, I told him I thought publishing it was a gutsy move by China's leading dissident. Clinton agreed and added that it would be a sign of progress if Wei was allowed to lead a normal life now that he had been released from prison.

Several hours later we sat down with the Chinese delegation and the Clinton-Jiang meeting got under way. During the traditional "camera spray" for press photographers before the meeting, a smiling Jiang shook hands with an uncharacteristically poker-faced Clinton. The President had decided to convey a cool relationship with the Chinese leader because of the uncertainty about what Jiang might say on human rights.

As the host, Clinton invited his guest to speak first. The Chinese president, who had spent part of the previous day visiting the huge Boeing plant on the outskirts of Seattle, was in an expansive mood. Reading from a prepared text, he put down two markers. "The world is unstable," he asserted, "and needs a strong U.S.-China relationship." And then more pointedly, "Countries should be free to choose their own systems and cultures," and not be pressured from the outside. Inviting Clinton to visit China, Jiang asserted that the President would be able to "see with your own eyes how in China economic development is our most important product."

Clinton responded by reminding Jiang that the United States purchases a third of China's exports and is therefore a very important trading partner for China as it seeks to expand its markets. He told the Chinese president he wanted to build a constructive relationship with him based on frank discussion of differences over trade, nonproliferation of weapons, and human rights. On human rights, he told Jiang he would be "very specific"—270 members of Congress had written to inform him that they would oppose the extension of MFN if they had to vote today.[12] Clinton warned that it would be harmful to U.S.-China relations if Congress had to debate the issue of human rights in the spring just before his decision on MFN. The President then proceeded to make an abbreviated version of the same appeal I had made to Qin Huasun two days earlier—urging his guest to consider releasing political prisoners on medical parole, allowing International Red Cross visits to Chinese prisons, conducting a dialogue with the Dalai Lama about the situation in Tibet, opening suspected prison labor facilities to inspection, and recognizing the right of emigration by the family members of dissidents.

Jiang offered a programmed and inflexible reply. Continuing to read from his prepared text, he produced a series of one-liners that did little to advance the dialogue. "The right to subsistence is the key Chinese contribution to human rights. Democracy and human rights have different meanings in the United States and China. Some people in the West care only about the small number of people who have violated the law in China, and not about the other 1.2 billion Chinese." When Clinton replied that he cared about the Chinese people and hoped their government would make a transition to the twenty-first century "consistent with the shared values of the world," Jiang responded that Clinton should make a speech to the Congress calling for MFN to be extended "because it is in the best interests of the U.S. and China."

The Clinton-Jiang meeting was a stand-off. While the Chinese continued to reject the linkage between trade and human rights, the President held his ground and succeeded in conveying both the specificity of his policy and the seriousness with which he was pursuing it. As Christopher pointed out in an interview with the *Washington Post* after the meeting, Clinton, unlike his predecessor, was "firm and specific" in demanding progress on human rights: "That's quite a different policy."[13] In view of the mounting pressure being brought to bear on the White House by American businesses impatient with the uncertainty surrounding MFN, Clinton's posture in Seattle was remarkably firm.

There was a flurry of activity on both sides. While holding the line on MFN, the White House shifted its position on a related economic issue. Earlier that week, the United States had announced it would again lift some of the sanctions it had imposed on China for selling missiles to Pakistan, clearing the way for the U.S. aerospace industry to sell additional satellite parts to China. For its part, China seemed to be sending a few tentative human rights signals even as it was rejecting Clinton's MFN policy. Ten days before the summit meeting, Chinese Foreign Minister Qian Qichen had made his comment to the press that China was considering allowing International Red Cross visits to political prisoners. Then a week after the summit, the Chinese freed two elderly Catholic bishops who were on the list of political and religious prisoners I had presented to the Justice Ministry in Beijing in October.[14] The conclusion I drew from these events was that Clinton was being tested by the Chinese to see how little they could do to get beyond MFN.

## Mixed Messages

After making this brief appearance in the center ring in Seattle, the human rights debate turned into a sideshow. The dominant theme of the Asia-Pacific Economic Conference (APEC), after all, was trade and the expansion of Asian markets. Fresh from his NAFTA victory, Clinton was stimulated by the APEC meetings to connect domestic economic issues with his interest in developing a post–Cold War framework for his foreign policy. With the end of the Soviet threat, military security was no longer the dominant issue. Instead, as the APEC talks demonstrated, global economics now ruled the day. Bob Rubin, the rising economic policy star in the Clinton White House, observed to the press that the President left Seattle "recognizing what a lot of private companies have recognized: we're dependent on world trade."[15]

As often happened during my time as assistant secretary, I got swept up for the next month and a half by a series of other crises that took me to Haiti and the Middle East in December and the Balkans in January. By the time I was able to reengage on China in mid-January 1994, I could sense that the ground under me had shifted. There were no more presidential warnings to the Chinese that they were in danger of losing MFN; instead, there were now daily messages by trade specialists and businesses that the United States was in danger of losing its China markets. Even some ardent Democratic congressional supporters of the Clinton executive order were beginning to say privately that the United States had put itself at a disadvantage with foreign competitors like Germany and France, which were pointedly rejecting the U.S. linkage between trade and human rights. I heard this view expressed in a closed-door briefing by several members of a congressional delegation headed by Dick Gephardt

(D-Mo.), who returned from China in January and told a group of administration officials, including me, that while their trip had reinforced the President's MFN message in their meetings in Beijing, they were concerned about where the policy was headed.[16]

The Chinese were receiving mixed messages. Through Christopher, Lord, and me, the State Department was continuing to emphasize that U.S. law explicitly conditioned the renewal of MFN on human rights progress. Christopher made this point himself when he joined me at a press briefing on January 30 to announce the publication of the State Department's Country Reports on Human Rights Practices for 1993.

But elsewhere in the administration, the rug was slowly being pulled out from under us. Bob Rubin told a group of journalists at a breakfast meeting on January 29 that trade should be separated from our concerns about human rights because "it is imperative that we have an economic relationship" with China.[17] On a trip to Beijing in January, Treasury Secretary Lloyd Bentsen succeeded in getting the Chinese to allow inspections of suspected prison labor facilities, but his overall message was that trade expansion was good for both countries. In the White House, Tony Lake held firm to the link between trade and human rights that he had helped to forge, but his deputy, Sandy Berger, began to express his concern about the policy's endgame.

Divisions within the administration were being exploited by powerful opponents of the policy. Former President George Bush and Brent Scowcroft, for example, in Beijing on a business trip in January, "gave an extensive private presentation to the Chinese leadership" about Washington's growing skepticism toward the Clinton policy, which no doubt stiffened the leadership's resolve to resist it.[18] Meanwhile, the confusing and mixed messages emanating from Washington made the job of the U.S. ambassador in Beijing extremely difficult. During the first two months of 1994, Stapleton Roy appealed repeatedly for a clearer mandate to negotiate with the Chinese about what was required under the executive order, but since the policy consensus had broken down, he never got what he was looking for. Above the growing debate, the President remained silent. Instead of moving decisively to impose discipline on his administration, Clinton allowed the mixed messages to chip away at his policy.

Despite the silence from the White House, Warren Christopher kept prodding the Chinese to make progress, reminding them of his responsibility to report to the President on MFN. On January 22 I flew to Paris with Christopher for another round of talks with Foreign Minister Qian Qichen. After an extensive discussion on the plane about where things stood and what my role would be during the endgame, I wrote in my notes that "Christopher clearly wants me 'at the point of the spear.' If I stay out in front on human rights— both in managing the details of our negotiations and staking out practical ways of testing human rights progress—I can store up credibility for the moment when we will have to make the recommendation to the President."

As the meeting got under way at the Ritz Hotel in Paris, Qian was the picture of suave self-confidence. Pamela Harriman, seated between me and Christopher, passed me a note asking whether we expected to get anything from the meeting, to which my scribbled answer was, "I hope so—time's running out." What we got was consistent with earlier meetings—just enough to test how little might satisfy the executive order.

Christopher was polite but firm. His main point was that the State Department human rights report, to be published the following week, would not be able to document significant human rights progress in China over the past year. Unless progress was made, the report could have negative consequences for MFN. In addition, Christopher observed to the glowering faces on the Chinese side of the table, "There is not yet sufficient progress to justify not raising China at the U.N. Human Rights Commission."

Qian reacted coolly, offering just enough to keep the talks alive. He agreed to look into several of the cases of dissident family members who wanted exit visas to travel to the United States, and he announced that his deputy, Liu Huaqiu, would travel to Washington the following week for talks at the White House and the State Department. Qian promised that Liu would be prepared to go over the list of prisoners I had given to the Ministry of Justice in Beijing and "other matters." He also invited me to return to China at the end of February.

I commented to Christopher and Lord that the session with Qian had been tough but was not a setback. The Secretary had certainly done his part to counter the mixed messages the Chinese were getting about MFN, and we had seen some movement on prisoner lists on the Chinese side. Meanwhile, there was good news on the domestic front. On an amendment by Senator John Kerry (D-Mass.) to the State Department authorization bill, the Senate voted 62–34 to endorse the President's policy linking MFN to human rights.[19]

But the benefit of these developments was short-lived. When Liu Huaqiu arrived in Washington for his meetings, it became clear that China had concluded that the battle over MFN would be settled by American business. At the White House, Liu told Bob Rubin that the French, the Germans, and the Canadians were all signing contracts with China worth billions, and that American companies were lining up to join them.[20] He made similar points in a meeting at the State Department with Peter Tarnoff, Winston Lord, and me, asserting brazenly that "the U.S. needs MFN more than China does." Almost as an afterthought, Liu turned to the unfinished human rights agenda of the Christopher-Qian meeting. He said I would be provided with more information about prisoners on my list in the next round of talks in Beijing and that further discussions could take place on prison labor and other issues.

No sooner had these inconclusive meetings in Paris and Washington ended than a set of disturbing reports began arriving from China. Dissidents and religious activists were being arrested in Shanghai, Beijing, and Tibet. Whether this was a result of tensions in the leadership as Deng's health continued to decline, growing labor unrest and dislocation of the workforce in China's volatile and inflationary economy, or the government's increasing confidence about MFN with all the positive trade messages coming out of the

White House and the economic agencies after APEC is still unclear—
but whatever the reason for the new crackdown, it was bad news.

As I prepared for my second trip to Beijing at the end of February,
Washington was speaking in a cacophony of voices about China.
Both extremes of the debate over what to do about MFN were repre-
sented, although the loudest voices by far were for scrapping the
Clinton policy.

Human rights groups were urging me to hang tough in my next
round of negotiations with the Chinese and not to "inflate" human
rights progress. Meanwhile, four separate congressional delegations
had returned from China trips in February, all favoring MFN extension based on progress they claimed to have observed. Senator
Max Baucus (D-Mont.) summarized this point of view in a speech on
the Senate floor citing a relaxation of tensions since Tiananmen,
downplaying the new crackdown on dissidents and calling for permanent extension of MFN.[21] These congressional maneuverings reflected a stepped-up campaign by the U.S.-China Business Council
and other China trade lobbyists to scrap the executive order. The
message the Chinese government was getting from this lobbying
campaign was so predictable that John Kamm, a Hong Kong–based
American businessman with contacts in the Chinese Ministry of Foreign Affairs, came to my office in late February to warn me that the
Chinese have become complacent on political prisoners and other
human rights issues "because they think they have MFN in the
bag."[22]

As I watched these developments unfold, I had a sinking feeling
that the MFN strategy was falling apart. The President's silence on
human rights for more than three months since Seattle was a sign
that the White House must have calculated the political cost of trying
to counter the economic lobby and decided it was too high. But even
apart from the President's passivity, it was increasingly clear that the
overall MFN strategy was coming too late to have a chance of making a difference in China. Immediately after the Tiananmen crisis
when the country's economy was in a slump, the United States
might have been able to join with other countries to use economic

measures more effectively to press for human rights progress. Now that China was attracting vast amounts of foreign investment, however, it was in a strong position to resist, particularly when the Clinton administration itself was reluctant to use its economic leverage to back up its human rights diplomacy.

## The Middle Kingdom

On February 27 I took off from Dulles Airport, flying through twelve time zones in the opposite direction from the sun, over the dark Atlantic, across Europe and the vast steppes of central Asia, then down into a smog-ridden Beijing Sunday morning. On the long ride into the city, the embassy car sped past rapidly vanishing fields and farmlands that were being gobbled up by miles of sprawling tin-roofed factories, warehouses, and buildings used for light industry. As the city came into view, giant cranes could be seen hovering over a skyline of rising steel skeletons and gleaming glass-skinned buildings. Despite this aura of modernity, I knew I was back in the capital of the fabled Middle Kingdom, to which foreigners had been traveling for centuries in search of the mysteries of Imperial China.

The car pulled into the compound of the ambassador's residence. Stapleton Roy greeted me and showed me to the same guest room I had stayed in during my last visit. He had told me then that this was the room where in 1989 Fang Lizhi had lived under embassy protection. Fang's story had been an emblem of the Tiananmen repression, and during my visit it would again resonate as China unleashed its latest crackdown on human rights.

The day after Tiananmen, Fang, an internationally renowned astrophysicist who was then China's most famous dissident and was often compared to Andrei Sakharov, had sought refuge in the American embassy. Three months earlier, he had been at the center of a widely publicized diplomatic incident during the state visit to China of President George Bush that had shown the unpredictability of the Chinese government's reaction to contacts by Chinese citizens with foreign officials in China. On February 26, Fang had been blocked by police from attending a banquet hosted by Bush at Beijing's Great Wall Sheraton Hotel, and the Chinese government had delivered a strong official protest in Washington over Fang's invitation. The embassy had invited Fang to the banquet as a low-keyed gesture to demonstrate the American commitment to human rights and freedom of association. Since Fang had published an article in the United States earlier that month without any consequences for him in China, embassy officials did not believe the Chinese would object to the invitation, which the ambassador, Winston Lord, had cleared first with Washington.[23] But the Fang incident in February later proved to be a harbinger of the Tiananmen crackdown in June.

I thought about Fang as Roy and I settled into chairs in his living room to go over the agenda of my meetings. I was groggy after only a couple of hours of fitful sleep, but stimulated by awareness of the importance of my trip. With the pressure mounting and the months dwindling before Clinton's MFN decision, I knew it was essential to try to find concrete evidence of progress on human rights in China.

Earlier that month, my office had published the State Department's annual human rights report on China. Its conclusion was bleak:

> The [Chinese] Government's overall human rights record in 1993 fell far short of internationally accepted norms as it continued to repress domestic critics and failed to control abuses of its own security forces. The Government detained, sentenced to prison or sent to labor camps, and in a few cases expelled from the country, persons who sought to exercise their rights of freedom of assembly and speech. The number of persons in Chinese penal institutions considered political prisoners by international standards is impossible to estimate accurately. . . . Physical abuse, including torture by police and prison officials persisted, especially in politically restive regions with minority populations, like Tibet.[24]

In light of China's human rights record, the ambassador and I both felt that the U.S. negotiating position on MFN depended on getting Washington to stick to the President's policy in the crucial months ahead. In our meetings, we would repeat to the Chinese the major political point that we had been making to them for six months: unlike his predecessor, President Clinton as a Democrat has the capacity to work with a Democratic Congress to move the annual MFN debate out of the center of U.S.-China relations. Clinton, we would say, has already taken two steps toward this goal—substituting an executive order for legislation that, if passed by Congress, would have been far tougher on China, and meeting with Jiang Zemin in Seattle. In return for Clinton's commitment to extend MFN without a messy fight in Washington, China should respond with immediate gestures demonstrating real progress on human rights.

Roy believed that China had actually made considerable progress since Tiananmen, and that it was time to begin measuring it. I was not so sure, but we agreed that new ways had to be found quickly to demonstrate that more progress could be made now. In the months since my last trip to Beijing, embassy officers had met several times with Wei Jingsheng to get his views about the political climate for dissidents following Wei's early release from prison the previous fall. During the planning of my visit, the possibility of my meeting with Wei had been discussed and included in an embassy cable that was sent to the State Department and the White House and reviewed by the China Desk. I raised the subject again now with Roy, and he had the embassy arrange for the meeting to take place that evening.

Wei Jingsheng was an intense and engaging former Red Guard who later became an electrician at the Beijing Zoo and a leading democracy activist. He had been arrested for advocating democracy in China in 1979 and released from prison in September 1993, six months before the end of his fifteen-year sentence. By letting Wei out early, the government was putting on its best face. It had an immediate goal: persuading countries still outraged by the Tiananmen massacre five years earlier to support Beijing's bid to host the 2000 Olympic Games. But the question remained: was Wei's release a sign of real progress, or just part of a Potemkin village public-relations campaign?

After his release, Wei had been relatively free, circulating articles to other dissidents, publishing an op-ed in the *New York Times,* and engaging in regular contacts with U.S. embassy officials.[25] Although he had been warned several times to stop meeting with foreign journalists, the government seemed to be tolerating Wei's activities, including his meetings with American diplomats.

As I entered the coffee garden of the China World Hotel with Deborah Kingsland, an embassy officer, we were hailed by Wei's assistant, Tong Yi, and made our way to a table near the center of the room. After Kingsland's introductions, Wei plunged immediately into a monologue on his favorite subject, the movement for democracy in China. Chain-smoking as he talked, he observed that the severe repression of earlier decades had been easing in the 1980s. Then the government had reversed itself in the Tiananmen crackdown. Now, he claimed, things might improve again if the United States and other countries held firm on human rights. "Without international pressure," Wei asserted, "I would still be in prison." My conversation with Wei yielded some useful insights into how China's internal democracy movement saw economic relations between the United States and China. The embassy's cable about the meeting reported that Wei was "torn on the issue of encouraging foreign investment. 'Too much foreign investment would bolster the status quo,' he said, 'but pulling out would harm the economy and the average Chinese.'" Wei's conclusion was that "foreign business should take a long term view and support democracy and therefore stability in China."

Getting access to the views of nonexiled dissidents like Wei was why U.S. diplomats made it a practice of having these kinds of meetings. In China, the Soviet Union, and other communist or authoritarian countries, such meetings were "standard operating procedure for us," Warren Christopher later pointed out.[26] The fact that I had been able to have a conversation with Wei in an open setting, apparently unhindered by the police, seemed a positive sign that I hoped would point the way toward a successful next round of discussions with my government interlocutors.

Things got off to a rocky start the next morning with Qin Huasun, who lost no time returning to his familiar protest against the linkage in U.S. policy of MFN with human rights. "The current problem was created by the U.S. side," he asserted, "and the U.S. side should correct its own mistake." Surprisingly, however, as the meeting went on we were able to move beyond rhetoric and get back to the details of the Clinton executive order, which Qin said he would report to his superiors so that they could prepare for the visit of Secretary Christopher later that month. Through Qin I delivered a letter to President Jiang Zemin signed by fifty-four U.S. senators, requesting that five ailing leaders of the Tiananmen democracy movement be released from prison on medical parole, and I ironed out with Qin an agreement on prison labor so that it could be signed by Christopher when he arrived in Beijing. At a press conference after the meeting, I told reporters that my human rights discussions "have become more businesslike and intense." The next day, a Chinese Foreign Ministry official was quoted by the *Asian Wall Street Journal* as saying that China "is willing to do what we can within the law. What we can't do, we'll tell the U.S. clearly."[27] During my four-hour meeting with Qin, the subject of Wei Jingsheng never came up, although by then Wei's meeting with me would certainly have been reported to the Ministry of Foreign Affairs and written into Qin's talking points if the government was planning to make an issue of it. The progress Stapleton Roy and I were looking for seemed possible.

Later that afternoon we got the first indication that we might not be in control of the situation. Patrick Tyler of the *New York Times* called the embassy to ask for comment on an interview he had just conducted with Wei about our meeting. Without my knowledge, Wei had taken a defiant and dangerous step. Going to the press, he had raised the stakes and risked playing into the hands of the hardliners, making it impossible for the government to ignore our meeting. Roy and I agreed that we would make no comment. That evening, I received a protest about the meeting at a banquet hosted by Deputy Foreign Minister Liu Huaqiu. Liu's message did not affect the overall positive tone of the evening, and gave little indication of the coming storm. He simply said that "meetings with so-called dissidents would bring trouble to the Ministry of Foreign Affairs and those in charge of the human rights question."

The next day I got a glimpse of the reformers' side of the power struggle going on inside the Chinese government. In meetings at the Ministry of Justice and the Chinese Academy of Social Sciences, I was told that "experts" were interested in revising China's counter-revolutionary laws. A fledgling law reform movement was apparently taking aim at speech crimes and other restrictions on freedom of expression "so that we can have more open debate of issues that are important to the people," as one scholar put it. At the academy, I heard that the 1993 World Conference on Human Rights (where Chinese diplomats had attacked the very idea that rights are universal), had actually emboldened China's internal reformers. One academy scholar who had been in the Chinese delegation in Vienna said that she had been impressed by the range of nongovernmental organizations at the conference, and had returned to Beijing with the idea of expanding the role of China's "citizen organizations."

But the storm clouds were growing darker. On the next leg of my trip, to Shanghai, Li Baodong, my Ministry of Foreign Affairs escort, warned that China would "retaliate" if the United States persisted in supporting an "anti-China resolution" the following week in the U.N. Human Rights Commission. I also learned at our Shanghai consulate that dissidents were being rounded up again for questioning, and that Western journalists were being told that China's best-known political prisoners were all "healthy," a sign that our diplomatic appeals to release them on "medical parole" had been denied.

Even as the storm was breaking in Shanghai, however, I was getting signals from the embassy in Beijing that my visit had moved the human rights agenda forward. I spoke with Stapleton Roy on a secure phone from the consulate, and he reported that progress was being made on the exit visa cases, that the Ministry of Justice had reaffirmed China's willingness to talk to the International Red Cross about possible prison visits, and that after his meeting with me, assistant justice minister Jia Jingping had confided to an embassy officer that "China's human rights conditions, including prison conditions, need to be brought up to civilized standards." Another embassy political officer reported that analysts from the Ministry of State Security's International Affairs Institute had told him that it was a positive sign on human rights that security officials had actually allowed Wei's meeting with me to take place. Buoyed by these reports, Roy had sent a cable to Christopher summarizing my Beijing talks. "Assistant Secretary Shattuck provided his interlocutors with the most detailed and comprehensive exposition of the concrete steps on human rights that would constitute 'overall significant progress' [under the executive order]." Roy's cable to the Secretary concluded that my meetings had "laid the foundation for your detailed substantive engagement on human rights issues and constructive discussion of the future of bilateral relations."

But the next day, the furies were unleashed. Wei was arrested in Beijing, and more dissident roundups began.[28] Clearly the hardliners were determined to gain the upper hand by discrediting my talks and heightening the tension between Beijing and Washington. I felt shaken by these developments, guilty at the role I might have unwittingly played in Wei's arrest, and used as a pawn by forces intent on blocking even the most minimal human rights progress in China. For the next several days, the international press was dominated by reports of the new Chinese crackdown and its negative effects on U.S.-China relations on the eve of Christopher's trip to Beijing. "Arrests in China Cast a Pall on Visit," read a typical front-page headline.[29] The *New York Times* announced that "China Arrests Leading Dissident Despite U.S. Warnings on Rights," setting off a flurry of press speculation about the growing power struggle inside the Chinese government.[30] Commenting on "the preemptive arrest of a dozen or more pro-democracy leaders in recent days," Patrick Tyler observed on March 7 that the ghost of Tiananmen was haunting the aging leaders, headed by Deng Xiaoping and his hardline premier, Li Peng, who had suppressed the stirrings of democracy five years earlier. "Although the new arrests may appear to be an affront to the Clinton Administration's push for human rights," Tyler wrote, "they also reflect the mounting tension in Chinese society as democracy activists begin to stir from the long dormancy that followed the massacre near Tiananmen Square in June 1989."[31]

If the power struggle in China centered around responding to the new pressures for democracy, another struggle was under way inside the U.S. government about how to respond to China. On the day the new dissident crackdown began, the *Wall Street Journal* carried a front-page article with the headline, "U.S. Sends China Mixed Signals on Trade; MFN Talks Pit Commercial Interests against Pursuit of Human Rights."[32] The story noted that a few hours before I had told the press in Beijing on March 1 that "further progress on human rights is needed if MFN is to be renewed in June," Jeffrey Garten, the U.S. undersecretary of commerce, had commented to the same reporters that "there are huge stakes for the United States here, and we're looking very much to deepen them in the long term." I was aware of Garten's visit and knew that it had been coordinated with the interagency China Steering Group in Washington. I later learned that Garten, like other administration visitors to China during this period, had reinforced my human rights message in his meetings with the Chinese. Nevertheless, there can be no doubt that the ardor with which U.S. commercial interests were being pursued in China encouraged the Chinese leadership to believe that trade would soon trump human rights in U.S. policy. As the roundups continued, undermining whatever diplomatic progress had been made on human rights, I knew that our own mixed signals were weakening our negotiating position.

The immediate question was what to do about Christopher's trip. The White House and the State Department had condemned the latest dissident arrests, and sentiment was building for canceling or postponing it to protest this latest crackdown on human rights. Mike McCurry, the State Department spokesman, told the press on March 6, "There is certainly a pattern of detentions that we find troubling and which certainly casts a pall over the secretary's coming visit."[33] Christopher was in Australia on his way to Japan and could have simply scrubbed China as the last stop on his itinerary. From Hong Kong, and later from Bangkok where I was holding talks with the government and meeting with Thai human rights groups, I argued against going forward. I called Winston Lord on a secure phone and discovered that he was undecided. Lord's uncertainty reflected the conflict between his personal commitment to human rights, forged during his ambassadorship in the pre-Tiananmen years when China's democracy movement was growing, and his sense of China's geopolitical importance, developed during his time as an aide to Kissinger during the Nixon administration, when the foundations of modern U.S.-China relations were laid.

Lord suggested I send a cable to Christopher, and to Sandy Berger in the White House, stating my views. In my cable I outlined the risks in going ahead with the trip: the possibility of more dissident detentions while Christopher was in Beijing; the possibility of no further human rights progress during the trip; and the likelihood that the United States would further weaken its negotiating position if the trip went forward at the very time when dissidents were being rounded up. Based on these risks, I recommended to Christopher that he consider "a change in your plans for the Beijing visit." Since the President had made a public statement from the White House condemning the crackdown as "obviously not helpful to our relations," I sensed that this was an opportunity to show the Chinese we were serious about human rights by suspending our diplomatic dialogue.[34] Berger told the Secretary from Washington that the White House would defer to his judgment. Stapleton Roy from Beijing, ultimately backed by Lord, argued for going ahead on the ground that the diplomatic cost of canceling the trip would be greater than the cost of proceeding. It was a close call. In the end, Christopher decided that "it would be more effective to tell the Chinese face-to-face that we disapproved of their actions," so he pressed ahead, signaling before he reached Beijing that he was appalled by the dissident roundups and "concerned that China was going in the wrong direction."[35]

## Eye of the Storm

I flew from Bangkok to Tokyo on March 11 to meet Christopher's party. The atmosphere was tense. Mike McCurry and Tom Donilon, the Secretary's chief of staff, had picked up reports of still more dissi-

dent arrests, and were increasingly worried about what we would encounter when we reached Beijing. The Washington press corps accompanying the Secretary was scrambling to find out how we
planned to respond to what was going on. A typical rumor, which
Elaine Sciolino of the *New York Times* spent all night trying to track
down by calling around to the hotel rooms of members of the official
party, was that the military-to-military dialogue that undersecretary
of defense for policy Frank Wisner was scheduled to initiate would be
canceled to protest the dissident arrests. Wisner's dialogue was not
canceled, but the flap over it showed the confusion and uncertainty
that threatened to overwhelm the Secretary's Beijing mission before
it even began.

A huge chess game was being played, and we were losing. The
Chinese side had the benefit of enforced unity and discipline, while
our side reflected the competition inside and outside our own government among trade, security, and human rights interests in the un-
ruly environment of American democracy. Assessing where things
stood on the eve of Christopher's trip, I wrote in my notes: "There is
speculation that the Chinese have decided not to do anything further
to respond to the executive order, or at least to reduce our expectations about what they will do, in an effort to get us to lower the
MFN bar. The detentions will make it even more difficult for us to
conclude that there has been 'overall significant progress' within the
meaning of the executive order. The Chinese know this, and seem to
be thumbing their noses at us."

Stapleton Roy sent Christopher a cable from Beijing setting the
scene for the trip and trying to put the best face on the situation.
While warning that "all the makings of a tense and unproductive
standoff are present," the ambassador asserted that "beneath the sur-
face, the Chinese are signaling that the door is [still] open for progress." The cable noted that the Chinese leaders were preoccupied
with stability on the eve of the National Peoples' Congress. Nevertheless, Roy claimed, we were finally getting our message across, and
had done "a superb job in preparing the ground on the human rights
front." The ambassador recommended that Christopher emphasize

in his meetings how much harder MFN extension had been made by Chinese actions against the dissidents. The Secretary should convey his personal indignation that a visit aimed at improving U.S.-China relations was being clouded by Chinese actions in conflict with that goal. Roy's cable concluded with a suggestion of prophecy that would soon prove true. The Chinese know our course on MFN is set, Roy noted, "but they are not immune from fanciful thinking that their old nemeses, Wall Street and the captains of American industry, may bail them out."

The Christopher trip was the Götterdämmerung of Clinton's policy on human rights in China. From the moment the secretary's plane touched down in Beijing on March 11, it was clear that the Chinese were determined to call the president's bluff on MFN by putting Christopher on the defensive and defying the executive order. The atmospherics were terrible. On the flight from Tokyo we received reports of more dissident arrests, bringing to eighteen the total of those rounded up just during the few days immediately before Christopher's arrival.[36] Two American journalists were detained by the police for eight hours when they went to the apartment of a well-known labor activist to try to interview him. At the airport and later at the China World Hotel, Chinese security agents made things as difficult as possible for their American counterparts, jostling them and blocking their way. Since the Chinese made no public welcoming statement when the secretary's party landed, Christopher dispensed with any statement on his part and went straight to the hotel to prepare for his meetings.

The next morning we were escorted by a long line of security vehicles through a bleak and deserted Tiananmen Square on the way to the Daioyutai Guest House. The center of the city had been turned into a ghost town for us, and all Chinese citizens had been blocked from coming anywhere near our motorcade. When we arrived at the government compound, Foreign Minister Qian Qichen greeted Christopher perfunctorily, and then opened their first diplomatic session by delivering a message from the newly dominant hardline leadership.[37] Foregoing the usual deference to a visitor, Qian began the exchange by saying he wanted to raise China's concerns first. He accused me of "interfering in China's internal affairs" by meeting with Wei Jingsheng; complained that the United States had not lifted the sanctions it had imposed against China after Tiananmen; asserted that the sale of F-16s to Taiwan under the Bush administration was in violation of previous U.S.-China agreements; and alluded to "other concerns" that he said he would raise later. As for MFN, he referred confidently to the broad support China was getting from the American business community for its renewal.

Christopher responded forthrightly to this preemptive strike. He said it was essential to the work of diplomats to meet with citizens in other countries who are not accused of crimes. By challenging Wei's right to have a conversation with me, he continued, China was losing an opportunity to show respect for basic freedoms of speech and association. The secretary observed that the ongoing roundup of dissidents had "cast a pall" over his visit, and then turned to ambassador Roy, who suggested that the foreign minister arrange a meeting for us with some of those detained. Christopher made clear that the United States was prepared to address other issues raised by China, but that the paramount issue now was human rights. MFN and human rights were linked by U.S. law, and under the terms of the executive order he would have to report in less than three months to President Clinton whether sufficient human rights progress had occurred in China for the President to recommend renewing China's MFN status. As matters now stood, human rights conditions in China would have to improve for this to happen.

The frosty atmosphere continued through the morning and over the elegant seven-course midday banquet that followed. As he was leaving, Christopher remarked to Qian that he wished "the meeting had been as good as the lunch." The normally urbane and affable Chinese Foreign Minister had lectured the American Secretary of State about China's views on human rights, but offered no further gestures in the seven areas of the executive order. In a private exchange at the end of the meeting, Christopher asked Qian whether he was "prepared to see a failure here," to which Qian only smiled and said nothing. One member of our party commented privately as we were walking out to the motorcade that the "Dynasty" wine the foreign minister had served us was on a U.S. list of banned Chinese export goods produced by prison labor—another sign that the Chinese had decided to thumb their noses at us.

But the Qian meeting was only a warmup for the full-scale collision that took place when Christopher met Li Peng. Li had been the architect of the Tiananmen crackdown and now was the head of China's newly resurgent hardline leadership. Although the secretary knew he might as well be talking to the wall, he left no doubt about the policy he was working to implement. He told Li that President Clinton was prepared to take new steps to improve U.S.-China relations, including lifting the restrictions on the sale of satellite parts and other high-technology exports. Before that could happen, however, the MFN issue would have to be resolved. But, Christopher added, "unless there is human rights progress, MFN is in serious jeopardy. What we're seeking here is not extraordinary, nor should it be regarded as pressure on China. What we're seeking is the most basic internationally recognized human rights under the Universal Declaration that China itself recognizes." Christopher told Li he had heard rumors that China thought the United States had already decided to renew MFN. Rumors like these, he emphasized, looking directly at the impassive Chinese premier, were erroneous. Much as President Clinton would like to renew MFN, he would not do so in violation of his own executive order.

Li replied by bluntly telling Christopher that he had "not received the response that I expected." Hinting, as Qian had done before him, that China knew the interests of American business better than American diplomats did, he said "the sky will not fall for China if MFN is revoked," but it will for the United States if China reciprocates, particularly for U.S. agriculture, timber, airline, telecommunications, and other major industries that are heavily dependent on the Chinese market. Li implied that Christopher was not qualified to question China's record on human rights, asserting that the secretary's role in "cleaning things up" after the Los Angeles riots showed that he was not objective about his own country. Christopher, who had chaired a widely praised commission that had recommended reforms of the Los Angeles Police Department after the brutal police beating of Rodney King in 1991, stared impassively at Li.[38] The Chinese premier then summarized his position by asserting flatly that "human rights are not universal, and China will not accept the human rights concepts of the United States."

Later, as we considered the diplomatic setbacks of Christopher's first day in China, Winston Lord remarked that we were in the throes of "a Middle Kingdom syndrome." For centuries, he said, Chinese leaders have roughed up foreign emissaries on the first day of a visit and then offered them just enough before their departure to remove the sting. Firing back at the Chinese government spokesman who had told American reporters that "U.S. actions and pressure" had poisoned the atmosphere of the trip, Lord produced the sound bite of the week when he quipped that the spokesman's efforts to blame the United States for China's own appalling human rights record was "a great leap of chutzpah." That evening, at a private dinner with Stapleton Roy, Tom Pickering (the U.S. ambassador to Russia), and me, Lord described how the Chinese government had accused him in February 1989 of interfering with China's internal affairs when, as ambassador, he had arranged for Fang Lizhi to be invited to the Beijing banquet hosted by President Bush. Just as they were trying to do now in the case of Wei Jingsheng, Lord observed, the Chinese had used the Fang Lizhi incident to try to put the United States on the defensive and create tensions inside the U.S. government over how to conduct human rights diplomacy in China.

The Chinese offensive continued on the second day, although it came from an unlikely source. In a meeting with the American Chamber of Commerce in Beijing, which Christopher opened to his traveling press corps, we heard confirmation of what the secretary had been told by Li Peng: the American business community was now actively campaigning inside China against Clinton's MFN policy. In a remarkable demonstration of openness in a country committed to the suppression of all forms of open political speech, the Secretary of State found himself being actively lobbied by a parade of U.S. business representatives in a Beijing hotel to cut the linkage between human rights and trade. I was struck by the contrast between China's reaction to my meeting with Wei Jingsheng in another Beijing hotel and Christopher's willingness to listen to American opponents of the policy he was trying to carry out, who were now being allowed to exercise their freedom of speech in front of the American press even at the risk of undermining their own government's negotiating position with the Chinese.[39]

As Lord had predicted, the atmosphere of the visit changed somewhat toward the end. President Jiang Zemin offered Christopher a peculiar combination of patronizing statements and passive quips—for example, suggesting that since he and the Secretary of State were both older than Clinton, they could help extricate the young American President from his China dilemma. He told Christopher that he admired Abraham Lincoln's leadership in holding together the United States while freeing the slaves, and recounted his own role in calming student demonstrators when he was mayor of Shanghai by reciting and analyzing for them the Gettysburg Address. Since MFN is mutually beneficial, he asserted, we should be able to resolve our conflict over human rights "within the framework of Chinese law." Before sending his visitor off to a final meeting with Foreign Minister Qian Qichen, Jiang reinforced Christopher's already rock-bottom expectations by quoting Confucius, "One cannot expect to become a fat man with only one good meal," and concluding with a line of Chinese poetry—"We can share the beauty of the moon even though we are thousands of miles apart."

The damage had been done. After the opening diplomatic bombast, Christopher's trip was universally characterized as a failure in the American press.[40] Ironically, the final meetings produced some modest human rights progress. After Christopher's second exchange with Qian Qichen and my own concluding session with Qin Huasun, we were able to announce an agreement between China and the United States to permit inspections by the U.S. Customs Bureau of a number of suspected prison labor facilities—as well as progress toward resolution of the emigration cases I had raised involving family members of dissidents, a limited accounting of the status of 235 prisoners and a promise of additional information on 106 more prisoners in Tibet, talks on the "technical problems" of receiving Voice of America broadcasts in China, and a commitment by China to accept the validity of the Universal Declaration of Human Rights.[41] In addition, Qian told Christopher that China would "soon" allow an imprisoned leader of the Tiananmen demonstrations, Wang Juntao, to travel to the United States "for medical treatment and reunion with his wife." Another imprisoned Tiananmen leader on our list, Chen Ziming, would be released on medical parole in May.

The field was stony, and the harvest modest. Despite these last-minute positive developments in Beijing, the following two months would be decisive in determining whether the Chinese would follow through on their commitments and reverse their crackdown on dissidents so that Christopher could certify to the President the "overall significant progress on human rights" required for MFN renewal. The question as we left China was what the rest of the administration would do to reinforce the message Christopher had delivered in Beijing.

The answer was: nothing.

## Endgame

Washington's reception for the Secretary of State on his return was almost as frosty as the greeting he had received a week earlier from the Chinese when he arrived in Beijing. Press commentary on the trip focused on the stormy early meetings and ignored the positive results of the final day. In a session with Strobe Talbott's senior State Department team two days after our return, Winston Lord and I worked with Mike McCurry to hammer out a press strategy to counter the growing perception that what had happened in Beijing was the diplomatic equivalent of the *Harlan County* fiasco five months earlier in Haiti. Our message, which we fanned out to deliver in a series of interviews, was that Christopher had held firm, progress had been achieved during the trip, and more was possible if Christopher's message was reinforced in the final months before the May deadline on MFN. Christopher himself came out swinging against his critics in testimony before a House Appropriations subcommittee on March 17. "The Chinese have been hearing mixed signals and needed to hear our position stated clearly and directly," he told the subcommittee, adding that "in my sessions with China, I pulled no punches and yielded no ground."[42]

Meanwhile, the Chinese were playing the growing controversy in the United States over MFN like a finely tuned fiddle. By rounding up dissidents and roughing up Christopher, they had succeeded in lowering U.S. expectations about what the policy could achieve, and making Christopher, Lord, and me the scapegoats for its failure. The U.S. foreign policy establishment, which had hailed the executive order as a brilliant political compromise when it was unveiled by Clinton in May 1993, now turned with a vengeance on those seeking to implement it. In a remarkable slap at Christopher the day after his return from Beijing, three former secretaries of state and a parade of other former officials and China experts called upon the administration to abandon its ten-month-old MFN policy at a forum in New York sponsored by the Council on Foreign Relations.[43]

Henry Kissinger's attack was especially biting, since it suggested that the policy would be a failure even if it achieved its human rights goals. Kissinger speculated that Beijing would harbor grudges for years to come, undermining the broader U.S.-China relationship. "How many such victories can we afford?" he asked.[44] Since no administration official was invited to participate in the forum, Clinton's policy went undefended at a critical time, when the Chinese were watching closely to see how seriously they should take it. One participant, Douglas H. Paal, who had directed Asia policy on the National Security staff of President George Bush, sounded a note from the same tune China was playing. "If you find a policy is not serving U.S. interests, then you sacrifice somebody and get rid of the policy. That's how we do it in Washington."[45]

Attacks from within the administration were just as strong as those from the outside. The China Steering Group, now chaired by Sandy Berger, began meeting regularly in the White House Situation Room. At its first meeting after Christopher's return, Berger urged participants to "hold firm, give the President flexibility and not let the policy unravel." But the appeal for unity was too late, since the economic agencies were already in active revolt against any further linkage between human rights and trade. On March 22, for example, the *Wall Street Journal* reported that Treasury Secretary Lloyd Bentsen had told the press that "we have to explore alternatives to see if we can work this out."[46] Comments like these reinforced China's confidence that MFN would be renewed even if no further human rights gestures were made. The growing discord of voices inside the U.S. government was a signal to China's finance minister, Liu Zhongli, that he had little to worry about. In a speech in Honolulu on March 19, Minister Liu summed up the Chinese perception of where things stood on MFN: "I think in the U.S. Congress there are different views, and I think in the U.S. administration there are different views. I think it is the view of U.S. business to solve this issue once and for all."[47]

The one person who could have stilled the cacophony was the President, but he continued to remain silent. In the ten months since he had promulgated his MFN policy, Clinton had been preoccupied by the economy, health care, and other domestic controversies, and only occasionally—before his Seattle meeting with Jiang Zemin, for example—had he reviewed the China policy framework created in the spring of 1993. With the May deadline fast approaching, it was now time to address the question he had left open when he forged the consensus around MFN and human rights: What would be the consequences for U.S.-China relations if the conditions in his executive order were not fulfilled?

There were increasingly clear indications of which way the President would go on the issue of MFN. In the months since NAFTA and the APEC meeting with Asian leaders in Seattle, Clinton had placed economic issues in the center of his foreign policy agenda, paving the way for American business to expand international trade and investment. More immediate, and perhaps more telling, was that the President had said nothing to reinforce Christopher's message to Beijing after the Secretary's return from China. Clinton's first public comment about the situation came in the opening statement of a news conference on March 24, when he indicated only that his administration would continue "to seek progress on human rights in China" as part of its effort "to build a more positive relationship with that very important nation."[48]

Three debates took place in the final eight weeks leading up to the president's MFN decision. The first involved the standard for assessing human rights progress in China. Should the assessment be objective, or should it simply be used to ratify a decision previously made to extend MFN? The second debate was over what consequences would follow if it was determined that the human rights conditions in the executive order had not been met. Should MFN be revoked if there was not enough progress? If not, should some alternative form of sanctions be imposed on China? The last "debate" was the most far-reaching, even though it never really took place: should Clinton's MFN policy be scrapped entirely and the linkage between human rights and trade severed permanently?

In the rapidly shifting sands of China policy, I felt that an honest assessment of the facts was fundamental. I decided early in these debates that I would resign if I was asked to sign off on an inflated assessment of human rights progress. Shortly after returning from Beijing, I told Ellen that if a train wreck was coming over China policy, I would not try to avert it by shading the truth about human rights in China. Fortunately, Lord and Christopher agreed with me that we should review the facts objectively and not inflate them, no matter what the outcome of the policy debate. On April 1, I discussed this issue with Mike Posner of the Lawyers Committee for Human Rights, one of the most experienced and thoughtful human rights leaders working on China. Mike agreed that it was essential to call the facts by their proper names, even if the policy was changing. Bad policy would be bad enough, he said, but the cause of human rights would be damaged irreparably by dishonest reporting. In a

China Steering Group meeting in the White House on April 4, I argued that we should not count as "progress" the release of dissidents who were detained during Christopher's trip, since they never should have been rounded up in the first place.[49] Sandy Berger supported me, but others in the room tried to dismiss my point as nitpicking. Nevertheless, as the spring wore on, the position Lord and I, backed by Christopher, had staked out was grudgingly accepted: we should use an objective standard of assessment. Applying this standard, China had met some, but not enough, of the conditions in the President's executive order.[50]

The debate over what consequences should follow from China's failure to demonstrate "overall significant progress" on human rights was far more difficult, at least for the human rights side. Taking place against a highly charged political backdrop of the Whitewater investigation, congressional battles over presidential nominations, and the deepening crises in Bosnia, Haiti, and Rwanda, this debate was skewed from the outset against further confrontation with China. Clinton did not need another crisis. In his early China Steering Group meetings, Sandy Berger made an effort to hold the Clinton team together, pointing out that there was a chance of getting more human rights gestures from China if the administration remained united around the President's policy, but no chance at all if we were publicly divided. This exhortation had no effect. National Economic Council Chairman Bob Rubin, Treasury Undersecretary Larry Summers, and Deputy U.S. Trade Representative Charlene Barshefsky, among others, were already mounting a campaign to renew MFN despite China's human rights record. By the end of March their voices were dominating the discussion, making it a foregone conclusion that unless the President surprised everyone by overruling them, MFN would be extended.

This still left open the question whether some form of sanctions should be imposed on China for its failure to meet the human rights conditions in the executive order. Once again, the State Department was alone in pressing the human rights case, although Christopher seemed increasingly resigned to the likelihood that the whole policy would be thrown out. After meeting with nine cabinet-level officials in the White House at the end of March and being greeted by silence when he appealed for them to support the policy he had worked faithfully to implement, the Secretary was convinced that the executive order was dead. "No one spoke in defense of continued linkage of China's trade status to its human rights progress," he later wrote. "It was as if the policy had died in my absence, or, as some at the meeting would have it, had never existed. All that remained was to arrange a decent burial."[51]

If the policy was to be scrapped, Lord and I argued that some form of sanctions was essential for the administration to preserve credibility on human rights. The China Steering Group debated the issue throughout April and May, looking at several options. Two alternative approaches, known as the "partial revocation" models, were to cut off MFN benefits for products made by Chinese state-owned enterprises, or to impose a fixed-percentage tariff surcharge across the board on all Chinese-made products. While not a substitute for full revocation, the two broad sanctions models were nevertheless appealing to Mitchell, Pelosi, Gephardt, and other key congressional architects of the trade and human rights linkage.

The Council of Economic Advisors, headed by Laura Tyson, ran computer analyses of the probable effects of these proposals on the Chinese economy. The council's conclusion gave the economic agencies all the ammunition they needed to shoot down both partial revocation approaches. In the case of targeted sanctions, the computer studies found that it would be impossible to separate state enterprises from private companies, because the two sectors were intertwined and the sanctions could easily be circumvented by false labeling. In the case of a tariff surcharge, the sanction would hit the very sectors that the U.S. trade policy was supposed to help: American joint ventures, Hong Kong businesses with strong international ties, and private enterprise.

Two other sanctions proposals were less controversial, but far less significant. The first was to ban the export of Chinese weapons into the United States, and the second was to reaffirm the limited sanctions imposed on China after Tiananmen. Both were acceptable to the economic agencies, and both became part of the final package announced by the President. Other noneconomic sanctions, such as suspending various high-level diplomatic exchanges, were rejected as inconsistent with the President's overall approach of promoting "engagement" with China.

As the day of decision approached, I could feel the air going out of our human rights policy. While I had succeeded in keeping our assessment honest, I knew I had lost the larger debate over sanctions, and the juggernaut of "delinkage" was hurdling forward without any debate. I left Washington on May 2 to try to get the United States engaged in an effort to stop the genocide in Rwanda. I returned a week later, overwhelmed and exhausted. On May 10 I spoke with my old friend, Representative Tom Lantos (D-Calif.), a survivor of the Holocaust and respected human rights leader in the Congress. Tom shared my despair about both the administration's inaction on Rwanda and its impending collapse on China, and he urged me to keep speaking up. The next day, I sent a memo to Christopher, Lake, and Berger making one last pitch for sanctions. "If the President renews and delinks with only the weapons sanction," I warned, "he will confront not only howls of protest from Congress, but legislation and a stiff fight. . . . The human rights community will be up in arms, and the Chinese leaders will believe they forced us down and we blinked." My appeal was ignored. The issue had already been decided.

On May 26, President Clinton announced that he was renewing China's MFN status, revoking his executive order, and breaking the link between U.S. trade and human rights policies toward China. Responding to questions from the press about why he had decided to reverse course so dramatically, the President argued that the new direction he was taking would be more likely to produce human rights progress than the path he was abandoning.

Clinton provided three justifications for his decision. Expanding trade and development, he argued, would lead to an improvement in the climate for human rights. By the same token, he said, engaging

China "in a growing web of political and economic cooperation and contacts" would be better "for advancing freedom" than a more confrontational approach. Finally, he asserted, "we are far more likely to have human rights advances in China when [our relationship] is not under the cloud of the annual review of MFN." Clinton remarked that the policy he was abandoning had grown out of "a frustration in the Congress that the previous administration had reestablished relationships too quickly after Tiananmen Square, and there seemed to be no other aggressive human rights strategy." Now, he asserted, "we have reached the end of the usefulness of that policy."[52]

It was an extraordinary statement. In a few words, the President had shifted the China human rights policy back to the economic arena where it had been before Tiananmen. The essence of the Chinese argument throughout the year that Clinton's MFN executive order had been in effect was that economic development, not human rights, must come first. Now we were implicitly agreeing with this position by reaffirming the view of China experts before Tiananmen that political freedom in China would *necessarily* follow from increased trade and foreign investment.

There was little evidence to support such a deterministic claim. As one human rights advocate put it just before Clinton announced his decision, "Those who advocate decoupling MFN status from China's performance on human rights commonly argue that Western economic ties with China, in and of themselves, promote freedom there. The obvious question to such economic determinists is: Where is the evidence?"[53] Or, as I had remarked in a speech explaining the President's old policy a month before it was abandoned, "Development of institutions of political freedom—free press, free speech, basic principles of humane treatment of individuals—come about through political and human rights reforms, and they are not necessarily going to result from trade and economic growth."[54] The one thing that was clear on May 26 was that American business interests opposed to the President's human rights policy had succeeded in making the case that it was costing them trade and investment opportunities in China. As an alternative to MFN, the administration announced that it would pursue its human rights interests in China through other means: diplomatic dialogue, resolutions at the U.N. Human Rights Commission, radio broadcasting, and voluntary "human rights principles" for companies to consider when doing business in China. In the wake of the enormous political and diplomatic costs of the MFN reversal, however, these alternatives amounted to thin gruel.

In the weeks after Clinton's MFN decision, I thought seriously about resigning. While this was neither the first nor the last time such a thought would cross my mind during my five and a half years as the government's chief human rights official, it was the most serious time. *Washington Post* columnist E. J. Dionne captured my dilemma in a May 31 op-ed, "Goodbye to Human Rights?" The article quoted a Clinton statement in 1992 that "the people of China 'are still denied their basic rights and liberties. They are denied the right to choose their own leaders; they are still imprisoned for simply calling for democracy; they continue to suffer torture and cruel, inhuman and degrading treatment and punishment.'" Dionne pointed out that all these conditions still existed. "Yet Clinton, after so many threats and promises, was forced to back down. In doing so he sent a message about all future American statements and undertakings about human rights: We may not really mean them. . . . [This] will not be lost on China's dictators, nor on dictators anywhere else."[55]

I recognized the dilemma the President had faced. On the one hand, he had made a specific commitment to use the leverage of MFN to press the Chinese government to respect human rights. On the other hand, he had promised to expand trade as part of a broader commitment to make economic issues the top priority of his administration. In 1993, he had persuaded himself that he could do both. Now he had been forced to confront the political reality that shapes many presidential decisions. As I thought about the question posed by the title of Dionne's article, I asked myself why I should accept the political calculation that had forced the President's hand. My constituency, after all, was made up of those whose human rights were being violated, and I was their voice inside the U.S. government. If I could no longer speak on their behalf, I should not continue to try to represent them.

For two weeks, I discussed my future with Ellen, going back and forth about whether to resign and take a stand for human rights outside the administration. My resignation would have been understood, although interpreted in different ways, by Washington insiders. Human rights groups would have seen it as an indication that the Clinton administration was a dead end for human rights; the press would have interpreted it as my being forced out as a scapegoat for the failure of Clinton's MFN policy; and administration officials would have regarded it as an inevitable clash between human rights idealism and the hard realities of governing. For my own part, I considered resigning to separate myself from a policy decision with which I disagreed.

In the end I chose to stay. I felt I could do more to advance the cause of human rights by continuing the battle to shape policies inside an administration that was struggling with the new realities of the post–Cold War world. I knew that by staying on there was a risk that I might be associated with policies or decisions, like the one Clinton had just made on MFN, with which I disagreed. But I decided my reputation was not the issue. Would the objectives I was pursuing be better addressed by others if I quit? In fact, the opposite seemed likely—a successor would be chosen who would be more malleable and less likely to take risks. To the amazement of Ellen and many others, I actually enjoyed the challenge of bureaucratic infighting, while maintaining my own values and identity. For me, the work itself and the possibilities it presented for making a difference in the lives of real people were what mattered. I wanted to keep fighting from within, even if the odds were stacked against me and the rewards often invisible.

In June 1994, the world was coming apart at the seams—in Rwanda, in Haiti, in Bosnia, and now in China—and the United States seemed unable or unwilling to lead an effort to put it back together. But over the next four years, as lessons were learned inside the Clinton administration about the growing importance of human rights in the post–Cold War world, we were able to help move to the center of U.S. foreign policy such essential objectives as stopping the violence in Haiti, Bosnia, and Kosovo; bringing war criminals to justice for genocide in Rwanda and the former Yugoslavia; promoting the rule of law in countries emerging from conflict or authoritarian rule; and supporting the struggles of people all over the world to build democracy and constitutional government. While China remained frozen, we were able to score two important human rights victories in the year after the MFN debacle—first by working with European countries that had never been willing to link their trade policies with human rights to muster the votes in the U.N. Human Rights Commission to prevent China from blocking a resolution criticizing its human rights record, and second, under the leadership of Hillary Clinton, by confronting China's repressive practices at the U.N. International Conference on Women in Beijing.[56]

Much of the work to advance these objectives was done behind the scenes. All of it justified for me my decision not to resign following the disastrous setback for human rights when Clinton reversed his early China human rights policy. In going out day after day to fight these battles instead of quitting after losing one, I was guided by the wisdom of one of the world's great freedom fighters, Vaclav Havel, whom I later came to know well when I served as U.S. ambassador to the Czech Republic. Havel declared: "I am not am optimist, because I do not believe all ends well. Nor am I pessimist, because I do not believe all ends badly. Instead, I am a realist who carries hope, and hope is the belief that freedom has meaning and is always worth the struggle."[57]

# CHAPTER 9

# STRATEGIES FOR PEACE

At 4:00 A.M. on February 17, 1999, the phone rang in the U.S. ambassador's residence in Prague. I answered groggily, having arrived home the day before after a long drive through a blinding blizzard from the European Command Headquarters of the U.S. Army in Stuttgart, where I had attended a briefing on how to deal with terrorism. The voice on the line was the embassy's regional security officer, who said he and his team needed to see me right away. Ten minutes later, I was told about a credible, specific, and immediate terrorist threat by nationals from a Middle Eastern country to the official American presence in Prague. What I had learned in Stuttgart came into sharp focus.

I huddled with my security team in a corner of the darkened music room. After hearing that report, I had no choice but to close the embassy. I called Washington to convey my decision to David Carpenter, the assistant secretary of state for diplomatic security, and then began working around the clock with the State Department and the Czech government to beef up security at embassy buildings and at Radio Free Europe (RFE), the Prague-based international broadcasting organization funded by the U.S. government. By the time I reopened the embassy three days later, Czech soldiers and police with automatic weapons had moved in to guard us, and the narrow, medieval street leading to the chancery building had been blocked off by police vehicles.

Defending against terrorist attacks was high on the agenda of U.S. ambassadors in the late 1990s. In February 1999, Prague was a city of more than passing interest to terrorists. A postcommunist democracy with a former dissident as president, the Czech Republic under Vaclav Havel was the host country of Radio Free Europe. As part of its post–Cold War mission, RFE had been instructed by the U.S. Congress to begin broadcasting into Iran, Iraq, and other Middle Eastern and Central Asian countries in the grip of repressive regimes and Islamic terrorists. The director of RFE, Tom Dine, had started transmitting the Iran and Iraq broadcasts from Prague just before I arrived as ambassador in 1998. During the next two years, RFE was the target of a series of terrorist threats. Although not conclusively connected to them, an Egyptian terrorist, Muhammad Atta, traveled at least once to Prague in 2000, and possibly again in June of the following year. On September 11, 2001, Atta seized control of an American Airlines passenger plane after its takeoff from Boston and flew it into the World Trade Center.

The terrorist attacks of September 11 were not directly related to the human rights wars of the 1990s. But they were rooted in the deadly environment of repression, poverty, underdevelopment, refugee flows, religious and ethnic conflict, mass violence, and state failure in which these wars were waged. The massive human rights crimes committed in Afghanistan, Sudan, Somalia, Rwanda, Haiti, Bosnia, Kosovo, and other failed states flashed across the global screen throughout the decade that preceded September 11 as warning signals of a world to come. By using Afghanistan as their base, Osama bin Laden, al Qaeda, and the September 11 attackers showed that terrorism thrives in conditions that also create human rights catastrophes. They were motivated by a fanaticism and hatred of the West that has deep historical roots, but they found their support in a contemporary environment in which state failures and human rights wars were proliferating.

Since the end of the Cold War, there has been a pattern to U.S. participation in sporadic efforts to contain these wars. At first, Washington is likely to deny that such a conflict will directly affect American interests or security. Secretary of State James Baker's notorious comment about the Bosnia crisis in 1991, "We have no dog in that fight," could have applied equally to the early official U.S. attitude toward the crises in Afghanistan, Rwanda, Haiti, Kosovo, and other human rights wars of the 1990s. Without development assistance and other forms of preventive action, the conflict expands, human rights crimes are committed, state failure occurs, and an entire region is destabilized. At that point, the United States sometimes reluctantly agrees to lead or join a humanitarian intervention. Meanwhile, the conflict becomes so complex that it cannot be resolved without a long-term commitment of international resources and personnel. But the United States is often unwilling to make such a commitment for fear of becoming stuck in a quagmire. As a result, the crisis persists.

To break this pattern of reluctant involvement, Americans need to recognize that the costs of *not* engaging can be greater than the benefits of remaining on the sidelines. The rise of the Taliban and al Qaeda in the vacuum created by international disengagement from Afghanistan in the late 1980s, after the Soviet occupation, was an example of what can happen when a failed state is ignored. After years of severe repression, human rights atrocities, and neglect by the international community to contain the growing crisis in Afghanistan, the eventual cost of intervening militarily in late 2001 to root out terrorism was enormous.[1]

U.S. military intervention in Afghanistan marked the beginning, not the end, of the stabilizing process. But after several months of successful military operations, the United States proved reluctant to lead a long-term international effort to rebuild a country devastated by years of war and crimes against the entire civilian population. By leaving development assistance and other crucial tasks of nation-building to others, and by failing to commit significant resources to Afghanistan beyond the battlefield, the Bush administration dangerously downplayed the U.S. security interest in preventing the recurrence of a human rights catastrophe.[2] A military campaign to combat terrorists in failed states cannot succeed unless it is accompanied by an international effort to promote human rights, democracy, and development in places where terrorism flourishes.

## Redefining International Security

The human rights wars of the 1990s foreshadowed the global instability of the early twenty-first century. In this environment, international security depends in large part on preventing state failure and heading off conflicts in states that *have* failed. The United States has the power and the responsibility to work with other countries to address these problems through a variety of means, ranging from preventive action to active intervention. To do so, we must start with the lessons of the last decade.

In Rwanda, the world stood by while 800,000 people were slaughtered over fourteen weeks in a genocide that raged through the country like wildfire. The Rwandan reign of terror was instigated by extremists bent on seizing power through ethnic extermination.

The world's response to Rwanda illustrated what happens when nothing is done to stop political opportunists from launching a human rights war. While Rwanda may have seemed remote at the time to most Americans and inconsequential to U.S. interests, its lesson is that genocide can have vast humanitarian, security, and geopolitical costs. Since 1994, U.S. taxpayers have spent more than a billion dollars on U.N. "peace operations" in and around Rwanda.[3] If some of these dollars had been spent earlier to strengthen the U.N. peacekeeping force, in response to warnings sent by its commander in February 1994 about the impending violence, many lives might have been saved and central Africa might have been spared the worst effects of a genocidal conflict.

In contrast to the total failure of peacekeeping in Rwanda, the deployment of a multinational force in Haiti was a turning point in U.S. policy toward post–Cold War human rights crises. Conducted without casualties, the Haiti operation was a first step toward freeing American policymakers from the peacekeeping straitjacket they had imposed on themselves after the failed Somalia mission of 1993.

Since the "Somalia-Vietnam Syndrome" had been a major factor in keeping the United States from intervening in Rwanda and Bosnia in 1994, the Haiti operation opened the way for the development of a new doctrine of "humanitarian intervention," and its implementation a year later by NATO in Bosnia in 1995, and in Kosovo in 1999. Haiti also demonstrated four important truths about managing and resolving human rights conflicts. First, security-driven approaches, such as forcibly repatriating refugees, are more likely to exacerbate a human rights conflict than to contain it. Second, an interventionist policy can succeed only if it has domestic political support and multinational participation. Third, intervention requires a commitment to nation-building, not just an "exit strategy." By providing insufficient resources, and withdrawing or reducing them too soon, the multinational coalition that intervened in Haiti failed to improve significantly the country's prospects for long-term progress. And fourth, to be successful, international support for the economic and democratic development of a postconflict society requires a committed internal political partner. The international partnership with Haiti's democratic government has been unstable from the beginning on both sides.

The early chapters of the Bosnia story contain lessons about how *not* to respond to a human rights war, but the later ones begin to show the way. The most important lesson of the four-year conflict in Bosnia is that the United States cannot stand on the sidelines and leave the problem to others. Nor can the United States act alone. The long slide toward war in Yugoslavia might have been halted by aggressive European and American diplomacy, backed by warnings to would-be aggressors about the consequences of territorial seizure and human rights abuse as the country began to splinter. Instead, local leaders like Milosevic and Tudjman were allowed to start their ethnic terrorism with impunity. When U.N. peacekeepers arrived in 1992, they might have been able to contain the conflict if they had been operating under rules of engagement that allowed them to respond immediately and forcefully to human rights crimes. Instead, these early peacekeepers were given a weak mandate that turned them into observers who entered into commitments they could not keep, which made them become appeasers and eventually hostages.

The turning point in Bosnia came in the summer of 1995, when the international rules of engagement were finally changed, diplomacy at last was backed by force, the spotlighting of human rights atrocities was used to begin to push the warring parties to the negotiating table, and a price was attached to the commission of war crimes. The legacy of Bosnia is that a human rights war can erupt anywhere, even in Europe. The lesson of that war is that only a well-coordinated, robust military and civilian intervention has a chance of stopping it.

China in the early 1990s was the scene of a very different kind of human rights crisis. A popular Chinese reform movement, coinciding with the fall of communist governments in Eastern Europe and the spread of democracy in other parts of the world, was systematically rooted out and suppressed by the communist regime following its military crackdown on the Tiananmen Square demonstrations in 1989. How should the United States have responded to the violent suppression of human rights by an authoritarian government in a large and important country in which Americans had a wide range of economic and security interests? This question was hotly debated by the Congress, the executive branch, the press, and the public in the years following the Chinese crackdown. Some saw threats to isolate China through sanctions as the best way to prod the Chinese government to lift the tight lid it had put on all forms of open political expression. Others saw this approach as counterproductive and urged the downplaying of human rights in U.S.-China relations.

A "China Syndrome" has plagued U.S. policymakers for decades. Wild swings from confrontation to passivity have served neither U.S. interests in promoting political reform in China, nor the interests of the internal reformers themselves. The only beneficiary of these conflicting approaches has been the Chinese government, which has been able to characterize the United States as alternately intruding on Chinese sovereignty, or accepting Chinese repression. The lesson of the China Syndrome is that neither confrontation nor passivity is an effective way of relating to a country as large and strategically important as China. In the case of human rights, oscillation should be replaced by sustained, U.S-led international engagement on all aspects of democratic development and civil society. This will require increased human rights reporting, the use of international institutions such as the U.N. Commission on Human Rights to focus on China's record, insistence on China's respect for international legal norms, and efforts to persuade China to develop an internal rule of law.

The terrain in which human rights wars were waged during the 1990s can now be mapped. Using this map, efforts to head off similar conflicts in the future can be planned, and the criteria and means for intervening more aggressively when containment fails can be spelled out. But if the map is to be used, human rights will have to be brought into the mainstream of U.S. foreign policy. American support for international human rights standards can enhance U.S. influence abroad. But when the United States fails to accept the treaties and international institutions that embody these standards, it undercuts its own influence and weakens its capacity to guard against the forces of disintegration that are a central feature of the twenty-first century. Until we redefine international security to include the global protection of human rights, we will face an ever-increasing threat of instability and terror emanating from failed states.

Failed states wracked by internal conflict are the human rights equivalents of black holes in space. They destroy freedom and draw civilian populations and other countries into the negative fields of energy that they project across entire regions. America's interest in preventing these human rights black holes from developing should be as great as our interest in stopping the spread of weapons of mass destruction. But our commitment to do so will take a far greater investment of diplomatic, economic, and military resources than we are willing to make today. To contain human rights wars, the United States must work with other countries and international institutions to develop strategies to anticipate and forestall them, stop them once they have started, and limit the long-term damage they can inflict across the globe.

The crisis in the Middle East is a case in point. The U.S. role in addressing the Israeli-Palestinian conflict over the last decade has fluctuated between intense involvement during the Clinton presidency and studied disengagement during much of the administration of George W. Bush. At the core of the conflict, human rights issues require close attention so that a formula can be developed to reduce the violence by appealing to the common and distinct interests of both parties. U.S. disengagement is simply not an option, and when it occurs the conflict inevitably deepens.

As the dominant superpower, the United States is under close scrutiny by the rest of the world. Because we have the resources to project our power militarily, transform the global economy, and export our culture to billions, the world is watching to see if we also have the will to work with other countries to prevent human rights wars. It is not enough simply to acknowledge that organized, wide-scale attacks against civilians can create a climate of terror or repression, as we recognized in the cases of Rwanda, Haiti, Bosnia, Kosovo, and Afghanistan. Nor is it enough to apologize to the victims of human rights terror for failing to come to their assistance, as President Clinton did in the case of Rwanda. To strengthen the international response to human rights wars, the President should announce in a presidential decision directive that it is the explicit policy of the United States to work with other countries, within the framework of the United Nations, to prevent or stop genocide and massive crimes against humanity. Incentives and rewards should be created for government officials to carry out missions aimed at achieving this objective.[4] Only then will the vast bureaucracies of the Pentagon, the State Department, and other agencies that are required to implement such a policy actually unite behind it.

In defining its broader post–Cold War role of promoting international security, the United States should adopt five core strategies for preventing genocide and crimes against humanity.

1. *Early warning and prevention.* The tools are at hand for creating an international system to provide early warning of human rights conflicts, and to take preventive action to stop them from expanding. The most important but least understood of these tools is development assistance, which must be sharpened and put to more effective use in preventing conflicts.

2. *Intervention.* An international capacity should be developed to intervene in human rights wars where preventive measures have failed to stop the outbreak of widespread violence against civilians. As a last resort, military intervention should be used, based on clear criteria for when, how, and what type of intervention is appropriate under what circumstances.

3. *Justice.* Institutions of justice should be created or strengthened so they can be brought to bear on a human rights conflict where genocide or crimes against humanity have been committed, with the aim of removing and punishing criminal leaders and breaking repetitive cycles of revenge and impunity.

4. *Building peace.* Nation-building in countries recovering from a human rights war is a long-term process. The most urgent task is to establish the conditions of domestic security, after which assistance should be provided to restore civil society, create institutions of democratic governance, and build the foundations for sustainable economic development.

5. *Reducing repression.* Repression destroys freedom, fuels frustration, and breeds terror. The international community, led by the United States, should press countries under authoritarian rule to make progress on human rights and democracy in order to forestall the outbreak of violence.

## Early Warning and Prevention

Conflict prevention is a vast subject. Although conventional wars between states have become less common in the post–Cold War era, conflicts *within* states have increased, claiming an estimated five million lives over the last decade, and turning many times that number of people into refugees and displaced persons.[5] In his Millennium Report to the U.N. General Assembly, Secretary-General Kofi Annan summarized a widely shared diagnosis and prescription for heading off these deadly intrastate conflicts over human rights: "Conflicts are most frequent in those states that are ill governed and where there are sharp inequalities between ethnic or religious groups. The best way to prevent them is to promote healthy and balanced economic development, combined with human rights, minority rights and political arrangements in which all groups are fairly represented."[6]

The rudiments of an international "early warning" system to head off the outbreak or recurrence of a human rights war now exist, but need to be developed much further if they are to work. The United Nations and regional coalitions like the Organization for Security and Cooperation in Europe (OSCE) and the Organization of American States (OAS) have the authority but not sufficient capacity to operate as effective early warning agencies. The United States has an interest in bolstering these organizations so they can act on the kind of warnings that were reported from the field in Rwanda, but ignored both by the United Nations and by governments months before the genocide broke out. Instead of undermining the United Nations by ignoring appeals for support, the United States should actively strengthen the capacity of U.N. peacekeeping forces like the ones that were deployed in Rwanda and Bosnia in 1993 and 1994 to disarm the genocide planners before the killing begins. This recommendation was at the heart of the report issued in 1999 by a U.N. panel on peace operations, chaired by Under-Secretary-General Lakhdar Brahimi.[7]

By the time the peacekeepers arrive, however, it is often too late. In order to make early warnings more effective, the United Nations and regional organizations should create a network of monitoring systems to direct the attention of the world to emerging human rights and refugee crises. The U.N. high commissioners for human rights and refugees both have the authority to establish field operations to report on human rights abuses, internally displaced persons, and other warning signals of increasing conflict.[8] If better supported financially and politically by the United States and other key U.N. members—and better connected to the policy process so that their findings and recommendations can influence the international response to conflicts—these international warning systems could monitor dozens of pre- or postconflict situations, and help deter the outbreak of violence. A strengthened OSCE could play a similar early warning role in Eastern and Central Europe through its high commissioner for national minorities and its Office of Democratic Institutions and Human Rights. Other regional organizations like the OAS and the recently established African Union could be much more active in heading off human rights crises if they were better supported and encouraged by U.S. multilateral diplomacy. There is an urgent need for a similar organization in the Middle East that could give moderate Arab governments a framework for pursuing democratic progress and regional peace.

The seeds of conflict are sown most easily in conditions of poverty, social and economic inequality, ethnic or religious enmity, lawlessness, repression of civil society, and other circumstances contributing to severe human rights abuse. Over the long run, these conditions can only be addressed through comprehensive social, economic, and political development undertaken by local leadership with full support by the international community. But there are also short-term measures that can be used to defuse a conflict and isolate those who are promoting it.

Once early warnings have been given, a diplomatic campaign can be mounted to create a coalition of countries to take more aggressive action. A wide range of tools is available for the coalition to prevent a human rights conflict from spreading. It can punish or isolate political leaders and their associates who are instigating violence and committing human rights crimes by denying them visas to travel, freezing their overseas assets, and blocking their access to government deposits in foreign banks. The coalition can support a U.N. or regional arms embargo to stop the flow of weapons into a conflict area, so long as all sides are disarmed and one side is not severely disadvantaged, as was the case with the Bosnian Muslims. (It must be recognized, however, that because of the size of the global arms trade, and the capacity of nonstate actors to circumvent embargoes, it is extremely difficult to control the supply of weapons to combatants determined to obtain them.) The United States and other countries in the coalition who are on the governing boards of the World Bank and the International Monetary Fund can also act to terminate international financing to governments supporting the conflict. World Bank loans or grants can be conditioned on taking specific steps toward peace, or on supporting international peace-building efforts to prevent the conflict from starting up again. Finally, the United States can condition its own economic assistance to a government of a country involved in an internal conflict on its taking steps to prevent the conflict from spreading, while isolating and punishing those engaged in violent aggression or repression against civilian populations.

The most extreme form of preventive action short of military intervention is to slap comprehensive sanctions on a human rights violator. Unilateral use of this strategic weapon, however, can often do more harm than good, generating sympathy for a repressive regime or further endangering the very people whom the sanctions are intended to help. The sanctions imposed by the United States on Haiti in 1991, in response to the military coup against Jean-Bertrand Aristide, did more harm to the Haitian people than to the military regime. Multilateral sanctions, on the other hand, can be an effective tool of preventive action because they involve the most sweeping form of international condemnation and have the most powerful practical influence. International sanctions against South Africa's apartheid regime in the 1980s, and against Serbia under Milosevic in the 1990s, undoubtedly contributed to ending the human rights conflicts in those countries and bringing about fundamental political change.

## Intervention

When a human rights crisis deepens and does not respond to preventive measures, more active forms of intervention may become necessary. A coalition of countries is the only effective instrument for intervening, not unilateral action by the United States or any other country acting alone. Coalitions confer legitimacy, provide resources, give political support, and reduce the risk that intervention will lead to greater conflict. Efforts should be made to secure the approval of the United Nations—as well as its participation and the involvement of its specialized agencies—in advance of an intervention to contain a human rights war. If these efforts fail, under the Genocide Convention a coalition of ratifying countries still has the authority in certain circumstances—and arguably even the obligation—to stop a genocide in progress.[9]

Intervention, especially intervention that might involve military action, is not to be taken lightly. The U.N. Charter is based on the principle of the sovereign equality of states,[10] under which a sovereign state is empowered to exercise exclusive jurisdiction within its borders, and other states are obligated not to intervene.[11] But when a state fails, and cannot protect the fundamental rights of its citizens enshrined in international law, intervention may be justified under an international responsibility to protect rights recognized by treaties like the Genocide Convention. By framing the right to intervene to stop or contain a human rights war as a *responsibility* to save the lives of people facing genocide or crimes against humanity, both sovereignty and human rights principles within the meaning of the U.N. charter are preserved.[12]

Military intervention is a last resort, and even then it is not a cure-all. There are many circumstances in which military intervention to protect human rights, even after the exhaustion of other means, is not appropriate, whether carried out by the United Nations or by an international coalition. These circumstances have less to do with sovereignty than with the risk of doing more harm than good. To assess whether military intervention should be undertaken as the final resort for containing a human rights war, four criteria should be used to determine whether, when, and what type of intervention might be justified.[13]

1. *Genocide or crimes against humanity.* The first and most important criterion is that genocide or crimes against humanity are

being committed with impunity. These crimes must involve ongoing or imminent large-scale killing with a genocidal purpose, or a purpose of ethnic, racial, political, or religious persecution, "which is the product of deliberate state action, state neglect, inability to act, or state failure."[14] The cases of Rwanda, Haiti, Bosnia, and Kosovo all fall within this criterion. Even where egregious human rights crimes are being committed, however, military intervention is justified only when three other conditions are satisfied.[15]

2. *Regional instability.* The conflict is causing major regional instability, which the neighboring countries want to contain by participating in an international intervention. The countries bordering on the former Yugoslavia all supported NATO's interventions in Bosnia and Kosovo, and the OAS unanimously supported the multinational force that intervened in Haiti. Had this support not been forthcoming, these interventions could have destabilized the region.

3. *No wider war.* Intervention is not likely to cause a broader conflict. If military intervention were to trigger a wider war— for example, by provoking other countries to enter into the hostilities, or by stimulating acts of terrorism—it would exacerbate the situation.

4. *Minimum necessary means.* The planned scale, duration, and intensity of the intervention are the minimum necessary to achieve the objective of saving lives. A military intervention to stop a human rights war should be as surgical as possible, and should not risk causing greater loss of life than would have occurred had the intervention not taken place.

These criteria should be applied to any proposed military intervention to stop a human rights war. Because military intervention carries a risk that it might do more harm than good, it must be undertaken only when *all* the criteria have been met to justify it. The U.S.-British military operation to change the regime in Iraq in the spring of 2003 did not meet these criteria. The intervention was strongly opposed by countries throughout the region and the Muslim world and was conducted unilaterally without United Nations Security Council approval. Twelve years earlier, the U.N.-sanctioned coalition forces that entered Iraq could have prevented Saddam Hussein from carrying out genocidal attacks against the Kurds and Shi'a Muslims in 1991 and 1992, but failed to do so. In 2003, despite Saddam Hussein's appalling record of continuing human rights abuse, there was no evidence that the earlier genocide was about to be renewed. Saddam's human rights record was used by President Bush to bolster a faltering case for intervention to disarm Iraq of its alleged stockpile of weapons of mass destruction.[16] Furthermore, the unilateral nature of the 2003 military operation made it far more difficult to stabilize the country, stimulated ongoing attacks against the intervening forces, increased the recruiting power of Islamic terrorist organizations, and shattered the cooperation necessary for humanitarian intervention.

An evolving doctrine of "humanitarian intervention" was the basis of four separate international military actions, led or supported by the United States, to protect human rights in the 1990s. In each of these cases humanitarian intervention might be defined as a combined military and civilian effort by a coalition of countries to protect a civilian population from severe human rights abuse at the hands of their own government. While the intervention altered the behavior of the abusive government, its purpose was to restore the legitimate authority of the state, not permanently to supplant it.

The first of these humanitarian interventions involved the United States working closely with the United Nations and the OAS in the summer and fall of 1994 to assemble the multinational military coalition that intervened in Haiti. The purpose of the coalition was to stop systematic political killings and other acts of persecution by a military junta and restore a democratically elected president. While the Haiti intervention succeeded in achieving these objectives, it ended too early and therefore failed to keep Haiti from sliding back into chaos. Two other interventions involved NATO's use of air power: in the fall of 1995, to back U.S. and European diplomacy aimed at ending the war in Bosnia, and later, in the spring of 1999, to force the Serbian government to stop expelling and killing Kosovar Albanians and to open the way for nearly a million refugees to return to their homes.[17] A fourth intervention was conducted by the United Nations in the fall of 1999. Led by Australian troops, its objective was to secure East Timor after the massive killings of Timorese by Indonesian paramilitaries—following a U.N.-administered referendum in which the people of East Timor had voted for independence from Indonesia.

These success stories are overshadowed by the massive failure of earlier international interventions in Bosnia and Rwanda, the major genocidal conflicts of the post–Cold War era. Two lessons stand out from these failures. First, genocide cannot be deterred or stopped by passive peacekeeping. As the Brahimi report pointed out, lightly armed troops with limited rules of engagement are no match for paramilitary forces whose objective is to kill or expel civilians because of their race, nationality, or religion.[18] The United Nations under the leadership of Secretary-General Kofi Annan has conducted reviews of the international peacekeeping failures in Bosnia and Rwanda.[19] It is incumbent on members of the U.N. Security Council, particularly the United States, to conduct similar internal reviews of their own failures in these situations and to see that the recommendations of these reports are implemented.[20]

The second lesson is that successful humanitarian interventions require a permanent international military force that is carefully trained and prepared for any contingency. It is not enough for countries to commit peacekeeping forces on an ad hoc basis as each crisis erupts. To maximize their prospect of success and minimize their likelihood of being taken hostage, international peacekeepers should train together and follow the same rules. The United States should support and contribute to the creation of an international standby force that can undertake humanitarian interventions under U.N. authority. Properly trained and deployed, a U.N. standby force could combine international legitimacy with rapid-reaction capacity, and become an effective instrument of humanitarian intervention.[21] Because the United Nations will not always agree and may not be able to act quickly enough, the United States should also encourage, support, and contribute to similar efforts to develop humanitarian intervention capacities among regional organizations, including NATO, the European Union, the OAS, the African Union, and the Association of Southeast Asian Nations.[22]

## Justice

Another lesson of the early peacekeeping failures in Bosnia and Rwanda is that where genocide or crimes against humanity have been committed, a human rights war cannot be brought to an end until justice is done. Revenge may offer survivors fleeting satisfaction, but only at the cost of an ongoing spiral of violence. Institutions of justice can provide victims with alternative means of righting the wrongs committed against them by holding accountable those who were responsible for instigating them. Justice is also important to innocent members of ethnic or religious groups involved in the conflict because it removes the stigma of guilt by association that can brand an entire group when its leaders have committed genocide.

Punishment of the perpetrators of human rights crimes can also serve as a warning to others who might plan to engage in similar acts in the future. Visible and effective international tribunals to try criminal leaders are important instruments not only for punishing those who start human rights wars, but also for *preventing* the outbreak of future conflicts. The arrests and trials of Slobodan Milosevic, Théoneste Bagosora, and other architects of genocide in Bosnia and Rwanda should make other leaders think twice before they unleash ethnic violence against civilian populations. One of the key lessons of Bosnia is that war criminals should be arrested early in the peace process, and peacekeepers instructed to assist in making arrests as part of their mandate to establish a secure environment so that other peacebuilding tasks can be tackled.

Over the last decade, efforts to create a system of international justice have resulted in the establishment of International Criminal Tribunals for the Former Yugoslavia and Rwanda, and the drafting of a treaty to set up a permanent International Criminal Court (ICC). The United States has been a leader in the creation of the tribunals, but an increasingly isolated opponent of the ICC. Throughout this period, international justice issues have stirred a far-reaching policy debate in the United States. On one side are those who argue that human rights conflicts in the post–Cold War world cannot be contained until the leaders who started them are held accountable for their crimes. On the other side are those who assert that the pursuit of justice can create impediments to peacemaking. An additional argument against the International Criminal Court has been made by the Bush administration, a parade of Pentagon officials, and Henry Kissinger.[23] They claim that the ICC will be used by opponents of U.S. policy to indict American officials for actions with which they disagree, such as the bombing of Afghanistan or Kosovo. The Bush administration also makes a more sweeping argument: the ICC would undermine American sovereignty.[24]

American opponents of international justice risk condoning future human rights crimes by blocking the creation of a permanent institution that can deter or prosecute those who commit them. The most significant lesson of Rwanda and Bosnia is that peace is not possible after genocide until those who planned it have been removed from the scene. In Serbia, the arrest and transfer of Milosevic to the International Criminal Tribunal for the Former Yugoslavia were essential steps in moving Serbia toward democracy. But this ad hoc tribunal is not a permanent institution with global jurisdiction, as is the International Criminal Court. If the ICC had attempted to bring Milosevic to justice, the Bush policy would have effectively prevented the United States from supporting his prosecution.

The International Criminal Court is an imperfect instrument of justice. But instead of working to scuttle it, American critics should redirect their efforts to strengthening its procedural protections against political bias. The United States would have had far greater leverage over the court's development by signing the ICC treaty than by withdrawing its signature and seeking to exempt all U.S. citizens from its jurisdiction, as the Bush administration has done.

The core of the administration's concern about the ICC is that an international court not controlled by the United States could pass judgment on the actions of American citizens. Leaving aside the fact that the International Court of Justice already has that power, the ICC is required to defer to national courts, not supplant them. The rules of the ICC give deference to national justice systems, and the United States has the strongest justice system in the world.[25] Only when a national system fails or refuses in bad faith to investigate a human rights crime would ICC jurisdiction come into play. To get to that point, as two astute commentators on the United States and the ICC have observed, "The United States would either have to be so biased that it could not evaluate the question of international crime, have no intention of investigating the claim, or be investigating only to protect the individual. Actions—official or unofficial—of a U.S. citizen that approached the gravity of an international crime would be addressed within the American judicial system."[26]

If the United States is unwilling to recognize ICC jurisdiction over genocide and crimes against humanity, it will undermine its ability to protect international security, as well as its claim of leadership to promote the values of democracy. As the commentators point out, "The U.S. attitude toward the ICC is linked to both domestic and international perceptions of the legitimacy of American leadership. . . . A state that relies upon the power of its political ideals can only stray so far from those ideals without losing the ability to inspire confidence internally and internationally."[27] By insisting that all Americans be given an ironclad immunity from prosecution by the International Criminal Court, however, the Bush administration has done just that.[28]

International justice by itself is not enough to punish and deter human rights crimes. Over the long run, it is essential to build indigenous national institutions that have the capacity to achieve the rule of law, support political freedoms, and protect the rights of minorities. When they are not paralyzed by politics, domestic courts are better suited than international tribunals to getting at the roots of human rights criminality. Quasi-judicial institutions, such as South

Africa's Truth and Reconciliation Commission, can provide an alternative way to address the legacy of systemic criminality in societies riven by racial, ethnic, or religious conflict and a history of deep-seated human rights abuse. International partnerships among countries and nongovernmental organizations can play a major role in supporting the creation of national institutions of justice and promoting the rule of law as a bulwark against future human rights catastrophes. For example, a new regional judicial training institute, established in Prague in 2000 by the American Bar Association's Central and Eastern European Law Initiative during the time I was serving as ambassador to the Czech Republic, is the kind of international partnership that can promote justice and the rule of law in countries emerging from repression and conflict.

## Building Peace

The hardest lesson to learn from the human rights wars of the 1990s is that building peace takes time. It also takes resources and a will to stay the course. In an era when the world lurches from crisis to crisis and the political attention span of most Americans is as short as the television news cycle, the United States has been reluctant to commit itself to sustained efforts to rebuild war-torn societies. After intervening in a human rights conflict, the United States often becomes more preoccupied with planning its exit strategy than with developing a plan for nation-building so that the cycle of violence can be broken. Nation-building is a complex and cooperative process best undertaken under the aegis of the United Nations or regional organizations, and not imposed unilaterally, as the Bush administration is doing in Iraq.

The first and most important task is to establish security arrangements and the institutions to support them. Without security there can be no peace. War criminals cannot be arrested. Civil society cannot be restored, elections cannot be conducted, and the economy cannot be built. One of the chief lessons of Bosnia and Kosovo is that to establish security, the military and civilian aspects of peace-building must be closely coordinated from the outset. If the civilian authority is weak and disconnected from the military command structure, as was the case in Bosnia following the Dayton Peace Accords, and in Kosovo during the early months of U.N. peacekeeping activities, the difficulties of creating a secure environment are compounded.

The two most important tasks to be tackled immediately after a human rights war—arresting war criminals and creating a civilian police force—fell between the cracks of the international authority structures in Bosnia and Kosovo. Particularly in Bosnia, where Radovan Karadzic, Mlatko Radic, and scores of other indicted war criminals roamed the country and were able to disrupt the peace process, security remained an elusive goal for years. The international peacekeeping force that entered Bosnia in December 1995 should have been explicitly ordered by its civilian political leaders to arrest all persons indicted by the International Criminal Tribunal for the Former Yugoslavia. Meanwhile, a poorly trained international civilian police force was unable to establish a close working relationship with the peacekeepers. By requiring international military and civilian leaders to coordinate their operations—for example, through integrated training programs and command structures—the gap between the two aspects of peace implementation can be narrowed. This is the way that a secure environment can be created so that other longer-term challenges can then be addressed.

A crucial aspect of military-civilian coordination during or immediately after a violent conflict is the delivery of emergency humanitarian assistance to refugees and displaced persons. In Bosnia, before the 1995 NATO intervention, and in Rwanda after the genocide, international humanitarian organizations were taken hostage by war criminals and *genocidaires*. Relief delivery convoys were continually hijacked and diverted from their destinations in Bosnia. In Zaire, the Rwandan refugee camps were taken over by leaders of the genocide. In both situations what was desperately needed was an international military force with strong rules of engagement and a mandate to protect the aid operations. The absence of such a force discredited the very humanitarian organizations that were at the forefront of peace-building.

Even as steps are taken to establish a secure environment, efforts need to be made to construct a foundation for the rule of law. The development of an indigenous police force and prison system is an essential part of this process, as is the training of domestic lawyers and judges who can begin to resolve social and economic disputes and enforce the criminal law. Both of these institutions will require extensive international support to overcome the legacy of repression, corruption, and chaos that plague all postconflict societies.

Reviving civil society is another long-term challenge of peace-building. Indigenous media and nongovernmental organizations are the backbone of a country's political culture. Often they are the first victims—and are sometimes forced to be the instruments—of repression and human rights conflict. Serbian state television and Radio Television Libres des Milles Collines were instrumental in spreading the religious and ethnic venom that poisoned Bosnia and Rwanda. Countering their message was essential if the reign of terror was to be halted in the Balkans and Central Africa, but little was done by the international community to block or undercut these media from propagandizing their captive audiences.

Nongovernmental organizations in Bosnia, Rwanda, Haiti, and Kosovo were hit hard by the destructive forces of genocide, ethnic cleansing, and state-sponsored terror that swept through their societies. In many ways these organizations found it as difficult to operate inside their own countries as did the Chinese dissidents who sought to organize political activities in China during the severe repression that followed the Tiananmen massacre. To help revive civil society, international assistance must be directed as soon as possible to the indigenous media and local nongovernmental organizations that have been shattered by human rights conflict.

As civil society slowly reemerges, the institutions of democratic governance can begin to be established. Because the United States has often been preoccupied by its search for an "exit strategy" after leading or participating in a humanitarian intervention, it has tended to push too early for the formalities of democracy before civil societies recovering from human rights wars are ready for them. The most visible of these processes, democratic elections, are also the most difficult and even the most dangerous to undertake. When an election is conducted too soon after the end of a war, it can be manipulated by war criminals or warlords. This was what happened in Bosnia when the United States insisted on conducting internationally supervised elections in September 1996, less than nine months after the ink was dry on the Dayton Accords. The unintended result was a ratification of the authority of hardline opponents of the peace process, and a firming up of the very ethnic divisions that the war criminals had used to propel themselves to power.[29]

The largest task of peace-building depends on all the others. Sustainable social and economic development is ultimately the only path for a society shattered by conflict to escape the conditions of poverty, inequality, lawlessness, hatred, and repression that caused the conflict. But development can be successful only when internal security, civil society, and democratic governance are all on the road to recovery, and the leaders who carried out a human rights war have been removed from the scene. War criminals too often have been allowed to benefit from international economic assistance extended to a postconflict society before they are arrested or sidelined. The deeply corrupt economy of the Milosevic era, for example, was sustained in Serbia by European investors who found loopholes in the U.N. sanctions regime.

When donors do not deliver enough development assistance to a society struggling to put a human rights conflict behind it, however, they can severely retard the process of recovery and create new problems of governance. When the international community failed to sustain nation-building assistance to Haiti after Aristide was restored, for example, the country began to slide back toward economic and political chaos in the late 1990s. More recently, in Afghanistan, while international donors have provided significant resources for peace-building tasks, the political development to which much of the assistance has been channeled has "fostered a weak central government and abetted the resurgence of fiefdoms headed by warlords."[30]

To avoid the opposite extremes of providing development assistance too early and to the wrong people, or too little and too late, the United States should work with other countries to coordinate international aid. Assistance should be given only to those who are committed to building peace. Incentives should be created for countries emerging from conflict to work with U.N. development agencies, and with regional organizations like the European Union, the Organization of American States, the Association of Southeast Asian Nations, and the African Union, as well as international economic agencies like the World Bank. That is the only path toward sustainable social and economic development for a postwar country.

## Reducing Repression

Often the clearest indicator of an impending human rights conflict is harsh political repression. Not only in a failed state like Afghanistan, but also in an authoritarian country like China, in Yugoslavia before its collapse, or in the autocratic regimes of the Middle East, the seeds of conflict find fertile ground.

Repression can breed political violence and terrorism. As President Kennedy warned the dictators of Latin America in 1962, "Those who make peaceful change impossible will make violent revolution inevitable."[31] It is necessary to remind the world's repressive regimes that they "stand on the wrong side of history," as Bill Clinton told Chinese President Jiang Zemin in 1997. But warnings are not enough: strategies must be developed for challenging repression from the outside by insisting that those who exercise it make progress on human rights.

The United States has a long record of inconsistency in its dealings with repressive governments. During the Cold War, it condemned communist regimes, but was willing to embrace right-wing authoritarian governments that suppressed critics and opponents. Since the end of the Cold War, the United States has often muted its concern about the human rights practices of certain repressive governments, such as Saudi Arabia, Egypt, and China, because of their importance to American economic and security interests. Today, as part of the war on terrorism, President Bush has signaled the world's repressive regimes that what they do on human rights is less important than what they do on terrorism. But if repression engenders instability, unrest, and more terrorism, long-term U.S. interests will be ill-served by this approach.

To protect the security of Americans, the United States should build an international coalition to promote human rights and democracy in authoritarian countries. We can no longer afford to ignore or downplay the way China, Saudi Arabia, Egypt, Pakistan, Uzbekistan, or other repressive governments treat their citizens. Finding appropriate and effective ways to press from the outside for reform will be essential if regional human rights conflicts are to be contained. In the Middle East, the United States must condemn the human rights abuses committed against Palestinians by Israelis, just as it condemns the terrorism launched against Israelis by Palestinians.

The many different ways of applying outside influence for human rights reform range from conducive to coercive, from diplomatic to economic, from unilateral to multilateral. How effective such efforts can be depends on how long, how broadly, and how consistently they are applied. A striking example of sustained external pressure for human rights reform was the use of international economic sanctions against the apartheid regime in South Africa during the 1980s. And while many factors were at work in the case of Serbia, U.N. sanctions played a role in spurring the internal democratic reforms of 2000 that finally ended the Milosevic era. These successes involved coordinated multilateral strategies in which the United States worked closely with other countries in pressing for human rights progress.

When the United States ignores the rest of the world and imposes or threatens unilateral sanctions on authoritarian regimes—as in the case of Cuba or China—it is less successful. President Clinton's China MFN policy was crippled by many factors, including the opposition of American business and the resistance of economic agencies inside the U.S. government to carrying it out, but its fatal flaw was its unilateral character. Had the United States led the way with other countries in developing and coordinating a human rights policy toward China in the immediate post-Tiananmen period, and had it demonstrated a willingness during the Clinton administration to sustain this multilateral diplomatic and economic pressure, the likelihood of human rights reform occurring in China would have increased.

Even without an economic component, a well-executed multilateral strategy can sometimes play a role in pressing an authoritarian regime to make progress on human rights. Among the tools for doing so are covenants and treaties that establish international standards, as well as U.N. human rights agencies and their counterparts in regional organizations. Although it has no enforcement powers, the U.N. Commission on Human Rights can shine an international spotlight on a repressive regime, as can the U.N. high commissioners for human rights and refugees and the U.N. special rapporteurs for particular issues like torture, extrajudicial executions, and racial discrimination. The U.N. Human Rights Committee, which reviews the compliance of countries with human rights treaties, is another instrument for identifying and publicizing abuses.

Unfortunately, these U.N. institutions have limited value as they are currently structured because they are vulnerable to authoritarian countries who gang up to resist international censure. Throughout the 1990s, China managed—by working with other repressive regimes on the commission and exerting pressure on small countries— to corral enough votes in the U.N. Commission on Human Rights to block a series of resolutions condemning its human rights record. China was able to succeed in its lobbying campaigns because the United States and other democratic countries were unwilling to apply high-level diplomatic resources to counter this kind of "lobbying for repression."[32] The United States and other democratic countries must work together to ensure that the Commission on Human Rights has a balanced membership and the resources to do its job. The same level and intensity of diplomatic effort must be put into a resolution challenging human rights abuses as a resolution before another U.N. body challenging nuclear proliferation or trade restrictions. At the same time, the United States should be on guard against efforts to exclude it from key international human rights institutions. That was what happened in 2001, when lack of preparation and interest by the incoming Bush administration, coupled with its opposition to human rights institutions like the International Criminal Court, led to the United States being voted off the commission for a year.[33]

## Human Rights at Home

Americans have been at the center of the international human rights movement since the days when Eleanor Roosevelt helped draft the Universal Declaration of Human Rights. The Bill of Rights has been a model for other democratic constitutions and an inspiration for rights revolutions the world over.

But there is another side of this story. The United States has been unwilling to adopt large portions of the international human rights agenda. It has declined to ratify—and sometimes even to sign— human rights treaties and has exempted itself from widely accepted standards of human rights behavior, such as the international condemnation of capital punishment.[34] This special status, long supported by American exceptionalists from Jesse Helms to George W. Bush, is self-defeating, making the United States seem arrogant and self-centered when it calls other countries to task for violating human rights.[35]

There are three underlying reasons for the gap between U.S. advocacy of human rights abroad and U.S. resistance to international human rights standards at home. First is a tradition of exceptionalism, in which Americans have tended to downplay or reject international human rights law. Not only has the United States failed to ratify many human rights treaties; the long and ongoing struggle for civil rights and civil liberties in the United States has only recently begun to make use of international human rights law and to forge ties with rights movements in other countries. Closely related to exceptionalism is the tradition of isolationism, which since the earliest days of the Republic has made Americans wary of "foreign entanglements."

The third reason for the perceived gap between what the United States preaches abroad and practices at home is unilateralism—the tendency for the United States to act on its own when pursuing its international objectives and not to be guided by multinational organizations or alliances.

Taken together, these three traditions have made the United States an ambivalent, and from the point of view of other countries, untrustworthy leader when it comes to human rights. While American power and global preeminence make the United States *the* indispensable player in any effort to prevent or stop a human rights war, the resistance of the U.S. government to ratifying treaties or supporting international institutions undermines U.S. effectiveness in leading such an effort.

The war on terrorism declared by President Bush after the attacks of September 11 brought all of these issues to a head. To be successful, the effort to uproot terrorism must ultimately include preventing massive human rights abuses like the ones that were committed for years with impunity by the Taliban and al Qaeda in Afghanistan. Instead, the strategy and tactics used by the Bush administration to prosecute the war on terrorism have condoned the suppression of human rights in the name of rooting out terrorists.

At the end of the first phase of the U.S. military operation in Afghanistan in February 2002, an astute commentator posed a disturbing question:

The question after September 11 is whether the era of human rights has come and gone. If that sounds alarmist, consider some of the evidence. Western pressure on China to honor human rights, never especially effective, has stopped altogether. Chinese support for the war on terror has secured Western silence about repression in the Xinjiang region. China now says it has a problem with Islamic fundamentalists and terrorists, and it is straining to link them to al Qaeda. A similar chill is settling over world politics. Australia's government uses the threat of terrorism to justify incarcerating Afghan refugees in a desert compound. Tajikistan and Uzbekistan have leveraged their provision of bases and intelligence into a carte blanche for domestic repression. Egypt, which for many years has used detention without trial, military courts and torture to keep control of militants, now demands an even freer hand.[36]

Meanwhile, the United States itself has pursued a variety of measures in the war on terror that have curtailed both domestic civil liberties and international human rights. These include the roundup and indefinite detention without charges of thousands of young men from Middle Eastern countries based solely on their ethnic and national profiles, the withholding of identities and information about those rounded up, the breakdown of constitutional search and seizure standards in criminal investigations built on electronic surveillance conducted for foreign intelligence purposes, the reduction of due process protections in proposed military trials of suspected terrorists, the indefinite detention of suspected al Qaeda and Taliban combatants in a remote military prison camp in Guantanamo, Cuba, and the designation of American citizens suspected of supporting terrorist groups as "enemy combatants" who can be stripped of their rights both to counsel and to access to the evidence on which their designation is based. "If you don't violate someone's human rights some of the time, you probably aren't doing your job," a U.S. law enforcement official told a *Washington Post* reporter in December 2002.[37]

The message of the post–September 11 antiterrorist strategy followed by the Bush administration seems to be that if the war on terror is to succeed, human rights have to get out of the way. Brave activists struggling to reform repressive countries are paying close attention to how the war on terrorism is conducted. If the global antiterrorism mandate is defined too broadly, there is a danger that these countries could return to chaos or tyranny.

Reformers in Indonesia, for example, face enormous challenges in trying to overcome decades of corrupt and dictatorial leadership. They are now worried, however, about the effect the new antiterrorism campaign will have on their cause, particularly after the October 2002 terrorist bombing of a nightclub in Bali. "Indonesian democrats have always depended on America as a point of reference that we could count on to support us," Indonesian commentator Wimar Witoelar told *New York Times* columnist Tom Friedman. "If we see you waffling [on human rights and democracy], whom do we turn to? It is like the sun disappearing from the sky and everything starts to freeze here again." In response to this warning, Friedman pointedly commented that "Indonesians are worried they're hearing America shift—from a war for democracy to a war on terrorism, in which the U.S. will judge which nations are with it or against it not by the integrity of their elections or the justice of their courts, but by the vigor with which their army or police combat al Qaeda. For Indonesia, where democracy is a fragile flower, anything that encourages a comeback by the long-feared but now slightly defanged army and police is not good news."[38]

People engaged in the struggle for freedom around the world depend on the United States not only for its military and economic power, but above all for its commitment to democratic values and human rights. From their point of view, there can be no international security until the campaign against terrorism is connected to a broader campaign for human rights, democracy, and development.


On December 2, 1993, I was escorted from the Cairo airport to a downtown hotel by an Egyptian police squadron of armed motorcyclists, agents in unmarked vehicles, and police sedans with sirens blaring. At the hotel, my security team posted a twenty-four-hour armed guard outside the door to my room. I had come to meet with Egypt's embattled human rights and civil society leaders. The first message I received, however, was from the Egyptian government. Its meaning was unmistakable: you're under our control.

At a dinner that night with the Arab Organization for Human Rights, I was briefed by Mansur Kikhia, a former Libyan foreign minister in the days when Libya had been a constitutional democracy. Kikhia talked about the severe repression of civil society in Egypt and most of the Arab world. A week later, he was abducted by Libyan agents thought to be collaborating with the Egyptian security services, and never seen again. Kikhia's message was later repeated to me at the Ibn Khaldun Center for Development Studies, an institute devoted to advocacy of civic participation in Egypt and throughout the Arab world. In response to their moderate call for reform, on June 30, 2000, the center's co-founder, Saad Eddin Ibrahim, a prominent sociology professor at the American University in Cairo, and twenty-seven of his associates were arrested for "receiving funding without authorization" to support their democracy-promotion activities.

Following his second trial, Ibrahim was sentenced to seven years in prison. On the day of his sentencing, July 29, 2002, the aging Egyptian democracy activist made an eloquent statement to the court in which he described the losing battle for civil society in many Arab countries that is going on in the shadows of the war on terrorism:

> Civil society is the space where citizens come together voluntarily, guided by their free will, to exercise their right to free speech, their right to disagree, their right to innovate, their right to try, and even their right to make mistakes. . . . Civil society as a space for liberty is an essential condition for initiative and creativity, and an essential precondition for sustained development. . . . Perhaps we are being persecuted because we have been pioneers in discussing openly and practicing what we preach about, and because we dared to say publicly what millions of Egyptians and Arabs think privately.[39]

The battle being fought by Saad Eddin Ibrahim and people like him around the world will ultimately determine the outcome of the war on terrorism. Their message is simple: the United States must practice what it preaches by supporting the struggle for human rights and civil society as the alternative to repression and terror. Theirs is a message of hope, but it is also a warning: if we allow the sacrifice of freedom in the name of fighting terror, in the long run we will only have more terror.

# CHRONOLOGY

**February 6** East German student last person killed attempting to escape over Berlin Wall.

**February 25–26** President George H. W. Bush visits China.

**February 27** Chinese police block prominent dissident Fang Lizhi from attending Bush banquet in Beijing, to which he had been officially invited by U.S. embassy.

**April 27** Death of Hu Yaobang, member of senior Chinese leadership previously sidelined for supporting political reform, sparks large student demonstration in Tiananmen Square.

**May 2** Tens of thousands march through Warsaw calling for reform.

**May 4** Massive demonstrations in Beijing and other major Chinese cities commemorating seventieth anniversary of 1919 democracy movement.

**May 13** Beijing demonstrators tell international press they plan to occupy Tiananmen Square until demands for political reform are met.

**May 15–18** Mikhail Gorbachev visits China.

**May 19** Zhao Ziyang, moderate member of Chinese leadership and general secretary of Communist Party, meets with demonstrators in Tiananmen Square.

**May 30** Tiananmen demonstrators erect "Goddess of Democracy," inspired by Statue of Liberty.

**June 3–4** Chinese army enters Tiananmen Square, killing hundreds of demonstrators; thousands killed in cities throughout China.

**June 9**    Deng Xiaoping praises Chinese military for suppressing "counterrevolutionary forces."

**June 24**    Zhao Ziyang dismissed. Replaced as general secretary by Jiang Zemin.

**June 28**    Slobodan Milosevic gives speech in Kosovo, marking 600th anniversary of Battle of Kosovo Polje, calling for creation of "Greater Serbia."

**July**    Bush sends National Security Advisor Brent Scowcroft on secret mission to Beijing to assure Chinese government that U.S.-China differences over human rights should not get in way of longstanding positive U.S.-China relationship.

**August**    Scowcroft mission becomes public. Strongly negative congressional response. Senate Majority Leader George Mitchell (D-Me.) denounces Bush policy as "embarrassing kowtowing to a repressive Communist government."

**August 19**    Mass flight of East Germans and Hungarians across Hungarian border with Austria.

**September 11**    Hungary opens border and suspends travel restriction treaty with East Germany.

**October 30**    400,000 demonstrate for democracy in Leipzig.

**November 4**    One million demonstrate in East Berlin.

**November 9**    Berlin Wall opened.

**November 16**    Czechoslovakia's Velvet Revolution begins. Students march and are attacked by police. In coming days more than one million gather on Wenceslas Square; communist government resigns.

**December 3**    Slovenia seals border with Serbia.

**December 20**    Vaclav Havel elected first postcommunist president of Czechoslovakia.

## 1990

**February 2**    South African president Willem de Klerk announces lifting of ban against African National Congress (ANC).

**February 11**    After twenty-seven years of imprisonment, ANC leader Nelson Mandela released from Robben Island prison.

**July**    Under pressure from Western aid donors, Rwandan president Juvenal Habyarimana agrees to establish multiparty democracy.

**September**   Anti-Tutsi tract, "Hutu Ten Commandments," published in Kigali by Leon Mugesera, a friend of Habyarimana, asserting that "Hutus should stop having mercy on Tutsis."

**October**   Rwandan army begins to train and arm Hutu militias known as Interahamwe ("those who stand together"). For next three years Habyarimana stalls on establishment of multiparty system with power sharing. Throughout period, thousands of Tutsis killed; opposition politicians and newspapers persecuted. Guerrillas of Tutsi-led Rwandan Patriotic Force (RPF) invade Rwanda from Uganda.

**December**   Slobodan Milosevic elected Serbian president on platform calling for creation of "Greater Serbia in Yugoslavia."

**December 16**   Jean-Bertrand Aristide wins Haiti's first democratic presidential election.

## 1991

**February 7**   Aristide inaugurated.

**June 25**   Slovenia and Croatia declare independence from Yugoslavia.

**June 27**   Yugoslav army attacks Slovenia.

**July 18**   Yugoslav army withdraws from Slovenia.

**July**   In Krajina region of Croatia, skirmishes escalate into war between Croats and rebel Serbs influenced by Milosevic and backed by Yugoslav army.

**July**   Secretary of State James Baker responds to press question about U.S. policy toward violent breakup of Yugoslavia: "We have no dog in that fight."

**September**   United Nations imposes arms embargo on former Yugoslavia.

**September 30**   Lieutenant-General Raoul Cedras orchestrates military coup against Aristide. Hundreds of Aristide supporters killed during first week, thousands more over next three years. Aristide exiled to United States.

**October 3**   Bill Clinton announces candidacy for President.

**October 7**   Bush White House spokesman Marlin Fitzwater states, "We don't know if Aristide will return to power."

**October**   Germany recognizes independence of Croatia and Slovenia.

**December**   European Commission, under pressure from Germany, announces it will recognize Croatia and Slovenia.

## 1992

**January**   Deng Xiaoping tours China's southern provinces, calling for economic revitalization and new efforts to attract foreign investment.

**January 2**   U.N. mediator (and former U.S. Secretary of State) Cyrus Vance negotiates cease-fire in Croatia.

**February 21**   U.N. Security Council votes to send peacekeeping troops to Croatia.

**February 29**   Boznia-Herzegovina declares independence. Bosnian Serbs proclaim separate state.

**March**   12,500 lightly armed U.N. troops sent to Croatia to supervise Croat-Serb cease-fire, watch over humanitarian shipments.

**April**   Bosnian Serbs begin three-year siege of Sarajevo.

**April 6**   European Commission recognizes Bosnia.

**April 7**   United States recognizes Bosnia.

**May 5**   Yugoslav army relinquishes command of 80,000 troops in Bosnia, effectively creating Bosnian Serb army.

**May 24**   President Bush orders U.S. Coast Guard to intercept all Haitians leaving island in boats and forcibly return them to Haiti.

**May 30**   United Nations imposes sanctions on Serbia for fomenting war in Bosnia and Croatia.

**July 3**   International airlift begins to Sarajevo.

**July**   At Democratic National Convention in New York, Bill Clinton attacks Bush foreign policy for supporting "the butchers of Beijing," endorses position taken by congressional Democrats that China's trade benefits should be linked to human rights improvements. Student leaders from Tiananmen democracy movement address convention.

**August 3**   Clinton criticizes Bush administration for "coddling dictators" in Haiti, Yugoslavia, and China. Accuses Bush of playing "racial politics" with Haiti refugee issue, asserting, "I wouldn't be shipping those poor people back."

**September 19**   United Nations expels Yugoslavia from General Assembly.

**September 30**   On anniversary of military coup, Haitians hand out leaflets and attend commemorative masses and meetings. In following weeks soldiers and paramilitary forces carry out arrests, beatings, and mass killings of Aristide supporters.

**November**  Prominent Hutu extremist Leon Mugesera appeals to Rwandan Hutus to send Tutsis "back to Ethiopia" via the rivers.

**November 3**  Clinton elected President.

**December**  CIA reports indicate that Clinton's campaign charge against Bush of coddling dictators has raised hopes of Haitians for refuge in United States. Boat-building accelerates in Haiti. Pressure mounts for Clinton to reverse his policy.

**December**  At roundtable policy discussion with American business leaders in Little Rock, Arkansas, Clinton asserts that he plans to promote both trade and human rights in China.

**December**  End-of-year estimate of 100,000 killed since 1991 in former Yugoslavia.

## 1993

**January 2**  International mediators Cyrus Vance and David Owen unveil plan to divide Bosnia into ten provinces, mostly along ethnic lines.

**January 20**  Clinton inaugurated.

**January**  Reversing campaign position, Clinton continues Bush policy of intercepting and returning Haitian refugees.

**February**  United Nations and Organization of American States establish Civilian Mission in Haiti to monitor human rights violations.

**March**  Bosnian Croats and Bosnian Muslims begin fighting over portions of Bosnia not seized by Bosnian Serbs.

**April and May**  U.N. Security Council declares six "safe areas" in Bosnia— Sarajevo, Tuzla, Bihac, Srebrenica, Zepa, and Gorazde.

**May 15–16**  Bosnian Serbs reject Vance-Owen plan in favor of independent Bosnian Serb state.

**May 25**  U.N. Security Council establishes International Criminal Tribunal for the Former Yugoslavia.

**May**  Secretary of State Warren Christopher travels to Europe to seek support for new U.S. proposal to lift arms embargo so that Bosnian Muslims can defend themselves, and to launch air strikes against Bosnian Serbs to break siege of Sarajevo. European leaders reject proposal because United States is unwilling to join them in committing ground forces to Bosnia.

**May 28**    Clinton signs executive order extending most favored nation (MFN) trade status to China for one year, setting forth specific human rights criteria that must be met for further renewal.

**June 2**    John Shattuck sworn in as assistant secretary of state for human rights and humanitarian affairs (title changed a year later to assistant secretary for democracy, human rights, and labor to reflect expanded responsibilities).

**June 14–25**    Shattuck leads U.S. delegation to U.N. World Conference on Human Rights in Vienna.

**June 16**    European and American mediators meet with Serbian president Slobodan Milosevic, Bosnian president Alija Izetbegovic, Croatian president Franjo Tudjman, and Bosnian Serb president Radovan Karadzic in Geneva. Proposal to split Bosnia in three ways. Izetbegovic walks out.

**July 3**    Governors Island Accord signed by Aristide and Cedras in New York, committing Cedras to cede power by October 15, and allowing Aristide to return by October 30.

**July**    Sarajevo siege intensifies. Bosnian Serb mortar and sniper attacks render city virtually defenseless.

**July 15**    Shattuck reports to Christopher growing evidence of genocide in central Bosnia, urges U.S. leadership to strengthen International Criminal Tribunal. Christopher calls for "unfettered tribunal."

**August 4**    Following months of chaotic negotiations, Habyarimana and Tutsi rebel forces sign peace accord in Arusha, Tanzania, calling for return of refugees to Rwanda and coalition Hutu-Tutsi government. U.N. peacekeeping troops (2,500) authorized to oversee implementation of Arusha accords.

**August**    U.N. Special Rapporteur for Extrajudicial Killings Bacre Ndiaye issues report on growing ethnic tensions in Rwanda, warns of possible genocide.

**September**    Wei Jingsheng released from prison in China six months before end of fourteen-year sentence for role in "Democracy Wall" movement. Release coincides with Chinese government's international lobbying to host 2000 Olympic Games.

**September 8**    Soldiers and paramilitaries fire on crowd in Port-au-Prince assembled to greet elected mayor, Evans Paul, returning after two years in exile. Four unarmed Haitians killed and dozens wounded.

**September 11**   Antoine Izmery, prominent businessman and Aristide supporter, dragged from church service by paramilitaries and assassinated in presence of U.N./OAS human rights monitors.

**September 25**   National Security Advisor Tony Lake meets with Chinese Ambassador Li Dayou at White House to outline new U.S. policy of "engagement" with China on all issues, including human rights.

**September 26**   Shattuck meets with Chinese assistant foreign minister Qin Huasun in New York to begin human rights "dialogue" and explain conditions of Clinton's executive order linking China's MFN trade benefits to improvements on human rights.

**September 30**   Christopher meets with Chinese foreign minister Qian Qichen in Washington. Qian invites Shattuck to continue human rights dialogue in Beijing in October.

**October 9–16**   Shattuck visits Beijing for meetings on MFN with Chinese government officials; travels to Tibet, southern China, and Hong Kong; and meets with local officials, intellectuals, academics, religious leaders, democracy advocates, and prisoners.

**October 11**   USS *Harlan County,* carrying two hundred U.S. and Canadian military engineers, turns back from landing in Port-au-Prince when paramilitaries demonstrate on dock.

**October 14**   Guy Malary, Aristide's minister of justice, assassinated in Port-au-Prince.

**October 15**   General Cedras refuses to cede power in defiance of Governors Island Accord deadline.

**October 16**   Eighteen U.S. Army Rangers participating in U.N. peacekeeping operation killed in Mogadishu, Somalia, during attempt to capture local warlord. CNN broadcasts film of Somalis dragging body of U.S. soldier through streets.

**October and November**   Congressional outcry against U.S. participation in U.N. peacekeeping.

**October 20**   Christopher meets with American business leaders on China MFN policy; asks for support in pressing China for human rights progress.

**November 9**   Bosnian-Croat shelling destroys centuries-old Mostar Bridge, symbol of ethnic harmony.

**November 15**   Clinton receives letter signed by 270 members of Congress stating they would oppose MFN extension if vote was taken today.

**November 16**   Chinese foreign minister announces China will give "positive consideration" to allowing International Red Cross visits to three thousand "counterrevolutionary prisoners."

**November 18**   Chinese democracy activist Wei Jingsheng publishes op-ed in *New York Times* renewing call for democracy in China.

**November 18**   Shattuck meets with Chinese assistant minister Qin Huasun in Seattle to go over again in detail human rights conditions in Clinton executive order on MFN.

**November 19**   Clinton meets with Chinese president Jiang Zemin in Seattle; delivers strong human rights message.

**November 28**   China releases from detention two Christian leaders of underground church movement.

**December 10**   Shattuck escorts Rwandan human rights activist Monique Mujawamariya to White House ceremony with President Clinton commemorating forty-fifth anniversary of Universal Declaration of Human Rights.

**December 11–15**   Shattuck travels to Haiti to gather information about human rights situation facing boat refugees returned to the country. Suggests need for review of U.S. forced return policy. *New York Times* reports Shattuck "rebuked" by State Department and White House for making statement.

**December 26**   Cedras regime paramilitaries set more than a thousand homes on fire in Cité Soleil area of Port-au-Prince, killing seventy.

## 1994

**January 4–8**   Albright, accompanied by Shattuck, conducts first cabinet-level human rights mission to former Yugoslavia, visiting Croat-Serb confrontation area in Vukovar and Eastern Slavonia, suspected mass grave site in Ovcara, and meeting with U.N. and Croatian officials.

**January 11**   General Romeo Dallaire, U.N. commander in Rwanda, sends urgent fax to U.N. headquarters in New York, warning that informant told him Hutu extremists are assembling arms caches and planning genocide. Dallaire denied permission to disarm extremists on grounds that such an action would exceed mission's authority; told instead to inform Rwandan president and ambassadors of Security Council member states in Kigali.

**January**   Robert Kaplan's *Balkan Ghosts* popularizes view of many U.S. policymakers that conflict in Yugoslavia is one of "ancient hatreds."

**January 22**   Shattuck accompanies Christopher on trip to Paris to discuss Bosnia situation with French foreign minister, and to meet with Chinese foreign minister to urge progress on human rights conditions for renewing MFN.

**End of January**   Former president George Bush and Brent Scowcroft tell Chinese in Beijing about Washington's growing skepticism concerning Clinton's MFN policy.

**January 29**   Clinton economic advisor Robert Rubin tells journalists that trade should be separated from human rights in U.S. relationship with China.

**January 30**   Chinese deputy foreign minister Liu Huaqiu provides first "accounting" of prisoners on list submitted by Shattuck in October.

**February 5**   Sixty-two killed, two hundred wounded by mortar round fired into crowded Sarajevo market.

**February 27–March 2**   Shattuck travels to Beijing, meeting with Chinese officials, academics, and intellectuals, as well as with Wei Jingsheng.

**Early March**   Chinese detain Wei Jingsheng and dozens of other dissidents in Beijing and Shanghai.

**March 3**   *Wall Street Journal* reports U.S. sending mixed signals on MFN: simultaneously Shattuck tells international press in Beijing that "further progress on human rights is needed if MFN is to be renewed in June," and Undersecretary of Commerce Jeffrey Garten tells press in Hong Kong that "there are huge [economic] stakes for the U.S. in China."

**March 4**   Clinton criticizes Chinese detention of dissidents as "obviously not helpful to our relations."

**March 12–14**   Christopher visits China, pressing Chinese government on Clinton's MFN policy.

**March 16**   Former U.S. officials, business leaders, and China specialists criticize Clinton's MFN policy at Council on Foreign Relations forum in New York.

**March 17**   Christopher tells House Appropriations Committee that "the Chinese have been hearing mixed signals and needed to hear our position clearly and directly," adding, "in my sessions in China, I pulled no punches and yielded no ground."

**March 18**   Bosnian Muslims and Bosnian Croats sign U.S.-brokered peace accord, establish Federation.

**March 19**    Chinese finance minister Liu Zhongli tells American business audience, "I think it is the view of U.S. business to solve [the MFN issue] once and for all."

**March 22**    Treasury Secretary Lloyd Bentsen tells press that "we have to explore alternatives" to current China MFN policy.

**March 24**    Clinton tells press he would "continue to seek progress on human rights in China" as part of an effort "to build a more positive relationship with that very important nation."

**March**    Prominent U.S. civil rights leader Randall Robinson begins hunger strike to protest U.S. policy of sending Haitian boat refugees back to Haiti.

**End of March**    International Criminal Tribunal threatened by pressure from five-power Bosnia Contact Group (United States, Great Britain, France, Germany, and Russia) to offer amnesty to indicted war criminals to induce them to enter peace negotiations.

**April 6**    Rwandan and Burundian presidents killed when Habyarimana's plane shot down near Kigali Airport.

**April 7**    Rwandan army and Hutu extremist paramilitary group Interahamwe set up roadblocks and go from house to house in Kigali, killing Tutsis and moderate Hutu politicians, including the prime minister. Thousands murdered on first day of genocide.

**April 8**    A thousand French, Belgian, and Italian troops sent to Kigali to guard evacuation of foreign nationals. Tutsi RPF launches offensive to rescue its troops based in Kigali under Arusha accords.

**April 17**    Dallaire makes appeal to U.N. headquarters for five thousand well-armed soldiers backed by strong mandate and broad rules of engagement.

**April 18**    Haiti policy review results in decision to develop new strategy for ending forcible return of refugees, as well as a determination to remove Cedras and restore Aristide.

**April 19**    Monique Mujawamariya comes to Washington to plead for help in stopping genocide in Rwanda.

**April 21**    United Nations Security Council cuts Rwandan peacekeeping force from 2,500 to 270 following murder of ten Belgian peacekeepers assigned to guard the prime minister.

**April 21**    Boat carrying four hundred Haitians evades Coast Guard, lands on Florida coast.

**April 26–29**    Nelson Mandela elected president of South Africa.

**April 30** U.N. Security Council adopts resolution condemning mass killings in Rwanda, but omits reference to "genocide."

**May** U.N./OAS International Civilian Mission in Haiti reports 340 extrajudicial killings.

**May 2** Discussion at State Department senior staff meeting of Powell-Weinberger Cold War Doctrine on use of force. Deputy Secretary of State Strobe Talbott suggests that the doctrine is outmoded, calls for review of post–Cold War circumstances where diplomacy could be backed by limited force.

**May 3–9** Shattuck trip to Rwanda, Burundi, Tanzania, Uganda, and Ethiopia. Hundreds of thousands of Rwandan refugees fleeing across borders to Tanzania, Burundi, and Zaire.

**May 3** Clinton issues Presidential Decision Directive 25, setting strict controls over U.S. participation in peacekeeping operations.

**May 17** U.N. Security Council votes to send new peacekeeping mission to Rwanda in resolution, stating that "acts of genocide may have been committed." Deployment delayed for more than a month over logistical and financing issues.

**May 26** Clinton extends MFN for China, severs link between trade and human rights.

**June 22** U.N. Security Council authorizes deployment of French forces to southwest Rwanda.

**June 30** Legislation barring U.S. military from assisting return of President Aristide to Haiti narrowly defeated in Congress following heavy lobbying by White House.

**July** Attacks on new Clinton Haiti policy continue in Congress, even among senior Democrats. Senator Sam Nunn (D-Ga.) says Haiti not "vital" to American interests.

**July** Tutsi RPF forces under General Paul Kagame capture Kigali, Hutu government flees to Zaire, and French troops withdraw. Estimates indicate 800,000 killed since April 7 in Rwanda genocide.

**July 3–4** More than 6,000 Haitians flee by boat from Haiti.

**July** Shattuck human rights trip to Turkey, Russia, and Kazakhstan. In meeting with Russian deputy foreign minister Sergei Lavrov on July 6, agreement reached on appointment of Richard Goldstone to be first chief prosecutor of International Criminal Tribunal for the Former Yugoslavia.

**July 31**   U.N. Security Council votes to authorize multinational force to use "all necessary means" to remove military regime in Haiti and facilitate return of Aristide. Unanimous vote by Organization of American States to back multinational force.

**August 3–7**   Shattuck trip to Rwanda, Burundi, and refugee camps in Zaire.

**September 14**   Shattuck briefs President Clinton on human rights situation in Haiti.

**September 15**   In televised address to nation, Clinton announces U.S. leadership of multinational military intervention in Haiti. Warns Haitian military regime, "Your time is up. Leave now or we will force you from power."

**September 16–19**   Former President Jimmy Carter, former Senator Sam Nunn, and General Colin Powell persuade Cedras and junta to agree to step down on eve of arrival of multinational force.

**September 19**   U.S. troops enter Haiti.

**October 15**   Aristide returns to Haiti.

**November 7**   Republicans sweep U.S. midterm elections.

**November**   U.N. Security Council creates International Criminal Tribunal for Rwanda, based in Arusha, Tanzania.

**Early December**   Shattuck visits Haiti, reports significant improvement in human rights situation.

**December 20**   Jimmy Carter negotiates cease-fire with Bosnian Serbs in exchange for replacement of Bosnian government troops around Sarajevo with U.N. lightly armed peacekeepers. Cease-fire broken by Bosnian Serbs two months later.

## 1995

**January**   In meetings in Beijing, Shattuck urges Chinese officials to make progress on human rights, informing them of U.S. intention to sponsor resolution on China at U.N. Human Rights Commission in April.

**February 27**   U.N. Security Council passes resolution calling on member states to arrest persons suspected of participating in Rwandan genocide.

**April**   U.N. Human Rights Commission for first time rejects effort by China to block vote on resolution introduced by the United States and European Union, criticizing China's human rights record. Resolution later defeated by one vote.

**May 1**   Croatia launches failed offensive to recapture Krajina region from rebel Serb forces. Serbs retaliate by shelling Zagreb, killing six civilians and wounding more than two hundred.

**May**   Tensions increase between United Nations and Rwandan government over failure to arrest genocide leaders in refugee camps and lack of international aid.

**May**   Shattuck travels to Rwanda with International Criminal Tribunal Chief Prosecutor Richard Goldstone to deliver U.S. funding for tribunal and assistance to Rwandan government for rebuilding its domestic justice system.

**May 24–25**   Bosnian Serbs defy U.N. order to remove heavy weapons around Sarajevo. NATO planes bomb Bosnian Serb ammunition depot. Serbs respond by shelling U.N. "safe areas," including Tuzla, where 71 civilians are killed and 150 wounded.

**May 26**   NATO planes attack more Bosnian Serb ammunition depots. Bosnian Serbs take 350 U.N. peacekeepers hostage. CNN broadcasts images of hostages chained to trees and telephone poles.

**June 2**   Bosnian Serbs shoot down U.S. F-16 over northern Bosnia.

**June 3**   NATO defense ministers, meeting in Paris, agree to create Rapid Reaction Force for Bosnia.

**June 4**   Hostages released after U.N. commander in Bosnia, General Bernard Janvier, secretly agrees in meeting with Bosnian Serb General Ratko Mladic to end NATO airstrikes on Bosnian Serb targets.

**June 7**   U.S. Marines rescue downed pilot of U.S. F-16.

**June**   European governments threaten to pull troops out of Bosnia.

**June 15–30**   As Bosnian government launches offensive to break siege of Sarajevo, Bosnian Serbs increase shelling of Sarajevo and "safe areas."

**July 6**   Shattuck meets in The Hague with Goldstone, briefed on impending indictment of Karadzic, Mladic, and other Bosnian Serb leaders for crimes against humanity.

**July 11**   Bosnian Serb forces under General Mladic overrun Srebrenica.

**July 12–13**   Twenty thousand Bosnian Muslim women and children separated from men and expelled on buses from Srebrenica; many raped, assaulted, and robbed by Bosnian Serb soldiers.

**July 14–16**  Seven thousand Bosnian Muslim men rounded up; held in schoolhouses, warehouses, and other buildings; assaulted, tortured, and shelled with hand grenades and rocket launchers; then shot in front of open pits. Hurem Suljic and a few others survive, escape to refugee camps in Tuzla.

**July 17**  Deputy commander of Dutch peacekeeping battalion in Srebrenica forced by Bosnian Serbs to sign "Declaration" that "evacuation [of the Srebrenica civilian population] was carried out by the Serb side correctly."

**July 17–20**  International Committee for Red Cross (ICRC) searches for missing men. Shattuck prepares for trip to Bosnia to support search.

**July 19**  British prime minister John Major announces emergency conference on Bosnia crisis. State Department postpones Shattuck trip to Bosnia.

**July 19**  Shattuck memo to Christopher reports ICRC being denied access to Bosnian Serb areas around Srebrenica; summary executions of Bosnian Muslim men and boys suspected.

**July 21–23**  Western allies, meeting in London, adopt U.S. position promising "decisive and substantial" NATO air strikes, with or without U.N. approval, to protect remaining "safe area" of Gorazde.

**July 25**  Richard Goldstone, chief prosecutor of International Criminal Tribunal, issues indictment of Karadzic and Mladic for genocide and crimes against humanity committed prior to Srebrenica.

**July 27–August 2**  Shattuck travels to Tuzla to interview Srebrenica refugees, helps break story of largest genocide in Europe since World War II.

**July–August**  Withdrawal of most of multinational force in Haiti.

**August 2**  CIA aerial photo analysts identify photographs of killing areas around Srebrenica described by Shattuck in report to White House.

**August 4**  Croatia launches new offensive to recapture Kraijina from rebel Serb regime allied with Milosevic. Following massive ethnic cleansing by Croatian army and shelling of civilians, 150,000 Serbs flee ancestral homes.

**August 10**  U.S. Ambassador to the United Nations Madeleine Albright displays photos of Srebrenica killing fields to U.N. Security Council.

**August 18**  U.S. diplomats, led by assistant secretary of state for European affairs Richard Holbrooke, launch new U.S. peace initiative and begin shuttling among leaders in region.

**August 19**  Three U.S. diplomats involved in peace initiative, Robert Frasure, Joseph Kruzel, and Nelson Drew, are killed when their armored personnel carrier crashes and explodes on a mountain road above Sarajevo.

**August 28**   Mortar shell fired into crowded Sarajevo market kills 37and wounds 85.

**August 30**   NATO planes launch massive air strikes against Bosnian Serb military targets.

**Early September**   Muslim-Croat Federation forces advance on Bosnian Serbs in central and western Bosnia.

**September 6–10**   Shattuck trip to Haiti to prepare for presidential election in December.

**September 14**   Milosevic pledges to Holbrooke that Bosnian Serbs will withdraw heavy weapons from around Sarajevo. NATO suspends air strikes.

**September 26**   Christopher and Holbrooke conclude "framework agreement" with Bosnian, Serb, and Croatian foreign ministers in New York, setting forth basic outlines of a peace plan. Holbrooke and Shattuck meet to discuss Shattuck's human rights missions to Bosnia in support of peace drive.

**September 27–October 1**   Shattuck conducts first U.S. mission to areas of fighting in western Bosnia and Krajina, visits refugees at risk, and uncovers new mass grave sites.

**October 2–4**   Meeting of Organization on Security and Cooperation in Europe in Warsaw. Shattuck briefs delegates on U.S. Bosnia peace strategy, led by Holbrooke, of spotlighting ongoing human rights abuses and confronting leaders in order to move them toward negotiations.

**October 5**   Bosnian parties agree to sixty-day cease-fire.

**October 12**   U.S. Ambassador to Bosnia John Menzies calls Shattuck from Sarajevo to report new ethnic cleansing and atrocities carried out by notorious Serb paramilitary leader "Arkan" and Bosnian Serbs in Banja Luka.

**October 15–17**   Shattuck returns to Bosnia to interview Muslim victims of new ethnic cleansing in Banja Luka, providing Holbrooke with fresh evidence of war crimes with which to confront Milosevic simultaneously in Belgrade.

**October 18–21**   Shattuck meets with Serb victims of Croatian atrocities and ethnic cleansing in Krajina, and confronts Croatian government with evidence of war crimes committed during recapture of Krajina.

**October 20**   Aerial photos later introduced into evidence in war crimes trial in The Hague indicate ongoing Bosnian Serb efforts to remove bodies from mass graves near Srebrenica and hide them in other locations.

**October 24**  Shattuck meets with Milosevic to demand that Bosnian Serbs release Muslim prisoners and provide access to Srebrenica and Banja Luka. Milosevic replies, "No problem."

**October 26–27**  Shattuck attempts to reach Banja Luka by U.N. helicopter. Blocked by shootings, bad weather.

**October 29**  Responding to U.S. pressure, Bosnian Serbs release 324 Muslim men rounded up in Banja Luka in September.

**November 1**  Bosnian peace talks open at Wright-Patterson Air Force Base in Dayton, Ohio.

**November 7–11**  Shattuck leads first international diplomatic mission across confrontation zone from Sarajevo to Banja Luka in order to implement freedom of movement, build confidence at peace talks.

**November 10**  Wei Jingsheng receives new fourteen-year sentence for advocating democracy and human rights in China.

**November 16**  Karadzic and Mladic reindicted for their roles in Srebrenica genocide.

**November 20**  Final Framework Agreement of Dayton Peace Accords requires "all parties to cooperate" with International Criminal Tribunal, but omits clause "and its orders." Military annex to agreement silent on whether NATO International Force will arrest indicted war criminals.

**November 21**  Balkan leaders sign Dayton Peace Accords.

**December 1**  NATO authorizes deployment of 60,000 troops to Bosnia.

**December 4**  Polls show majority of Americans oppose sending U.S. troops to Bosnia.

**December 5**  First U.S. troops arrive in Bosnia.

**December 8**  Presidential election in Haiti won by Rene Preval. First peaceful democratic transition of power in Haitian history, as Aristide prepares to complete term, succeeded by Preval. Shattuck participates in U.S. observer mission headed by USAID director Brian Atwood.

**December 11**  Commander of U.S. forces in Bosnia, Admiral Leighton Smith, announces in press interview he will "absolutely not" order troops to arrest persons indicted by the International Criminal Tribunal.

**December 12**  International Criminal Tribunal for Rwanda announces first indictments against eight persons charged with genocide and crimes against humanity.

**December 13**  Legislation to cut off funds for U.S. mission in Bosnia defeated in Senate.

## 1996

**January 22**   Shattuck leads first international diplomatic mission to Srebrenica, opening area for investigation by International Criminal Tribunal and later meeting with Milosevic to inform him no evidence exists that killings occurred during hostilities, as Milosevic and Bosnian Serbs contend.

**February**   Two Bosnian Serb officers arrested by Bosnian government are charged with war crimes, turned over to tribunal prosecutors, and flown to The Hague by NATO.

**February–June**   NATO commanders continue to bar the use of international troops to arrest war crimes suspects.

**June**   Goldstone and Dutch defense minister Hans von Mierlo propose to Shattuck the creation of an elite commando team to arrest persons indicted by International Criminal Tribunal. Plan opposed by Pentagon.

**July**   U.S. pressure on Milosevic results in removal of Karadzic from office as Bosnian Serb president and enforcement of Dayton policy that persons under indictment by tribunal cannot hold political office. Karadzic and other indicted war criminals remain at large in Bosnia, continuing to influence political events.

**September**   First Bosnian elections following Dayton peace process. Shattuck participates in U.S. observer delegation headed by Richard Holbrooke.

**November**   Mass repatriation of refugees to Rwanda and dispersal of others throughout Zaire as Rwandan army shuts down refugee camps along Rwandan border.

**November 8**   Clinton elected to second term.

**December**   Rwanda begins genocide trials.

## 1997

**January 10**   Rwandan mayor Jean-Paul Akayesu first person to be tried for genocide by International Criminal Tribunal for Rwanda.

**January**   Rwandan troops enter eastern Zaire, join forces with Congolese rebel leader Laurent Kabila to overthrow Zairean dictator Mobutu Sese Seko, and pursue Hutus fleeing from refugee camps.

**April**   Mobutu overthrown. Kabila proclaims Democratic Republic of the Congo with support of Rwandan troops.

**June 5–7**   U.S. Ambassador to the United Nations Bill Richardson leads delegation, including Shattuck, to meet with Kabila.

**June 8–11**   Shattuck travels through refugee areas in eastern Zaire to report on atrocities committed by Rwandan forces against fleeing Hutus. Meets with Paul Kagame in Kigali. Urges end of reprisal killings.

**October**   Student demonstrations protesting failure of Serbia to reopen universities in Kosovo broken up violently by Serb police.

**November**   Wei Jingsheng released from prison, sent to United States.

## 1998

**February–March**   Serb police and paramilitaries conduct raids in Kosovo, burning houses, emptying villages, and killing ethnic Albanians in actions ostensibly aimed at Kosovo Liberation Army.

**March**   Clinton trip to Rwanda, accompanied by Shattuck. Clinton apologizes to Rwandans that United States did not try to stop genocide.

**May**   Holbrooke travels to Belgrade to arrange dialogue between Milosevic and Kosovo leader Ibrahim Rugova. Dialogue breaks down as raids continue; dozens killed in village of Decani.

**June**   Shattuck accompanies Clinton on trip to China. Clinton tells Jiang Zemin that the Chinese government's human rights record puts it "on the wrong side of history."

**June 23–24**   In separate meetings Holbrooke warns Milosevic and Kosovo Liberation Army commanders against escalation of violence.

**July**   Kosovo Diplomatic Observer Mission begins patrols of Kosovo to report on freedom of movement and security conditions. Reports that more than 100,000 Kosovars had been driven from their homes following Serb shelling of villages.

**September 5–7**   Shattuck and former Senator and Republican presidential candidate Bob Dole sent by White House and Secretary of State Madeleine Albright to Kosovo to report firsthand on escalating human rights crisis. They meet later with Milosevic to warn him of consequences of continuing attacks on civilians.

**September 24**   NATO takes first steps toward military intervention in Kosovo, approving contingency plans for air strikes and monitoring ceasefire.

**September 29**   U.N. High Commissioner for Refugees Sadaka Ogata reports 200,000 civilians displaced within Kosovo, 60,000 without shelter.

**October**   Holbrooke negotiates withdrawal of Serb forces from Kosovo.

**November 19**   Shattuck sworn in as U.S. Ambassador to Czech Republic.

**December 23**   Serbian army and security police undertake new military action in Kosovo, which is condemned by the United States.

## 1999

**January 15**   Bodies of forty-five ethnic Albanians discovered in village of Racak.

**January 29**   Contact Group (United States, France, Great Britain, Germany, and Russia) meets in London, urges Serbs and ethnic Albanians to attend peace talks in Rambouillet, France.

**February**   U.S. official presence in Prague targeted by specific, credible, immediate terrorist threat from Middle East country. After consultation with Washington, Shattuck closes embassy.

**March**   Czech Republic becomes new member of NATO.

**March 15**   Albanian delegation to Rambouillet agrees to cease-fire, but Serbs reject proposal.

**March 20**   Serbian army and security police launch major offensive in Kosovo, driving tens of thousands more from villages, shelling civilians, and setting fire to houses.

**March 21**   Holbrooke delivers "final warning" to Milosevic in Belgrade, who makes no concessions.

**March 24**   NATO air strikes begin.

**Late March**   Over 800,000 Kosovar refugees pour into Albania and Macedonia; thousands killed by Serb forces in Kosovo.

**May 27**   Milosevic indicted by International Criminal Tribunal chief prosecutor Louise Arbour for crimes against humanity.

**March 24–June 10**   NATO air war results in withdrawal of all Serb forces from Kosovo.

**June**   U.N. peacekeeping force enters Kosovo. Ethnic Albanian refugees return; Serb civilians flee.

**June**   Muhammad Atta reportedly visits Prague.

**July**   Petition for Milosevic to resign circulates in Belgrade. A year later, Milosevic loses bid for reelection. In October 2001 he is arrested on order of Serbian judge and flown to The Hague to stand trial before the International Criminal Tribunal.

# STATE DEPARTMENT ORGANIZATIONAL CHART

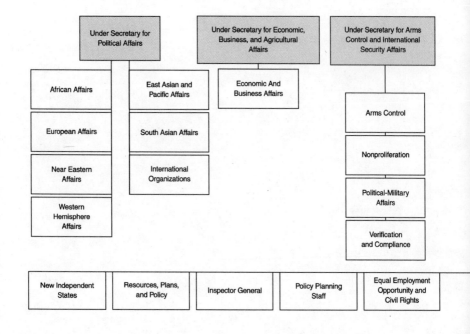

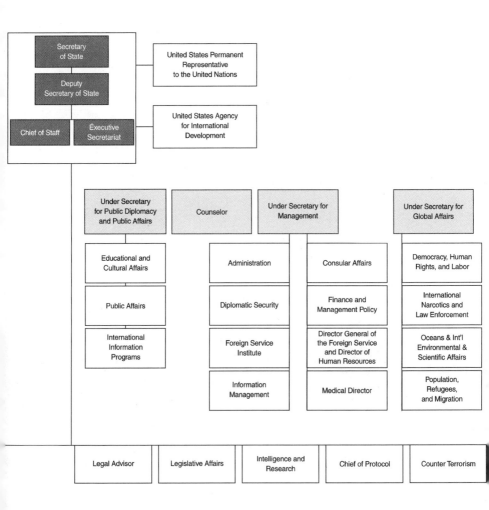

# NOTES

## Introduction

1. Francis Fukayama, *The End of History and the Last Man* (New York: Free Press, 1992).

2. R. J. Rummel, *Death by Government* (New Brunswick, N.J.: Transaction, 1994), p. 21.

3. Preamble, Universal Declaration of Human Rights, U.N. General Assembly, Dec. 10, 1948, clause 2.

4. Ibid., clause 3.

5. According to a February 2002 report of the U.S. General Accounting Office, "The United States directly contributed an estimated $3.45 billion to support U.N. peacekeeping from fiscal years 1996 through 2001. . . . [In addition,] U.S. indirect contributions that benefited U.N. peacekeeping were about $24.2 billion. Although there is no common definition within the U.S. government on what constitutes indirect contributions, we defined indirect contributions as U.S. programs and activities that (1) are located in the same area as an ongoing U.N. peacekeeping operation, (2) have objectives that help the peacekeeping operation achieve its mandated objectives, and (3) are not an official part of the U.N. operation. The largest indirect contribution ($21.8 billion) stemmed from U.S. military operations and services that helped provide a secure environment for U.N. operations." U.S. General Accounting Office, *U.N. Peacekeeping: Estimated U.S. Contributions, Fiscal Years 1996–2001* (Washington, D.C.: Government Printing Office, GAO-02-294, Feb. 2002), pp. 1–2.

6. The title and role of my position was expanded in early 1994 to assistant secretary for democracy, human rights, and labor.

7. In 1963, I found it was easy to replace both my driver's license and my draft card when I returned home.

## 1. Rwanda: The Genocide That Might Have Been Prevented

1. "Two African Presidents Killed in Plane Crash," *Washington Post,* Apr. 7, 1994, p. A18; "Troops Rampage in Rwanda," *New York Times,* Apr. 8, 1994, p. A1.

2. "Thirty-seven Who Saw Murder Didn't Call the Police," *New York Times,* Mar. 27, 1964, p. A1.

3. *Report of the Independent Inquiry into the Actions of the United Nations during the 1994 Genocide in Rwanda* (New York: United Nations, A/54/549, Dec. 15, 1999), p. 1. See also Alison Des Forges, *"Leave None to Tell the Story":* *Genocide in Rwanda* (New York: Human Rights Watch, 1999), pp. 15–16, which estimates that while some of the casualties from April to July 1994 were "from causes other than genocide," three-quarters of the Tutsi population was wiped out by the 1994 genocide.

4. *Peace Operations: U.S. Costs in Support of Rwanda* (Washington, D.C.: General Accounting Office, Letter Report GAO/NSIAD-96-38, Mar. 3, 1996).

5. Quoted in David Halberstam, *War in a Time of Peace* (New York: Scribner's, 2001), p. 264.

6. Quoted in Laura Silber and Allan Little, *Yugoslavia: Death of a Nation* (London: Penguin/BBC Books, 1996), p. 201.

7. See Philip Gourevitch, *We Wish to Inform You That Tomorrow We Will Be Killed with Our Families: Stories from Rwanda* (New York: Farrar, Straus, and Giroux, 1998), pp. 47–48.

8. Des Forges, *"Leave None to Tell the Story,"* p. 37. See also Gourevitch, *We Wish to Inform You,* p. 47.

9. Des Forges, *"Leave None to Tell the Story,"* pp. 36–37.

10. Linda Melvern, *A People Betrayed: The Role of the West in Rwanda's Genocide* (London: Zed Books, 2000), pp. 10–11.

11. Ibid., p. 10.

12. Des Forges, *"Leave None to Tell the Story,"* p. 38. See also Gerard Prunier, *The Rwanda Crisis, 1959–94: History of a Genocide* (London: Hurst, 1995), p. 12; Gourevitch, *We Wish to Inform You,* pp. 50–52.

13. Melvern, *A People Betrayed,* p. 13.

14. Ibid., pp. 14–15.

15. See Gourevitch, *We Wish to Inform You,* p. 59.

16. Des Forges, *"Leave None to Tell the Story,"* p. 41.

17. Ibid.

18. See Gourevitch, *We Wish to Inform You,* p. 73.

19. See Melvern, *A People Betrayed,* pp. 28–31.

20. Reprinted in African Rights, *Rwanda: Death, Despair and Defiance* (New York: African Rights, 1995), pp. 42–43.

21. Quoted in Gourevitch, *We Wish to Inform You,* p. 96. For background on the Hutu Ten Commandments see Samantha Power, *"A Problem from Hell": America and the Age of Genocide* (New York: Basic Books, 2002), pp. 339–340.

22. See Power, *"Problem from Hell,"* p. 336.

23. While those responsible for Habyarimana's murder have never been definitively identified, the view of two journalists on the scene is that it was Hutu extremists who shot down his plane. See Scott Peterson, *Me against My Brother* (London: Routledge, 2000), p. 268; Bill Berkeley, *The Graves Are Not Yet Full: Race, Tribe, and Power in the Heart of Africa* (New York: Basic Books, 2001), p. 259.

24. Report by W. B. Ndiaye, Special Rapporteur on Extrajudicial, Summary or Arbitrary Executions, on His Mission to Rwanda from 8 to 17 April 1993, E/CN.4/1994/7 (Aug. 11, 1993), paragraph 64. "The cases of inter-communal violence brought to the Special Rapporteur's attention indicate very clearly that the victims of the attacks, Tutsis in the overwhelming majority of cases, have been targeted because of their membership of a certain ethnic group, and for no other objective reason" (paragraph 79).

25. See Melvern, *A People Betrayed,* pp. 82–97; Peterson, *Me against My Brother,* pp. 290–293.

26. Facsimile from Major General Romeo Dallaire, Force Commander, United Nations Assistance Mission for Rwanda, to Major General Maurice Baril, United Nations Peacekeeping Operations, "Request for Protection for Informant," Jan. 11, 1994, quoted in Gourevitch, *We Wish to Inform You,* pp. 103–104.

27. Ibid., p. 104.

28. See Alan J. Kuperman, *The Limits of Humanitarian Intervention: Genocide in Rwanda* (Washington, D.C.: Brookings, 2001), p. 78.

29. Power, *"Problem from Hell,"* p. 344.

30. Gourevitch, *We Wish to Inform You,* p. 105.

31. Power, *"Problem from Hell,"* p. 344.

32. *Frontline,* "The Triumph of Evil," 1998. Available online at *www.pbs.org/wgbh/pages/frontline/shows/evil/interviews/riza.html.*

33. *Report of the Independent Inquiry into the Actions of the United Nations*

*during the 1994 Genocide in Rwanda,* Dec. 15, 1999, p. 30. Available online at *www.reliefweb.int/library/documents/Rwandagenocide.pdf.*

34. Quoted in Philip Gourevitch, "The Genocide Fax," *New Yorker,* May 11, 1998. In a moving article written five years after the genocide, General Dallaire spoke of the consequences of international inaction in Rwanda as "inexcusable by any human criteria." Romeo A. Dallaire, "The End of Innocence: Rwanda 1994," in Jonathan Moore, ed., *Hard Choices: Moral Dilemmas in Humanitarian Intervention* (Lanham, Md.: Rowman and Littlefield, 1998), pp. 71–87.

35. Gourevitch, *We Wish to Inform You,* pp. 114–115.

36. Elizabeth Neuffer, *The Key to My Neighbor's House: Seeking Justice in Bosnia and Rwanda* (New York: Picador, 2001), p. 126.

37. Memorandum of Frank Wisner to Sandy Berger, May 5, 1994 (declassified), quoted in Power, *"Problem from Hell,"* pp. 371–372.

38. Power, *"Problem from Hell,"* p. 372.

39. Presidential Decision Directive 25, "U.S. Policy on Reforming Multilateral Peace Operations," May 3, 1994. PDD 25 lists eighteen factors for U.S. policymakers to consider when determining whether to support a U.N. peacekeeping resolution in the U.N. Security Council: nine when no U.S. soldiers are involved, nine more for determining whether the "even stricter standards" are met for allowing "U.S. personnel [to] participate in a given peace operation," including three "even more rigorous factors" when the operation is "likely to involve combat."

40. Quoted in Power, *"Problem from Hell,"* p. 342.

41. See Melvern, *A People Betrayed,* pp. 165–166.

42. Instruction Cable to Ambassador Madeleine Albright, Apr. 15, 1994 (declassified), quoted in Power, *"Problem from Hell,"* pp. 367–368.

43. The Convention on the Prevention and Punishment of the Crime of Genocide, article 1. The State Department press briefing on April 29 showed how tortuous the official description of what was happening in Rwanda became.

*Question:* A British aid agency, Oxfam, today described what was happening [in Rwanda] as genocide. Does the State Department have a comment on that, or a view as to whether or not what is happening is genocide?

*Ms. Shelley* [*State Department press briefer*]: As I think you know, the use of the term "genocide" has a very precise legal meaning, although it's not strictly a legal determination. . . .

*Question:* Does determining that genocide has or has not happened, does that also require the U.S. government to do certain things, like to try to stop it?

*Ms. Shelley:* Again, my understanding of the issue is whereas there is not an absolute requirement if a determination of genocide is made to intervene directly in the particular crisis under international law—and particularly under the 1948 Genocide Convention—there are several ways which are outlined—several avenues that are outlined—in that for proceeding under international law to investigate and ultimately take actions related to the crime of genocide.

Transcript, State Department Press Briefing by Christine Shelley, Deputy Press Spokesperson, U.S. Department of State, April 29, 1994, pp. 3–4. Typical of the internal bureaucratic opposition to officially characterizing the Rwanda situation as genocide was an internal memorandum prepared by the Office of the Secretary of Defense on May 1, in preparation for an interagency meeting on Rwanda. Under the heading "Genocide Investigation," the memo cautions against supporting "language that calls for an international investigation of human rights abuses and possible violations of the genocide convention. Be careful. Legal at State was worried about this yesterday—genocide finding could commit the U.S. government to actually 'do something.'" Quoted in Power, *"Problem from Hell,"* p. 359. Although this memo mischaracterizes the State Department Legal Adviser's objection to official use of the term "genocide" as based on "legal" rather than "policy" issues, it certainly reflects the bureaucracy's nervousness over this issue.

44. These rough estimates are based on the stark fact that approximately 800,000 Rwandans were murdered over a period of about 110 days.

## 2. Rwanda: The Struggle for Justice

1. U.N. Security Council Resolution S/RES/918, May 17, 1994.

2. When the APCs finally arrived in Uganda, they remained in storage until the end of July because there were no available trucks large enough to transport them to Rwanda. See Linda Melvern, *A People Betrayed: The Role of the West in Rwanda's Genocide* (London: Zed Books, 2000), p. 196.

3. CBS, *Face the Nation,* Apr. 10, 1994.

4. John Shattuck, "Justice for Rwanda," *Boston Globe,* May 25, 1994, p. A21.

5. The other co-signers were George Moose, Legal Adviser Conrad Harper, and Assistant Secretary for International Organizations Douglas Bennet.

6. Conrad, Bennet, Moose, and Shattuck Memorandum to the Secretary of State, May 21, 1994 (declassified).

7. Rwanda Paper, Office of the Secretary of Defense, May 1, 1994 (declassified), quoted in Samantha Power, *"A Problem from Hell": America and the Age of Genocide* (New York: Basic Books, 2002), p. 359.

8. Quoted in Bill Berkeley, *The Graves Are Not Yet Full: Race, Tribe, and Power in the Heart of Africa* (New York: Basic Books, 2001), p. 265.

9. Three Catholic priests and two Protestant clergymen have been charged by the International Criminal Tribunal for Rwanda with separate acts of genocide and crimes against humanity for allegedly collaborating with the killers of their congregations during the genocide. "Trials Test the Faith of Rwandans," *New York Times,* May 12, 2002, p. A15.

10. On September 26, 1994, a Rwandan national, Elizaphan Ntakirutimana, was arrested in Laredo, Texas, on charges of genocide. Associated Press Worldstream, Sept. 27, 1994. Nine years later Ntakirutimana was convicted of genocide by the International Criminal Tribunal for Rwanda. *New York Times,* February 20, 2003, p. A3.

11. Richard J. Goldstone, *For Humanity: Reflections of a War Crimes Investigator* (New Haven: Yale University Press, 2000), p. 110.

12. Ibid., p. 111. Goldstone points out that the prime minister's "fears over the exclusion of the death penalty became a reality when, during 1998, the Rwandan government executed less-guilty persons while the tribunal was sentencing the real leaders to life imprisonment. There was really no way to resolve this problem" (p. 112).

13. See generally Arthur Helton, *The Price of Indifference: Refugees and Humanitarian Action in the New Century* (Oxford, Eng.: Oxford University Press, 2002).

14. By 2000, the International Criminal Tribunal for Rwanda had sixty detainees, including eight who had been convicted after trial proceedings. See *www.ictr.org.*

## 3. Haiti: A Tale of Two Presidents

1. Evans Paul was defeated for reelection as mayor in 1995, but went on to create his own political party and become a leading opponent of Aristide.

2. Quoted in Bob Shacochis, *The Immaculate Invasion* (New York: Viking, 1999), p. 19.

3. Morris Morley and Chris McGillion, *Political Science Quarterly* (Fall

1997), quoted in David Halberstam, *War in a Time of Peace* (New York: Scribner's, 2001), p. 268.

4. "Executive Order Formalizes U.S. Embargo on Haitian Trade," U.S. Department of State Dispatch, Nov. 4, 1991. One observer commented: "President Bush, underwriter of the island's nascent democracy, swiftly announced that the coup would not stand, then just as quickly receded into embarrassed silence when informed by his staff that his own crew in Port-au-Prince not only had foreknowledge of the putsch, but had allowed it to advance without a word. The United States had been Janus-faced in its intentions toward the island ever since." Shacochis, *Immaculate Invasion*, p. 9.

5. Halberstam, *War in a Time of Peace*, p. 270; Shacochis, *Immaculate Invasion*, p. 29.

6. Halberstam, *War in a Time of Peace*, p. 270.

7. Colin Powell, *My American Journey* (New York: Random House, 1995), p. 544.

8. Elizabeth Drew, *On the Edge: The Clinton Presidency* (New York: Simon and Schuster, 1994), p. 138.

9. Remarks of Governor Bill Clinton, Los Angeles World Affairs Council, Aug. 3, 1992.

10. Francis Fukayama's popular commentary at the end of the Cold War predicted the global expansion of liberal democracy and democratic capitalism. See Fukayama, *The End of History and the Last Man* (New York: Free Press, 1992).

11. Drew, *On the Edge*, p. 332.

12. Ibid., p. 139.

13. Halberstam, *War in a Time of Peace*, p. 269.

14. U.N. General Assembly Resolution A/Res/47/20B, Nov. 24, 1992.

15. "Mistakes Cited in El Salvador," *Washington Post*, July 16, 1993, p. A16. See also Leigh Binford, *The El Mozote Massacre: Anthropology and Human Rights* (Tucson: University of Arizona Press, 1996), pp. 63–66.

16. U.S. Department of State, *Country Reports on Human Rights Practices for 1992* (Washington, D.C.: Government Printing Office, Feb. 1993), p. 421.

17. "Haitian Military and Aristide Sign Pact to End Crisis," *New York Times*, July 4, 1993, p. A1. See also Drew, *On the Edge*, pp. 332–333.

18. Halberstam, *War in a Time of Peace*, p. 271.

19. Drew, *On the Edge*, p. 333. Christopher was in the middle, "at times more inclined to [the use of force] than the Pentagon" (p. 333). In his memoir, Christopher observes that "it became clear that despite their commitments,

Cedras and his junta had no intention of adhering to the [Governors Island] provisions. . . . Many of us began to understand that no matter what Cedras said, he would never leave power until forced to do so." Warren Christopher, *In the Stream of History* (Stanford, Calif.: Stanford University Press, 1998), p. 175.

20. Halberstam points out that "what was especially pernicious about the incident was that the thugs on the dock were being choreographed by Cedras's security people, controlled by Emmanuel Constant, still on the CIA payroll." *War in a Time of Peace,* p. 272.

21. Colin Granderson, "Military-Humanitarian Ambiguities in Haiti," in Jonathan Moore, ed., *Hard Choices: Moral Dilemmas in Humanitarian Intervention* (Lanham, Md.: Rowman and Littlefield, 1998), p. 107.

22. U.S. Department of State, *Country Reports on Human Rights Practices for 1993* (Washington, D.C.: Government Printing Office, Feb. 1994), p. 408.

23. See Drew, *On the Edge,* p. 335.

24. *New York Times,* Dec. 15, 1993, p. A7.

25. One of the leading critics of U.S. interdiction policy, and the lead counsel in several of these cases, was Harold Koh, a Yale Law School professor whom I recruited five years later to be my successor as assistant secretary of state for democracy, human rights, and labor.

26. In the first two weeks of December, 220 Haitians were interdicted at sea by the Coast Guard, 25 percent more than were picked up during the entire month of November. *New York Times,* Dec. 16, 1993, p. A6.

27. "U.S. Aide to Seek New Policy on Fleeing Haitians," *New York Times,* Dec. 15, 1993, p. A7.

28. Ibid.

29. *New York Times,* Dec. 16, 1993, p. A6.

30. Although my position was attacked by anonymous officials in the administration, it was strongly reinforced by commentary in the press. A *New York Times* editorial, "The Truth Rebuked on Haiti," opened with the following paragraph: "John Shattuck is the State Department's highest human rights official. He is also an honest man. After a firsthand look at the deteriorating situation in Haiti, Mr. Shattuck concluded that the collapse of efforts to restore President Jean-Bertrand Aristide had intensified repression, and that a new wave of refugees would soon be on the way. He urged the Clinton Administration to review its policy of turning back every boat that attempts to flee Haiti. He wanted to assure that those with a legitimate claim to asylum get a fair chance to present their cases. What he got was an official rebuke." *New York*

*Times,* Dec. 17, 1993, p. A38. Similarly, the columnist Murray Kempton pointed to the gap between rhetoric and policy on human rights in Haiti: "The candidate Bill Clinton denounced the president for cruelty and then, as soon as he took office, mandated the same policy on a 'temporary' basis. Nine months later, Assistant Secretary of State John Shattuck visited Haiti. What he saw there impelled him to say aloud that the blockade ought to be reconsidered. He returned to find that he had incensed the White House with a statement the customarily anonymous spokesman called 'completely wrong and outrageous.' Shattuck's conscience had been so much too lively for the company around him as to earn him official denunciation as a rogue." *Newsday,* Dec. 19, 1993, p. A20.

31. U.S. Department of State, *Country Reports on Human Rights Practices for 1994* (Washington, D.C.: Government Printing Office, Feb. 1995), p. 422.

32. Taylor Branch, *Parting the Waters: America in the King Years, 1954–63* (New York: Simon and Schuster, 1988), was awarded the Pulitzer Prize for History in 1989. A second volume, *Pillar of Fire: America in the King Years, 1963–65,* was published in 1998. A third volume of Branch's monumental King trilogy is expected in 2004.

33. Associated Press, Apr. 22, 1994. The AP reported that "State Department spokesman Mike McCurry said today that a boatload of 411 Haitians off Florida will not be turned back as is customary with U.S. repatriation policy. The migrants were to be brought ashore by the Coast Guard and processed by the Immigration and Naturalization Service because of 'extraordinary circumstances,' including the fact that their 65-foot freighter was severely overcrowded, many passengers were in poor physical condition and the boat 'was without adequate safety equipment.'"

34. U.S. Department of State, *Country Reports on Human Rights Practices for 1994,* describes the killings as follows: "At the end of April, military authorities in Gonaïves, who were seeking a pro-Aristide activist, opened fire on a wide area of beach in the slum area of Roboteau, killing as many as 26 persons. They asserted the action was in response to a terrorist attack on a police station, but there was no evidence of any such attack" (p. 422).

35. Christopher, *Stream of History,* p. 177.

36. Ibid.

37. Comparing Aristide's regime with that of its predecessors, the 1991 State Department Human Rights Report, issued by the Bush administration, documented that "there were fewer instances of abuse by soldiers, which re-

sulted in a greater sense of personal security [under Aristide]." U.S. Department of State, *Country Reports on Human Rights Practices for 1991* (Washington, D.C.: Government Printing Office, Feb. 1992), p. 633.

38. "U.S. Making Moves for Haiti Action," *New York Times,* July 15, 1994, p. A1.

39. U.N. Security Council Resolution 940, adopted July 31, 1994.

40. George Stephanopoulos, *All Too Human* (Boston: Little, Brown, 1999), p. 305. See also Halberstam, *War in a Time of Peace,* pp. 279–280.

41. Christopher, *Stream of History,* p. 180.

42. Halberstam, *War in a Time of Peace,* p. 280.

43. Christopher, *Stream of History,* p. 181.

44. Ibid.

45. Perry's remark was relayed by Talbott at a State Department senior staff meeting on September 20, 1994.

46. Christopher, *Stream of History,* p. 181.

47. "Beyond the U.S. Raid: Haiti Is Still a Minefield," *New York Times,* Oct. 3, 1994, p. A10. See also "U.S. Troops Conduct Arms Search in Haiti, *New York Times,* Oct. 2, 1994, p. A20.

48. Ray Kelly served as New York City police commissioner from 1992 to 1994. From 1996 to 1998 he was undersecretary of the treasury for enforcement, and subsequently commissioner of the U.S. Customs Service. In 2002 he was appointed again to serve as New York City police commissioner by Mayor Michael Bloomberg.

49. See Roger Fatton Jr., *Haiti's Predatory Republic: The Unending Transition to Democracy* (New York: Lynne Rienner, 2003); Peter Dailey, "Haiti: The Fall of the House of Aristide," *New York Review of Books,* March 13, 2003, p. 41.

50. See Marlye Golin-Adams and David M. Malone, "Haiti: A Case of Endemic Weakness," in Robert I. Rotberg, ed., *State Failure and State Weakness in a Time of Terror* (Washington, D.C.: Brookings Institution Press, 2003), pp. 287–301.

## 4. Bosnia: The Pariah Problem

1. One exception was Roy Gutman, a *Newsday* reporter who had won a Pulitzer Prize two years before for his investigative reporting that uncovered the existence of concentration camps in the Serb areas of Bosnia. Gutman pub-

lished a story on August 8 reporting that my "interviews with survivors from Srebrenica and its sister enclave of Zepa turned up 'substantial new evidence of genocide and crimes against humanity.'" "Big Atrocity: Serb Militia Chief Said to Have Role," *Newsday,* Aug. 8, 1995, p. A7.

2. David Rohde, *Endgame: The Betrayal and Fall of Srebrenica* (New York: Farrar, Straus, and Giroux, 1997), pp. ix–xi.

3. The mortar round was reportedly fired by the Bosnian Serb forces surrounding Sarajevo, although this has never been proven.

4. Laura Silber and Allan Little, *Yugoslavia: Death of a Nation* (London: Penguin/BBC Books, 1996), p. 201.

5. In a speech on August 4, 1992, Clinton called for "collective action, including the use of force, if necessary," to liberate the Serb concentration camps, adding that the United States should "be prepared to lend appropriate support, including military, to such an operation." *New York Times,* Aug. 5, 1992, p. A12.

6. See, e.g., "Vance-Owen Bosnia Move Is Surprise for Washington," *New York Times,* Jan. 31, 1993, p. A10; "The Limping Vance-Owen Effort," *Los Angeles Times,* Feb. 15, 1993, p. B7; "Allies Still Balk at Air Strikes, Arms Aid," *Washington Post,* May 7, 1993, p. A29; "Road to Bosnia: Left to Waterloo, Right at Munich," *Los Angeles Times,* May 9, 1993, p. M1.

7. Warren Christopher, *In the Stream of History* (Stanford, Calif.: Stanford University Press, 1998), p. 345.

8. Ibid.

9. "Allies Still Balk at Air Strikes, Arms Aid," *Washington Post,* May 7, 1993, p. A29.

10. Aryeh Neier, *War Crimes: Brutality, Genocide, Terror and the Struggle for Justice* (New York: Random House, 1998), p. 124.

11. On August 25, 1992, George Kenney, the acting Yugoslav desk officer, had resigned, asserting that "I can no longer in clear conscience support the [Bush] Administration's ineffective, indeed counterproductive, handling of the Yugoslav crisis." *Washington Post,* Aug. 26, 1992, p. A1. A year later, on August 4, 1993, Marshall Harris, the Bosnia desk officer, also resigned. In a letter to Christopher he stated, "I can no longer serve in a Department of State that accepts the forceful dismemberment of a European state and that will not act against genocide and the Serbian officials who perpetrate it." *New York Times,* Aug. 5, 1993, p. A8.

12. U.N. Security Council Resolution 827, May 25, 1993.

13. Convention on the Prevention and Punishment of the Crime of Genocide, article 1: "The Contracting Parties confirm that genocide, whether committed in time of peace or in time of war, is a crime under international law which they undertake to prevent and punish."

14. The *New York Times* reported that "Mr. Boutros-Ghali . . . angered Washington in August when he asserted a right to veto any NATO plan to carry out air strikes in Bosnia and Herzegovina, a move that convinced the Administration that he was trying to control American foreign policy." "U.N. Chief Has to Direct Peace Efforts at U.S., Too," *New York Times*, Oct. 16, 1993, p. A1.

15. U.S. Department of State, *Report on Human Rights Practices for 1993* (Washington, D.C.: Government Printing Office, Jan. 1994), pp. 831–832.

16. "Envoy Comments after Visiting Mass Grave: Vows Continued Support for War Crimes Tribunal," *Los Angeles Times*, Jan. 7, 1994, p. A6.

17. Three years later, Boorda tragically committed suicide following his investigation by a Navy panel for allegedly misrepresenting his military medals.

18. Robert Kaplan, *Balkan Ghosts: A Journey through History* (New York: St. Martin's, 1993).

19. Richard Holbrooke notes: "Kaplan has repeatedly stated that he did not intend to have this effect. . . . In his preface, Kaplan says that 'nothing I write should be taken as a justification, however mild, for the war crimes committed by ethnic Serb troops in Bosnia, which I heartily condemn.'" Holbrooke, *To End a War* (New York: Random House, 1998), p. 22n.

20. E. J. Dionne, "Goodbye to Human Rights?" *Washington Post*, May 31, 1994, p. A17.

21. "France Held Secret Talks with Serbs," *New York Times*, June 23, 1995, p. A7: "The terms of the deal hammered out by the French generals are now clear. The meeting on June 4 in Zvornik, which took place just over a week after the hostages were seized, was followed by a statement on June 9 in which the United Nations abruptly declared it would strictly abide by peacekeeping principles—a firm signal that no more NATO air strikes would occur." See also "U.N. Bosnia Deal Alleged," *Newsday*, June 24, 1995, p. A10.

22. Holbrooke, *To End a War*, p. 65.

23. An editorial in the *Economist* sharply criticized the United States for failing to use the same military strength and precision with which it had rescued Lieutenant O'Grady to try to stop the war in Bosnia. "How Bill Clinton Missed His Chance Yet to be Commander-in-Chief (U.S. Rescue of Air Force

Pilot Scott O'Grady in Bosnia vs. American Support for Peacekeeping in Bosnia)," *Economist,* June 17, 1995, pp. 15–16.

### 5. Bosnia: Facing Reality

1. "France Held Secret Talks with Serbs," *New York Times,* June 23, 1995, p. A7. See also "U.N. Bosnia Deal Alleged," *Newsday,* June 24, 1995, p. A10.

2. See Samantha Power, *"A Problem from Hell": America and the Age of Genocide* (New York: Basic Books, 2002), p. 400.

3. Richard Holbrooke, *To End a War* (New York: Random House, 1998), p. 70.

4. David Rohde, *Endgame: The Betrayal and Fall of Srebrenica* (New York: Farrar, Straus and Giroux, 1997), pp. 326–327. The text of the "Declaration" contains a handwritten addition by Major Franken stating that the document referred only to those convoys "actually escorted by U.N. forces."

5. Holbrooke, *To End a War,* p. 71.

6. Ibid., p. 107.

7. The German press reported that "the International Committee of the Red Cross [was] trying to gain access to [the Srebrenica refugees], but although this had been promised by the Bosnian Serb leadership, it had yet to be granted." Deutsche Presse-Agentur, July 18, 1995.

8. Very little intelligence information was available to me. I was told that CIA aerial photographs were "unproductive," although a month later they were used to verify the information I had by then gathered myself from eyewitness survivors of the Srebrenica genocide.

9. During the following months, security was constantly an issue on my Balkan trips, and the diplomatic security officers assigned to my missions always did an outstanding job under extremely difficult conditions.

10. See Warren Zimmermann, *Origins of a Catastrophe* (New York: Random House, 1996). Zimmermann was the last U.S. ambassador to Yugoslavia.

11. See Indictment for Crimes against Humanity and Grave Breaches and Violation of the Laws or Customs of War of November 1995, filed by the Prosecutor of the International Criminal Tribunal for the Former Yugoslavia against Dario Kordic, Tihomir Blaskic, Mario Cerkez, Ivan Santic, Pero Skopljak, and Zlatko Aleksovski; and Second Amended Indictment of April 1997 filed by the Prosecutor against Tihomir Blaskic. See *www.un.org/icty.*

12. Quoted in Holbrooke, *To End a War,* pp. 32–33.

13. Ibid., p. 190.

14. "Prisoner Release Comes after U.S. Pressure on Milosevic," *Deutsche Presse-Agentur,* Oct. 31, 1995; "Bosnian Serbs Free Muslim Civilians, *New York Times,* Nov. 1, 1995, p. A10.

## 6. Bosnia and Kosovo: Breaking the Cycle

1. Statement by Sadako Ogata, United Nations high commissioner for refugees, at the Humanitarian Issues Working Group of the International Conference on the Former Yugoslavia, Geneva, Switzerland, Oct. 10, 1995.

2. International Criminal Tribunal for the Former Yugoslavia, Prosecutor against Radislav Krstic, Case no. IT-98-33, Exhibit 161/6, Proceedings of May 25, 2000. See *www.un.org/icty.*

3. "Administration Rejects Call to Lift Serbia Sanctions during Talks," *New York Times,* Oct. 29, 1995, p. A16.

4. Richard Holbrooke, *To End a War* (New York: Random House, 1998), p. 160.

5. Jane Perlez, Dateline Banja Luka, "Bosnian Serbs Free 300 Muslim Civilians in Prisoner Exchange," *New York Times,* Nov. 1, 1995, p. A10.

6. Speaking of Milosevic, Burns commented, "I don't think it's possible to say that someone who championed a war three and four years ago has gone through a process of complete redemption and is an entirely different person." Associated Press, *Ottawa Citizen,* Nov. 1, 1995, p. A12.

7. See, e.g., "Bosnia: Justice Collides with Peace," *Economist,* Nov. 18, 1995, p. 58.

8. General Framework Agreement for Peace, annex 6, chapter 3, article 13. See *www.nato.int/ifor/gfa/gfa-home.htm.*

9. The military annex of the Framework Agreement, *which applied only within Bosnia,* required each of the *Bosnian* parties to "comply with any order or request of the International Tribunal for the Former Yugoslavia for the arrest, detention, surrender or access to persons . . . who are accused of violations within the jurisdiction of the Tribunal." Framework Agreement, annex 1A, article 9. Because of Milosevic's pressure, however, no similar requirements were imposed on Serbia or Croatia.

10. For example, IFOR had the right "to help create secure conditions for the conduct by others of other tasks associated with the peace settlement" (Framework Agreement, annex 1A, article 6, paragraph 3, clause (a)) and "to do all that the Commander judges necessary and proper, including the use of

military force, to protect the IFOR and to carry out the responsibilities listed above in paragraph . . . 3" (article 6, paragraph 5).

11. As Holbrooke points out, Smith and his deputy, General Michael Walker, "made clear that they intended to take a minimalist approach to all aspects of [Dayton] implementation other than force protection. Smith signaled this in his first extensive public statement to the Bosnian people, during a live call-in program on Pale [Bosnian Serb] Television—an odd choice for his first local media appearance. During the program, he answered a question in a manner that dangerously narrowed his own authority. He later told *Newsweek* about it with a curious pride: 'One of the questions I was asked was, "Admiral, is it true that IFOR is going to arrest Serbs in the Serb suburbs of Sarajevo?" I said, "Absolutely not, *I don't have the authority to arrest anybody.*"' [Emphasis added.]" Holbrooke, *To End a War,* p. 328. He *did* have the authority, but not the will to use it.

12. As the *New York Times* reported as early as November 3, the issue of arresting war criminals had already been informally resolved before Dayton: "One issue that has been settled, American officials said, was whether the international force [that will be] sent to monitor the peace accord will make an active effort to find and arrest war crimes suspects in Bosnia. They will not." "Panel Seeks U.S. Pledge on Bosnia War Criminals," *New York Times,* Nov. 3, 1995, p. A1. The State Department's public view on the issue was more forward leaning. On December 6, Nick Burns, the State Department spokesman, told the press that "IFOR would apprehend Karadzic and Mladic and others indicted, if they were 'encountered.' Pressed on the point, he said IFOR would seek them out." Quoted by Deutsche Presse-Agentur, Dec. 6, 1995.

13. Framework Agreement, annex 1A, articles 1–5.

14. See, e.g., *New York Times,* Jan. 22, 1996, p. A3; *Washington Post,* Jan. 22, 1996, p. A1.

15. See *www.un.org/icty/glance/keyfig-e.htm.*

16. See *www.un.org/icty/glance/profact-e.htm.*

## 7. The China Syndrome

1. For a vivid description of the Tiananmen Square massacre and its aftermath, see Nicholas Kristoff and Sheryl WuDunn, *China Wakes: The Struggle for the Soul of a Rising Power* (New York: Random House, 1994), pp. 77–91.

2. See James Mann, *About Face: A History of America's Curious Relationship with China, from Nixon to Clinton* (New York: Knopf, 1999), p. 6.

3. Ibid., p. 135.

4. Kristoff and WuDunn, *China Wakes,* pp. 77–79, 82–85.

5. See Mann, *About Face,* pp. 205–209.

6. Winston Lord, "Misguided Mission," *Washington Post,* Dec. 9, 1989, p. A28.

7. Quoted in Mann, *About Face,* p. 223.

8. Associated Press, June 5, 1989.

9. Ibid.

10. See Mann, *About Face,* pp. 198–200, 211–216.

11. Ibid., pp. 228–229.

12. Patrick Tyler, *A Great Wall* (New York: Public Affairs Press, 1999), p. 383.

13. Ibid., pp. 386, 389; Mann, *About Face,* p. 262.

14. See Mann, *About Face,* p. 275. In a speech on December 12, 1991, "A New Covenant for American Security," Clinton said: "We should use our diplomatic and economic leverage to increase the material incentives to democratize and raise the costs for those who won't. We have every right to condition our foreign aid and debt relief policies on demonstrable progress toward democracy and market reforms. In extreme cases, such as that of China, we should condition favorable trade terms on political liberalization and responsible international conduct."

15. From the right, Patrick Buchanan and other conservative Republicans, led in the House by Rep. Gerald Solomon (R-N.Y.), pushed the Bush administration to stop "playing footsie with Li Peng and Deng Xiaoping, . . . the gentlemen who sent tanks to roll over the children in Tiananmen Square." Buchanan quoted in Mann, *About Face,* p. 261.

16. The final vote was 60–38 to override the veto, six votes short of the required two-thirds' majority. Nine Republicans joined 51 Democrats in support of the override, but the Bush administration was able to persuade four Democrats from farm states to oppose it. A week earlier, on March 18, the House had voted 357–61 to override Bush's veto, with 110 Republicans joining 247 Democrats in favor of the override. "U.S. Senate Backs Bush on Trade Status," *Facts on File,* Mar. 19, 1992, p. 199.

17. CNN Transcript of Little Rock Economic Conference, Dec. 14, 1992.

18. Ibid.

19. Ibid.

20. Executive Order 12850 required the Secretary of State to "make a recommendation to the President to extend or not to extend MFN status to China for the 12-month period beginning July 3, 1994." In order to recommend extension, the Secretary was requested to make a positive finding on

both of the "mandatory conditions," and to find "overall significant progress" with respect to the remaining five.

21. Mann, *About Face,* pp. 281–282.

22. Reuters, May 28, 1993.

23. Ibid.

24. Henry Kissinger, "Why We Can't Withdraw from Asia," *Washington Post,* June 15, 1993, p. A22.

25. Presidential Statement on Most Favored Nation Status for China, Office of the White House Press Secretary, May 28, 1993.

26. See Mann, *About Face,* p. 283.

27. For President Clinton's warning, see transcript of Press Conference by President Bill Clinton and President Jiang Zemin, Office of the White House Press Secretary, Oct. 29, 1997.

28. "No Chemicals on Chinese Vessel, State Department Says," *Los Angeles Times,* Sept. 5, 1993, p. A1. See also Tyler, *A Great Wall,* pp. 396–400.

29. Tyler, *A Great Wall,* p. 396; Mann, *About Face,* pp. 285–286.

30. Mann, *About Face,* p. 289.

31. The same article reporting Haig's outburst pointedly noted: "Not far from Mr. Haig's hotel suite, a recently released political prisoner provided some contrast. The prisoner was held for more than two years in solitary confinement and thought for a time that he had lost his mind in isolation. His health is broken, his life shattered by his pamphleteering for democracy in 1989. He asked that his name not be used. After listening to a description of Mr. Haig's view, he said that keeping up the pressure on the Chinese leadership to respect human rights has been one of the greatest influences on its behavior. 'It would be very sad if the United States changed its policy in this way,' he said." *New York Times,* Oct. 28, 1993, p. A14.

32. *Washington Post,* Nov. 7, 1993, p. C1.

33. Ibid.

34. *South China Morning Post,* Oct. 20, 1993, p. A1.

35. See Mann, *About Face,* pp. 286–287.

36. *New York Times,* Dec. 12, 1993, p. A10.

37. Ibid.

## 8. China: Collision Course

1. *New York Times,* Oct. 21, 1993, p. A8.

2. See, e.g., John Kruger and Charles Lewis, op-ed, "When Big Money Talked, Clinton Retreated to George Bush's Policy," *Washington Post,* Nov. 7,

1993, p. C3. See also Nicholas Kristoff and Sheryl WuDunn, *China Wakes: The Struggle for the Soul of a Rising Power* (New York: Times Books, 1994), pp. 416–417.

3. In November 1993, for example, the *New York Times* noted in an editorial: "Washington has reminded Beijing that . . . a last-minute flurry of human rights gestures would not be enough to assure renewal of low tariff privileges . . . China already knows through diplomatic channels what moves would be most welcome. On human rights these include following through on Red Cross visits and medical release, as provided under Chinese law, for ailing prisoners like Wang Juntao, the democracy activist; Gao Yu, a journalist detained as she was about to depart for a U.S. visit; and Bao Tong, a top aide to the former Communist Party leader Zhou Ziyang." "Coddling China, Constructively," *New York Times*, Nov. 18, 1993, p. A26.

4. Schifter had held my position as assistant secretary of state for human rights and humanitarian affairs in the Bush administration in the aftermath of Tiananmen, and had conducted earlier bilateral talks on human rights with the Chinese.

5. "Christopher Welcomes Chinese Move on Red Cross Visits to Prisoners," Associated Press, Nov. 16, 1993. Section 1(b) of Executive Order 12850 called for "ensuring humane treatment of prisoners, such as by allowing access to prisons by international humanitarian and human rights organizations."

6. Chinese law allows the release of ailing prisoners under "medical parole" at the discretion of the authorities.

7. Section 1(b) of the executive order called for progress in "protecting Tibet's distinctive religious and cultural heritage."

8. One of the two mandatory conditions in the executive order required the President to certify that "extension [of MFN] will substantially promote [the] freedom of emigration objectives" of section 402 of the Trade Act of 1974 (19 U.S.C. 2432 (a) and (b)). E.O. 12850, section 1(a).

9. The other mandatory condition required certification that "China is complying with the 1992 bilateral agreement between the United States and China concerning prison labor." Ibid.

10. A nonmandatory condition of the executive order called for progress in "permitting international radio and television broadcasts into China." Ibid., section 1(b).

11. Wei Jingsheng, "The Wolf and the Lamb," *New York Times*, Nov. 18, 1993, p. A23.

12. The President had received a letter dated November 15 from 270 mem-

bers of the House of Representatives informing him that "We stand firmly behind your Executive Order and believe that we must hold the Chinese government accountable to the conditions you have outlined."

13. *Washington Post,* Nov. 20, 1993, p. A18.

14. *New York Times,* Nov. 28, 1993, p. A20.

15. *Los Angeles Times,* Nov. 22, 1993, p. A1.

16. Gephardt's delegation included notable Democratic liberals Norm Dicks (D-Wash.), Mike Synar (D-Okla.), Clarence Brown (D-Ohio), Rose DeLauro (D-Conn.), and Fortney ("Pete") Stark (D-Calif.). They were debriefed by Sandy Berger, Mickey Kantor, Treasury Undersecretary Jeff Garten, Winston Lord, and myself.

17. *New York Times,* Jan. 30, 1994.

18. Patrick Tyler, *A Great Wall* (New York: Public Affairs Press, 1999), pp. 404-405.

19. The Kerry amendment was a substitute for an even tougher amendment offered by Sen. Jesse Helms (D-N.C.) that would have enacted the original Mitchell bill conditioning MFN on both human rights and nonproliferation progress.

20. James Mann, *About Face: A History of America's Curious Relationship with China, from Nixon to Clinton* (New York: Knopf, 1999), p. 296.

21. "Senator Asks End to Threats to China," *New York Times,* Jan. 27, 1994, p. A11.

22. Kamm's human rights work was later the subject of a *New York Times Magazine* article. Tina Rosenberg, "John Kamm's Third Way," *New York Times Magazine,* Mar. 3, 2002.

23. Fang Lizhi, "China's Despair and China's Hope," *New York Review of Books,* Feb. 2, 1989.

24. U.S. Department of State, *Country Reports on Human Rights Practices for 1993* (Washington, D.C.: Government Printing Office, Feb. 1994), p. 605.

25. Wei Jingsheng, "The Wolf and the Lamb," p. A27.

26. Mann, *About Face,* p. 299.

27. *Asian Wall Street Journal,* Mar. 3, 1994, p. A20.

28. At first Wei was detained for a day and then released, only to be rearrested on April 1, held without charges for more than a year, finally tried summarily at the end of 1995 for plotting to overthrow the Communist Party, sentenced to thirteen years in prison, and then effectively exiled in November 1997, when he was released on medical parole on the condition that he leave the country. He is now living in the United States.

29. *Washington Times,* Mar. 7, 1994, p. A1.

30. *New York Times,* Mar. 5, 1994, p. A1.

31. "Behind Beijing Arrests, the View That Stability Is Everything," *International Herald Tribune,* Mar. 7, 1994, p. A1.

32. *Wall Street Journal,* Mar. 3, 1994, p. A1.

33. *Asian Wall Street Journal,* Mar. 7, 1994, p. A1.

34. Clinton spoke at a White House press conference with visiting Ukrainian president Leonid M. Kravchuk on March 4, indicating that "the United States had 'sent a very stern statement' to Beijing, and adding that 'we strongly disapprove of what was done, and it obviously is not helpful to our relations.'" *New York Times,* Mar. 5, 1994, p. A1.

35. Warren Christopher, *In the Stream of History* (Stanford, Calif.: Stanford University Press, 1998), p. 154.

36. As the arrests continued, the embers of the democracy movement that had been extinguished in 1989 showed a glimmer of new light. A group of seven leading Chinese scientists and intellectuals sent a petition to President Jiang Zemin calling for an end of the repression. "We appeal to the authorities to bravely end our country's history of punishing people for their ideology, speech and writing and release all those imprisoned because of their ideology or speech." The petition concluded that "only after human rights are respected . . . will the society have a true stability." *New York Times,* Mar. 11, 1994, p. A1.

37. Two days earlier the U.S. division chief of the Chinese Ministry of Foreign Affairs had told a U.S. embassy officer that his ministry and the Chinese security police had been criticized by a "senior leader" (undoubtedly Li Peng) for allowing Wei to meet with me, and that with Deng Xiaoping no longer in the picture, there were no other "elders" in the Chinese leadership who were as heavily invested in Sino-American relations.

38. Christopher had served as chairman of a commission to investigate the Los Angeles Police Department after the brutal police beating of Rodney King in 1991, and was widely praised for the thoroughness and honesty of the commission report: *Report of the Independent Commission on the Los Angeles Police Department,* July 9, 1991. As the veteran journalist Lou Cannon observed, "Warren Christopher and his competent band of lawyers performed a public service in exposing the excesses of the LAPD and the deficiencies of its chief." Cannon, *Official Negligence: How Rodney King and the Riots Changed Los Angeles and the LAPD* (New York: Times Books, 1997), p. 147.

39. The next day the U.S. press was full of stories about the meeting. A typi-

cal headline read, "Christopher Confronts Double Whammy: U.S. Business-men and Chinese Leaders Protest the Use of Trade Policy to Force Human Rights Reform." *Washington Times,* Mar. 13, 1994, p. A2.

40. "China Rejects Call from Christopher for Rights Gains," read a front-page headline in the *New York Times* on Sunday, March 13, for example.

41. In a remarkably candid comment, Qin told me at the beginning of our three-hour meeting on March 13 that the Wei Jingsheng incident would have ended with the deputy foreign minister's mild protest at the banquet in my honor on March 1 if Wei had not publicized his meeting with me, and if "anti-Chinese opinions had not been expressed in the press."

42. "Christopher Is Drawing Fire in Washington on China Visit," *New York Times,* Mar. 18, 1994, p. A1.

43. "Ex U.S. Officials Oppose China Trade, Human Rights Link," *Washington Post,* Mar. 16, 1994, p. A24.

44. Ibid.

45. Ibid.

46. "Cacophony of Voices Drowns Out Message from U.S. to China; Beijing Is Able to Exploit Washington Infighting over MFN Status," *Wall Street Journal,* Mar. 22, 1994, p. A5.

47. Ibid., p. A6.

48. *New York Times,* Mar. 25, 1994, p. A12.

49. In a memo to Christopher on April 21, I pointed out that in the eleven months since the executive order was signed, China had released eleven politi-cal prisoners but detained fifty others.

50. On March 15 Lord and I prepared a report entitled "MFN Checklist and Followup" for Christopher to use at a White House Principals Meeting. The report indicated that while the two mandatory conditions of the executive order (prison labor and emigration) had been met, there was not "overall significant progress" in the other specified areas (Universal Declaration of Hu-man Rights, accounting of prisoners, release of prisoners, humane treatment of prisoners, Tibet, and international broadcasting). This was the assessment two months later when the President announced his decision on MFN.

51. Warren Christopher, *Chances of a Lifetime* (New York: Scribner's, 2001), p. 242.

52. Press Conference of the President, The White House, May 26, 1994.

53. Aryeh Neier, "Watching Rights," *Nation,* Apr. 18, 1994, p. 512.

54. USIA Wireless File, Apr. 22, 1994, p. 11.

55. *Washington Post,* May 31, 1994, p. A17.

56. On March 8, 1995, the U.N. Human Rights Commission voted 22–22 in a tie that, under the rules of the commission, resulted in the defeat of China's motion to take "no action" on a resolution co-sponsored by the European Union and the United States criticizing China's human rights record. The resolution itself was then narrowly rejected by one vote, but this marked the first time since Tiananmen that China had been defeated in the Human Rights Commission on a procedural motion so that a resolution on the merits could be brought to a vote. Six months later, in September 1995, China's human rights record was criticized by First Lady Hillary Rodham Clinton at the U.N. International Conference on Women in Beijing.

57. Havel made the statement in a press conference in 1990, the text of which is quoted in *Europa,* June 10, 2001, p. 18.

## 9. Strategies for Peace

1. On February 5, 2002, Secretary of Defense Donald Rumsfeld, in testimony before the Senate Armed Services Committee, estimated that the *monthly* cost of "tracking down al Qaeda and Taliban pockets of resistance in Afghanistan" would be $1.8 or $1.9 billion through 2003. Rumsfeld's cost estimate was for Afghanistan alone, and did not include the vastly larger costs associated with the international hunt for al Qaeda. Transcript of hearing, *www.defenselink.mil/speeches/2002/s20020205-secdef.html.*

2. As of November 2002, "the per capita per year allocation [of international assistance] for Afghanistan [was] far smaller than in many other post-conflict situations—$42 for Afghanistan versus $195 for East Timor, $288 for Kosovo, and $326 for Bosnia." Arthur C. Helton and Jennifer Seymour Whitaker, "Nationbusting from Afghanistan to Iraq," *International Herald Tribune,* Nov. 15, 2002, p. 8.

3. See U.S. General Accounting Office, *U.N. Peacekeeping: Estimated U.S. Contributions, Fiscal Years 1996–2001* (Washington, D.C.: Government Printing Office, GAO-02-294, Feb. 2002); U.S. General Accounting Office, "Peace Operations: U.S. Costs in Support, 1994–95" (Washington, D.C.: Government Printing Office, GAO/NSIAD-96-38, Mar. 6, 1996).

4. A dramatic example is the case of Hiram Bingham IV, a Foreign Service officer who received a special posthumous award on June 28, 2002, from the American Foreign Service Association for his "constructive dissent" during World War II. Bingham issued more than 2,500 visas to Jews and other anti-Nazi refugees in Marseilles in 1940 and 1941, in violation of State Department refugee restrictions in effect at the time. Bingham's son was interviewed about

the award on National Public Radio's *All Things Considered* on June 27, 2002. See *http://npr.org/cf/cmn/segment_display.cfm?segID*.

5. Millennium Report of the U.N. Security-General, executive summary (Sept. 2000), p. 5.

6. Ibid.

7. Report of the Panel on U.N. Peace Operations S/2000/809 (New York, 1999), also known as "The Brahimi Report."

8. The U.N. high commissioner for human rights is empowered to "plan, support and evaluate human rights field presences and missions." Mission Statement of the U.N. High Commissioner for Human Rights, Activities and Programmes Branch, paragraph (f), Geneva, 2000. The Mission of the U.N. high commissioner for refugees is "to ensure that everyone can exercise the right to seek asylum and find safe refuge in another state, and to return home voluntarily." Mission Statement of the U.N. High Commissioner for Refugees, published at *www.unhcr.ch/cgi-bin/texis/vtx/ho*.

9. Under article 1 of the Convention on the Prevention and Punishment of the Crime of Genocide, "The contracting parties confirm that genocide, whether committed in time of peace or time of war, *is a crime under international law which they undertake to prevent* and to punish" (emphasis added).

10. Charter of the United Nations, article 2, section 1.

11. Ibid., article 2, section 7.

12. Gareth Evans and Mohamed Sahnoun argue that responding to human rights wars requires the debate about sovereignty and nonintervention "to be turned on its head. The issue must be reframed not as an argument about the 'right to intervene' but about the 'responsibility to protect.' And it has to be accepted that although this responsibility is owed by sovereign states to their own citizens in the first instance, it must be picked up by the international community if that first-tier responsibility is abdicated, or if it cannot be exercised." Evans and Sahnoun, "The Responsibility to Protect," *Foreign Affairs* 81, no. 6 (Nov./Dec. 2002): 101.

13. Similar criteria have been recommended by the International Commission on Intervention and State Sovereignty in its final report, *The Responsibility to Protect* (Ottawa: International Development Research Centre, 2001). See also Evans and Sahnoun, "Responsibility to Protect," pp. 102–105.

14. Evans and Sahnoun, "Responsibility to Protect," p. 103.

15. Ibid., pp. 104–105.

16. Address of President George W. Bush to the U.N. General Assembly, Sept. 12, 2002.

17. The NATO intervention was legitimate, despite its lack of authority

from the U.N. Security Council, because the Genocide Convention authorizes ratifying states to take appropriate measures to stop a genocide in progress. Ironically, this is the very provision that U.S. government lawyers were concerned about during the Rwanda genocide.

18. Report of the Panel on U.N. Peace Operations, executive summary, p. 2.

19. Report of the Secretary General on Srebrenica pursuant to U.N. General Assembly Resolution 53/35 (1998); Final Report of the International Committee of Inquiry on Rwanda pursuant to U.N. General Assembly Resolution 1013 (1995).

20. The Dutch government has published a report on the conduct of its peacekeeping forces in Srebrenica in July 1994. See "Srebrenica, A 'Safe' Area—Reconstruction, Background, Consequences and Analyses of the Fall of a Safe Area," a report conducted by the Netherlands Institute for War Documents at the request of the Government of the Netherlands (2002).

21. There is growing support among influential U.S. nongovernmental organizations for the creation by the United Nations of trained standby military forces for peacemaking and peace enforcement. In August 1994, for example, the American Bar Association, in an effort spearheaded by my father, adopted a resolution calling for such a standby force. See H. Francis Shattuck, Jr., "Recommendation and Report on Peacemaking and Peace Enforcement," in Louis B. Sohn, H. Francis Shattuck, Jr., and John E. Noyes, eds., *The United Nations at Fifty* (Washington, D.C.: American Bar Association, 1997), pp. 45–55.

22. The African Union, a successor organization to the Organization of African Unity, was created in 2002 and includes authority in its mandate for an African standby peacekeeping force. *Boston Globe,* July 8, 2002, p. A7. And at a meeting of the Asian Pacific Economic Forum on September 10, 1999, the chairman of the Standing Committee of the Association of Southeast Asian Nations, Surin Pitsuwan of Thailand, affirmed that "the ASEAN stands ready to extend support to Indonesia in a resolution of the East Timor crisis," including by the deployment of a U.N. peacekeeping force. *Financial Times,* Global News Wire, Sept. 11, 1999.

23. Kissinger's interest in this issue is not academic. He is being sought by a Chilean court for questioning in connection with a prominent human rights case in Chile. The case involves the disappearance and death of an American citizen, Charles Horman, after the military coup that overthrew the democratically elected government of Salvador Allende and brought General August Pinochet to power in 1973. See *New York Times,* Mar. 28, 2002, p. A13.

24. See, e.g., "American Foreign Policy and the International Criminal Court," remarks prepared for delivery by Undersecretary of State for Political Affairs Marc Grossman to the Center for Strategic and International Affairs, Washington, D.C., May 6, 2002.

25. U.S. negotiators at the 1998 Rome Convention that drafted the ICC treaty succeeded in establishing the principle of complementarity, which obliges the ICC to defer to national justice systems "investigating or prosecuting a case in good faith." Statute of the International Criminal Court, part 2, article 17 (1999). See *www.un.org/law/icc/statute/99_corr/2.htm*.

26. Sarah Sewall and Carl Kaysen, *The United States and the International Criminal Court: The Choices Ahead*, CISS Occasional Paper, American Academy of Arts and Sciences, Cambridge, Mass., Mar. 2002, p. 6.

27. Ibid., p. 13.

28. "U.S. Presses for Total Exemption from War Crimes Court," *New York Times*, Oct. 9, 2002, p. A7.

29. The main nationalist parties from all three ethnic groupings—the Bosnian Serb SDS, the Croatian Democratic Union, and the Muslim Party of Democratic Action—all retained power in the elections, while the reform parties were uniformly defeated.

30. Arthur C. Helton and Jennifer Seymour Whitaker, "Nation-Busting from Afghanistan to Iraq," *International Herald Tribune*, Nov. 15, 2002.

31. Address to Latin American Diplomatic Corps., Mar. 13, 1961, archived in Theodore C. Sorensen, *Let the Word Go Forth: The Speeches, Statements and Writings of John F. Kennedy, 1947–1963* (New York: Delacorte Press, 1988), p. 352.

32. In 1995, the one year in which China's "no action" tabling motion failed, the United States, the European Union, and other democratic countries coordinated their efforts to censure China more effectively than usual by agreeing early on the text of a resolution and making high-level diplomatic contacts to try to secure its adoption. See also "U.N. Fears 'Bloc' Voters Are Abetting Rights Abuses," *New York Times*, Apr. 28, 2002, p. A20.

33. "U.S. Dumped from U.N. Human Rights Commission," UPI Newswire, Apr. 3, 2001.

34. In addition to the Rome Treaty on the International Criminal Court, from which President Bush withdrew the U.S. signature in 2002, the United States has not ratified the International Convention on the Elimination of All Forms of Discrimination against Women; the Convention on the Rights of the Child; the International Covenant on Economic, Social and Cultural

Rights; the International Convention on the Protection of the Rights of Migrant Workers; the Optional Protocol to the Convention on the Rights of the Child on the Sale of Children, Child Prostitution and Child Pornography; the Optional Protocol on the Rights of the Child on the Involvement of Children in Armed Conflict; and the Optional Protocol to the International Covenant on Civil and Political Rights Aimed at the Abolition of the Death Penalty.

35. In 1994, when I published the first U.S. report to the U.N. Human Rights Committee concerning U.S. compliance with the International Covenant on Civil and Political Rights, I was criticized by several prominent conservatives for stating in my introduction that the United States continues to face its own human rights problems. See, e.g., Midge Decter, "The State Department vs. America," *Commentary* (Nov. 1994): 65; "Officials Make First Formal Defense under '92 Treaty," *Washington Post,* Mar. 30, 1995, p. A19.

36. Michael Ignatieff, "Is the Human Rights Era Ending?" *New York Times,* Feb. 5, 2002, p. A22.

37. Dana Priest and Bart Gellman, "U.S. Decries Abuse but Defends Interrogations," *Washington Post,* Dec. 26, 2002, p. A1.

38. Thomas L. Friedman, "The War on What?" *New York Times,* May 8, 2002, p. A31.

39. Statement of Saad Eddin Ibrahim at his sentencing by the High State Security Court, South Cairo District, July 29, 2002, *www.democracy-egypt.org/files/Family/07–31–02UpdateSEI Statement.htm.*

# ACKNOWLEDGMENTS

As my former colleague Richard Holbrooke notes in the introduction to his personal account of the successful effort he led to end the war in Bosnia, "a memoir sits on the dangerous intersection of policy, ambition and history." Having now written such a book myself, I am acutely aware of the dangers that lurk at this juncture, and the challenges of getting the story straight. Many have helped me along the way, but I alone am responsible for any flaws that remain in the final product.

Of the countless people who have shaped my views about freedom and human rights, three stand at the core. My father, to whom this book is dedicated, taught me what it means, and why it matters, to fight for what you believe in. He and his fellow Marines defended freedom in its darkest hour during World War II. My first wife, Petra Tölle Shattuck, introduced me to the restless search for human rights, which she began in the shadow of the Holocaust in postwar Germany, where she grew up, and continued until the day she died in 1988, never to know the awful truth that genocide would strike again, simultaneously in Europe and in Africa. Ellen Hume, my wife and partner in all aspects of life, encouraged me to work for human rights, even at the risk of overwhelming our family during my eight years of endless travel and frequent frustration. Ellen's passion, wisdom, and judgment inspired me to stay the course and take a stand for freedom.

I am grateful to those who spurred me to write this book and provided invaluable advice and assistance as it began to take shape. Crystal Nix, Jonathan Moore, and George Moose read and commented on early drafts of the Rwanda chapters. The Haiti material was reviewed by Taylor Branch, who generously took time from his own writing to give a boost to mine. Steve Coffey, Peter Eicher, and Crystal Nix made contributions to the Bosnia chapters. Winston Lord and Susan O'Sullivan contributed their experience and good judgment in looking over what I had written about China. Jonathan Moore drew on his own wealth of knowledge in reviewing and suggesting changes to the concluding chapter.

I am especially indebted to Harold Koh, Joshua Rubenstein, and Roger Shattuck for their willingness to read an early draft of the entire manuscript and provide me with thoughtful and penetrating comments, many of which formed the basis for revisions.

Early encouragement, inspiration, and insight came from the many colleagues and friends with whom I have discussed the issues in this book over the years. These include Madeleine Albright, Scott Armstrong, Alex Arriaga, Hava Beller, Sandy Berger, Derek and Sissela Bok, Sam Brown, Holly Burkhalter, Nick Burns, Pru Bushnell, Wesley Clark, Nick Danforth, Drew S. Days III, Tom Dine, Bob Dole, Don Edwards, Bennett Freeman, Ken Galbraith, Peter Galbraith, Bob Gelbard, Nancy Gertner, Morton Halperin, Vaclav Havel, Arnold Hiatt, Richard Holbrooke, Geri Laber, Tony Lake, Tom Lantos, Arnie Miller, Chuck Muckenfuss, Mark Munger, Aryeh Neier, Jim O'Brien, Jim O'Dea, Sadaka Ogata, John O'Sullivan, Jiri Pehe, Michael Posner, Samantha Power, John Reinstein, Mary Robinson, Josiah Rosenblatt, Ken Roth, David Scheffer, Eric Schwartz, Eli Segal, Dan Serwer, Lee Sigal, Gare Smith, Cornelio Sommarurga, Arnold Steinhardt, Bill Swing, Strobe Talbott, Sherman Teichman, Jan Urban, Dorothea von Haeften, Ike Williams, and Tim Wirth.

Two former chief prosecutors for the International Criminal Tribunals for the Former Yugoslavia and Rwanda, Louise Arbour and Richard Goldstone, provided insight and technical advice about issues of international justice both during and after the time I served in government. I am also thankful to the many staff members of the tribunals with whom I have met over the years, most recently to Peter McCloskey for information about evidence on the public record in the Yugoslav tribunal.

I want to thank my colleagues at the Kennedy Library for their support and forbearance during this project, particularly Doris Drummond, Allan Goodrich, Deborah Leff, Tom McNaught, Karen Mullen, Tom Putnam, Frank Rigg, Sandy Sedacca, Maria Stanwich, and Victoria Tise.

Jane Dietrich and Paul Hilburn were helpful in guiding the manuscript through the State Department's classified review process. It should be obvious that the opinions and characterizations in this book are my own and do not necessarily represent official positions taken by the United States Government.

The book would never have emerged from the drafting stage without the wise counsel and gentle prodding of Jill Kneerim, who brought it to the attention of Harvard University Press and Michael Aronson, whose deft touch and good judgment are what make a great editor. I am also grateful to Benno Weisberg, Julie Carlson, and Donna Bouvier for helping with the editorial process, and to Roger Falcon, Jeremy Freeman, and Philip Dufty for their research assistance.

Finally, I have felt the support and inspiration of my family each step of the way, from six years of living this book to two years of writing it. In fact, I undertook the writing project in part so they would know what I had been doing during those eight long years of our lives together, when I was so often missing in action. Jessica (whose writing far outshines my own), Becca, and Peter read portions of the manuscript and lovingly gave their father straight feedback. Susannah kept me laughing and focused on the things that count in life. Ellen talked me through the book and read every page. Our partnership was indivisible, but in many ways they had the harder job.

# INDEX